Collectible Magazines

Collectible Magazines

IDENTIFICATION

AND PRICE GUIDE

SECOND EDITION

DAVID K. HENKEL

HarperCollins*Publishers*

HarperCollins books may be purchased for educational, business, or sales promotional use. For information please write: Special Markets Department, HarperCollins Publishers Inc., 10 East 53rd Street, New York, NY 10022.

SECOND EDITION

Library of Congress Cataloging-in-Publication Data has been applied for.

ISBN 0-380-80876-5

00 01 02 03 04 RRD 10 9 8 7 6 5 4 3 2 1

Acknowledgments

✠

The Back Issue (Collectible Magazines)
P.O. Box 743
Ridgefield Park, NJ 07660

Diane Cismowski
Lyndhurst, NJ

Darryl and Mary Henkel
Celebrity Photos
28 Orchard Street
Ridgefield Park, NJ 07660

Dennis C. Jackson
The Illustrator Collector's News
P.O. Box 1958
Sequim, WA 98382

Don Smith
National Geographics
3930 Rankin Street
Louisville, KY 40214

TV Guide Specialists
Box 20
Macomb, IL 61455

Contents

✣

Collectible Magazines

Introduction

❊

During the past few years magazine collecting has seen an explosion in growth and interest from the world of collecting as well as the general reading public. With the tremendous success of cable television's replaying the great TV shows and movies of the past, and the new and dynamic network TV shows such as *The X-Files, Xena: Warrior Princess, Hercules, Star Trek: The Next Generation, Buffy the Vampire Slayer, Sabrina the Teenage Witch,* and yes, even animated shows such as *Pokemon,* there is an ever-growing market for photos, features, posters, and interviews from these shows. Magazines are the number one source for most of this material—both vintage magazines and those just off the press.

Certain new magazines may quickly disappear from newsstands, swiftly appreciating in value in the marketplace of the collector. Today, an entire collectors' convention may be held based on only one specific theme. There is so much interest in magazine collecting that quite often this theme can be based on a single magazine title, or magazine collecting type, such as Famous Monsters of Filmland or *Playboy.* At a Famous Monsters convention, collectors of horror magazines will travel from across the nation or even across the ocean to purchase the issues needed to complete their collection. At the *Playboy* or *Glamour* conventions, collectors not only will pay top dollar for needed issues but will also pay for the opportunity to speak with and obtain autographs from the models themselves. For many, collecting magazines has become a lifestyle that is both relaxing and exciting.

A bonus to the magazine collector and investor is that the hobby is growing, not only among the collecting world but also among the general reading population, which quite often finds people purchasing a magazine that catches their eyes. It is hard today not to find a collector's shop or mall antiques show that does not offer back-issue magazines. Drawn by a complete spectrum of magazine covers and features that span the grotesque to the sublime, Americans find it hard not to pick up and purchase a magazine of interest, be it the most recent newsstand copy or an issue published fifty or sixty years ago. Today, readers purchase an estimated 1 billion magazine issues per year in the United States alone, and this figure does not include the millions of back issues sold to collectors.

To the new collector, welcome to the hobby. To all seasoned collectors, sit back in an easy chair and enjoy viewing the values on all those magazines you saved despite the many voices advising you to throw them out.

Using the Guide

※

The Effect of Internet Auctions on Magazine Values

As there have been literally tens of thousands of magazine titles and millions of different issues published within the last hundred years, it would be impossible to list and individually value all of them. Such an undertaking would require a price guide consisting of hundreds of volumes. Furthermore, the vast majority of back-issue magazines published within the past century hold very little, if any, value. In this guide we have focused on those magazines that are currently most in demand.

Values listed in this guide reflect prices paid for issues from mail-order dealers, from back-issue magazine and comic shops, at conventions, through classified ads in trade papers, and from collector-to-collector purchases. We do not include prices realized through Internet auctions. The reason for this is that items at auction may fetch a price much higher (sometimes five to ten times higher) than their accepted collector's value. However, these events are beginning to happen more and more frequently, as an increasing number of collectors gain access to the Internet.

Internet auction sites can be an extremely viable and exciting way of buying and selling. In many ways, Internet auctions are resetting the values of magazines and are changing the way collectors and dealers are looking at the magazine marketplace. Dealers are finding that listing magazines on the Internet can greatly reduce their overhead. As a result, "Mom and Pop" stores are closing down all over the nation. For the dealer, the Internet auction can greatly reduce his expenses by eliminating overhead such as rent, advertising, and mail-order catalogs. Today, it is hard to find a dealer who is not participating on an Internet auction site and who does not have his or her catalog available on the Web. Dealers are learning that for literally pennies a listing they can achieve record-breaking prices not only for the rare and established valuable magazines but also for magazines that would have gone ignored in their stores. Collectors, on the other hand, find that in an instant they can view items of interest being offered by sellers from all over the world. The collector no longer needs to go through the slow process of buying a trade paper, picking out the dealers who carry what they are interested in, mailing payment for a catalog, and then hoping that the items listed are still available. With the Internet auction your desired collectible is staring you right in the eye (most auctions feature photos of the items up for bid) and it's definitely available . . . to the highest bidder. The danger and the reward lie in the bidding. Daily bidding can become much like gambling, and the bidding can be extremely competitive. It is very easy to get caught up in the heat of a bidding war. Be sure to bid only what you can afford or the price that you can easily live with the day after the auction.

To many sellers the Internet auction is like the stock market; each day the seller can view his or her item(s) and see if the minimum bid price is rising . . . and more often than not rising swiftly to unheard-of prices. This guide is an excellent source for information about what price you should open your auction at. The high values we list can be used on any magazine in very good or better condition as your opening bid. Use a lower value for magazines in less than very good condition. To increase your chances of selling your magazine, use our description column to inform the potential bidder of each issue's contents. For issues that you wish to sell that are not in this guide, take your time and list all subjects of interest. In most cases, this bit of added attention will net you very good results.

Throughout this guide, after certain values there will appear the symbol (+). This informs the reader that this particular issue is presently in greater demand than other similar issues, and its listed value is soon expected to rise.

All magazines in this guide are listed according to specific collecting themes—they are then listed alphabetically by title. Each title is then listed by year and issue date or issue number. When applicable, both issue date and number are listed. Within certain magazine sections the cover subject may be listed, followed by a detailed description of that issue's contents. Occasionally, information from the Year, Issue/Number,

Description columns may be missing—this absence of information indicates material that was either not applicable or not available at press time. Prices listed in this guide represent a retail price range based on actual sales throughout the United States, Canada, and Europe. Prices apply to magazines in very good to near mint condition.

On our value charts we have occasionally included a column marked Cameo. A cameo is an article that is less than one full page in length.

Protecting Magazines

The easiest way of protecting both new and old magazines is to just use common sense when reading or looking through your collection. Many a novice collector has damaged his or her own issues while reading by folding the cover backward, thereby creating a cover crease, or spilling a few drops of a soft drink on pages while showing his or her prize issues to a friend. Remember that magazine collecting is not only a wonderful and greatly rewarding hobby, but also an investment for the future. Treat every issue carefully and you'll be rewarded when you decide to sell. After the proper handling of your magazines, the next best way to preserve the condition is to place them individually in specially designed plastic magazine bags backed by acid-free cardboard inserts, and then store them together in acid-free boxes. Magazine bags, cardboard inserts, and boxes come in a wide variety of sizes to accommodate the many different sizes of magazines. They can be purchased through the mail, at comic book shops, back-issue magazine stores, conventions, and on the Internet. Mail-order suppliers selling these necessary supplies regularly advertise in comic books, magazines, and trade publications. Consider well where you will store your magazines—a basement may be too humid, and an attic quite often is too dry. If your basement is damp and has a history of flooding, or if your attic is too hot and dry during the summer months, do not store your magazines in these places. Humidity and excessive dryness will quickly destroy your magazines. Attics and basements are also places where mice or squirrels will find paper goods to chew up for their nests. The best places to store magazines is anywhere within the daily living area of the collector . . . for example, your bedroom closet, in filing cases or bookshelves, or boxes placed under your bed. If the temperature in your home is right for you, it will also be right for your magazines.

Magazine Grades

Poor: Any magazine that is suffering from excessive flaking of the covers and or pages to the point of the magazine falling apart when handled; this is generally caused by being stored in an excessively dry place for a long time. Many magazines published during the years 1941–1945 (World War II era) were made with a cheaper grade of paper, and if not stored properly will quickly begin to deteriorate. Any magazine that has been clipped and/or has pages or cover missing. Teen and movie magazines from the fifties and sixties are the issues that are most likely to suffer this sort of damage. Many a fifties movie or teen magazine will look perfect from the outside but will be completely clipped and destroyed on the inside. Any magazine that has been more than moderately water damaged, has its cover and/or pages written on to the point that the markings seriously affect the quality of the cover subject or obliterate the inside text or photos, or is in any way marked or greatly defaced. Issues in this poor condition are worthless. The only exceptions are magazines that still contain, in at least good condition, collectible illustrations, pinups, vintage ads, photos, or rare articles. When these exceptions are found, they should be carefully removed from the magazine and placed in protective plastic sleeves with an acid-free cardboard backing. They can then be added to your collection or offered for sale.

Good: A good-condition magazine is a copy that has been well read and handled often, and shows the wear. Color from the cover may be fading. There may be some light water staining, minor tears, spine fraying, cover separating from spine, and chipping from its cover and pages. Pages will be showing signs of yellowing.

Fine: Magazines in fine condition will show sharp covers with no fading of color photos and no stains or chipping. Cover will be firmly attached to spine. Some very light wear may exist. A subscription label may be on the cover but does not affect cover subject. Pages will be white and will fit tightly within the magazine.

Mint: Mint copies are issues that are nearly flawless and are as first printed and received by newsstands. A subscription copy can be mint if it is received in a mailing envelope and does not have a subscription label attached to the cover. Very few magazines from before 1955 can be found in this condition, and when found should be treated as small treasures and receive the utmost of care.

Sports Magazines

✥

Values of sports magazines are determined primarily by three factors, besides condition: (1) historical importance, (2) greatness of subject, and/or (3) regional interest. An example of the first factor would be Bobby Thomson's "shot heard round the world" in the 1951 National League baseball playoffs—he was an average player at the center of a very dramatic, historic moment in sports history. The second factor would not be confined only to great athletes of the past and present but would also include, say, great horses of the past, such as Man O' War, Secretariat, and others. As an example of the third factor, the value of a magazine focusing on the Boston Red Sox would be higher in the Massachusetts area than in California. Sometimes two—or all three—of these factors might be present. Take, for example, Willie Mays's great over-the-shoulder catch in the 1954 World Series. A magazine from 1954 featuring this great star at this great moment would indeed have great value in the collectors' marketplace, particularly in the New York area.

The hottest trends in what would be considered sport-related magazines are wrestling and martial arts magazines. At present, the current demand greatly outweighs the supply. Just a few years ago these magazines were seldom even offered for sale as collectors' back issues. Today dealers are frantically seeking new sources of supply. The demand is not caused so much by the high resale value of wrestling and karate magazines (most sell from $2 to $5 each) as by the fact that they sell extremely quickly to collectors and fans of all ages.

The 1960s gave birth to such magazines as *Black Belt* and *Karate Illustrated,* and after the martial arts boom in the early 1970s, many more magazines began to pop up regularly on the newsstands. *Inside Kung*

Fu, Inside Karate, Fighting Stars (dedicated to celebrity martial artists), *Official Karate, Professional Karate, MA Training, Karate International, Journal of Asian Martial Arts, Martial Arts Movies,* and numerous others have graced the magazine racks over the last three decades and have kept martial arts, movies, TV shows, and stars in the foreground.

Wrestling magazines have been around since the 1950s, and any issue in fine or better condition from this era is a rare find and will sell at a high price. With the continued growth of the wrestling profession, its increased visibility on cable television, and the mass marketing of celebrity wrestlers' toys, dolls, gum cards, videos, and endorsements, the wrestling magazine has come of age and is now considered a true sports collectible.

SPORTS MAGAZINE VALUES

(By Decade)

Decade	Value ($)
Wrestling	
1959 and earlier	10–20+
1960–1965	10–15
1966–1969	7–12
1970–1979	5–10
1980–1987	3–6+
1988–present	2–4+

Decade	Value ($)
Martial Arts and Karate	
Pre-1970	5–10+
1970–1979	4–8+
1980–1989	4–6+
1990–present	2–4+

Note: Issues containing covers featuring Bruce Lee double the listed value.

September 1977

February 1978

August 1983

January 1997

December 1994

July 1995

August 1976

January 1988

August 1987

#14, 1976

#15, 1976

#19, 1976

#23, 1977

#24, 1977

#31, 1978

April 1994

January 1988

September 1986

Decade	Value ($)
Boxing	
Pre-1900	25–50
1901–1910	20–40
1911–1930	12–30
1931–1941	7–15
1942–1950	5–12
1951–1960	5–10
1961–1970	4–8
1971–1979	2–5
1980–present	2–4+
Auto and Car Racing	
Pre-1910	50–100
1911–1920	25–50
1921–1930	10–20
1931–1940	7–15
1941–1950	5–10
1951–1960	2–5
1961–present	1–2
Baseball	
1900–1910	25–50
1911–1920	20–40
1921–1930	15–30
1931–1940	12–25
1941–1950	10–20
1951–1960	10–15
1961–1970	2–4

Decade	Value ($)
1971–1980	2–3
1980–present	1–2

Football

Pre-1930	10–20
1931–1940	7–12
1941–1950	5–10
1951–1960	4–8
1961–1970	3–5
1971–1980	2–4
1981–present	1–2

Other Sports/Athletic Events

Pre-1910	10–20
1911–1920	10–15
1921–1930	8–12
1931–1940	4–8
1941–1955	3–7
1956–1960	2–4
1960–1969	1–3
1970–present	1–2

SPORTS ILLUSTRATED
(THE TWENTY MOST VALUABLE ISSUES)

Year	Issue/Number	Description	Value ($)
1954	August 16/#1	Eddie Matthews	100–200+
1954	August 23/#2	Golf, Yankees, Mickey Mantle	150–300+

Year	Issue/Number	Description	Value ($)
1954	August 30	Swimsuit Cover, Yankees	15–30
1954	September 7	Sailing/Robin Roberts	15–30
1954	October 11	Marilyn Monroe and Joe DiMaggio, Leo Durocher, World Series	25–50+
1955	January 3	Roger Bannister, Willie Mays	25–50
1955	April 11	Willie Mays and Leo Durocher	50–100+
1955	June 27	Duke Snider	50–100+
1955	July 11	Yogi Berra	100–200+
1955	August 1	Ted Williams	100–200
1955	August 15	Ed Matthews	25–50
1955	October 24	Hopalong Cassidy	25–50
1956	April 9	Baseball Special	30–60
1956	May 14	Al Kaline	25–50
1956	June 18	Mickey Mantle	50–100
1956	August 20	Ed Matthews, Ted Williams	25–50
1956	September 10	Whitey Ford, Yankees	25–50
1956	October 1	Mickey Mantle, World Series	50–100
1957	March 4	Mickey Mantle	50–100
1957	July 8	Ted Williams, Stan Musial, All-Star Special	50–100

Detective, Romance, True Story, and Men's Adventure Magazines

⁂

There are basically two types of buyers of these types of magazines. The first is collectors of dramatic, unusual, or violent cover artwork. The most sought-after covers are those depicting female bondage, covers that had their heyday in the 1960s. Issues of men's adventure magazines showing Nazis or Japanese soldiers tormenting half-naked women on the cover have seen their values triple in the past couple of years. Detective magazines that feature scantily clad seductive females who are either being threatened or are themselves about to commit a crime are becoming almost impossible to find except from professional magazine dealers. The most valuable issues are those from the 1940s and very early 1950s. The second type of buyer is mainly interested in reading the stories—generally issues from 1960 to the present. Values for this type of magazine are constant. A detective or romance magazine issue that features a cover photo or illustration of female bondage is considered to be "Outstanding Cover Copy." All other issues are considered a "Reading Copy."

DETECTIVE, ROMANCE, TRUE STORY, AND MEN'S ADVENTURE MAGAZINE VALUES

Pre-1930	Value ($)
Reading Copy	10–20
Outstanding Cover Copy	20–50

#2, circa 1959

September 1973

June 1972

December 1971

November 1963

March, #1, 1963

Spring 1957

October 1962

June 1967

August 1925   *October 1925*   *June 1930*

March 1939   *August 1944*   *May 1940*

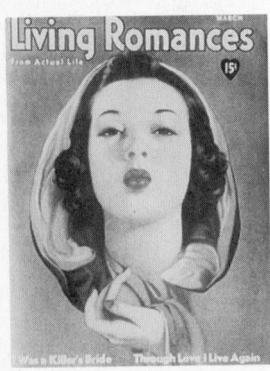

March, #2, 1940   *December 1937*   *June 1940*

May 1940

November 1940

October 1940

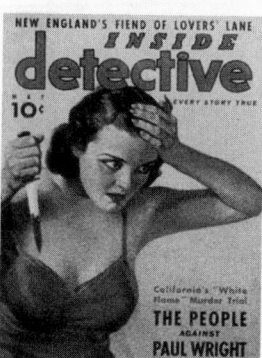

May 1938

September 1940

December 1940

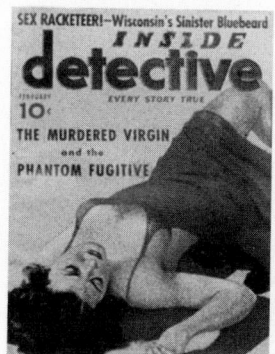

February 1938

October 1951

April 1950

1930–1940	Value ($)
Reading Copy	5–15
Outstanding Cover Copy	20–40

1941–1950	
Reading Copy	5–10
Outstanding Cover Copy	20–40

1951–1960	
Reading Copy	3–8
Outstanding Cover Copy	8–15
Covers featuring Nazis or Japanese soldiers tormenting a female	20–40+

1961–1971	
Reading Copy	3–6
Outstanding Cover Copy	5–10
Covers featuring Nazis or Japanese soldiers tormenting a female	15–30+

1972–1979	
Reading Copy	1–3
Outstanding Cover Copy	3–10

1980–present	
Reading Copy	1–2
Outstanding Cover Copy	3–10

Illustrated Magazines

The vast majority of mainstream magazines from just before the turn of the century to the present hold very little value (fifty cents to a couple of dollars each). What sets certain issues apart is whether or not they include covers, ads, posters, or illustrations by artists and illustrators of note. These issues are fascinating paper time machines that propel one into other times and ages. They present attitudes, fashions, illustrations, advertising, photographic, and a slice of history—they cover the spectrum from yellow journalism to slick high fashion.

It is impossible to list and price every issue ever published in the past hundred years, as there have been thousands of American publications and millions of different issues. Values for old magazines also vary a great deal. For example, say you find a pile of old magazines and they are sixty to seventy years old; most of the magazines will be worth $2 to $5 each, while other issues may have retail values of $10 to well over $100 each. What makes some of these issues more valuable than others is something on or in them that is salable to a collector, dealer, or general buyer. Many old magazines have multiple value. For instance, a mid-1920s *Ladies Home Journal* may have a cover by Norman Rockwell, an advertisement by Maxfield Parrish, a Marvis Perfume ad, an article by F. Scott Fitzgerald, a paper doll page, auto ads, and on and on. Each of these separate items has value to the specialized collector looking for that certain type of old magazine.

Quite often a seller will acquire an old issue that is technically in poor condition and as such should be worthless. He will then take the time to inspect each page slowly and carefully to see if the issue contains valuable illustrations. Quite often, a magazine that seemed worthless can be a valuable and salable collectors' item. In cases such as this, the seller or buyer will carefully remove the illustrations, discarding the rest of the magazine, and mat and frame them.

During the Golden Age of Illustration (about 1895 to 1930), magazine covers, ads, and story illustrations were created by a wide variety of highly paid illustrators. These illustrated items make up most of an old magazine's value. Illustrator-oriented items are sought not only nation-wide, but also worldwide.

The most exciting and least expensive way to acquire old magazines that may contain valuable illustrations is to seek them out at flea markets, garage sales, and estate sales, and to place small inexpensive ads in your local penny-saver publication. Most sellers at these venues have acquired their magazines while cleaning out the attic, basement, or garage of an aged relative, friend, or client, without a clue to their real value. Always ask the seller if he or she has more issues than what they are presently offering. It is not uncommon for the seller to have much, much more back at home or at a warehouse waiting to be thrown away. Both you and the seller will be glad that you asked. This type of buying adventure is still to be had, but it is quickly becoming a thing of the past. As more and more people be-come aware of the true values of magazines, there will be fewer opportuni-ties to acquire large numbers of magazines at very low prices.

The most reliable sources for these magazines continue to be back-issue magazine shops, mail-order dealers, paper shows, Internet auction sites, and local mall collectors' shows. One of the best sources for buying, sell-ing, or just learning about old magazines is the *Illustrator Collector's News,* located at P.O. Box 1958, Sequim, WA 98382 (Illustrator Collector's Hot-line: 360-452-3810 e-mail: ticn@olypen.com). You can also visit their Web site at http://www.olypen.com/ticn/. A one-year subscription to this inter-esting and informative publication is $17 for first class posting. This publi-cation also offers very inexpensive classified advertising.

For more info regarding issues that may not be listed in this guide, call the guide's hotline: 201-641-7212, or e-mail henkellang@aol.com.

THE TWELVE MOST COLLECTIBLE ILLUSTRATORS

The following is a list of today's most popular illustrators. Magazines that feature their illustrations bring high prices. There are thousands of other minor illustrators whose work appears in magazines of the past

100 years; some bring very high values and some do not. There are also hundreds of other illustrators who are becoming more popular every day, and their prices have not yet been established. Pinup artists and illustrators from the 1930s through the 1950s are becoming very much in demand. Some of the more popular of this growing group of illustrators are Rolf Armstrong, Zoe Mozert, Earl Moran, Eoch Bolles, Billy De Vorss, Gil Elvgren, and Earl MacPherson.

Besides doing thousands of magazine illustrations, the following twelve illustrators created many calendars, playing cards, book illustrations, art prints, and a great variety of illustrated paper items.

Illustrator	Years Worked	Value ($)
Maxfield Parrish	1895–1936	20–225
Norman Rockwell	1914–1975	2–600+
Alberto Varga	1920–1974	5–125+
George Petty	1932–1955	5–100
Rose O'Neal	1896–1935	5–100
Harrison Fisher	1890–1935	5–75
Erté	1916–1936	10–100
Coles Phillips	1907–1927	2–35
Rolf Armstrong	1914–1932	10–80
J. C. Leyendecker	1896–1951	5–90
F. X. Leyendecker	1886–1924	5–100
Jessie Wilcox Smith	1900–1934	5–45

ALBERTO VARGA
MAGAZINES FEATURING VARGA WORK

(A Sampling)

Year	Issue	Description	Value ($)
Dance			
1931	June	Cover: Pavlova	75–100
	August	Cover: Spanish Girl	75–125
Esquire			
1940	October	Centerfold: Love at Second Sight	30–70
1941	January	Centerfold: Double Trouble	30–70
	February	Centerfold: Lullaby for a Dream	30–70

February 1927

February 1927

Year	Issue	Description	Value ($)
1943	January	6-page Calendar Special	50–100
	February	Centerfold: Song for a Soldier	30–75
1946	January	Centerfold: Miss January	25–50
	February	Centerfold: Saints Be Praised	25–50

Ladies' Home Journal

Year	Issue	Description	Value ($)
1942	November	¼-page Sealy ad	10–20
1943	November	Jergen's ad	15–30

Mademoiselle

Year	Issue	Description	Value ($)
1941	February	Calendar ad	10–25

Motion Picture

Year	Issue	Description	Value ($)
1924	February	Leatrice Joy	35–75

Newsweek

Year	Issue	Description	Value ($)
1940	October 23	Feature Article	10–20

Theatre

Year	Issue	Description	Value ($)
1920	February	Cover	50–100

ROSE O'NEAL
MAGAZINES FEATURING O'NEAL WORK

(A Sampling)

Rose O'Neal is the most famous woman illustrator of all time. She is primarily known for her Kewpie art, though her talents were much broader than just Kewpies. Her old paper items sell very well, and there is a large number of faithful followers who avidly hunt for her old illustrations and magazine covers. When Rose O'Neal material is offered for sale, it generally sells immediately.

Year	Issue	Description	Value ($)

Appleton's Magazine

Year	Issue	Description	Value ($)
1905	December	Illustration	20–40

Art Decorations

Year	Issue	Description	Value ($)
1922	April	Article	10–20

Year	Issue	Description	Value ($)
Broadway			
1908	August	Jell-O ad	25–50
Christian Herald			
1909	April	Jell-O ad	20–40
Cosmopolitan			
1903	August	Illustration	15–30
1928	September	Illustration	15–30
1930	November	Illustration	20–40
1931	September	Illustration	20–40
Delineator			
1928	May	Kewpie Illustration	25–50
	July	Kewpie Illustration	25–50
Everybody's			
1908	August	Illustration	15–30
Good Housekeeping			
(Most containing four pages of Kewpie illustrations.)			
1914	May	Kewpies Are Coming	20–40
	August	Kewpies and Little Tibby's Tree	20–40
	September	Kewpies and Young McShanes	20–40
1915	January	Kewpies and Old Father	15–30
1916	April	Kewpies and Little Tommy Todd	15–30
1917	December	Kewpies and Forgotten Toys	15–30
1918	January	Kewpies and Their Winter Industry	15–30
	July	Kewpies and Liberty's Birthday	15–30
1919	May	Kewpies and the Haunted House	20–40
Hearst's Magazine			
1928	June	Illustration	15–30

December 1906

February 1927

Year	Issue	Description	Value ($)
Hobbies			
1946	June	Illustration	10–20
Ladies Home Journal			
1927	April	Kewpies	10–20
Munsey			
1905	December	Illustration	15–30
Puck			
1897	September 15	Cover	50–100
	December 22	Illustration	20–40
1898	January 5	Illustration	20–40
	February 9	Illustration	35–75
1900	January 9	Illustration	15–30
	April 11	Illustration	25–50
1903	March 11	Illustration	20–40
1904	March 30	Illustration	20–40
	April 20	Illustration	20–40
1926	April	Illustration	10–20
1927	February	Illustration	10–20
Smart Set			
1912	September	Illustration	25–50
Woman Citizen			
1925	December	Article	10–20
Woman's Home Companion			
(Dotty Darling and Kewpies)			
1910	September	Kewpie: Just How It Happened	30–75
1911	February	D.D.'s Kewpish Valentine	20–40
	March	Kewpies Teach D.D. to Fly	20–40
Woman's World			
1932	November	Oxydol ad	15–30

GEORGE PETTY
MAGAZINES FEATURING PETTY WORK

(A Sampling)

Year	Issue	Description	Value ($)
Esquire			
1933	August	Pinups: Darling and Pardon Me, Miss	20–40
1934	June	Pinup: Oh, Mr. Feinberg	20–40
1935	February	Old Gold cigarette ad: Stymied by a Stupid	10–25
	March	Old Gold cigarette ad: Wearied by a Windbag	10–25
	April	Old Gold cigarette ad: Pawed by a Pudgy-Widgy	10–25
	May	Old Gold cigarette ad: Shanghaied by a Silly Salt	10–25
	June	Old Gold cigarette ad: Tortured by a Tele-Phoney	10–25
	July	Old Gold cigarette ad: Bothered by a Beach Bore Pinup: Tired Folks	20–40
	August	Old Gold cigarette ad: No-Noed by a Nifty Number	10–20
	September	Old Cigarette ad: Marooned with a Mental Mummy	10–20
	October	Old Gold cigarette ad: Hitched to a Humrummy	10–20
	November	Old Gold cigarette ad: Riled by a Raccoon Rah-Rah	10–20
	December	Old Gold cigarette ad: Smacked by a Sappy Santa	10–20
1939	December	Pinup: Well	30–60
1940	January	Pinup: So He Pointed Out	25–50
1941	January	Pinup: Remember Me	25–50
	February	Pinup: Yes, Yes, Yes	25–50
	March	Pinup: No It Isn't That	25–50
1946	September	½-page Springmaid Fabrics ad	7–15

Year	Issue	Description	Value ($)
1955	January	Pinup: Lady Fair	15–30
1971	October	Girl on Swing cover illustration	7–15

Intimate Romances

1948	August	Ad	10–20

True

1945	January	Pinup: Miss Pouty	15–30
	February	Pinup: Miss Athlete	15–30
	March	Pinup: Miss Clinging Vine	15–30
	April	Pinup: Miss Career Girl	15–30
	June	Pinup: Miss Bashful	15–30
	July	Pinup: She Wolf	15–30
	August	Pinup: Miss Pixie	15–30
	September	Pinup: Miss Self Salesman	15–30
	October	Pinup: Miss Exclusive	15–30
	November	Pinup: Miss Bewitching	15–30
	December	Pinup: Miss Wrong Number	15–30

Vogue

1937	October 1	Ad	10–20

NORMAN ROCKWELL
MAGAZINES FEATURING ROCKWELL WORK

(A Sampling)

Year	Issue	Description	Value ($)

American Boy

1916	December	Cover	50–100
1917	June	Cover	50–100
	July	Cover	50–100
	December	Cover	50–100
1918	May	Ad	20–40
1919	July	Ad	20–40
1920	April	Cover	35–75
	December	Cover	35–75

American Magazine

1918	November	Cover	50–100
1919	April	Cover	50–100

Year	Issue	Description	Value ($)
1919	July	Cover	50–100
1921	May	Cover	40–80
	October	Cover	40–80
1922	February	Cover	40–75
1923	March	Cover	35–70

Boy's Life

Year	Issue	Description	Value ($)
1913	September	Cover	200–400
	October	Cover	125–300
	November	Cover	125–300
	December	Cover	125–300
1914	January	Cover	100–250
	February	Cover	100–250
	March	Cover	100–250
1915	May	Cover	100–225
	August	Cover	100–225
1919	February	Cover	100–225
	July	Cover	100–225
1921	July	Cover	100–200
1926	February	Cover	100–200
1927	February	Cover	50–110
1929	February	Cover	50–110
1931	February	Cover	50–110
1933	February	Cover	50–110
1934	February	Cover	50–100
	April	Cover	50–100
1935	February	Cover	50–100
	July	Cover	50–100
1936	February	Cover	45–90
1940	February	Cover	35–70
1941	February	Cover	25–50
1942	February	Cover	25–50
1943	February	Cover	25–50
1949	February	Cover	20–40
1950	February	Cover	20–40
1953	February	Cover	20–40
1959	February	Cover	20–40
1963	February	Cover	15–30
1965	February	Cover	15–30

Year	Issue	Description	Value ($)
1971	March	Cover	12–25

Collier's

1919	March 1	Cover	75–100
	March 19	Cover	75–100
	April 19	Cover	75–100
1937	January 5	Ad	10–20
	April 10	Ad	10–20

Country Gentleman

1917	August 25	Cover	50–100
	October 6	Cover	45–90
1918	April 6	Cover	40–80
1919	April 26	Cover	40–80
1920	May 8	Cover	40–80
1921	June 4	Cover	35–70
1922	May 18	Cover	35–70

Design Arts & Education

1980	March/April	Cover	10–20

Family Circle

1967	December	Cover	10–20
1968	December	Cover	10–20

Grade Teacher

1945	September	Cover	25–50
1946	November	Cover	25–50
1948	January	Cover	20–40

Judge

1917	January 15	Cover	150–300
1917	July 7	Cover	150–300

Ladies' Home Journal

1928	April	Cover	25–50
1930	August	Ad	5–10
1932	April	Cover	25–50

Look

1966	June 14	Cover	10–20

Year	Issue	Description	Value ($)
McCall's Magazine			
1964	December	Cover	10–20
Newsweek			
1970	December 28	Cover	10–20
Reader's Digest			
1937	November	Ad	5–10
1957	April	Ad	5–10
	August	Ad	5–10
	December	Ad	5–10
1958	April	Ad	3–6
	June	Ad	3–6
	July	Ad	3–6
	August	Ad	3–6
	September	Ad	3–6
	October	Ad	3–5
	November	Ad	3–5
1959	January	Ad	3–5
	February	Ad	3–5
	November	Ad	3–5
	December	Ad	3–5
Saturday Evening Post			
1916	May 20	Cover	500–1,000
	June 3	Cover	200–400
	August 5	Cover	150–300
	September 16	Cover	125–250
1917	January 13	Cover	100–200
	May 12	Cover	100–200
	June 16	Cover	100–200
	September 15	Ad	15–30
	October 6	Ad	10–20
1918	January 26	Cover	75–150
	February 23	Ad	10–20
	August 10	Cover	75–150
1919	June 28	Cover	100–200
	October 4	Cover	75–150
	December 20	Cover	75–150
1920	January 17	Cover	75–150

Year	Issue	Description	Value ($)
1920	May 1	Cover	75–150
	May 15	Cover	75–150
	July 10	Ad	10–20
	July 31	Cover	75–150
	August 28	Cover	75–150
	December 4	Cover	300–600
1921	January 29	Cover	75–150
	March 12	Cover	75–150
	June 4	Cover	75–150
	July 9	Cover	75–150
	August 13	Cover	75–125
	October 1	Cover	75–125
	December 3	Cover	75–125
1922	January 14	Cover	75–150
	February 19	Cover	75–150
	April 8	Cover	75–150
	April 22	Cover	75–150
	May 20	Cover	75–150
	June 10	Cover	75–150
	September	Cover	200–400
	October 7	Ad	10–20
	November 11	Ad	10–20
	December 9	Cover	100–200
1923	February 3	Cover	75–150
	April 28	Cover	50–100
	May 26	Cover	75–150
	June 23	Cover	75–150
	August 18	Cover	50–100
	October 13	Ad	10–20
	November 10	Cover	50–100
	December 8	Cover	50–100
1924	July 19	Cover	50–100
	September 27	Cover	50–100
	October 18	Cover	75–150
	November 1	Ad	10–20
	December 6	Cover	50–100
1925	January 31	Cover	50–100
	April 18	Cover	50–100

June 1926

August 1908

March 20, 1915

November 1918

February 9, 1918

August 3, 1918

January 29, 1913

April 25, 1914

Year	Issue	Description	Value ($)
1925	May 16	Cover	50–100
	June 27	Cover	50–100
	July 11	Cover	50–100
	August 29	Cover	50–100
	September 19	Cover	50–100
	November 21	Cover	100–200
1926	March 27	Cover	50–100
	April 26	Cover	100–200
	August 19	Cover	100–200
	October 2	Cover	50–100
	December 4	Cover	125–225
1927	June 4	Cover	50–125
	August 13	Cover	75–150
	September 24	Cover	75–125
	October 22	Cover	75–125
	December 3	Cover	60–120
1928	January 21	Cover	50–100
	April 14	Cover	100–200
	May 5	Cover	50–100
	May 26	Cover	75–125
	June 23	Cover	50–100
	July 21	Cover	50–100
	August 18	Cover	60–120
	December 8	Cover	50–100
1929	March 9	Cover	200–750
	April 20	Cover	100–200
	May 4	Cover	50–100
	June 15	Cover	50–100
	July 13	Cover	50–100
	August 3	Cover	200–400
	September 28	Cover	40–75
	December 7	Cover	75–150
1930	April 12	Cover	40–75
	May 24	Cover	100–200
	November 8	Cover	100–200
	December 6	Cover	40–75
1931	January	Cover	30–60
	March 28	Cover	75–125
	April 18	Cover	30–60

Year	Issue	Description	Value ($)
1931	June 13	Cover	25–50
	July 25	Cover	75–125
	September 5	Cover	75–125
	November 7	Cover	75–125
	December 12	Cover	75–125
1932	January 30	Cover	25–50
1933	June 17	Cover	25–50
	October 21	Cover	25–50
1934	June 30	Cover	50–100
	September 22	Cover	25–50
	October 20	Cover	25–50
1935	February 9	Cover	25–50
	March 9	Cover	25–50
	July 13	Cover	25–50
	November 16	Cover	25–50
	December 21	Cover	75–150
1936	May 30	Cover	25–50
	July 11	Cover	25–50
	September 26	Cover	25–50
	October 24	Cover	25–50
	November 21	Cover	35–100
1937	December 19	Cover	35–100
1938	April 23	Cover	25–50
	October 8	Cover	50–100
	December 17	Cover	25–50
1939	March 18	Cover	20–40
	April 29	Cover	20–40
	November 4	Cover	20–40
	December 16	Cover	40–80
1940	March 30	Cover	20–40
	April 27	Cover	25–50
	August 24	Cover	20–40
	December 28	Cover	20–40
1941	October 4	Cover	35–75
	December 20	Cover	35–75
1942	February 7	Cover	35–75
	March 21	Cover	35–75
	June 27	Cover	20–40

Year	Issue	Description	Value ($)
1943	May 29	Cover	10–20
	June 26	Cover	10–25
	September 4	Cover	10–25
1944	January 1	Cover	20–40
	March 4	Cover	20–40
	September 16	Cover	25–50
1945	May 26	Cover	100–200
	August 11	Cover	25–50
	October 14	Cover	20–40
1946	August 3	Cover	20–40
	October 5	Cover	20–40
	November 16	Cover	20–40
	December 7	Cover	20–40
1947	January 11	Cover	20–40
	March 22	Cover	20–40
	May 3	Cover	20–40
1948	January 24	Cover	20–40
	April 3	Cover	30–60
	October 30	Cover	20–40
	December 25	Cover	20–40
1949	July 9	Cover	30–60
	November 5	Cover	35–75
1950	October 21	Cover	20–40
	November 18	Cover	20–40
1951	November 24	Cover	20–40
1952	February 16	Cover	20–40
1953	October 11	Cover	20–40
1954	January 9	Cover	20–40
1955	March 12	Cover	20–40
1956	May 16	Cover	15–30
1957	May 25	Cover	25–50
	June 29	Cover	25–50
	September 7	Cover	20–40
1958	August 30	Cover	20–40
	November 8	Cover	20–40
1959	October 24	Cover	25–50
1960	September 17	Cover	20–40
1961	April 1	Cover	15–30

Year	Issue	Description	Value ($)
1961	November 25	Cover	10–20
Town and Country			
1918	May	Fisk Tire ad	30–60
1919	August	Fisk Tire ad	30–60
True Story			
1955	June	Ad	5–10
	August	Ad	5–10
1956	August	Ad	5–10
Vanity Fair			
1921	March	Ad	30–60
1922	February	Ad	30–60
1926	November	Ad	20–40
Vermont Life			
1947	Summer	Cover	20–40
Woman's Home Companion			
1921	July	Ad	10–20
1923	March	Ad	10–20
1926	December	Ad	10–20
1927	May	Ad	10–20
1938	August	Ad	10–20
1945	November	Ad	10–20
1955	October	Ad	5–10

MAXFIELD PARRISH
MAGAZINES FEATURING PARRISH WORK

(A Sampling)

Year	Issue	Description	Value ($)
Atlantic Monthly			
1921	June	Hires ad	25–50
Agricultural Digest			
1934	November	Cover	20–40
American Heritage			
1970	December	Illustration	5–10

February 1928

June 1918

Year	Issue	Description	Value ($)
The Bookseller			
1914	May 1	Illustration	15–30
Century			
1900	December	Fisk Tire ad	15–30
Collier's			
1904	December 3	Cover	25–50
1906	November 17	Frontispiece	25–50
1908	January 25	Frontispiece	30–60
1929	January 5	Cover	50–100
Harper's Bazaar			
1895	December	Cover	50–100
1922	March	Jell-O ad	25–50
Nebraska Educational Journal			
1928	October	Cover	20–40
Pictorial Review			
1922	January	Jell-O ad	50–100
Progressive Farmer			
1952	June	Cover	20–40
St. Nicholas			
1898	December	Illustration	10–20
1900	November	Illustration	10–20
Town & Country			
1918	May	Fisk Tire ad	25–50
1919	August	Fisk Tire ad	25–50
Vanity Fair			
1922	February	Jell-O ad	40–80
Vogue			
1917	September 1	Fisk Tire ad	30–60
Woman's Home Companion			
1918	March	Djer-Kiss ad	40–80
Worlds Work			
1919	December	Fisk Tire ad	25–50
1921	June	Hires ad	20–40

Year	Issue	Description	Value ($)
Yankee			
1936	December	Cover	25–50
1968	December	Cover	7–15
1977	May	Cover	5–10
1979	December	Cover	2–5

JOSEPH CHRISTIAN
AND FRANK XAVIER LEYENDECKER
MAGAZINES FEATURING LEYENDECKER WORK

(A Sampling)

Joseph Christian Leyendecker and Frank Xavier Leyendecker were among the nation's most prolific magazine cover illustrators, their work spanning nearly seventy years. Joseph Christian Leyendecker's covers were published from 1896 to 1951, and his brother Frank Xavier Leyendecker's were published from 1886 to 1924. Both brothers today have a large following of collectors. Joseph Christian did more published illustration work than almost anyone, with the exception of Norman Rockwell. In the early years Norman Rockwell emulated Leyendecker's style. In the first quarter of this century Leyendecker art was predominant in the form of magazine covers, advertising, story illustrations, books, and posters.

Joseph Christian Leyendecker had a rather large cult/art following of Americans who framed his magazine art to hang in their homes in the 1910s and 1920s. Many of the colorful ads Joseph Christian created adorned the walls in the rooms of many college men of those days. His strong and bold art helped create the fashion trends that influenced millions of men and women. There are still those who remember the days of steel-jawed Arrow Shirt Man and the Kuppenheimer man. These fantasy men were women's answers to the Gibson Girl.

Both brothers were born in Germany and traveled with their family to Chicago in 1882. There they both displayed an extraordinary talent for drawing at an early age. By the time they were teenagers and had acquired some formal training, the doors to small ad agencies in Chicago opened up to them. After a few years of art training in Paris—at the Academie Du Julian—the brothers returned home with newly honed skills and began illustrating for many of the high-paying magazines of the day. Frank died early in his career (1924); much of his early work was as good as if not better than his older brother's. Many experts believe his true potential was never fully realized.

Year	Issue	Description	Value ($)
Arts and Decoration			
1922	November	Frank Xavier cover	20–30
Collier's			
1901	Anniversary Issue	Frank Xavier cover	50–100
1902	July 5	Frank Xavier cover	50–100
	December 20	Frank Xavier cover	50–100
1903	February 20	Frank Xavier cover	30–75
	June 27	Frank Xavier cover	30–75
	July 25	Frank Xavier cover	30–75
1904	February 13	Frank Xavier cover	50–100
	March 5	Joseph Christian cover	30–75
	May 7	Joseph Christian cover	25–50
	May 14	Frank Xavier cover	40–80
	June 18	Joseph Christian cover	30–60
	July 4	Frank Xavier cover	35–75
	August 4	Frank Xavier cover	35–75
1907	January 19	Joseph Christian cover	25–50
	February 23	Joseph Christian cover	25–50
	March 23	Joseph Christian cover	30–60
	April 27	Joseph Christian cover	30–60
	May 25	Joseph Christian cover	30–60
	August 17	Frank Xavier cover	50–100
	August 31	Frank Xavier cover	50–100
	September 14	Joseph Christian cover	25–50
	September 19	Joseph Christian cover	25–50
	October 26	Joseph Christian cover	25–50
	November 9	Frank Xavier cover	50–100
	December 7	Joseph Christian cover	25–50
	December 21	Joseph Christian cover	35–75
1908	April 18	Frank Xavier cover	40–80
1909	January 9	Frank Xavier cover	40–80
	August 28	Joseph Christian cover	25–50
	October 16	Joseph Christian cover	25–50
1910	January 29	Frank Xavier cover	50–100
	February 26	Frank Xavier cover	50–100

Year	Issue	Description	Value ($)
1910	March 12	Frank Xavier cover	50–100
	April 30	Frank Xavier cover	50–100
	December 10	Frank Xavier cover	50–100
1912	June 19	Frank Xavier cover	40–80
1914	May 30	Frank Xavier cover	40–80
	September 12	Joseph Christian cover	25–50
	November 28	Joseph Christian cover	25–50
1915	February 20	Frank Xavier cover	40–80
	May 29	Frank Xavier cover	40–80
	June 19	Joseph Christian cover	20–40
	September 11	Frank Xavier cover	40–80
	October 9	Joseph Christian cover	20–40
	December 11	Joseph Christian cover	20–40
1916	January 8	Joseph Christian cover	20–40
	April 22	Joseph Christian cover	30–60
	June 24	Joseph Christian cover	25–50
	September 23	Joseph Christian cover	25–50
	October 23	Joseph Christian cover	25–50
1917	January 6	Joseph Christian cover	25–50
	April 14	Joseph Christian cover	25–50
	April 28	Joseph Christian cover	25–50
	July 7	Joseph Christian cover	25–50
	November 10	Joseph Christian cover	25–50

Inland Printer

Year	Issue	Description	Value ($)
1896	November	Joseph Christian cover	125–200
1897	January	Joseph Christian cover	125–200
	February	Joseph Christian cover	100–200
	March	Joseph Christian cover	100–200
	August	Joseph Christian cover	100–200
	September	Joseph Christian cover	100–200

Saturday Evening Post

Year	Issue	Description	Value ($)
1899	May 20	Joseph Christian cover	30–60
1900	May 26	Frank Xavier cover	30–60
1901	March 23	Frank Xavier cover	25–50
	June 22	Frank Xavier cover	25–50
1902	May 31	Frank Xavier cover	20–40
1910	January 1	Joseph Christian cover	20–40

Year	Issue	Description	Value ($)
1910	February 12	Joseph Christian cover	20–40
1912	April 6	Joseph Christian cover	20–40
	May 25	Joseph Christian cover	20–40
	June 22	Joseph Christian cover	20–40
	July 6	Joseph Christian cover	30–60
	September 28	Frank Xavier cover	30–60
	October 12	Frank Xavier cover	30–60
1914	January 3	Joseph Christian cover	15–30
	June 13	Joseph Christian cover	15–30
	July 4	Joseph Christian cover	15–30
	August 22	Frank Xavier cover	40–80
	September 19	Joseph Christian cover	15–30
	October 3	Joseph Christian cover	15–30
	October 24	Joseph Christian cover	15–30
	November 21	Joseph Christian cover	20–50
	November 28	Joseph Christian cover	20–50
	December 19	Joseph Christian cover	20–50
1915	January 2	Joseph Christian cover	20–40
	April 3	Joseph Christian cover	20–40
	May 22	Joseph Christian cover	20–40
	June 12	Joseph Christian cover	15–30
	July 24	Joseph Christian cover	20–40
	August 7	Joseph Christian cover	20–40
	December 11	Joseph Christian cover	15–30
	December 25	Joseph Christian cover	15–30
1916	January 1	Joseph Christian cover	15–30
	March 11	Joseph Christian cover	15–30
	April 15	Joseph Christian cover	15–30
	April 22	Joseph Christian cover	25–50
	May 6	Joseph Christian cover	20–40
	June 17	Joseph Christian cover	20–40
	July 1	Joseph Christian cover	20–40
	August 26	Joseph Christian cover	35–75
	December 8	Joseph Christian cover	15–30
1921	January 1	Joseph Christian cover	15–30
	March 26	Joseph Christian cover	10–25
	June 11	Joseph Christian cover	10–25
	December 10	Joseph Christian cover	10–25

Year	Issue	Description	Value ($)
1921	December 24	Joseph Christian cover	10–25
	December 31	Joseph Christian cover	10–25
1929	March 30	Joseph Christian cover	20–30
	June 8	Joseph Christian cover	20–30
1934	March 10	Joseph Christian cover	20–30
	July 7	Joseph Christian cover	20–30
	December 1	Joseph Christian cover	20–40
	December 29	Joseph Christian cover	20–40
1937	January 2	Joseph Christian cover	10–25
	February 20	Joseph Christian cover	15–25
	May 15	Joseph Christian cover	15–25
	July 3	Joseph Christian cover	15–25
	December 18	Joseph Christian cover	15–30

JESSIE WILCOX SMITH
MAGAZINES FEATURING SMITH WORK

(A Sampling)

Year	Issue	Description	Value ($)
American Heritage			
1956	December	Illustration	10–20
Collier's Magazine			
1905	November 25	Cover	25–50
Good Housekeeping			
1932	December	Illustration	10–20
1933	February	Cover	20–40
Ladies' Home Journal			
1905	April	Cover	20–40
McLure's Magazine			
1905	February	Illustration	20–45

Media Magazines

✠

A media magazine is any magazine that features news of the day on its cover and in its stories. These media magazines are in general very difficult to sell unless they feature spectacular, tragic, or history-making events of the day. Such titles as *Time, Newsweek, Look, Pic, Click,* and even *The National Enquirer* fall into this category. Below we have valued average media magazines—that is, issues that do not feature an outstanding cover or special story. Exceptional issues will be issues that feature major national or international events, such as the sinking of the *Titanic* or the *Lusitania,* the San Francisco earthquake, the assassination of presidents or world leaders, the beginning or ending of a world war, combat covers from major battles, the birth and progress of famous people (for example, the Dionne quintuplets), historic accomplishments of people such as Charles Lindbergh and other heroes, or of infamous people such as Machine Gun Kelly, Bonnie and Clyde, or Adolf Hitler. These issues will have a value considerably higher than that of an average media magazine. A good starting price for these special issues is 100 to 500 percent of the listed average issue value for that time. It is also important to note that a magazine will sell for whatever the present market will bear. Marketing your magazine to collectors that have a fervent interest in the subject matter featured in your issue will always bring you higher prices. Values on specific subjects can be greatly affected by current events. For example, when the movie *Titanic* was released, any magazine that had the slightest mention of this tragic event saw its value literally go through the roof. Now that *Titanic* mania has somewhat abated, these magazines have also settled down to a lower value. A great place to test the current market for these special issues is an Internet auction. The cost to list your magazines is minimal and the benefits can be tremendous.

AVERAGE MEDIA MAGAZINE VALUES

Issues	Value ($)
Pre-1913	10–25
1913–1928	10–20
1929–1938	10–15
1939–1945	10–25
1946–1955	6–12
1956–1959	4–7
1960–1965	2–5
1966–1975	2–4
1976–1985	1–2
1986–present	Less than 1

General Circulation Magazines

❄

Any magazine that can be found on most newsstands and in many homes that does not fall into any specific collecting category is a "general circulation magazine" or "average magazine." Such titles as *Redbook, Cosmopolitan, Vanity Fair, Elle, Reader's Digest, Saturday Evening Post, Woman's Day, Collier's, The New Yorker,* and countless others that do not contain collectible illustrations or celebrity covers, stories, or photos have a minimal value. The buyers of this type of magazine usually are only willing to pay a very modest price.

The best way to price general circulation magazines is by their age, and for issues published before 1960, by their condition. Issues before 1960 in truly fine to mint condition can sell for up to 100 percent more than the values listed below.

GENERAL CIRCULATION MAGAZINE VALUES

Issues	Value ($)
Pre-1913	10–25
1913–1928	10–20
1929–1938	10–15
1939–1945	10–25
1946–1955	6–12
1956–1959	4–7
1960–1965	2–5
1966–1975	2–4
1976–1975	1–2
1986–present	Less than 1

August 6, 1938

May 27, 1939

November 25, 1939

June 1941

February 1951

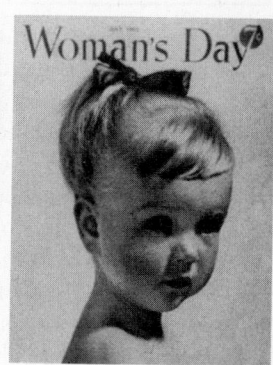

July 1952

January 1959

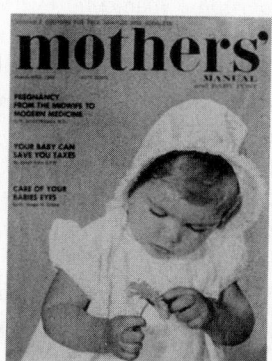

March 4, 1965

July 1945

National Geographic Magazine

※

If you have ever read *National Geographic,* you have discovered a means of knowledge through travel, adventure, and exploration; showcasing scientific achievements not only from this earth, but from the doorstep of the infinitesimal up the stairway to the universe, this magazine can open the door to learning. You may be a student, a lawyer, a doctor, or perhaps a person who likes to read or collect things; no matter, it is important to know that this magazine has been popular for nearly a century. *National Geographic,* with its comprehensive stories and excellent illustrations, will continue to be published as long as ideals of those honorable gentlemen who started the National Geographic Society are continued, as long as there are frontiers to explore, expeditions to sponsor, and dreams to fulfill.

The National Geographic Society, in Washington, D.C., has sold and circulated *National Geographic* magazine every month since January 1896 (except for the years 1897 and 1917, when one magazine was issued to cover a two-month period). There were nine publications of this magazine issued between 1888 and 1891, before the first monthly in 1896. Also, in 1891 and running through the year 1895 there were twenty-seven brochures produced, making a total of thirty-six early publications. In those early years the magazine was redbrick in color, and some of these issues are still around. Altogether, there are six different cover designs up to the present.

If you have been thinking of collecting magazines, it would be best to give these magazines some serious thought. A complete set consisting of everything published by the National Geographic Society (all being originals) has a value of $30,000 to $85,000. Few hobbies give people as much satisfaction as collecting old *National Geographics*. The recent growth in the number of *National Geographic* collectors is astonishing, and the ranks are getting bigger every day. Currently, the circulation of the magazine is above 20 million. With circulation this high, there are more and more people demanding the earliest issue numbers. The type of collection you wish to arrange is entirely up to you. Some collectors try to acquire all the issues, while others add the maps and pictorial supplements. There are collectors who are not satisfied until they add the book publications also.

For the past twenty-five years the most reliable source for buying and selling *National Geographic* magazine has been the mail-order dealer Don Smith, located at 3930 Rankin Street, Louisville, KY 40214. Mr. Smith has continuously offered many of the early issues and is regarded as "the source" for acquiring copies of the magazine and all other National Geographic Society publications from the nineteenth century to the most current issue. He, at present, offers an excellent reference guide, *National Geographic Magazine for Collectors 1888–1990's* for $12.00. More common issues, 1920 to the present, can still, on occasion, be found in old book and magazine stores. The Salvation Army, Goodwill, and other nonprofit secondhand stores are also excellent sources for the more common issues. These secondhand stores will generally sell common issues for as low as $.25 to $1 per copy. Other sources include library book sales, garage/yard sales, estate sales, flea markets, and your local magazine recycling center. Often a seller at a garage sale, flea market, or library sale will actually give you the remaining issues for free at the end of the day. In my experiences with small-town magazine recycling centers, I have found that most are more than happy to put aside issues of *National Geographic* for you. Many laypeople find it difficult to see any issue of this wonderful magazine being trashed and this attitude can work for the beginning collector on a tight budget. Finally, Internet auctions are also excellent places to find complete runs at often very fair prices for the common issues, and rarer issues at competitive prices for those collectors who can afford them.

Within our listing of *National Geographics*, we have given the contents for the 100 most popular issues. These 100 issues are not among the most valuable or scarce issues, but are rather the issues that are sought after and purchased by collectors more often than other issues. To date there is no reference book that lists in chronological order the contents for all issues of *National Geographic*. An excellent source listing contents by subject is *The Quick Reference Guide to National Geo-*

graphic 1955–1990, by Jack Hobart; it can be purchased by sending $8 (U.S.) to Geoimages Publishing Company, P.O. Box 45677, Los Angeles, CA 90045.

Note: In 1964 the National Geographic Society published reprint issues of the original magazine from 1888 through 1907. These reprints are clearly marked "reprint" on the front covers.

NATIONAL GEOGRAPHIC MAGAZINE VALUES

Year	Issue/Cover Subject	Value ($)
1888	Vol. 1, #1	5,000–13,000
1888–1889	Vol. 1, #2	3,000–5,000
	Vol. 1, #3	3,000–5,000
	Vol. 1, #4	3,000–4,500
1890	Vol. 2, #1–5	200–500
1891–1892	Vol. 3, #1–5	200–400
1892–1893	Vol. 4, #1–5	250–500
	Vol. 4, #6, #7	200–400
1893–1894	Vol. 5, #1–6	150–350
1894–1895	Vol. 6, #1–5	200–350
	Vol. 6, #6–9	200–300
1896	January–March	100–250
	April–December	100–200
1897	January, February, April–December	100–200
	March	225–400
1898	January, February, April–December	100–200
	March	200–400
1899	January, February	100–175
	March, April, May	300–400
	June, July	175–250
	August–December	100–200
1900	January–December	100–200

Year	Issue/Cover Subject	Value ($)
1901	All months	90–180
1902	August	150–225
	All other months	100–180
1903	All months	100–150
1904	January, March, May, November	100–200
	All other months	75–125
1905	January, February, March	125–200
	April, May	50–100
	June–December	40–75
1906	All months	25–50
1907	All months	20–40
1908	All months	20–40
1909	October—Discovery of the Pole	35–50
	All other months	20–40
1910	All months	20–40
1911	April, May, June	10–20
	July—Reptiles of the Lands	20–40
	All other months	20–40
1912	January, February, March	20–40
	September—Headhunters of the North Luzon	10–20
	October–China	10–20
	All other months	10–20
1913	April—In the Wonderland of Peru	25–40
	September—Ancient Egypt	10–20
	All other months	10–20
1914	January—Northern Africa	20–30
	May—Birds of Town and Country	10–20

Year	Issue/Cover Subject	Value ($)
1914	November—Young Russia	10–15
	All other months	10–15
1915	May—American Wildflowers	8–15
	August—American Game Birds	8–15
	All other months	5–10
1916	February—Flowers and Berries	8–15
	May	8–15
	June—Common American Wildflowers	8–12
	November	8–15
	All other months	5–10
1917	October—Our Flag Number	15–20
	All other months	4–8
1918	May	8–15
	All other months	4–8
1919	February	5–10
	March—Dogs	10–20
	All other months	4–8
1920	May—Common Mushrooms of the U.S.	6–12
1921	March—America in the Air	5–10
	June—Grass and Their Flowers	5–10
	All other months	4–8
1922	July	6–12
	All other months	4–8
1923	May—The Tomb of Tutankhamen	8–15
	October	5–10
	November	8–15
	All other months	4–8

Year	Issue/Cover Subject	Value ($)
1924	June—Flowers and Berries	5–10
	October—Goldfish	5–10
	All other months	4–8
1925	May—Ferns as a Hobby	5–10
	July—Flowers and Berries	5–10
	December	6–12
	All other months	4–8
1926	January—Pigeons	5–10
	April—Slime Molds	5–10
	August—Jellyfish	5–10
	All other months	4–8
1927	April—Fowl	6–12
	May	5–10
	July—Moths and Butterflies	5–10
	All other months	4–8
1928	January—Seeing America with Charles Lindbergh	6–12
	May—To Bogota and Back by Air with Charles Lindbergh	6–12
	All other months	4–8
1929	July—Insects	5–10
	All other months	4–8
1930	March—Fowl	5–10
	June—First World Airship Flight	5–10
	August—Air Conquest of Antarctica	5–10
	All other months	4–8
1931	March—Tropical Fish	6–9
	All other months	3–7
1932	All months	3–7
1933	July—Eagles, Hawks, and Vultures	5–10

Year	Issue/Cover Subject	Value ($)
1933	All other months	3–7
1934	May—Common Birds of North America	5–10
	September—Flags of the World	5–10
	October—Exploration of the Stratosphere, Wild Geese, Ducks and Swans	5–10
	All other months	3–7
1935	February—Birds of the Night	4–8
	All other months	3–7
1936	February—Man's Oldest Ally . . . The Dog	5–10
	November—Trains	5–10
	All other months	3–7
1937	January—Field Dogs	5–10
	April—Colonial Williamsburg	6–12
	May—Butterfly Migrants	6–12
	October—Hounds	6–12
	All other Months	4–8
1938	May—Monkeys	5–8
	November—Cats	6–12
	December	4–8
	All other months	3–7
1939	August—Flowers and Berries	4–8
	December—Cathedrals of England	4–8
	All other months	3–7
1940	January—Whales, Porpoises, and Dolphins	4–8
	February—Rubber	4–8

Year	Issue/Cover Subject	Value ($)
1940	March—Classic Lands	4–8
	July—The National Gallery of Art	4–8
	All other months	3–7
1941	October—Ancient Egypt	8–14
	December—Working Dogs	6–12
	All other months	3–7
1942	February—Dinosaurs	5–10
	April—California Wildflowers	5–10
	All other months	3–7
1943	February—Lions, Tigers, and Leopards	5–10
	June—Insignia of the U.S. Armed Forces	8–15
	October—Decorative Medals and Service Ribbons	6–12
	November—Non-Sporting Dogs	6–12
	December—War Insignia	5–10
1944	March—The Greek Way	6–9
	July—Indians of the Western Plains	6–9
	All other months	4–6
1945	January—Indians of the North Pacific Coast	6–9
	October—Wrens of Australia	5–8
	All other months	4–6
1946	November—The Roman Way	4–8
	All other months	4–6
1947	July—The World of Your Garden	5–7
	September—Bird Dogs	5–8
	October—Antarctica	5–7

Year	Issue/Cover Subject	Value ($)
1947	November—The Northern Lights	5–7
	All other months	4–6
1948	February—Indians of the Far West	4–8
	March—The Circus	5–10
	September—American Painting of the National Gallery	6–9
	December—Prehistoric Paintings of Lascaux	5–8
	All other months	4–6
1949	April—The British Way	4–8
	May—Flags of the Americas	4–8
	July—Shells	8–12
	August—Vegetables	6–8
	All other months	4–6
1950	June—The Vienna Treasures	5–7
	October—Peru and Bolivia	5–8
	December—Gems	5–10
	All other months	4–6
1951	January—Ancient Mesopotamia	5–7
	February—American Paintings	5–8
	September—Fruit	5–7
	November—Minerals	5–7
	All other months	4–6
1952	January—The National Gallery of Art	5–10
	All other months	4–6
1953	September—The Coronation of Queen Elizabeth II	5–8
	All other months	4–6

Year	Issue/Cover Subject	Value ($)
1954	July—Conquest of Mt. Everest	5–8
	October—Uranium	5–8
	All other months	4–6
1955	May—The Grand Canyon	5–8
	July—Lhasa and Tibet	5–8
	September—Literary England	5–8
	November—Egyptian Archaeology	5–8
	All other months	4–6
1956	January—Monkeys, Dodo Birds	5–7
	June—Alaska	5–7
	All other months	2–5
1957	April—Modern Rome	3–6
	December—Old Testament Times	3–7
	All other months	2–5
1958	May—The National Parks	2–7
	August—Dogs Who Work for Man	2–7
	December—Dead Sea Scrolls	2–7
	All other months	2–4
1959	June—Modern Germany	3–6
	September—The Soviet Union	3–6
	All other months	2–5
1960	February—The Drowned City of Port Royal	3–6
	September—Africa	3–6
	December—Japan	3–6
	All other months	2–5

Year	Issue/Cover Subject	Value ($)
1961	January—The White House	3–6
	March—Ireland	3–6
	April—The Civil War	3–6
	All other months	2–5
1962	March—Journey to Outer Mongolia	2–5
	June—John Glenn's Orbits	2–6
	September—Brazil	2–6
	All other months	2–5
1963	May—India	2–6
	August—Disneyland	2–5
	September—Australia	2–5
	October—75th Anniversary Special	2–5
	All other months	2–4
1964	January—The National Capitol	2–5
	March—The Last Full Measure: President Kennedy's Funeral	2–5
	November—Profiles of the President Part I	2–5
	All other months	2–4
1965	January—Profiles of the President Part II	2–5
	May—Profiles of the President Part III	2–5
	August—Sir Winston Churchill	2–4
	October—Profiles of the President Part IV	2–5
	All other months	2–4
1966	January—Profiles of the President Part V	3–6
	March—Moscow, The U.S.S.R.	3–6

Year	Issue/Cover Subject	Value ($)
1966	July—Our National Parks	3–6
	August—Bayeux Tapestry	3–6
	All other months	1–4
1967	March—The National Gallery of Art	2–5
	December—Where Jesus Walked	2–4
	All other months	1–4
1968	All months	1–4
1969	March—Seashells	1–4
	December—*Apollo 11*	1–4
	All other months	1–3
1970	March—Japan	1–4
	June—Rome	1–4
	August—Planets	1–4
	December—Pollution	1–4
	All other months	1–3
1971	All months	1–3
1972	October—The Amazon	2–4
	All other months	1–3
1973	January—Search for the Oldest People	2–4
	October—Chile	2–4
	All other months	1–3
1974	January—Gold	1–4
	May—The Universe	1–4
	All other months	1–4
1975	June—Alaska	2–5
	July—Food	2–4
	December—The Maya: Children of Time	3–6
	All other months	1–3
1976	January—In the Steps of Moses	2–5

Year	Issue/Cover Subject	Value ($)
1976	July—This Land of Ours	1–4
	August—Venezuela	1–4
	September—Exploring the New Biology	1–4
	December—Whales	1–4
	All other months	1–3
1977	February—Egypt	2–4
	September—Leonardo da Vinci	2–4
	All other months	1–3
1978	August—Dinosaurs	2–4
	December—First Atlantic Balloon Crossing	2–4
	All other months	1–3
1979	July—Our National Parks	2–4
	All other months	1–3
1980	June—The Mystery of the Shroud	2–4
	All other months	1–3
1981	January—Mt. Saint Helens	1–3
	February—Special Report on Energy	1–3
	July—Saturn: The Riddle of the Rings	1–3
	All other months	1–2
1982	February—Napoleon	1–3
	September—Our National Forests, the Bahamas	1–3
	All other months	1–2
1983	June—The Universe	1–3
	All other months	1–2
1984	March—The Laser, Eagle Holograph Cover	2–5
	All other months	1–2
1985	January—The Planets	1–3

Year	Issue/Cover Subject	Value ($)
1985	November—Early Man Holograph Cover and Feature	1–3
	All other months	1–2
1986	December—The *Titanic*	2–4
	All other months	1–2
1987	December—The Oldest Known Shipwreck	2–4
	All other months	1–2
1988	January—100 Years of the National Geographic Society	1–2
	February—Australia	1–2
	September—100 Years of the National Geographic Society	1–2
	October—The Peopling of the Earth	1–2
	November—Exploring the Earth	1–2
	December—McDonald's Holographic Back Cover Ad	2–4
	All other months	1–2
1989	All months	1–2
1990	All months	1–2
1991	All Months	1–2
1992–present	All months	1–2

Consecutive Run Values

1888–present	$25,000–75,000
1896–present	15,000–30,000
1900–present	15,000–25,000
1908–present	3,000–5,500

Life Magazine

❖

Life magazine has long been one of the most collected magazines. For fifty years *Life* was the one magazine that could be found in nearly every household. Today values on *Life* continue to steadily increase; issues that were quite common just a few years ago are doubling and tripling in value and disappearing from back-issue magazine dealers' inventories.

Life magazine was first published in 1883, and it featured art from noted American illustrators from 1899 until late 1936. Issues from 1899 to the end of the illustrator period (Fall 1936) can have a value of $25 to $100. Issues prior to this period (1883–1899) generally have a value of $10 to $50.

Life magazine as we know it today was first published in November 1936. Its new, larger format featured spectacular photographs by world-famous photographers. Its pages brought startling images of world events into the homes of millions of Americans, offering photos of tragedies and celebrations, record-breaking moments in sports, and countless other events that captured America's attention for more than sixty years.

Today, back issues of *Life* can be found in nearly every back-issue magazine store, antique shop, flea market, or paper collectors' show, although not nearly in the quantities that were available just a few years ago. Back issues of this fine magazine are beginning to disappear into the hands of collectors and the days of finding a nice stack of *Life* magazines at a garage sale are quickly coming to an end.

LIFE MAGAZINE VALUES

Year	Issue	Cover Subject	Value ($)
1936	November 23	Fort Peck Dam	30–60
	November 30	West Point	20–40
	December 7	Skiing	15–30
	December 14	Archbishop of Canterbury	10–20
	December 21	Granddaughter of Lord Beaverbrook	10–20
	December 28	Metropolitan Opera Ballet	10–20
1937	January 4	Franklin D. Roosevelt	10–20
	January 11	Japanese Soldiers	12–25
	January 18	Henry and Edsel Ford	5–10
	January 25	English Lion	4–8
	February 1	Vassar Tennis	4–8
	February 8	Wyoming Winter	10–20
	February 15	Japan's General Senjuro Hayashi	15–30
	February 22	St. Louis Fountain Triton	4–8
	March 1	Laboratory Mice	5–10
	March 8	Sun Valley Ski Lift	10–20
	March 15	The British Coronation Throne	10–20
	March 22	Parachute Test	5–10
	March 29	Easter Singers	5–10
	April 5	Dog	4–8
	April 12	English Centenarian	4–8
	April 19	S.S. *Queen Mary*	10–20
	April 26	Rooster	4–8
	May 3	Jean Harlow	35–70
	May 10	Boy with Marbles	10–20
	May 17	Dionne Quintuplets	20–40
	May 24	Spring Lambs	5–10
	May 31	The Golden Gate Bridge	20–40
	June 7	Saddle Shoes	5–10
	June 14	Senator James Lewis	4–8
	June 21	Reno Divorcée	4–8
	June 28	The Beach	4–8
	July 5	July Corn	5–10
	July 12	Mannequin	5–10
	July 19	Harlem Street Shower	10–20

Year	Issue	Cover Subject	Value ($)
1937	July 26	Polo Pony	5–10
	August 8	Nun	6–12
	August 9	Watermelon Wagon	6–12
	August 16	Camper on a Boat	6–12
	August 23	Transoceanic Airplane	10–20
	August 30	Frog Hunt	5–10
	September 6	Harpo Marx	15–30
	September 13	Steel Master	5–10
	September 20	The Hands of Yehudi Menuhin	4–8
	September 27	Nelson Eddy	10–20
	October 4	Legionnaire's Living Room	5–10
	October 11	USC Football Captain Chuck	5–10
	October 18	Veils in Fashion	4–8
	October 25	Hunting Dog	5–10
	November 1	Alfred Lunt and Richard Whorf	3–5
	November 15	Lightship Engineer	5–10
	November 22	*Life*'s Birthday Baby	10–20
	November 29	The U.S. Capitol	4–8
	December 6	Japanese Soldier	10–20
	December 13	Locomotive Repair	8–16
	December 20	Chorus Girl	7–15
	December 27	Comtesse d'Haussonville	5–10
1938	January 3	Swedish Skater	5–10
	January 10	Koalas	5–10
	January 17	Oil Tankers	4–8
	January 24	Alpine Skiers	5–10
	January 31	Student Nurses	5–10
	February 7	Gary Cooper	6–12
	February 14	Egypt's Queen	5–10
	February 21	Carl Sandburg	5–10
	February 28	Monte Carlo Fireworks	5–10
	March 7	High School Girls	6–12
	March 14	Jane Froman	3–7
	March 21	Marriage Clinic Couple	3–6
	March 28	German Bugler	5–10
	April 4	Anthony Eden	3–6
	April 11	Fashion	3–5
	April 18	Paulette Goddard	10–20
	April 25	Tom Winsett/Brooklyn Dodgers	6–12

Year	Issue	Cover Subject	Value ($)
1938	May 2	John N. Garner	3–6
	May 9	Fashions of Summer	3–6
	May 16	Chinese Soldier	5–10
	May 23	Errol Flynn	15–30
	May 30	Czech General Jan Sirvoy	4–8
	June 6	Youth Problems	4–8
	June 13	Gertrude Lawrence	5–10
	June 20	Rudolph Valentino	15–30
	June 27	Franklin D. Roosevelt	10–20
	July 4	West Point Wedding	5–10
	July 11	Shirley Temple	30–50
	July 18	Camisoles in Fashion	5–10
	July 25	Queen Elizabeth	10–20
	August 1	Garment Workers at Play	4–8
	August 8	Divers	5–10
	August 15	Sumerian High Priest	4–8
	August 22	Fred Astaire and Ginger Rogers	20–40
	August 29	Goodbye to Summer	5–10
	September 5	Fall Fashions	3–5
	September 12	Hungarian Police	3–5
	September 19	James A. Farley	3–6
	September 26	Country Fair Baker	6–12
	October 3	Czech Soldier	6–12
	October 10	Legion Drum Majorettes	5–10
	October 17	Carole Lombard	15–30
	October 24	Columbia College's Sid Luckman	5–10
	October 31	Raymond Massey	8–15
	November 7	California Gubernatorial Candidate Culbert Olsen	3–6
	November 14	Brenda Duff Frazier	3–6
	November 21	Japanese Boy	5–10
	November 28	*Life* Birthday Baby	7–15
	December 5	Ballerina Yvette Chauvire	5–10
	December 12	Champion Labrador Retriever	5–10
	December 19	Mary Martin	10–20
	December 26	Lutist Mrs. Otto Baldauf	3–6
1939	January 2	Wimples in Fashion	3–7
	January 9	Romanian Boy	3–7

Year	Issue	Cover Subject	Value ($)
1939	January 16	Lucius Beebe	3–6
	January 23	Bette Davis	20–35
	January 30	Air Cadet	4–8
	February 6	Peruke Hairstyle	3–6
	February 13	Norma Shearer	10–20
	February 20	France's Chief of Staff	5–10
	February 27	On a Nassau Beach	5–10
	March 6	Tallulah Bankhead	10–20
	March 13	World's Fair Sculpture	15–30
	March 20	Rep. Joseph Martin	3–6
	March 27	Spring Shower	5–10
	April 3	Realistic Dolls	5–10
	April 10	Texas Ranger	6–12
	April 17	Hildegarde	5–10
	April 24	Neville Chamberlain	7–14
	May 1	Joe DiMaggio	20–40+
	May 8	Cottons in Fashion	2–6
	May 15	Anne Morrow Lindbergh	5–10
	May 22	World's Fair Guide	15–30
	May 29	Eleanor Roosevelt	10–20
	June 5	Statue of Liberty	10–20
	June 12	June Week at Annapolis	3–6
	June 19	USC Sprinter Payton Jordon	3–6
	June 26	Reds in Fashion	3–7
	July 3	Swimsuits in Fashion	5–10
	July 10	Japanese Home Guard	6–12
	July 17	Lord Halifax	5–10
	July 24	Ann Sheridan	5–10
	July 31	Diana Barrymore	10–25
	August 7	U.S. Official Paul McNutt	3–6
	August 14	Actress Sandra Lee Henville	3–6
	August 21	Boy Meets Girl	4–8
	August 28	Alice Marble	3–6
	September 4	Rosalind Russell	5–10
	September 11	Benito Mussolini	12–20
	September 18	British Soldier	5–10
	September 25	Britain's General Edmund Ironside	4–8

Year	Issue	Cover Subject	Value ($)
1939	October 2	Cordell Hull	3–6
	October 9	Kids' Football	3–6
	October 16	German U-boat	10–20
	October 23	War and Fashion	5–10
	October 30	Veloz and Yolanda	3–6
	November 6	Planes over England	10–20
	November 13	Claudette Colbert	10–20
	November 20	German Warship	6–12
	November 27	Arturo Toscanini	3–7
	December 4	UCLA Coed and Date	3–7
	December 11	Betty Grable	15–30
	December 18	Canadian General Andrew McNaughton	4–8
	December 25	Merry Christmas	3–7
1940	January 1	Queen Elizabeth	6–12
	January 8	Bowdoin House Party	3–7
	January 15	USC's Basketball Star Ralph Vaughn	3–7
	January 22	Dutch East Indians	3–7
	January 29	Starlet Lana Turner	10–20
	February 5	Swedish Aviators	3–7
	February 12	Valentine's Day Hat	3–7
	February 19	Romania's King Carol and Son Mihai	3–6
	February 26	Carhop	3–6
	March 4	Springtime Hats	4–8
	March 11	French Soldier	5–10
	March 18	Chorus Girl	5–10
	March 25	Sir Neville Henderson	3–6
	April 1	N.Y. Giants Baseball Rookie John Rucker	4–7
	April 8	Actress Anna Neagle	3–7
	April 15	Government and Youth	3–6
	April 22	Dude Outfit	3–5
	April 29	Winston Churchill	5–10
	May 6	British Aerial Gunner	5–10
	May 13	Silk Shawls in Fashion	3–7
	May 20	French General Maxime Weygand	3–7

Year	Issue	Cover Subject	Value ($)
1940	May 27	German Soldier	6–12
	June 3	Statue of Liberty	7–15
	June 10	Emperor Hirohito	5–10
	June 17	General Motor's William Knudson	3–6
	June 24	Italy's Marshall Rodolfo Graziani	3–7
	July 1	Red Cross Girl	4–8
	July 8	Admiral Harold Stark	3–7
	July 15	Rita Hayworth	10–20
	July 22	Tank Commander	7–15
	July 29	Girl Lifeguard	4–8
	August 5	U.S. Vacations	3–6
	August 12	Republican Vice President Nominee Charles McNavy	3–5
	August 19	Parachute Trainee	3–7
	August 26	Couple at Jasper National Park	3–7
	September 2	Dionne Quintuplets	15–30
	September 9	Singer Carol Bruce	3–6
	September 16	Flight across America	4–8
	September 23	Air Raid Victim	3–7
	September 30	Wendell Willkie	5–10
	October 7	Gary Cooper	5–10
	October 14	Jinx Falkenburg	3–6
	October 21	Sweaters in Fashion	4–8
	October 28	U.S. Sailor	3–7
	November 4	San Diego Campaign Rally	2–5
	November 11	Michigan's Tom Harmon	2–5
	November 18	Franklin D. Roosevelt	6–12
	November 25	Fur Coats in Fashion	3–5
	December 2	Balloonists	10–20
	December 9	Ginger Rogers	20–35
	December 16	Greek Soldier	3–6
	December 23	Couple Dressed for a Party	3–5
	December 30	Britain's Desert Fighters	7–14
1941	January 6	Katharine Hepburn	10–25+
	January 13	Bathing Suits in Fashion	4–8
	January 20	U.S. Ski Trooper	4–8

Year	Issue	Cover Subject	Value ($)
1941	January 27	Winston Churchill II and His Mother, Pamela	5–10
	February 3	Joseph Goebbels and Hermann Goering	10–20
	February 10	Lord Halifax	3–7
	February 17	Actress Cobina Wright, Jr.	3–5
	February 24	New Zealanders	4–8
	March 3	Fashion	4–8
	March 10	Washington Worker	2–5
	March 17	Panama Canal Defense	5–10
	March 24	Veils in Fashion	2–5
	March 31	U.S. Navy's New Dive-Bomber	6–12
	April 7	Spring Showers	4–8
	April 14	New York Harbor	5–10
	April 21	U.S. Cavalryman	2–5
	April 28	Red in Fashion	2–4
	May 5	John Harvard	2–4
	May 12	Army Parachutist	3–6
	May 19	Floppy Hats in Fashion	2–4
	May 26	Army Nurse	3–6
	June 2	Sunday School	2–4
	June 9	The Duke and Duchess of Windsor	10–20
	June 16	British Soldier with His First U.S. Soda	5–10
	June 23	Lazy Fishing	3–6
	June 30	Mme. Chiang Kai-shek	3–7
	July 7	General George Patton	10–20
	July 14	Sand Sailing	3–7
	July 21	British Air Chief Marshal Sir Robert Brooke	3–7
	July 28	Circus Family	4–8
	August 4	British Women Auxiliary	3–5
	August 11	Rita Hayworth	10–20
	August 18	U.S. Marine	5–10
	August 25	Fred Astaire and Son	10–20
	September 1	Ted Williams	5–10
	September 8	Smith College Girl	3–5

Year	Issue	Cover Subject	Value ($)
1941	September 15	British Captain Lord Louis Mountbatten	5–10
	September 22	Brazilian Dancer Eros Volusia	2–4
	September 29	Radio's Quiz Kid Gerald Darrow	3–5
	October 6	Farmer's Daughter	3–6
	October 13	Lana Turner and Clark Gable	15–30
	October 20	Pan American Clipper	3–7
	October 27	Air Raid Spotter	3–6
	November 3	West Point Cadet	3–5
	November 10	Gene Tierney	10–15
	November 17	Texas Football	2–4
	November 24	How to Knit	2–4
	December 1	B-17 Bomber	6–12
	December 8	General Douglas MacArthur	7–15
	December 15	Junior Miss	3–7
	December 22	American Flag	3–6
	December 29	U.S. Aerial Gunner	3–6
1942	January 5	Wanted . . . 50,000 Nurses	2–4
	January 12	Pacific Coast Defense	3–6
	January 19	North Atlantic Patrol	3–6
	January 26	Air Force Women's Auxiliary	3–6
	February 2	Thunderbolt Fighter	6–12
	February 9	Versailles Nightclub Chorus in New York	2–4
	February 16	Singer and Soldier	2–4
	February 23	Guns for Merchantmen	4–8
	March 2	Ginger Rogers	15–30
	March 9	Barrage Balloon	5–10
	March 16	Infantryman	3–6
	March 23	Making Plane Models	2–4
	March 30	Shirley Temple	25–50
	April 6	Tail Gunner	10–20
	April 13	General Brehon Somervell	2–4
	April 20	Slacks in Fashion	2–4
	April 27	Nelson Rockefeller	2–4
	May 4	Chinese Air Cadet	4–8
	May 11	Ruffles in Fashion	2–4

Year	Issue	Cover Subject	Value ($)
1942	May 18	Cadet Bomber	4–8
	May 25	Spring Planting	2–5
	June 1	Hedy Lamarr	10–25
	June 8	Nurse's Aide	2–4
	June 15	General Joseph Stilwell	2–4
	June 22	War Bride	3–6
	June 29	USO Belle	3–5
	July 6	American Flag	3–6
	July 13	Air Corps Gunnery School	4–8
	July 20	Short Coat in Fashion	2–4
	July 27	Atlantic Convoy	5–10
	August 3	General MacArthur's Son	2–5
	August 10	General Claire Chennault	5–10
	August 17	Guerrilla Warfare Expert	3–7
	August 24	Johnny Jeep	3–5
	August 31	Torpedo Boat *Ensign*	5–10
	September 7	Cargo Glider	2–4
	September 14	U.S. Official Leon Henderson	2–4
	September 21	Iran's Queen Fawzia	2–4
	September 28	Admiral William Leahy	2–4
	October 5	Hats in Fashion	2–4
	October 12	California Assembly	2–4
	October 19	Sandbagged Sphinx	3–7
	October 26	Actress Joan Leslie	2–4
	November 2	Praise the Lord and Pass the Ammunition Phrasemaker Captain William Maguire	3–7
	November 9	Infantry Mountain Trooper	3–7
	November 16	Vests in Fashion	2–4
	November 23	New England Church	2–4
	November 30	Eighteen-year-old Awaiting Draft	3–6
	December 7	Marine Ace Major John L. Smith	3–6
	December 14	Coast Guard Skipper	2–5
	December 21	Lonely Wife	2–4
	December 28	Madonna	2–4
1943	January 4	Assistant to the President Jimmy Bymes	2–4

Year	Issue	Cover Subject	Value ($)
1943	January 11	Kids' Uniforms	2–4
	January 18	Rita Hayworth	10–20
	January 25	Eddie Rickenbacker	10–20
	February 1	Dating in Casablanca	2–4
	February 8	Plane Spotter	3–6
	February 15	Princess Elizabeth	6–12
	February 22	Army Air Observer	3–5
	March 1	Bow Ties in Fashion	2–4
	March 8	General Brehon Somervell	2–4
	March 15	WAVES	3–6
	March 22	General George Kenney	3–5
	March 29	Joseph Stalin	5–10
	April 5	Montgomery Berets in Fashion	2–4
	April 12	Jefferson Memorial	2–4
	April 19	Soldier's Farewell	5–10
	April 26	Junior Army-Navy Organization	2–4
	May 3	Matching Dress and Parasol in Fashion	2–4
	May 10	PT Boat Skippers	5–10
	May 17	Boy Welder	2–4
	May 24	Actress Peggy Lloyd	2–4
	May 31	Saudi Arabian King Ibn Saud	2–4
	June 7	Captain Joe Foss	2–4
	June 14	High School Graduation	2–5
	June 21	Igor Sikorsky with Helicopter	3–6
	June 28	War Souvenir	3–6
	July 5	America's Combat Dead	5–10
	July 12	Roy Rogers and Trigger	20–40
	July 19	Air Force Auxiliary Pilot	3–6
	July 26	8th Air Force B-24	7–15
	August 2	British Admiral Sir Max Kennedy	2–5
	August 9	Steelworker	2–5
	August 16	Japanese Soldiers	6–12
	August 23	Lindy Hoppers	2–4
	August 30	Anthony Eden with His Dog Nipper	2–4

Year	Issue	Cover Subject	Value ($)
1943	September 6	American Soldiers Hunting Japanese	6–12
	September 13	Leotards in Fashion	2–4
	September 20	Cambridge Don Charles Seltman	2–4
	September 27	Harvester	2–4
	October 4	U.S. Ambassador to Governments-in-exile Anthony Biddle	2–4
	October 11	Half Hats in Fashion	2–4
	October 18	Wartime Romances	2–4
	October 25	Mary Martin	10–20
	November 1	Thunderbolt Fighter	10–20
	November 8	British Field Marshal Jan Smuts	2–4
	November 15	Fur-lined Coats in Fashion	2–4
	November 22	Foot Soldiers	5–10
	November 29	General Ira Eaker	2–5
	December 6	Earmuffs in Fashion	2–4
	December 13	Chinese Muslim	2–3
	December 20	U.S. Pilot's Wife	3–5
	December 27	Wounded Soldier with Nurse	5–10
1944	January 3	Alaska Holiday	2–5
	January 10	Bob Hope	10–20
	January 17	Historian Charles Beard	2–4
	January 24	Margaret Sullavan	5–10
	January 31	British Air Chief Marshal Sir Arthur Tedder	3–6
	February 7	George Bernard Shaw	3–6
	February 14	Wall of Fame Facade of Earl Carroll Theatre	2–4
	February 21	Patrice Munsel	2–4
	February 28	Actress Ella Raines	2–4
	March 6	Admiral Chester Nimitz	5–10
	March 13	Junior School Dance	2–4
	March 20	Ballerina Nana Gollner	2–4
	March 27	Landing Craft	5–10
	April 3	Pooch	2–4
	April 10	British Air Marshal Arthur T. Harris	2–5
	April 17	Esther Williams	6–12

Year	Issue	Cover Subject	Value ($)
1944	April 24	Princess Elizabeth	5–10
	May 1	Homecoming	3–6
	May 8	Hattie Carnegie Suit in Fashion	2–4
	May 15	British General Sir Bernard Montgomery	5–10
	May 22	Model Mother and Son	3–5
	May 29	General Carl Spaatz	2–4
	June 5	U.S. Infantrymen	5–10
	June 12	Bombs Falling on Italy	5–10
	June 19	General Dwight D. Eisenhower	4–8
	June 26	Statue of Liberty	4–8
	July 3	Back from the Front	4–8
	July 10	Admiral Chester Nimitz	5–10
	July 17	Peasant Clothes in Fashion	2–4
	July 24	Jennifer Jones	5–10
	July 31	Soviet Marshal Georgi Zhukov	3–8
	August 7	Geraldine Fitzgerald	2–5
	August 14	Airborne Infantry Officer	4–8
	August 21	Amphibious Tractors	4–7
	August 28	Pedal Pushers in Fashion	2–5
	September 4	Cordell Hull	2–5
	September 11	Nazi Prisoners	5–10
	September 18	Thomas E. Dewey	3–5
	September 25	A Letter to GIs	4–8
	October 2	General Lucian Truscott	3–5
	October 9	Helena Rubenstein's Dali Room	3–5
	October 16	Lauren Bacall	10–25
	October 23	Soviet Scientist Alexei Kryov	2–4
	October 30	U.S.S. *Iowa*	5–10
	November 6	Celeste Holm	4–8
	November 13	General Charles de Gaulle	4–8
	November 20	Thanksgiving	5–10
	November 27	Gertrude Lawrence	2–4
	December 4	B-29s over Formosa	6–12
	December 11	Judy Garland	20–35
	December 18	Fredric March	5–10
	December 25	Madonna and Child	2–5
1945	January 1	Soldier Cleaning Gun	4–8
	January 8	Scarves in Fashion	2–4

Year	Issue	Cover Subject	Value ($)
1945	January 15	General George Patton	10–25
	January 22	St. John's University Basketball	2–4
	January 29	Wounded Soldier	6–12
	February 5	Florida Fashion	2–4
	February 12	Soviet Soldier	3–6
	February 19	Ski Clothes in Fashion	3–5
	February 26	Winter Soldiers	5–10
	March 5	Flying over San Francisco's Presidio	3–7
	March 12	General William Simpson	3–5
	March 19	Dutch Girl	3–6
	March 26	Carol Lynn	3–5
	April 2	Subdeb Clubs	3–4
	April 16	General Dwight D. Eisenhower	3–6
	April 23	Harry S Truman	4–8
	April 30	War Artists	5–10
	May 7	The German People	4–8
	May 14	Victorious Yank	5–10
	May 21	Winston Churchill	3–6
	May 28	Starlet Barbara Bates	3–5
	June 4	War Loan Drive	2–4
	June 11	Teenage Boys	2–3
	June 18	Girl Scouts in Washington	5–10
	June 25	Kindergarten Graduation	3–5
	July 2	Pacific Fleet Destroyers	4–8
	July 9	Bathing Suits in Fashion	3–5
	July 16	Audie Murphy	10–20
	July 23	Actress Peggy Ann Garner	10–15
	July 30	Playing on the Beach	3–5
	August 6	Junior Sailors	2–4
	August 13	Jet Plane	3–6
	August 20	General Carl Spaatz	2–3
	August 27	Ballet Swimmer	2–3
	September 3	House Party	2–3
	September 10	Autoworker	2–3
	September 17	General MacArthur	5–10
	September 24	Colonel Jimmy Stewart	8–15

Year	Issue	Cover Subject	Value ($)
1945	October 1	June Allyson	5–8
	October 8	General Robert Eichelberger	2–3
	October 15	Fall Jewelry in Fashion	2–3
	October 22	Ohio State's Paul Sarringhaus	2–3
	October 29	Autumn	3–6
	November 5	Fleet's In	3–6
	November 12	Ingrid Bergman	4–8
	November 19	Big Belts in Fashion	2–4
	November 26	Champion Afghan	2–4
	December 3	Spencer Tracy	4–8
	December 10	Party Dresses in Fashion	2–3
	December 17	Paulette Goddard	10–20
	December 24	Procession to Bethlehem	2–4
	December 31	Mountain Climbing	3–6
1946	January 7	Winston Churchill's Paintings	3–5
	January 14	Southern Resort Fashion	2–3
	January 21	Cardinal Spellman	2–3
	January 28	Actress Jan Clayton	2–3
	February 4	Bob Hope and Bing Crosby	10–20
	February 11	Lincoln Memorial	2–3
	February 18	Dorothy McGuire	3–6
	February 25	Pointer	2–4
	March 4	Figure Skater	2–4
	March 11	Senator Arthur Vandenberg	2–3
	March 18	Eiffel Tower	2–3
	March 25	Actress Lucille Bremer	2–3
	April 1	St. Louis Cardinals' Red Barrett	3–6
	April 8	Clown Lou Jacobs	4–8
	April 15	Spring Fashions	2–3
	April 22	Denver High School	2–3
	April 29	Marble Pagoda in Peking	2–3
	May 6	Margaret Leighton	2–3
	May 13	Northwest Vacation	2–4
	May 20	Ice Capades	2–4
	May 27	Ozark Farmer	2–4
	June 3	Children in Church	2–4
	June 10	Donna Reed	8–15
	June 17	Play Dresses	2–4

Year	Issue	Cover Subject	Value ($)
1946	June 24	Chief Justice Fred Vinson	2–3
	July 1	Sailing Season	2–4
	July 8	Basque Shirts in Fashion	2–3
	July 15	Water Gadgets	2–3
	July 22	Mrs. Cornelius Vanderbilt Whitney with Coachman	2–3
	July 29	Vivien Leigh	20–35
	August 5	Radio's Juvenile Jury Participant	2–3
	August 12	Loretta Young	7–15
	August 19	Old Faithful	3–6
	August 26	College Fashions	2–3
	September 2	Vacation's End	2–3
	September 9	Jane Powell	3–6
	September 16	West Point's Glen Davis and Felix Blanchard	2–4
	September 23	Dachshund	3–6
	September 30	Jeanne Crain	5–10
	October 7	Bing Crosby and Joan Caulfield	5–10
	October 14	Fall Fashions	2–4
	October 21	Gloria Grahame	2–3
	October 28	One-Room School	3–6
	November 4	Arab Policeman with Camel in Palestine	2–4
	November 11	High School Model Shirley Arnow	2–3
	November 18	Party Raincoats in Fashion	2–3
	November 25	LIFE's 10th Anniversary Issue	4–8
	December 2	Ingrid Bergman	3–6
	December 16	Jet Pilot	3–6
	December 23	Teresa Wright	2–4
	December 30	Dorothy Kristen	2–3
1947	January 6	Annapolis Drag	2–3
	January 13	Resort Fashions	2–3
	January 20	Homesteading Veteran	2–3
	January 27	Nantucket Lighthouse	5–10
	February 3	Actress Susan Douglas	2–3
	February 10	Occupation of Germany	2–4
	February 17	Water Skier	2–3

Year	Issue	Cover Subject	Value ($)
1947	February 24	Texas Coed	2–3
	March 3	Renaissance Man in Armor	3–6
	March 10	Father's Day Bath	2–5
	March 17	Youth Center Director	2–3
	March 24	Eskimo Baby	2–4
	March 31	Spring Hats in Fashion	2–3
	April 7	Sunday School	2–4
	April 14	Pretty Girls	2–4
	April 21	Student Veteran	2–3
	April 28	Actress Bambi Linn	2–3
	May 5	Riding Clothes in Fashion	2–3
	May 12	Bulgarian Prime Minister Georgi Dimitrov	2–3
	May 19	Teenager's Sundae	3–5
	May 26	Medieval Castle	3–5
	June 2	Jane Greer	2–4
	June 9	Ballerina Ricky Soma	2–3
	June 16	Cape Hatteras Bay	3–6
	June 23	Bathing Suits in Fashion	2–4
	June 30	Ancient and Modern Mayan Sculpture	5–10
	July 7	Little Girl on a Merry-go-round	4–8
	July 14	Elizabeth Taylor	15–30
	July 21	Americans in Heidelberg	2–4
	July 28	Princess Elizabeth	5–10
	August 4	Portrait of a Man in a Red Cap	3–5
	August 11	Actress Ella Raines	2–3
	August 18	Lord Louis Mountbatten	4–8
	August 25	Model Gail Sullivan	2–3
	September 1	Auto Racer John Cobb	3–4
	September 8	Lady Sarah Fitzalan-Howard	2–3
	September 15	Madame Du Barry	2–4
	September 22	Fall Fashions	2–4
	September 29		2–5
	October 6	F. D. Roosevelt at 13	4–8
	October 13	Katrina von Oss in Allegro	2–4
	October 20	Child Listening to Folk Songs	3–6
	October 27	Admiral Lewis Douglas	2–3

Year	Issue	Cover Subject	Value ($)
1947	November 3	Ballerinas Ruth Koesun and Melissa Hayden	2–4
	November 10	Rita Hayworth	5–10
	November 17	Boxers	3–6
	November 24	Subdeb Pamela Helene Dudley Curran	2–3
	December 1	Gregory Peck	5–10
	December 8	Boyhood Portrait of the Duke of Windsor	3–6
	December 15	Nightclub Girls	3–5
	December 22	Christmas Carols	3–6
	December 29	Pretty Girl in Miami	2–4
1948	January 5	Pakistan's Muhammed Ali Jinnah	2–3
	January 12	Midwinter Accessories in Fashion	2–3
	January 19	Violinist Marcia Van Dyke	2–3
	January 26	Resort Fashions	2–3
	February 2	Maine Schoolboy	2–4
	February 9	Robert A. Taft	2–3
	February 16	Actress Joan Tetzel	2–3
	February 23	Skiing	2–4
	March 1	Harold E. Stassen	2–3
	March 8	Model Gaby Bouche	2–3
	March 15	Sir Laurence Olivier	5–10
	March 22	Thomas E. Dewey	3–6
	March 29	Basket Handbags in Fashion	2–3
	April 5	Baseball Rookies	5–10
	April 12	Barbara Bel Geddes	4–7
	April 19	Winston Churchill	4–8
	April 26	Collegians in Bermuda	2–3
	May 3	Career Girl	2–3
	May 10	Governor Earl Warren	2–3
	May 17	Mrs. David Niven	3–4
	May 24	Senator Arthur Vandenberg	2–3
	May 31	Television Ingenue Kyle MacDonnell	3–6
	June 7	Hooded T-shirts in Fashion	3–5

Year	Issue	Cover Subject	Value ($)
1948	June 14	Actress Phyllis Calvert	2–3
	June 21	Cape Cod Weekend	3–6
	June 28	Member of Kent School Crew	2–3
	July 5	F-84 Thunderjets	5–10
	July 12	Small-Town Girl	3–5
	July 19	Fun on the Beach	3–5
	July 26	Children's Ballet School	2–4
	August 2	Olympic Sprinter Mel Patton	3–5
	August 9	Marlene Dietrich	10–20
	August 16	Little Fisherman	3–6
	August 23	Young Hunter with Pet Deer	3–5
	August 30	Actress Colleen Townsend	2–3
	September 6	The Good Life in Madison, Wisconsin	2–4
	September 13	Marshal Tito	2–4
	September 20	Actress Joan Diener	2–3
	September 27	SMU's Doak Walker	2–3
	October 4	Big Industry in America	2–3
	October 11	Actress Rita Cotton	2–3
	October 18	Fur Jackets in Fashion	2–3
	October 25	University of California Football Fans	2–3
	November 1	General Lauris Norstadt	2–3
	November 8	Actress Helena Carter	2–3
	November 15	Ingrid Bergman	3–6
	November 22	Harry S Truman	3–6
	November 29	Dinner Hats in Fashion	2–3
	December 6	Montgomery Clift	5–10
	December 13	Dwight D. Eisenhower	5–8
	December 20	Teenage Fun	3–5
	December 27	The Story of Christ	3–6
1949	January 3	Famous Baby Dwight D. Eisenhower II	2–4
	January 10	Debutante Joanne Connelley	2–4
	January 17	Resort Fashions	3–4
	January 24	Skier Emile Allais	3–4
	January 31	Champion Cocker Spaniel	3–6

Year	Issue	Cover Subject	Value ($)
1949	February 7	Winston Churchill's Memoirs	3–7
	February 14	Viveca Lindfors	2–4
	February 21	Dean Acheson	2–4
	February 28	Children's Costume Clothes	3–4
	March 7	Marge and Gower Champion	2–3
	March 14	Dorothy McGuire's Baby	3–6
	March 21	Fashion Wardrobe	2–4
	March 28	Actress Joy Lansing	2–4
	April 4	U.S. Official Paul Hoffman	2–3
	April 11	Boy on Fence During Spring along the Mississippi	4–8
	April 18	Mary Martin	4–8
	April 25	Paris Fashion	2–4
	May 2	West Point's Arnold Galiffa	2–3
	May 9	Missouri Coed Jane Stone	2–4
	May 16	Little Boxer	4–8
	May 23	Sarah Churchill	3–6
	May 30	Baby Franklin D. Roosevelt	3–6
	June 6	Summer Play Clothes in Fashion	3–6
	June 13	Actress Marta Toren	2–3
	June 20	High School Graduate	2–4
	June 27	Inland Sailing	2–4
	July 4	Beach Holiday	2–4
	July 11	Olympian Bob Mathias	2–3
	July 18	Hollywood Child Sharon Harmon	3–6
	July 25	Girl in Plastic Beach Boat	3–5
	September 1	Joe DiMaggio	20–40+
	September 8	Straw Hats in Fashion	2–3
	September 15	Actress Brynn Noring	2–3
	September 22	Cowboy	3–6
	September 29	College Fashions	2–5
	October 3	North Carolina's Charlie Justice	2–3
	October 10	J. Robert Oppenheimer	2–4
	October 17	Actress Jeanne Crain	5–10
	October 24	Sweden's Ideal Pretty Girl	2–5
	October 31	Princess Margaret	2–4

Year	Issue	Cover Subject	Value ($)
1949	November 7	Alfred Lunt and Lynn Fontanne	3–7
	November 14	Pearls in Fashion	2–3
	November 21	Actor Ricardo Montalban	4–7
	November 28	Dancer Nita Bieber	2–4
	December 5	General Hoyt Vandenberg	2–3
	December 12	Beauty on Fifth Avenue	3–6
	December 19	Little Girl Clothes in Fashion	2–5
	December 26	God the Creator from the Sistine Chapel	2–5
1950	January 2	Gibson Girl Look	4–8
	January 9	Actress Norma de Landa	2–3
	January 16	Young Skater	3–6
	January 23	Man-Tailored Shirts in Fashion	2–3
	January 30	Childbirth without Fear	2–4
	February 6	Eva Gabor	5–10
	February 13	Indonesian Woman	3–5
	February 20	Gregory Peck	5–10
	February 27	Atomic Explosion	10–20
	March 6	Actress Marsha Hunt	3–4
	March 13	Spring Fashions	2–3
	March 20	Artist Edward John Stevens, Jr.	2–3
	March 27	Model Anne Bromley	2–4
	April 3	Iris Mann and David Cole on Broadway	2–4
	April 10	Young Horsewoman	2–4
	April 17	Dwight D. Eisenhower	3–6
	April 24	Inexpensive Blouses in Fashion	2–4
	May 1	Actress Ruth Roman	3–5
	May 8	Jackie Robinson	20–40
	May 15	Beach Fashions	3–5
	May 22	The Duke and Duchess of Windsor	5–10
	May 29	Mrs. William O'Dwyer	2–3
	June 5	Actress Stasia Kos	2–3
	June 12	Hopalong Cassidy (William Boyd)	12–25
	June 19	Children's Beach Fashions	3–4
	June 26	Actress Cecile Aubry	2–3

Year	Issue	Cover Subject	Value ($)
1950	July 3	Washington at Trenton	3–6
	July 10	Actress Miroslava Stern	2–3
	July 17	Jet Pilot	2–4
	July 24	Boy Scout	5–10
	July 31	24th Division Soldiers	3–6
	August 7	Actress Peggy Dow	2–3
	August 14	Admiral John Hoskins	2–3
	August 21	Broadway Chorines	2–3
	August 28	General Douglas MacArthur	10–20
	September 4	Two Marines on Reconnaissance	3–6
	September 11	American Elegance in Fashion	2–3
	September 18	Ezio Pinza	2–4
	September 25	Swedish Red Cross Girl	2–4
	October 2	U.S. Official Stuart Symington	2–3
	October 9	Jean Simmons	6–12
	October 16	Winnetka High School Girl	2–4
	October 23	Ed Wynn	3–6
	October 30	Faye Emerson	2–4
	November 6	Horse Show Rider	2–3
	November 13	SMU's Kyle Rote	2–4
	November 20	Girl of Shilluk Tribe	2–4
	November 27	UCLA Homecoming Queen	2–4
	December 4	Berlin Girl	2–4
	December 11	Lilli Palmer and Rex Harrison	4–8
	December 18	General George Marshall	2–3
	December 25	Girls Painting	3–5
1951	January 1	U.S. Official Charles E. Wilson	2–3
	January 8	Starlet Janice Rule	2–3
	January 15	Rose Parade Grand Marshal	2–3
	January 22	Air Warning Supervisor	2–3
	January 29	Actress Betsy von Furstenberg	2–4
	February 5	N.Y.C. Police Commissioner Thomas F. Murphy	2–3
	February 12	Veiled Hats in Fashion	2–3
	February 19	Adoption of Linda Joy	2–4
	February 26	Debbie Reynolds	10–20
	March 5	Dior Fashions	2–4

Year	Issue	Cover Subject	Value ($)
1951	March 12	Actor Paul Douglas	2–4
	March 19	Navy Couple	2–4
	March 26	Child Choir Singers	2–4
	April 2	Jet-setter Mercedes Spradling	2–3
	April 9	General Omar Bradley	4–8
	April 16	Esther Williams	5–10
	April 23	Dalai Lama	5–10
	April 30	General Matthew Ridgeway	2–3
	May 7	Actress Phyllis Kirk	2–3
	May 14	Michigan's Senator Blair Moody and Sons	2–3
	May 21	Beach Fashions	2–4
	May 28	Paratroopers	5–10
	June 4	Model Ursula Theiss	2–3
	June 11	Actress Vivian Blaine	2–4
	June 18	Iran's Royal Crown	2–3
	June 25	Actress Janet Leigh	10–20
	July 2	Sergeant John Pittman	2–4
	July 9	Summer Party in Charlotte, North Carolina	2–3
	July 16	TV Actress Dagmar	2–4
	July 23	Swimmer Mary Freeman	2–4
	July 30	Singer Gary Crosby	2–3
	August 6	Vacationing High School Girl	2–4
	August 13	Dean Martin and Jerry Lewis	10–20+
	August 20	Swimmer Barbara Hobelmann	2–3
	August 27	Model Rosemary Coover	2–4
	September 3	Gina Lollobrigida	5–10
	September 10	Japanese Prime Minister	2–3
	September 17	Chorus Girl	2–4
	September 24	Gene Tierney	4–8
	October 1	Princess Elizabeth	4–8
	October 8	Baby Malayan Snow Loris	2–4
	October 15	Zsa Zsa Gabor	3–6
	October 22	Bronc Rider Casey Tibbs	2–4
	October 29	TV Prop Girl	2–3
	November 5	Ginger Rogers	10–20
	November 12	Anthony Eden	2–3

Year	Issue	Cover Subject	Value ($)
1951	November 19	Lynn Fontanne, Katharine Cornell, and Helen Hayes	4–8
	November 26	Photography Contest Winner Regina Fisher	2–4
	December 3	Christmas Lingerie in Fashion	2–4
	December 10	Harry S Truman	4–8
	December 17	Vivien Leigh and Laurence Olivier	5–10
	December 24	Nativity	2–4
1952	January 7	Hairstyles	2–3
	January 14	Augustus John	2–3
	January 21	Dwight D. Eisenhower	3–6
	January 28	Model, Pianist, and Painter Phyllis Newell	2–3
	February 4	Skater Barbara Ann Scott	2–4
	February 11	Olympic Skier Henri Oreiller	2–3
	February 18	Queen Elizabeth II	5–10
	February 25	Gloves in Fashion	2–3
	March 3	Patrice Munsel	2–3
	March 10	Actor Brandon de Wilde	2–5
	March 17	Broadway Chorus Girl	3–6
	March 24	Democratic Presidential Candidates	2–4
	March 31	Li'l Abner Characters	2–5
	April 7	Marilyn Monroe	25–50
	April 14	Italian Fashions	2–3
	April 21	MarshalTito	2–4
	April 28	Ike and Mamie Eisenhower's Wedding Photo	3–5
	May 5	Actress Diana Lynn	2–3
	May 12	General Matthew Ridgeway	2–3
	May 19	Actress Miriam Charriere	2–3
	May 26	Stewart Granger	3–6
	June 2	Children's Party Outfits	2–3
	June 9	Bridal Model Martha Boss	2–4
	June 16	Dwight D. Eisenhower	3–6
	June 23	Mail-Order Fashions	2–3
	June 30	Nancy Kefauver	2–3

Year	Issue	Cover Subject	Value ($)
1952	July 7	Arlene Dahl	4–8
	July 14	Hangover Victim	2–3
	July 21	Dwight D. Eisenhower	2–5
	July 28	British Starlets Joan Elan, Dorothy Bromiley, and Audrey Dalton	2–4
	August 4	Adlai Stevenson	2–4
	August 11	Actress Joan Rice	2–3
	August 18	Marlene Dietrich and Daughter Maria Riva	7–15
	August 25	College Fashions	2–4
	September 1	Ernest Hemingway	5–10
	September 8	Fall Fashions	2–4
	September 15	Rita Gam	2–3
	September 22	LST at Polar Base	2–4
	September 29	Jackie Gleason TV Chorus Girls	10–20
	October 6	Mrs. Peter Thieriot at San Francisco Opera Opening	2–3
	October 13	Mamie Eisenhower	3–5
	October 20	Actress Lucia Bose	2–3
	October 27	Jon Linbergh	2–4
	November 3	New UN Assembly Building	2–3
	November 10	Duck Hunter Jean Huston	2–4
	November 17	Dwight D. Eisenhower and Mamie Eisenhower	3–6
	November 24	Jewelry in Fashion	2–4
	December 1	Actress Suzanne Cloutier	2–3
	December 8	The Earth Is Born	3–6
	December 15	Refugee Homecoming Queen	2–4
	December 22	Midget Horse	2–3
	December 29	Salzburg Marionettes	2–4
1953	January 5	$15,000 House	2–4
	January 12	Resort Fashions in Majorca	2–3
	January 19	U.S. Officials Charles E. Wilson and George M. Humphrey	2–4
	January 26	Fashion Stylist Sigrid Soelter	2–3
	February 2	Dwight D. Eisenhower's Inauguration	3–7

Year	Issue	Cover Subject	Value ($)
1953	February 9	Miracles of the Sea	3–6
	February 16	Coldstream Guard	2–4
	February 23	Prettiest Teacher	3–6
	March 2	Formosan Soldiers	3–6
	March 9	Stoles in Fashion	2–3
	March 16	Joseph Stalin and Georgy Malenkov	3–6
	March 23	Starlet Elaine Stewart	2–3
	March 30	Coronation Fashion	2–3
	April 6	Lucille Ball, Desi Arnaz, and Children	30–65
	April 13	Delicate Arch in Utah	3–6
	April 20	Marlon Brando	7–15
	April 27	Queen Elizabeth II	6–12
	May 4	Masai Warrior	2–4
	May 11	Denim in Fashion	3–6
	May 18	Indiana Coed	2–4
	May 25	Marilyn Monroe and Jane Russell	25–50
	June 1	Brooke Hayward	2–3
	June 8	Roy Campanella	10–20
	June 15	Coronation of Elizabeth II	10–20
	June 22	Miss College Graduate	5–6
	June 29	Cyd Charisse	5–10
	July 6	Actress Terry Moore	12–20
	July 13	Sir Edmund Hillary and Tenzing Norgay	10–20
	July 20	Senator John F. Kennedy	7–15
	July 27	Can-Can Lingerie in Fashion	2–4
	August 3	Actress Nicole Naurey	2–3
	August 10	Irish Fashions	3–6
	August 15	Actresses Barbara, Madelyn, and Alice Whittlinger	2–3
	August 24	Mormon Ballerinas on Connecticut Beach	2–4
	August 31	Donna Reed	5–10
	September 7	Stegosaurus and Brontosaurus	5–10
	September 14	Casey Stengel	10–20
	September 21	Photographer's Daughter	2–4

Year	Issue	Cover Subject	Value ($)
1953	September 28	De Cuevas Ball	2–3
	October 5	New Citizens	2–3
	October 12	Bare Backs in Fashion	2–4
	October 19	Prehistoric Mammals	4–8
	October 26	Actress Vikki Dougan	2–3
	November 2	Sir Winston Churchill	3–6
	November 9	Singer Jill Corey	2–4
	November 16	Greece's Queen Frederica	2–3
	November 23	College Art Student	2–3
	November 30	Queen Triggerfish	2–3
	December 7	Audrey Hepburn	15–30
	December 14	Richard M. Nixon	4–8
	December 21	Pajamas in Fashion	2–4
	December 28	Madonna and Child in St. Marks	2–4
1954	January 4	Regulus Missile	2–3
	January 11	Debutante Wardrobe	2–3
	January 18	U.S. Officials Leverett Saltonstall, William Knowland, and Richard M. Nixon	2–4
	January 25	Dancer Diane Sinclair	2–4
	February 1	Tropical Wardrobe	2–4
	February 8	Sea Turtle	2–4
	February 15	Italian Hairdo	2–3
	February 22	Disney Moviemaking	10–20
	March 1	Actress Rita Moreno	5–10
	March 8	Winston Churchill's Granddaughter	3–5
	March 15	Mrs. Winthrop Rockefeller	2–3
	March 22	Emperor Penguin	2–4
	March 29	Actress Pat Crowley	1–2
	April 5	The Desert	2–4
	April 12	Subteen Fashions	1–2
	April 19	H-Bomb Test	4–8
	April 26	Grace Kelly	10–25
	May 3	Rarest Stamps	4–8
	May 10	Bavaria's Neuschwanstein Castle	2–5

Year	Issue	Cover Subject	Value ($)
1954	May 17	Starlet Dawn Addams	2–4
	May 24	Actress Kaye Ballard	2–4
	May 31	William Holden	3–6
	June 7	Arctic Tundra	3–6
	June 14	California Fashions	3–6
	June 21	Las Vegas Chorus Girl	3–6
	June 28	Bathing Suits in Fashion	3–6
	July 5	Fourth of July	3–6
	July 12	Actress Pier Angeli	5–10
	July 19	Eva Marie Saint	5–10
	July 26	Army Counsel Joseph Welch	1–2
	August 2	Arabian Nights at Jones Beach Theater	3–6
	August 9	Boy Cowpuncher with His Father	3–6
	August 16	Africa's Spirited Children	2–3
	August 23	Philip, Duke of Edinburgh	2–4
	August 30	Singer Anna Maria Alberghetti	2–4
	September 6	Dior Fashions	1–2
	September 13	Judy Garland	15–25
	September 20	Tropical Rain Forest	4–8
	September 27	Hydrofoil	1–2
	October 4	Wesley Girl and UN Guide	1–2
	October 11	Mountain Climber	3–6
	October 18	Tacoma Congressional Campaigner	1–2
	October 25	The Big Ten Look of Coeds	2–4
	November 1	Actress Dorothy Dandridge	1–2
	November 8	New Jersey Deer	1–2
	November 15	Gina Lollobrigida	4–8
	November 22	Actress Judy Holliday	4–8
	November 29	Broadway Twins Tani and Dran Seitz	2–3
	December 6	Jet Age Man	2–3
	December 13	Pope Pius XII	1–2
	December 20	Measureless Space	2–5
	December 27	Joseph and Mary	2–4
1955	January 3	Food Shopping	1–2
	January 10	Greta Garbo	5–10

Year	Issue	Cover Subject	Value ($)
1955	January 17	Soviet Soldiers Eye the Girls	3–6
	January 24	Tahitian Girl Bathing	3–6
	January 31	Spencer Tracy	3–5
	February 7	Vigil of Indian Girl in Hindustan	
	February 14	Photographer's Family	1–2
	February 21	Princess Margaret	1–2
	February 28	Actress Shelley Winters	2–4
	March 7	Golden Buddha	2–4
	March 14	Convoy Shepherd	1–2
	March 21	Actress Sheree North	5–10
	March 28	Kilauea Volcano	3–6
	April 4	Confucianism Festival Boats	1–2
	April 11	Grace Kelly	10–20
	April 18	Frigate Figurehead	2–4
	April 25	Sir Anthony Eden and Lady Clarissa	2–3
	May 2	Oklahoma Dancers	4–8
	May 9	Pakistani Muslim Girl	2–3
	May 16	Happi Coats in Fashion	1–2
	May 23	Actress Leslie Caron	5–10
	May 30	Rare Playing Cards	2–3
	June 6	Henry Fonda	5–10
	June 13	Scranton Mother and Sabbath Candles	1–2
	June 20	Las Vegas Dancers	2–4
	June 27	The *Constitution* and Its Crew	2–4
	July 4	The Fourth of July	3–6
	July 11	Susan Strasberg	3–6
	July 18	Audrey Hepburn	15–30
	July 25	Cathy Crosby	2–4
	August 1	Nikolay Bulganin, Dwight D. Eisenhower, Edger Faure, and Anthony Eden	1–2
	August 8	Golfer Ben Hogan	1–2
	August 15	General Douglas MacArthur	4–7
	August 22	Sophia Loren	10–20
	August 29	Grandson with Grandfather	2–4

Year	Issue	Cover Subject	Value ($)
1955	September 5	Dior Fashions	1–2
	September 12	Joan Collins	5–10
	September 19	Guys and Dolls	3–5
	September 26	Harry and Bess Truman	3–6
	October 3	Rock Hudson	3–6
	October 10	Princess Margaret	1–2
	October 17	Princess Ira Furstenberg and Gondolier	1–2
	October 24	Cecil B. DeMille	2–4
	October 31	Partygoer Mrs. Averall Clark, Jr.	2–4
	November 7	Europe's First True Human: Swanscombe Man	1–2
	November 14	Dwight D. Eisenhower	2–4
	November 21	Actress Judy Tyler	1–2
	November 28	Carol Channing	4–8
	December 5	Man-Made Mink in Fashion	1–2
	December 12	Neanderthal Bear Cult	2–3
	December 19	Suits of Armor for Children	2–3
	December 26	Christianity Special Issue	2–4
1956	January 9	Riviera Fashions	1–2
	January 16	Anita Ekberg	7–15
	January 23	Harry S Truman	3–6
	January 30	Henry Ford III	2–3
	February 6	Shirley Jones	15–30
	February 13	Harry S Truman and General MacArthur	7–15
	February 20	Claire Bloom	3–6
	February 27	Eskimo Family	3–6
	March 5	Kim Novak	5–10
	March 12	Dwight D. Eisenhower	3–5
	March 19	Sir Winston Churchill	3–5
	March 26	Julie Andrews	4–8
	April 2	Teenage Telephone Tie-up	3–6
	April 9	Grace Kelly	5–10
	April 16	Berber Girls	1–2
	April 23	Jayne Mansfield	15–30
	April 30	Margaret Truman and Husband	2–3
	May 7	Lazy Susan Sunbathers	2–3

Year	Issue	Cover Subject	Value ($)
1956	May 14	Gainsborough Look in Fashion	1–2
	May 21	Beach Towels	1–2
	May 28	Deborah Kerr and Yul Brynner	5–10
	June 4	Primping in Ancient Sumer	1–3
	June 11	Carroll Baker	4–8
	June 18	Air Age Special Issue	3–6
	June 25	Mickey Mantle	20–40+
	July 2	Actress Stephanie Griffin	1–2
	July 9	Debutante Beatrice Lodge	1–2
	July 16	Gary Cooper and Tony Perkins	3–6
	July 23	The Battle of Buena Vista	1–3
	July 30	Pier Angeli	3–6
	August 6	Stricken S.S. *Andrea Doria*	10–20
	August 13	Dirndls in Fashion	1–2
	August 20	Audrey Hepburn	10–20
	August 27	Adlai Stevenson and Eleanor Roosevelt	5–10
	September 3	Slave Auction	5–10
	September 10	Actress Siobhan McKenna	1–2
	September 17	S.S. *Andrea Doria* Salvage	7–15
	September 24	Actress Janet Blair	1–2
	October 1	Egyptian Artist	1–2
	October 8	Masonic Grand Masters	2–4
	October 15	Elizabeth Taylor	10–20+
	October 22	Bather of Valpincon	1–3
	October 29	Plane Crash Rescue	3–6
	November 5	Dwight D. Eisenhower	2–3
	November 12	Rosalind Russell	2–4
	November 19	Wounded Egyptian Soldier	2–3
	November 26	Ingrid Bergman	2–4
	December 3	Flag on Sunken U.S.S. *Arizona*	6–12
	December 10	Olympic Sprinter Bobby Morrow	1–2
	December 17	Baptism	1–2
	December 24	American Woman Special Issue	3–6
1957	January 7	Richard M. Nixon and Hungarian Refugee Children	5–10
	January 14	*Li'l Abner* Chorus	1–3

Year	Issue	Cover Subject	Value ($)
1957	January 21	Harold Macmillan	1–2
	January 28	B-52	3–6
	February 4	Audrey Hepburn	10–20
	February 11	Vacationing Swimmer	1–2
	February 18	Julie London	2–4
	February 25	Masked Dancer	1–2
	March 4	Queen Elizabeth II and the Duke of Edinburgh	3–6
	March 11	John F. Kennedy	5–10
	March 18	Beatrice Lillie and Ziegfeld Follies Chorus	1–2
	March 25	Princess Caroline of Monaco	5–10
	April 1	Model Marie-Helene Arnaud	1–2
	April 8	Flying Blue Brothers	1–2
	April 15	Ernie Kovacs	6–12
	April 22	Carol Lynley	5–10
	April 29	Drag Race	1–2
	May 6	Sophia Loren	5–10
	May 13	Bert Lahr	4–8
	May 20	Air Force Vertijet	1–2
	May 27	Knights of Columbus	1–2
	June 3	Making of a Satellite	1–2
	June 10	Helicopter Safari	1–2
	June 17	*Mayflower II* Voyage	1–2
	June 24	Prince Juan Carlos of Spain	1–2
	July 1	Billy Graham	2–4
	July 8	King Ranch Roundup	1–2
	July 15	Maria Schell	2–4
	July 22	Dr. Hannes Lindemann in a Transatlantic Canoe	1–2
	July 29	Babysitter	2–4
	August 5	Debutante Julia Williamson	2–3
	August 12	Mai Britt	3–5
	August 19	Four DuPonts	1–2
	August 26	San Simeon's Pool	1–2
	September 2	Balloonist	3–6
	September 9	N.Y. Street Gang	3–6
	September 16	Cincinnati Police Chief	2–3
	September 23	Suzy Parker	1–2

Year	Issue	Cover Subject	Value ($)
1957	September 30	Kay Kendall and Husband, Rex Harrison	2–4
	October 7	U.S. Troops in Little Rock	2–4
	October 14	Milwaukee Parade for Braves and Manager Fred Honey	2–4
	October 21	U.S. Scientists Plot *Sputnik* Orbit	2–4
	October 28	Queen Elizabeth II Opens Canada's Parliament	2–4
	November 4	Elizabeth Taylor and Daughter	5–10
	November 11	Air-Supported Dome for Swimming	1–2
	November 18	Rocket Designer Wernher von Braun	2–4
	November 25	Elsa Martine	2–4
	December 2	Nikita Khrushchev	2–3
	December 9	Richard M. Nixon	2–4
	December 16	Mary and Jesus	2–4
1958	January 6	Space Pilot Scott Crossfield	2–4
	January 13	Revolution in Petrograd	2–4
	January 20	Texas Senator Lyndon B. Johnson	2–3
	January 27	Ski Fashions	1–2
	February 3	Shirley Temple and Her 3-year-old Daughter	10–25
	February 10	Ralph Bellamy	2–4
	February 17	Tracking a U.S. Satellite	2–3
	February 24	Fishing in Germany	1–2
	March 3	Sally Ann Howes	2–4
	March 10	Yul Brynner	3–6
	March 17	McGuire Sisters	5–10
	March 24	Soviet and U.S. High School	2–3
	March 31	Science Teachers	1–2
	April 7	Sugar Ray Robinson and Carmen Basilio	5–10
	April 14	Actress Gwen Verdon	1–2
	April 21	Jacqueline, Caroline, and John F. Kennedy	3–6

Year	Issue	Cover Subject	Value ($)
1958	April 28	Willie Mays in San Francisco	10–20
	May 5	Cancer Patient and Radiation Machine	1–2
	May 12	Former Iranian Queen Soraya	1–2
	May 19	Margaret O'Brien	3–6
	May 26	Venezuelan Rioters Attack Richard M. Nixon's Car	1–2
	June 2	Charles de Gaulle	1–2
	June 9	French Veteran	1–2
	June 16	Children in Swings	2–3
	June 23	Seniors with Yearbooks	1–2
	June 30	Sherman Adams and Dwight D. Eisenhower	1–2
	July 7	Lebanese Rebels	1–2
	July 14	Oklahoma Wheat	2–3
	July 21	Roy Campanella	5–10
	July 28	Marines in Lebanon	2–4
	August 4	General James M. Gavin	1–2
	August 11	Couple Sailing	1–3
	August 18	Anne Frank	3–6
	August 25	Two Airline Stewardesses	1–2
	September 1	Commander William Anderson of the Submarine *Nautilus*	2–4
	September 8	Galapagos Tortoise and Flycatcher	1–2
	September 15	Bing Crosby's Four Sons	2–4
	September 22	George Burns and Gracie Allen	5–10
	September 29	Gun Draw	2–4
	October 6	Actress France Nuyen	1–2
	October 13	British Field Marshal Montgomery	3–3
	October 20	Mamie Eisenhower	1–2
	October 27	College of Cardinals	1–2
	November 3	Aga Khan	1–2
	November 10	Pope John XXIII	1–2
	November 17	Nelson and Happy Rockefeller	1–2
	November 24	Kim Novak	3–8
	December 1	Ricky Nelson	25–50
	December 8	N.Y. Society Women	1–2

Year	Issue	Cover Subject	Value ($)
1958	December 15	Prehistoric Explosion	1–3
	December 22	U.S. Entertainment Special Issue	2–4
1959	January 5	New Generation in Shanghai	1–2
	January 12	Senator Hubert Humphrey	1–3
	January 19	Fidel Castro	3–6
	January 26	Saber-toothed Cat	2–4
	February 2	Pat Boone	4–8
	February 9	Shirley MacLaine with Daughter	2–4
	February 16	Miami Chorus Girls	2–4
	February 23	Gwen Verdon	1–2
	March 2	Princess Luciana Pignatelli	1–2
	March 9	Jack Paar	2–4
	March 16	Brazilian Jaguar	3–5
	March 23	ID Cards of a Soviet Agent	1–2
	March 30	Debbie Reynolds in Spain	4–8
	April 6	Wagons on the Oregon Trail	3–6
	April 13	Weightless in Space Test	1–3
	April 20	Marilyn Monroe	20–40
	April 27	Early California Bear Hunt	2–4
	May 4	Dalai Lama	3–8
	May 11	Old West Silver Queen Baby	2–4
	May 18	Jimmy Hoffa	2–4
	May 25	Mr. and Mrs. Sherman Adams	1–2
	June 1	Boating in Kansas	1–3
	June 8	Audrey Hepburn	10–20
	June 15	Space Monkeys Able and Baker	2–4
	June 22	First Air Force Academy Graduates	2–3
	June 29	Zsa Zsa Gabor and Her Ghostwriter	2–4
	July 6	Gardner McKay	1–2
	July 13	Old Age	1–2
	July 20	Ingemar Johnsson and Fiancée	1–3
	July 27	Peace Ships	2–3
	August 3	Kingston Trio	3–6
	August 10	Wives of Mikoyan, Nixon, Khrushchev, and Kozlov	2–3

Year	Issue	Cover Subject	Value ($)
1959	August 17	Mai Britt	2–4
	August 24	Senator and Mrs. John F. Kennedy	2–4
	August 31	Rip Van Winkle	2–4
	September 7	Bill Lundigan and Gene Barry	2–3
	September 14	Astronauts	7–15
	September 21	Astronauts' Wives	3–6
	September 28	Migrating Ducks	2–4
	October 5	Nikita Khrushchev with Iowa Farmer	2–4
	October 12	Family Doctor	2–3
	October 19	Mums and Missiles in Peking	2–4
	October 26	Quiz Star Charles van Doren	1–2
	November 2	Jackie Gleason	10–20
	November 9	Marilyn Monroe	15–30
	November 16	Jewelry in Fashion	1–2
	November 23	Mary Martin	2–3
	November 30	Pretty Postage Stamps	1–2
	December 7	Shah's Fiancée Farah Diba	1–3
	December 14	Hawaiian Volcano Erupts	3–6
	December 21	Dwight D. Eisenhower in Pakistan	2–4
	December 28	The Good Life Special Issue	2–4
1960	January 11	Actress Dina Merrill	1–2
	January 18	Ghanaian Speaker of the House	1–2
	January 25	Father Marquette Conquers Manitou	2–3
	February 1	Dinah Shore	2–4
	February 8	U.S. Olympic Skiers	1–2
	February 15	Navy Bathyscaphe	1–2
	February 22	Henry and Jane Fonda	4–8
	February 29	Olympic Ski Jumper	1–2
	March 7	Hypnosis	1–2
	March 14	Princess Margaret and Anthony Armstrong	2–3
	March 21	Billy Graham in Africa	3–6
	March 28	Hubert Humphrey and John F. Kennedy	2–3

Year	Issue	Cover Subject	Value ($)
1960	April 4	Marlon Brando	3–7
	April 11	Silvana Mangano	1–2
	April 18	Elopers Gamble Benedict and Andrei Porumbeau	1–2
	April 25	Tourists on Lover's Leap	2–3
	May 2	Trampoliners	2–3
	May 9	Yvette Mimieux	3–7
	May 16	Princess Margaret	2–4
	May 23	Minuteman Statue	1–2
	May 30	Nikita Khrushchev	1–3
	June 6	Lee Remick	3–5
	June 13	Hayley Mills	15–25
	June 20	L.A. Freeway	1–2
	June 27	Alaskan Walrus	2–4
	July 4	U.S. Politics Special Issue	1–2
	July 11	Nelson Rockefeller and His Grandchildren	1–2
	July 18	Ina Balin	1–2
	July 25	Kennedy Demonstration	1–3
	August 1	Giraffes and Children in New-Style Amusement Park	2–3
	August 9	Richard and Patricia Nixon	2–3
	August 15	Marilyn Monroe and Yves Montand	10–20
	August 22	U.S. Olympic Swimmers	1–3
	August 29	Record Free-Fall	1–3
	September 5	Ernest Hemingway	2–4
	September 12	U.S. Olympic Gymnasts	1–2
	September 19	Grandma Moses	2–5
	September 26	Norell Fashions	1–2
	October 3	President Dwight D. Eisenhower	1–2
	October 10	Doris Day	5–10
	October 17	Henry Cabot Lodge and Wife	1–2
	October 24	Nancy Kwan	2–5
	October 31	Halloween	3–6
	November 7	The Earth in the Magnetic Field	2–4
	November 14	Sophia Loren	3–6
	November 21	Victorious John F. Kennedy	5–10
	November 28	Carroll Baker	3–6

Year	Issue	Cover Subject	Value ($)
1960	December 5	Baltimore Colts Kickoff	2–4
	December 12	Jill Haworth and Sal Mineo	5–10
	December 19	President Kennedy and Wife	2–4
	December 26	25th Anniversary Special	2–4
1961	January 6	Civil War Cavalry Charge	5–10
	January 13	Clark Gable	5–10
	January 20	Cancer Surgeon	1–2
	January 27	Kennedys	3–6
	February 3	Queen Elizabeth II in India	3–6
	February 10	Astrochimp Ham	1–2
	February 17	Shirley MacLaine	2–4
	February 24	UN's Dag Hammarskjold	1–2
	March 3	John Glenn	10–20
	March 10	Maurice Chevalier and Bing Crosby	3–5
	March 17	Model Sheila Finn	1–2
	March 24	Puppets of Jack Paar and Ed Sullivan	2–4
	March 31	Cherub	2–3
	April 7	Ocean Fishing	1–2
	April 14	Mrs. Clark Gable and Son John	2–4
	April 21	Cosmonaut Yury Gagarin	5–10
	April 28	Elizabeth Taylor	5–10
	May 5	Anna Maria Alberghetti with Puppets	2–4
	May 12	Alan Shepard Pick Up at Sea	3–6
	May 19	Alan Shepard	4–8
	May 26	Jackie Kennedy in Canada	4–8
	June 2	Fidel Castro	2–4
	June 9	J.F.K. with Charles de Gaulle	2–4
	June 16	Princess Hohenioche	1–2
	June 23	Princess Grace	5–10
	June 30	Leslie Caron	3–5
	July 7	Dwight D. Eisenhower	2–3
	July 14	Ernest Hemingway	2–4
	July 21	Rio Slum Child	2–3
	July 28	Brigitte Bardot	10–20
	August 4	JFK	3–6

Year	Issue	Cover Subject	Value ($)
1961	August 11	Sophia Loren	4–8
	August 18	Mickey Mantle and Roger Maris	10–20
	August 25	West Berliners	1–2
	September 1	Jacqueline Kennedy	2–4
	September 8	U.S. Tank Soldier	3–5
	September 15	Civilian Fallout Suits	2–3
	September 22	Hurricane Carla	2–4
	September 29	Dag Hammarskjold's Coffin	1–2
	October 6	Elizabeth Taylor	5–10
	October 13	African Warrior	2–4
	October 20	Communist Leaders	2–3
	October 27	G.I. in Training	2–3
	November 3	A Daughter's Goodbye to National Guardsman	2–4
	November 10	Nikita Khrushchev	1–2
	November 17	Minnesota Vikings	2–3
	November 24	One-year-old JFK	1–3
	December 1	Italian Fashions	1–2
	December 8	Plum Pudding Flambé	1–2
	December 15	Chartres Cathedral	1–2
	December 22	Splendid Outdoors Special Issue	1–2
1962	January 5	Lucille Ball	10–20
	January 12	Community Fallout Shelter	2–4
	January 19	Iceboating	1–3
	January 26	Robert Kennedy	2–4
	February 2	John Glenn	10–20
	February 9	Seattle World's Fair	2–4
	February 16	Rock Hudson	2–4
	February 23	Shirley MacLaine	2–4
	March 2	John Glenn Back from Space	10–20
	March 9	Motorcade for John Glenn	10–20
	March 16	Richard M. Nixon	3–6
	March 23	Desert Housing Development	2–3
	March 30	Robert Frost	2–3
	April 6	Stretching the Dollar	1–2

Year	Issue	Cover Subject	Value ($)
1962	April 13	Elizabeth Taylor and Richard Burton with Baseball Cards	75–150
	April 20	Audrey Hepburn	6–12
	April 27	Moonsuit Test	2–3
	May 4	Seattle World's Fair Monorail	2–5
	May 11	Bob Hope	3–6+
	May 18	Scott Carpenter and Wife	2–3
	May 25	Prince Juan Carlos Weds His Princess	2–3
	June 1	Rene Carpenter Watching Scott Take Off	1–2
	June 8	Ticker Tape Parade Special	1–2
	June 15	Natalie Wood	5–10
	June 22	Marilyn Monroe	10–20
	June 29	Massachusetts Senatorial Candidates	2–4
	July 6	Balloon	2–4
	July 13	JFK in Mexico	3–6
	July 20	H-Bomb Fireball	3–6
	July 27	Elsa Martinelli	1–2
	August 3	Astronaut Bob White with His Son	2–4
	August 10	Janet Leigh	5–10
	August 17	Marilyn Monroe	10–20
	August 24	Soviet Space Capsules	2–3
	August 31	Reenactment of the Great Mail Robbery	2–4
	September 7	Caroline Kennedy	1–2
	September 14	The Takeover Generation Special Issue	1–3
	September 21	Iran Earthquake Victims	2–4
	September 28	Don Drysdale	2–4
	October 5	Jackie Gleason with Sue Ane Langdon	7–15
	October 12	Pope John XXIII	1–3
	October 19	Special California Issue	2–4
	October 26	The Human Body	2–3
	November 2	U.S. Navy off Cuba	2–4

Year	Issue	Cover Subject	Value ($)
1962	November 9	U Thant and British Ambassador	1–2
	November 16	Indian Soldier	1–2
	November 23	Bounty of Food Special Issue	1–2
	November 30	Sid Caesar	5–7
	December 7	The Human Body	2–4
	December 14	Marlon Brando	2–4
	December 21	The Sea Special Issue	2–4
1963	January 4	Greek Statue	2–3
	January 11	Ann-Margret	5–8
	January 18	The Trojan Horse	3–5
	January 25	Vietcong Prisoners	3–6
	February 1	Alfred Hitchcock	3–5
	February 8	Greek Statue	2–4
	February 15	Moving Lincoln's Body	3–6
	February 22	Alice and Ellen Kessler	1–2
	March 1	Snakes	2–4
	March 8	Jean Seberg	3–6
	March 15	Fidel Castro	3–6
	March 22	*Polaris* Sub Commander John L. From, Jr.	2–5
	March 29	Costa Ricans	2–4
	April 5	Spartans Stand at Thermopylae	3–6
	April 12	Helen Klaben Lost in the Yukon	3–6
	April 19	Elizabeth Taylor and Richard Burton	5–10
	April 26	Young Jackie Kennedy	2–4
	May 3	Alexander the Great	4–8
	May 10	Bay of Pigs	5–10
	May 17	Nelson and Happy Rockefeller	2–3
	May 24	Gordon Cooper	1–2
	May 31	Gordon and Trudy Cooper	1–2
	June 7	Pope John XXIII	1–2
	June 14	St. Peter's	1–2
	June 21	Shirley MacLaine	2–4
	June 28	Medgar Evers's Widow	2–3
	July 5	Pope Paul VI	1–2

Year	Issue	Cover Subject	Value ($)
1963	July 12	Steve McQueen	5–8
	July 19	Greek Sculpture	3–4
	July 26	Tuesday Weld	5–10
	August 2	Sandy Koufax	3–6
	August 9	Averell Harriman and Nikita Khrushchev	1–2
	August 16	Hospital Vigil over President Kennedy	4–8
	August 23	Frank Sinatra and Frank, Jr.	10–20
	August 30	Paris Fashions	1–3
	September 6	Washington March Leaders	1–2
	September 13	Special Russia Issue	2–3
	September 20	U.S. Team on Mt. Everest	3–6
	September 27	Astronauts Frank Borman, Thomas Stafford, and James Lovell	3–6
	October 4	DNA Molecule	2–3
	October 11	Vietnam's Madame Nhu	2–4
	October 18	Grand Duchess Anastasia and Family	2–4
	October 25	Yvette Mimieux	3–6
	November 1	Senator Barry Goldwater	2–3
	November 8	President Johnson's Former Aide Bobby Baker	1–2
	November 15	South Vietnam Soldiers	5–10
	November 22	Elizabeth Ashley	2–3
	November 29	John F. Kennedy	2–3
	December 6	John F. Kennedy's Family Waiting to Join Funeral Procession	2–4
	December 13	Lyndon B. Johnson	1–2
	December 20	The Movies Special Issue	4–7
1964	January 3	S.S. *Lakonia*'s Fire at Sea	2–4
	January 10	General Douglas MacArthur	2–4
	January 17	Pope Paul VI	2–3
	January 24	Canal Zone Rioters	2–3
	January 31	Geraldine Chaplin	2–4

Year	Issue	Cover Subject	Value ($)
1964	February 7	British Commando with Tanganyikan Mutineers	2–4
	February 14	Olympic Ski Jumper	1–2
	February 21	Lee Harvey Oswald	2–4
	February 28	Armed Turks on Cyprus	2–3
	March 6	Cassius Clay	2–4
	March 13	World War I British Wounded	2–5
	March 20	Ambassador Henry Cabot Lodge in Saigon	2–3
	March 27	Charles de Gaulle with President Lopez Mateos of Mexico	1–2
	April 3	Carol Channing	2–4
	April 10	Alaskan Earthquake	5–8
	April 17	General Douglas MacArthur's Hat	2–4
	April 24	Richard Burton	2–5
	May 1	The N.Y. World's Fair Opens	4–8
	May 8	Campaign Buttons	1–2
	May 15	Luci Baines Johnson	1–2
	May 22	Barbra Streisand	3–6
	May 29	Jacqueline Kennedy	2–3
	June 5	Cremation of Nehru	2–3
	June 12	U.S. Officer on Patrol in Vietnam	3–5
	June 19	LBJ's Beagles	2–4
	June 26	Pennsylvania Governor Wiliam Scranton	1–2
	July 3	Robert Kennedy with Kennedy Family Children	2–3
	July 10	Lee Harvey Oswald with His Wife Marina	3–6
	July 17	Carroll Baker with Masai Warriors	2–5
	July 24	Senator Barry Goldwater with His Wife	2–3
	July 31	Olympic Drive	1–2
	August 7	Marilyn Monroe	10–20
	August 14	LBJ	1–2

Year	Issue	Cover Subject	Value ($)
1964	August 21	South Vietnam's General Khanh	2–4
	August 28	The Beatles	10–20
	September 4	LBJ and Daughter	1–2
	September 11	Japan Special Issue	2–4
	September 18	Sophia Loren	2–4
	September 25	Saturn V Rocket	2–4
	October 2	John F. Kennedy's Assassination	3–5
	October 9	Olympic Swimmer	1–2
	October 16	Berlin Escape	2–4
	October 23	Leonid Brezhnev	1–2
	October 30	Olympic Gold Medalist Don Schollander	1–2
	November 6	Shirley Eaton	1–2
	November 13	LBJ and Hubert Humphrey	1–2
	November 20	Soviet Marshal Rodion Malinovsky and General A. P. Beloborodov	1–2
	November 27	Vietnam G.I.s	4–8
	December 4	Congo Missionary Dr. Paul Carlson	1–2
	December 11	The Rockettes	2–3
	December 18	Elizabeth Taylor	3–7
	December 25	The Bible Special Issue	2–5
1965	January 8	California Foods	1–2
	January 15	Ted Kennedy	1–2
	January 22	Peter O'Toole	2–4
	January 29	LBJ's Inauguration	1–2
	February 5	Winston Churchill's Casket Carried by Grenadier Guard	2–4
	February 12	Mercenaries Mop Up in the Congo	2–4
	February 19	Albert Schweitzer	2–4
	February 26	North Vietnam Postage Stamp	2–4
	March 5	Aftermath of Malcolm X's Death	2–4
	March 12	Julie Andrews	3–5
	March 19	Civil Rights in Selma	2–4
	March 26	Martin Luther King, Jr.	3–4

Year	Issue	Cover Subject	Value ($)
1965	April 2	*Gemini*'s Splashdown	5–8
	April 9	Robert Kennedy on Mountain Summit	2–3
	April 16	Aboard the U.S. Copter *Yankee*	2–5
	April 23	Frank Sinatra	10–20
	April 30	Fetus	2–4
	May 7	John Wayne	5–10
	May 14	Skateboarding	1–2
	May 21	Ku Klux Klan Defense Lawyer	1–2
	May 28	N.Y. Congressman John Lindsay	1–2
	June 4	German Measles Blood Test	1–2
	June 11	Waterloo	3–5
	June 18	Astronaut Ed White in Space Walk	4–8
	June 25	Indian Tiger	2–4
	July 2	Wounded Marine Evacuated in Vietnam	10–20+
	July 9	Yachting on the Riviera	1–2
	July 16	John F. Kennedy	1–2
	July 23	Adlai Stevenson	1–2
	July 30	Mickey Mantle	5–10
	August 6	U.S.S. *Oklahoma City* Shelling Vietcong	3–5
	August 13	Lady Bird Johnson	1–2
	August 20	Draft Inductees	1–2
	August 27	Riots in Watts	2–4
	September 3	Astronaut Charles Conrad Lifting Off	2–4
	September 10	Expectant Mother	1–2
	September 17	Indian Soldier	1–2
	September 24	Baja California as Seen from Spaceship	2–4
	October 1	Eskimo Game	2–3
	October 8	Hawaiian Beauty Elizabeth Logue	1–2
	October 15	Pope Paul VI in Yankee Stadium	1–3

Year	Issue	Cover Subject	Value ($)
1965	October 22	Mary Martin in Vietnam	2–4
	October 29	The Temples of Abu Simbel	2–4
	November 5	John F. Kennedy	2–3
	November 12	New York City Mayor-elect John Lindsay	1–2
	November 19	Manhattan Power Blackout	3–6
	November 26	Vietcong Prisoner	5–10
	December 3	LBJ with Princess Margaret	1–2
	December 10	Texas Linebacker Tommy Nobis	1–2
	December 17	Vatican	1–2
	December 24	The City Special Issue	1–2
1966	January 7	Sean Connery	5–10
	January 14	North Vietnam's Ho Chi Minh and Prime Minister Pham Van Dong	3–6
	January 21	Indian Prime Minister Shastri Lies in State	1–2
	January 28	Actress Catherine Spaak	1–2
	February 4	Sammy Davis, Jr., Harry Belafonte, and Sidney Poitier	2–4
	February 11	Wounded GIs in Vietnam	10–20+
	February 18	Model of the Flu Germ	1–2
	February 25	Sunrise Mission over South Vietnam	7–15+
	March 4	Bust of Roman Citizen	2–4
	March 11	Batman	10–20
	March 18	Barbra Streisand	3–6
	March 25	LSD Capsule	1–2
	April 1	Charlie Chaplin and Sophia Loren	2–4
	April 8	Captain Pete Dawkins	2–4
	April 15	Louis Armstrong	2–4
	April 22	Injured Monk in Vietnam	2–4
	April 29	Julie Christie	2–4
	May 6	Jacqueline Kennedy	1–2
	May 13	Mod Male Fashions	2–4
	May 20	Bugging Device	1–2

Year	Issue	Cover Subject	Value ($)
1966	May 27	Discotheque	1–3
	June 3	Bust of Marcus Aurelius	2–4
	June 10	Elizabeth Taylor	3–6
	June 17	Angela Lansbury	2–3
	June 24	Prescription Pills	1–2
	July 1	Moonscape	2–4
	July 8	Claudia Cardinale	3–5
	July 15	Young Black Militants	1–2
	July 22	Birth	2–4
	July 29	Murderer's Fingerprints	1–3
	August 5	*Gemini 10* Docking with *Agena 10*	2–4
	August 12	Texas Store Windows Shattered by Sniper	2–4
	August 19	Luci Johnson and Pat Nixon	1–2
	August 26	Strike Fever	1–2
	September 2	Paris Fashion	1–2
	September 9	Psychedelic Artist	2–4
	September 16	Sophia Loren	2–4
	September 23	Chinese Imperial Magistrate and Guards	1–2
	September 30	Rex Harrison	1–2
	October 7	Ian Fleming	2–5
	October 14	Pro Football Mayhem	1–2
	October 21	Zebra	1–2
	October 28	Wounded Marine	5–10
	November 4	LBJ in Vietnam	1–3
	November 11	Jean-Paul Belmondo	1–2
	November 18	Robert Kennedy	1–2
	November 25	Frame 230 of John F. Kennedy Assassination Film Footage	2–3
	December 2	Actress Melina Mercouri	1–2
	December 9	Draftees	2–4
	December 16	Restoring *The Last Supper*	2–4
	December 23	Photography Special Issue	2–4
1967	January 6	Black Leopard	2–3
	January 13	Navy Patrol over Mekong River	4–8

Year	Issue	Cover Subject	Value ($)
1967	January 20	China's Red Guard	1–2
	January 27	Bathing Suits in Fashion	1–2
	February 3	Astronauts Roger Chaffee, Ed White, and Gus Grissom	2–4
	February 10	Gus Grissom's Caisson at Arlington Cemetery	2–4
	February 17	Underground Culture Leader	1–2
	February 24	Elizabeth Taylor	2–5
	March 3	Leonardo da Vinci Sketch	2–3
	March 10	U.S. Paratroopers over Vietnam	3–6
	March 17	Charlie Brown and Snoopy	3–5
	March 24	Easter in Jerusalem	3–5
	March 31	Infant	1–3
	April 7	Hanoi Air Raid Alert	3–6
	April 14	Sharon Percy Weds John D. Rockefeller IV	1–2
	April 21	The Individual	1–2
	April 28	U.S. Pavilion at Expo '67	1–2
	May 5	Mia Farrow	1–3
	May 12	Truman Capote, Scott Wilson, and Robert Blake	1–3
	May 19	Astronaut Wally Schirra	1–3
	May 26	General Lew Walt	1–2
	June 2	China's Cultural Red Guards	1–3
	June 9	Sir Francis Chichester	1–2
	June 16	Israeli Troops Take Prisoners in Gaza	2–3
	June 23	Israeli Soldier Cools Off in the Suez Canal	2–3
	June 30	Aleksey Kosygin and LBJ	1–2
	July 7	LBJ	1–2
	July 14	Princess Lee Radziwill	1–2
	July 21	Kidnapped U.S. Official in Vietnam	4–8
	July 28	Newark Riot Victim	3–6
	August 4	Troops Patrol Detroit	2–3
	August 11	U.S.S. *Forrestal* Disaster	2–4
	August 18	Veruschka	2–4

Year	Issue	Cover Subject	Value ($)
1967	August 25	Marine and Young Vietnamese Friend	7–15+
	September 1	Posters	1–2
	September 8	Carl Yastrzemski	5–10
	September 15	Svetlana Alliluyeva	1–2
	September 22	Svetlana Alliluyeva	1–2
	September 29	Antiballistic Missile Test	1–2
	October 6	S.S. *Queen Mary*	2–3
	October 13	Ingrid Bergman	2–3
	October 20	U.S. POW in Vietnam	6–12
	October 27	GI at Con Thien	7–15
	November 3	Runaway Kids	1–2
	November 10	Leningrad Music Hall Girls	2–3
	November 17	Jacqueline Kennedy in Cambodia	1–2
	November 24	Governor Connally, Kennedys in San Antonio	1–2
	December 1	The American Indian	2–4
	December 8	Pearl Bailey	2–3
	December 15	Human Heart Recipient Louis Washansky	1–2
	December 22	The Wild World Special	
1968	January 5	Katharine Hepburn	2–4
	January 12	Faye Dunaway	2–4
	January 19	Human Heart and Surgeon	1–2
	January 26	Diet Pills	1–2
	February 2	Aleksey Kosygin	1–2
	February 9	Captured Vietcong Guerrilla	5–10
	February 16	North Vietnamese Soldiers	5–10
	February 23	Olympic Gold Medalist Figure Skater Peggy Fleming	1–3
	March 1	Georgia O'Keeffe	1–2
	March 8	Black Child	1–2
	March 15	Boris Karloff	15–30
	March 22	Ho Chi Minh	5–10
	March 29	Jane Fonda	5–10
	April 5	King Tut	2–4
	April 12	Martin Luther King, Jr.	2–4

Year	Issue	Cover Subject	Value ($)
1968	April 19	Mrs. Martin Luther King, Jr.	1–2
	April 26	Phillipe Thyraud de Vosjoli	1–2
	May 3	James Earl Ray	2–4
	May 10	Paul Newman	1–3
	May 17	The Generation Gap	1–3
	May 24	John Lindsay	1–2
	May 31	Egyptian Goddess Serket	2–4
	June 7	Eugene McCarthy	1–2
	June 14	Robert F. Kennedy	2–4
	June 21	James Earl Ray and Sirhan Sirhan	1–2
	June 28	Jefferson Airplane	15–30
	July 5	Presidency Special Issue	1–2
	July 12	Starving Children of Biafra	1–2
	July 19	Young American Nomads on Crete	1–2
	July 26	American and Soviet Flight Attendants	1–2
	August 2	George Wallace, Nixon, Reagan Air Traffic Jams	1–2
	August 9	Air Traffic Jams	1–2
	August 16	Richard Nixon and Wife	2–4
	August 23	Security Chiefs at Chicago Convention	1–2
	August 30	Czech Freedom Fighters	1–2
	September 6	Hubert Humphrey and Edmund Muskie	1–2
	September 13	The Beatles	10–20
	September 20	Arthur Ashe	1–2
	September 27	Swedish Fashions	1–2
	October 4	Probing the Sea	2–3
	October 11	Pope John XXIII	1–2
	October 18	Paul Newman and Joanne Woodward	1–2
	October 25	*Apollo* 7	5–10
	November 1	Jacqueline Kennedy and Aristotle Onassis	1–2
	November 8	Vietnam War Victim	6–12

Year	Issue	Cover Subject	Value ($)
1968	November 15	Nixon	1–2
	November 22	Frederick Douglass	2–4
	November 29	Egyptian Soldier Tests Soviet Tank	2–3
	December 6	Police Violence at the Chicago Convention	1–2
	December 13	Baltimore Colts	2–4
	December 20	Mark Twain	2–4
	December 27	Picasso Special Issue	2–4
1969	January 10	The Incredible Year Special Issue	2–3
	January 17	Sirhan Sirhan	1–2
	January 24	Catherine Deneuve	1–2
	January 31	Aerial View of the Washington Monument	1–2
	February 7	Lloyd Bucher of the U.S.S. *Pueblo*	2–4
	February 14	Barbra Streisand	3–5
	February 21	Nixon	2–4
	February 28	Herons	1–2
	March 7	Nixon	2–4
	March 14	Lunar Module on *Apollo 9*	4–7
	March 21	Woody Allen	1–2
	March 28	Orangutan	1–3
	April 4	Sensuality in the Arts	1–3
	April 11	Dwight D. Eisenhower's Bier	2–4
	April 18	Mae West	2–4
	April 25	Harvard Professor	1–2
	May 2	Judy Collins	3–6
	May 9	Peter Falk	2–4
	May 16	High School	1–2
	May 23	Rowan and Martin	3–5
	May 30	Ambulance	1–2
	June 6	The Moon's Surface	3–6
	June 13	Human Embryo and Mother and Infant	2–3
	June 20	Joe Namath	2–3
	June 27	American Dead in Vietnam	5–10

Year	Issue	Cover Subject	Value ($)
1969	July 4	Neil Armstrong	5–10
	July 11	Dustin Hoffman	2–3
	July 18	Youth Communes	1–2
	July 25	Neil Armstrong	5–10
	August 1	Ted Kennedy	1–2
	August 8	American Flag on the Moon	5–8
	August 15	Dollar Squeeze	1–2
	August 22	N.Y. Fashions	1–2
	August 29	Norman Mailer	1–2
	September 5	Peter Max	6–12
	September 12	Coretta Scott King	1–2
	September 19	Children	1–2
	September 26	N.Y. Mets	5–10
	October 3	Ballet Dancer	1–2
	October 10	Revolution	1–2
	October 17	Naomi Sims	1–2
	October 24	Dissent	1–2
	October 31	Marijuana	1–2
	November 7	Paul McCartney and Family	5–10
	November 14	Green Beret	5–10
	November 21	Johnny Cash	2–4
	November 28	The U.S. Mail Mess	1–2
	December 5	African Antelope	1–2
	December 12	*Apollo 12* Moon Walk	5–10
	December 19	Charles Manson	3–6
	December 26	'60s Special Issue	3–6
1970	January 9	Into the '70s Special Issue	2–4
	January 23	Johnny Carson	2–4
	January 30	Snow Monkey	1–2
	February 6	Robert Redford	1–2
	February 13	The Dollar Bill	1–2
	February 20	Architect Turned Clown	1
	February 27	The Spirit of American Cinema	2–3
	March 6	Gold Medalist Skier Billy Kidd	1–2
	March 13	Hemlines in Fashion	1–2
	March 20	Former Nun	1
	March 27	Credit Cards	1
	April 3	Lauren Bacall	2–3

Year	Issue	Cover Subject	Value ($)
1970	April 10	Denton Cooley and Micael DeBakey	1–2
	April 17	Zero Population Growth Campaign Button	1
	April 24	Jim Lovell	1–2
	May 1	Chapel Hill Coed	1–2
	May 8	Spiro Agnew	1
	May 15	Wounded Kent State Student	5–10
	May 22	Our Forgotten Wounded	2–4
	May 29	Brenda Vaccaro	1–2
	June 5	A Bear Market	1
	June 12	Palestinian Training Camp for Kids	2–3
	June 19	Dennis Hopper	1–2
	June 26	Americans in a Spanish Prison	1–2
	July 3	Iowa Boy Scouts	2–3
	July 10	California Girls at the Beach	2–4
	July 17	Rose Kennedy with Ted and Joan	1
	July 24	Candice Bergen	2–4
	July 31	Bebe Rebozo	1
	August 7	LBJ, Robert Kennedy, and JFK	1–2
	August 14	Summer Nomads	1–2
	August 21	Midiskirts in Fashion	1–2
	August 28	Pornography	2–3
	September 4	Liberty Congratulates Woman Voter	2–3
	September 11	Angela Davis	2–3
	September 18	Engelbert Humperdinck	3–5
	September 25	Male Plumage in Fashion	1
	October 2	Martha Mitchell	1
	October 9	Egypt's Abdel Nasser	2–4
	October 16	Spiro Agnew	1
	October 23	Muhammad Ali	5–10
	October 30	Dick Cavett	1
	November 6	Nixon at 14	2–3
	November 13	Nixon	1

Year	Issue	Cover Subject	Value ($)
1970	November 20	Oberlin Students in Coed Dorm	1–2
	November 27	Khrushchev	1
	December 4	Khrushchev	1
	December 11	Health Food	1
	December 18	Buckley and Families	1
	December 25	Prize-Winning Pictures Special Issue	1
1971	January 8	The New Shape of America Special Issue	2–3
	January 22	Tricia Nixon	1–2
	January 29	Bob Hope	2–4
	February 5	The New Army	2–3
	February 12	Jacqueline Onassis	2–4
	February 19	Rita Hayworth	2–4
	February 26	Snowmobiles	1–2
	March 5	Joe Frazier and Muhammad Ali	1–2
	March 12	Explosion among South Vietnamese Soldiers	5–10
	March 19	Frazier Beating Ali	2–3
	March 26	Walter Cronkite	2–4
	April 2	Pregnant High Schooler	1–2
	April 9	J. Edgar Hoover	1–2
	April 16	Paul and Linda McCartney	5–10
	April 23	Jane Fonda	3–6
	April 30	Chinese Children Marching	1–2
	May 7	Germaine Greer	1
	May 14	Carol Burnett	2–4
	May 21	LBJ with Grandson	1–2
	May 28	Chris Brown	1
	June 4	Christina Ford	1
	June 11	Ted and Joan Kennedy	1
	June 18	Tricia Nixon	1
	June 25	Frank Sinatra	7–15
	July 2	American Indians	3–6
	July 9	Photography Contest Winner	1–2
	July 16	Bess Myerson	2–4
	July 23	Clint Eastwood	5–10
	July 30	Chou En-lai	1–2

Year	Issue	Cover Subject	Value ($)
1971	August 6	Ann-Margret	2–4
	August 13	The Woman Problem	1
	August 20	Princess Anne	1–2
	August 27	Game Plan for the Dollar	1–2
	September 3	Americans Outdoors Special Issue	2–4
	September 10	TV's 25th Anniversary Special	3–6
	September 17	Heart Transplant Patient	1–2
	September 24	The Jackson Five with Their Parents	15–30
	October 1	The Human Brain	1–3
	October 8	Americans Stop for New Cars	1–2
	October 15	The Opening of Disney World	3–5
	October 22	The Brain	2–4
	October 29	David Cassidy	12–25
	November 5	Edmund Muskie	1–2
	November 12	Bobby Fisher	1–2
	November 19	Barred Window to Keep Crime Out	1–2
	November 26	Chemistry of Madness	1–2
	December 3	Los Angeles Rams and the Baltimore Colts	2–3
	December 10	Cybill Shepherd	2–4
	December 17	Children Special Issue	1–3
	December 31	The Year in Pictures	1–3
1972	January 14	Dallas Cowboys Roger Staubach and Tom Landry	2–4
	January 21	Single U.S. Vietnam Casualty in a Week	2–5
	January 28	John Wayne	5–10
	February 4	Howard Hughes	1–2
	February 11	Nina van Pallandt	1
	February 18	Japanese Olympic Ski Jumper	1–2
	February 25	Elizabeth Taylor	2–4
	March 3	Mao Tse-tung	1–2
	March 10	Marlon Brando	1–2
	March 17	Dropout Wife	1–2
	March 24	Wilt Chamberlain and Kareem Abdul-Jabbar	1–2

Year	Issue	Cover Subject	Value ($)
1972	March 31	Jacqueline Onassis	2–4
	April 7	The Oscars	2–4
	April 14	Broiling Steak	1
	April 21	Charlie Chaplin and Wife	1–2
	April 28	The Marriage Experiment	1–3
	May 5	Olympic Gymnast Cathy Rigby	2–4
	May 12	Vietnam Soldier Carrying Wounded Buddy	10–20+
	May 19	The Population Riddle	1–2
	May 26	Cornelia Wallace with George	1–2
	June 2	Raquel Welch	10–20
	June 9	Bella Abzug	1
	June 16	Girl with Hula Hoop	1–2
	June 23	Aleksandr Solzhenitsyn	1
	June 30	Young Crusaders for Jesus	1–2
	July 7	Senator George McGovern	1
	July 14	Mick Jagger	10–20
	July 21	McGovern	1
	July 28	The Bare Look in Fashion	2–4
	August 4	Flip Wilson	2–4
	August 11	Skyjackers Escape Hatch	1–2
	August 18	Mark Spitz	2–3
	August 25	Pat Nixon	2–3
	September 1	Autoworker	1
	September 8	Marilyn Monroe	4–8
	September 15	Israeli Olympic Team	2–4
	September 22	Frank Shorter	1
	September 29	POW Wife	2–4
	October 6	Dallas Cowboys Tackle Bob Lilly	2–3
	October 13	S.S. *Lusitania*	5–10
	October 20	Youngster	1–2
	October 27	Dr. Edward Land	1
	November 3	Joe Namath	1
	November 10	U.S. Navy POW	4–8
	November 17	Nixon	1
	November 24	Governor George Wallace	1
	December 1	Harry S Truman	1–2

Year	Issue	Cover Subject	Value ($)
1972	December 8	Diana Ross	10–20
	December 15	Christmas Special Issue	2–3
	December 29	The Year 1972 in Pictures	2–3

Note: Between 1973 and 1977 *Life* magazine did not issue a weekly magazine; instead they issued the following special issues:

Year	Value ($)
Spirit of Israel	2–4
The Year in Pictures (1973)	2–4
One Day in the Life of America	3–6
The Year in Pictures (1974)	2–4
The 100 Events That Shaped America	3–6
The Year in Pictures (1975)	2–4
Remarkable American Women	2–4
The Year in Pictures (1976)	2–4
The New Youth	2–4
The Year in Pictures (1977)	3–6

Note: In 1978 *Life* magazine goes monthly.

Year	Issue	Cover Subject	Value ($)
1978	October	Balloon	2–4
	November	Mickey Mouse	1–2
	December	Prince Charles	1–2
1979	January	Shar-Pei Dog	1–2
	February	Lingerie Fashions	2–3
	March	Lesley-Anne Down	2–4
	April	Eclipse	2–3
	May	Three-Mile Island	1–2
	June	Marlon Brando	1–2
	July	Whale	2–4
	August	Microsurgeon	1
	September	Pope John Paul II	1–2
	October	Dolly Parton	3–5
	November	Ted Kennedy	1
	December	The Decade in Pictures Special	2–4

Year	Issue	Cover Subject	Value ($)
1980	January	Ayatollah Khomeini	1–2
	February	Mary Astor	1–3
	March	Mickey Rooney	2–4
	April	Hare Krishna Children	1
	May	Man-made Gene	1–2
	June	Sunday Cat	1–3
	July	Cape Hatteras Lighthouse	1–3
	August	Miss Piggy	2–4
	September	Summer Sun	1–2
	October	Chinese Child	1–2
	November	Walter Cronkite	1–2
	December	Child Cancer Patient	1–2
1981	January	The Year in Pictures	1–2
	February	Swimsuit Fashions	2–4
	March	Jimmy Lopez	1
	April	Meryl Streep	1–2
	May	Ronald Reagan	1–2
	June	Planets	1–3
	July	Dying Lake	1–2
	August	Girl under Waterfall	2–3
	September	Artificial Heart	1–2
	October	Marilyn Monroe	3–5
	November	Fetus	1–2
	December	Brooke Shields	10–20
1982	January	The Year in Pictures	1–2
	February	Christie Brinkley	3–6
	March	Elizabeth Taylor	2–3
	April	Handgun	1–2
	May	Laser Surgeon	1–2
	June	Polar Bear	1–2
	July	Raquel Welch	10–20
	August	Marilyn Monroe	4–8
	September	Liver Transplant	1
	October	Arnold Schwarzenegger	1–2
	November	Test-Tube Baby	1–2
	December	Princess Diana	1–2

Year	Issue	Cover Subject	Value ($)
1983	January	The Year in Pictures	2–3
	February	Brooke Shields	10–20
	March	Prince Rainier and Children	1–2
	April	Embryo Hand	1–3
	May	Debra Winger	2–4
	June	Star Wars	5–10
	July	Glacier National Park	2–4
	August	Willie Nelson	2–3
	September	The Best and Worst Cars Ever	2–3
	October	Nancy Reagan	2–3
	November	JFK	1–2
	December	Barbra Streisand	2–4
1984	January	The Year in Pictures	2–3
	February	The Beatles	2–4
	March	Daryl Hannah in Bathing Suits	2–5
	April	Penguins	1–2
	May	History of Cocaine	1–2
	June	Harrison Ford and Kate Capshaw	3–5
	July	Dan Pisner and Quintuplets	1
	August	Grizzly Bear	2–3
	September	Michael Jackson	5–10
	October	Doonesbury Wedding	1–2
	November	John Jr. and Caroline Kennedy	1
	December	Princess Diana and Prince Andrew	5–10+
1985– present	All issues		1–4

Entertainment Magazines:
Movie/TV Magazines

⁂

What Are Movie/TV Magazines?

Many different types of magazines and issues fall into the collecting category of a movie/TV magazine. Any magazine that features a cover, stories, interviews, the latest facts or photos on a movie or television star is classified as a movie/TV magazine. The classic movie magazines such as *Photoplay, Screen Stars, Movie Mirror, Modern Screen, Motion Picture, Silver Screen,* and many others have since the silent era delighted many people, not just the seasoned collector. TV magazines first appeared on the newsstands in the early fifties, often including features about movie stars and cinema highlights. Magazines such as *Cosmopolitan, Esquire, Woman's Day, Ladies' Home Journal, Redbook,* and other similar magazines are considered movie/TV magazines only when they feature a TV or movie celebrity on the cover and include a story within on that celebrity. The basic rule is that any magazine, be it on travel, health, beauty, home improvements, sports, or any other subject, that highlights a star on its cover becomes a movie/TV magazine. Thus, a common, uncollected magazine, when featuring a star, quickly enters into the realm of collectibles.

What Makes a Movie/TV
Magazine Valuable?

The primary elements that make a movie/TV magazine valuable are the cover subject and the stories. Movie and TV magazines are collected basically by collectors and fans interested in particular stars, movies, and television shows. For example, Frank Sinatra, Princess Diana, Marilyn Monroe, and now Lucy Lawless (*Xena*), Sarah Michelle Gellar (*Buffy, the Vampire Slayer*), and Melissa Joan Hart (*Sabrina the Teenage Witch*) have remained strong collectible figures within the magazine marketplace. If an issue has an exceptional cover—say, a cover of a very young Frank Sinatra, or of Marilyn Monroe looking even more alluring than usual, or perhaps one of Shirley Temple or a young Judy Garland looking sweeter than ever—that issue can sell for up to double or even triple the value listed in our value column. Throughout this section we have listed the values for the average issues, as well as the magazines that feature the current most popular collectible celebrities. What makes a movie or TV magazine valuable? Content and how much any one collector is willing to pay to add a particular issue to his or her collection.

Buying Movie/TV Magazines

Vintage and classic movie magazines, namely issues prior to 1950, are becoming more and more difficult to find. Titles and issues that just a few years ago were easy to find and inexpensive to purchase are now disappearing from the marketplace. One reason for this is that dealers and collectors have been extremely aggressive in hunting them down. The wonderful days of the recent past when it was common to find an intriguing stack of vintage movie magazines at an estate sale, garage sale, or flea market for a low price have all but vanished. This does not mean that the collector should give up hope. Somewhere, somebody *is* cleaning an attic, basement, or closet and is deciding if he or she should throw them out or have a garage sale. Other than garage sales and flea markets, the most reliable sources, of course, are mail-order dealers, magazine stores, and trade publications (many trade publications can be found at the larger bookstores such as Barnes and Noble). Other reliable sources are comic book shops, back-issue magazine and old book stores, local want ads, movie and memorabilia conventions, public auctions, and paper collectible shows. Many major malls throughout the United States and Canada hold annual collectible shows. It is advisable to call the malls in your area to find out about any upcoming events. Today, the newest and most exciting places to find back issues of movie/TV magazines are the many Internet auction sites. Collectors and dealers are enthusiastically being drawn to such sites as eBay. An issue that has eluded a collector for years can suddenly be put up for auction; a minimum bid is

October 1934

November 1931

December 1932

January 1935

April 1932

April 1938

November 1944

March 1938

March 1940

June 1932

May 1943

January 1938

March 1938

May 1947

May 1936

Summer 1937

January 1938

October 1937

Steppin' Out,
January 27, 1999, $47.00

American Film *Magazine,*
November 1977, $84.00

given, and in most cases a photo of the magazine's cover is displayed. Surprisingly enough, vintage magazine prices attained on the Internet have remained modestly conservative while newer magazines (1970s to present) have been breaking sales records. For example, a one-month-old issue of *Steppin' Out,* featuring Lucy Lawless as Xena, with an original cover price of $3.95 sold for $47.00, and a 1977 issue of *American Film* featuring a young Brooke Shields sold for $84.00. On these auction sites the collector can key in his or her favorite star, movie, or TV program, and view sometimes hundreds if not thousands of related issues and items currently up for bid from sellers all around the world. The Internet is an excellent source for finding foreign issues, much sought after by American collectors, that just a short time ago were all but impossible to locate. In general, buying magazines on the most popular stars, such as Roy Rogers, Frank Sinatra, Marilyn Monroe, Judy Garland, and Howdy Doody on the Internet can be expensive as the competition for these issues is high. So if you're collecting the big stars, be prepared to pay. On the other hand, if you're looking for lesser known or not so popular stars, real bargains can be found.

Selling Movie/TV Magazines

Many collectors and dealers of movie and TV magazines, when selling, should first put together a detailed listing or catalog of all issues, including the titles, dates, and contents. This listing can then be made available to collectors throughout the world via an inexpensive classified ad in a trade paper such as *Film Collectors World, PCM, The Comic Buyers*

June 1945

September 1943

February 1938

December 1930

August 1930

November 1942

April 1941

August 1951

September 1938

February 1952

July 1947

November 1951

November 1954

February 1938

March 1933

August 1940

October 1940

December 1941

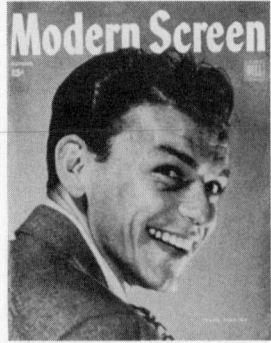

October 1945

March 1977

June 1938

May 1943

October 1944

March 3, 1938

Summer 1949

Spring/Summer 1972

February 1942

Guide, and others. Ads can also be placed in many local Want Ad publications. Often you pay only a small percentage of the sale price for these local want ads, and only if their ad sells your collection. You may consider attending a mall show or convention, or even driving your inventory to the local flea market. At most flea markets, you will be pleasantly surprised to see just how many people are interested in movie and TV magazines. Highest prices will be achieved by selling your magazines to hard-core collectors, who are generally found through the trade papers and paper shows. Lower prices are expected by the buyer at flea markets, so when selling there price your issues competitively.

If you have Internet services I strongly advise you to place a sampling of the issues on an Internet auction site such as eBay before you offer your magazines up for sale in any other venue. In the past couple of years it has not been uncommon for a movie or TV magazine with an accepted selling value of, say, $10 to sell through one of these auctions for five to ten times that amount. The cost of listing is generally less than $1 per item, plus a very small percentage fee when the item sells. Many back-issue magazine stores that once offered movie and TV magazines are no longer offering them in the shop, since they can get much higher prices on the Internet. For example, fairly recent back issues of *People* and *US* that are nearly impossible to sell in a retail store, flea market, garage sale, trade paper, or convention are selling at record prices on Internet auctions. In particular, an issue of *People* magazine, May 30, 1978, featuring Olivia Newton-John, which has a general value of $3 to $10, sold on eBay for $39, and an issue from August 2, 1976, featuring the Carpenters, with a general value of $4 to $8, recently sold for $26.

MOST COLLECTIBLE
FEMALE STARS OF THE THIRTIES

	Value ($)			
Subject	Cover and Feature	Cover Only	Feature Only	Cameo
Joan Crawford	15–30	10–25	10–20	5–15
Bette Davis	15–30	10–25	10–20	7–15
Olivia de Havilland	10–20	10–20	5–15	5–10
Olivia de Havilland/ Gone with the Wind	50–75	30–60	10–25	6–12

Subject	Value ($)			
	Cover and Feature	**Cover Only**	**Feature Only**	**Cameo**
Marlene Dietrich	10–25	10–25	10–20	5–10
Alice Faye	7–15	7–15	5–10	5–10
Greta Garbo	20–40	15–30	10–20	5–10
Judy Garland	25–60	15–30	10–20	5–10
Judy Garland/ The Wizard of Oz	100–250	100–200	30–60	20–40
Jean Harlow	20–40	20–40	10–20	5–10
Katharine Hepburn	10–25	10–25	10–20	5–15
Vivien Leigh	15–20	10–25	5–10	5–10
Vivien Leigh/ Gone with the Wind	100–200	75–150	20–40	5–10
Carole Lombard	10–20	10–20	5–10	5–10
Ginger Rogers	15–30	15–30	10–15	5–10
Ginger Rogers and Fred Astaire	20–40	15–30	10–20	6–12
Elizabeth Taylor	25–50	25–50	10–20	10–20
Shirley Temple	30–75	30–60	15–30	10–20
Mae West	15–30	15–30	7–15	5–10

MOST COLLECTIBLE MALE STARS OF THE THIRTIES

Subject	Value ($)			
	Cover and Feature	**Cover Only**	**Feature Only**	**Cameo**
Fred Astaire	15–30	15–30	10–20	6–10
Astaire and Rogers	20–40	15–30	10–20	6–12
Gene Autry and Western Stars	25–75	20–50	5–15	5–10

Subject	Value ($)			
	Cover and Feature	Cover Only	Feature Only	Cameo
Humphrey Bogart	20–40	20–40	5–15	5–10
James Cagney	25–50	20–40	5–12	5–10
Gary Cooper	10–20	10–20	5–10	5–10
Jackie Cooper	15–20	10–25	6–12	5–10
Bing Crosby	10–20	10–20	5–12	5–10
Disney Themes	50–100	30–75	20–30	10–20
W. C. Fields	10–25	10–25	5–15	5–15
Errol Flynn	20–40	15–30	5–10	5–10
Clark Gable	10–25	10–20	10–20	5–10
Clark Gable Gone with the Wind	50–125	50–100	15–25	10–20
Laurel and Hardy	50–100	50–100	10–30	10–20
Boris Karloff	50–125	50–100	10–25	10–20
Peter Lorre	15–30	15–30	7–15	5–10
Bela Lugosi	50–100	20–50	10–20	10–20
Marx Brothers	25–75	25–50	10–20	5–10
Basil Rathbone	15–35	15–30	10–20	5–10
Edward G. Robinson	10–20	10–20	5–12	5–10
Mickey Rooney	10–20	10–20	5–15	5–10
Three Stooges	100–250	100–200	40–75	20–40

MOST COLLECTIBLE FEMALE STARS OF THE FORTIES

Subject	Value ($)			
	Cover and Feature	Cover Only	Feature Only	Cameo
Lauren Bacall	10–20	10–20	5–12	5–10
Joan Crawford	10–20	10–20	10–20	5–10

June 1939

June 1956

April 1955

February 1956

1951 Annual

February 1955

January 1955

August 1954

April 1955

July 1938

December 1953

October 1955

April 1957

January 1953

March 1954

July 1992

September 1954

June 1955

Subject	Value ($)			
	Cover and Feature	Cover Only	Feature Only	Cameo
Bette Davis	10–25	10–25	10–20	5–10
Judy Garland	10–25	10–20	10–20	5–10
Betty Grable	10–20	10–20	5–12	5–10
Katharine Hepburn	10–20	10–20	5–15	5–10
Dorothy Lamour	10–20	10–20	5–10	5–10
Vivien Leigh	10–20	10–20	10–20	5–12
Carole Lombard	10–20	10–20	5–10	5–10
Ginger Rogers	10–25	10–20	5–12	5–10
Rogers and Astaire	10–25	10–20	5–15	5–10
Elizabeth Taylor	15–35	15–35	5–10	5–10
Shirley Temple	20–40	20–40	5–15	5–10

MOST COLLECTIBLE MALE STARS OF THE FORTIES

Subject	Value ($)			
	Cover and Feature	Cover Only	Feature Only	Cameo
Abbott and Costello	50–125	50–100	10–20	5–10
Fred Astaire	10–20	10–20	5–10	5–10
Astaire and Rogers	10–20	10–20	5–15	5–10
Humphrey Bogart	10–20	10–15	5–10	5–10
James Cagney	10–20	10–15	5–10	5–10
Bing Crosby	10–15	10–15	5–10	5–10
Disney Themes	40–80	40–80	15–30	5–10

Subject	Cover and Feature	Cover Only	Feature Only	Cameo
		Value ($)		
Errol Flynn	10–20	10–20	5–10	5–10
Clark Gable	10–20	10–15	5–10	5–10
Roy Rogers and Western Stars	25–60	25–50	6–12	5–10
Frank Sinatra	50–100	25–75	10–20	5–10
Three Stooges	100–200	100–200	20–40	10–20
John Wayne	30–75	30–75	10–20	6–12

MOST COLLECTIBLE FEMALE STARS OF THE FIFTIES

Subject	Cover and Feature	Cover Only	Feature Only	Cameo
		Value ($)		
Joan Crawford	5–15	5–10	4–8	4–8
Bette Davis	5–15	5–15	5–10	4–8
Annette Funicello	20–40	15–30	10–20	4–8
Judy Garland	10–20	10–20	5–15	5–10
Grace Kelly	5–10	5–10	5–10	4–8
Jayne Mansfield	10–25	10–25	10–25	8–15
Marilyn Monroe	20–75	20–50	10–25	8–20
Betty Page	50–100+	5–100+	20–40+	4–8
Elizabeth Taylor	10–20	10–20	10–15	4–8
Shirley Temple	15–30	15–30	10–20	5–10
Natalie Wood	10–20	10–20	10–20	5–10

MOST COLLECTIBLE MALE STARS OF THE FIFTIES

	Value ($)			
Subject	**Cover and Feature**	**Cover Only**	**Feature Only**	**Cameo**
Abbott and Costello	5–15	6–12	6–12	4–8
Humphrey Bogart	6–12	6–12	5–10	4–8
James Dean	20–40	20–40	20–30	5–10
Disney Themes	10–20	10–20	10–15	5–10
Rock Hudson	5–10	5–10	5–10	4–8
Elvis Presley	20–40	20–40	15–30	6–12
Frank Sinatra	20–40	20–40	10–20	5–10
Three Stooges	50–100	50–100	10–20	5–10
John Wayne	10–20	10–20	10–15	4–8

MOST COLLECTIBLE FEMALE STARS OF THE SIXTIES

	Value ($)			
Subject	**Cover and Feature**	**Cover Only**	**Feature Only**	**Cameo**
Jane Fonda	6–15	6–12	5–10	3–6
Jane Fonda/Barbarella	10–20	10–20	10–15	3–6
Brigitte Bardot	10–20	10–20	5–10	3–6
Barbara Eden	10–20	10–20	6–12	4–8
Annette Funicello	10–30	10–20	8–15	3–6
Judy Garland	10–20	10–15	5–10	3–6
Jayne Mansfield	10–15	10–15	10–15	3–6
Marilyn Monroe	10–20	10–20	8–15	4–8

August 10, 1957

Winter (#57), 1970

Autumn 1963

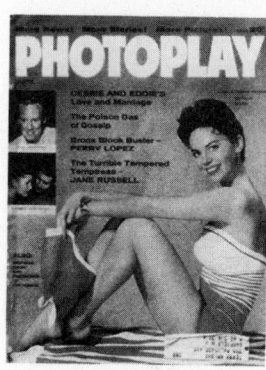

June 1956

January 1969

November 1977

September 1963

May 1967

January 1992

November 1990

June 22, 1998

November 1994

May 13, 1998

February 7, 1998

November 1997

#289/#290, 1995

June 23, 1997

Subject	Value ($)			
	Cover and Feature	Cover Only	Feature Only	Cameo
Betty Page	25–50	25–50	10–20	4–6
Elizabeth Taylor	5–10	4–8	4–8	3–6
Shirley Temple	6–12	6–12	6–12	4–8
Raquel Welch	15–40	15–30	4–8	3–6
Natalie Wood	5–10	5–10	4–8	3–6

MOST COLLECTIBLE MALE STARS OF THE SIXTIES

Subject	Value ($)			
	Cover and Feature	Cover Only	Feature Only	Cameo
Beatles	15–30	10–20	10–20	3–6
Elvis Presley	5–15	5–10	5–10	3–6
Frank Sinatra	10–20	5–15	3–7	2–5
Three Stooges	25–50	25–50	5–10	4–8

MOST COLLECTIBLE FEMALE STARS OF THE SEVENTIES

Subject	Value ($)			
	Cover and Feature	Cover Only	Feature Only	Cameo
Lynda Carter	5–10	5–10	4–7	2–4
Linda Blair	5–10	5–10	5–10	3–6
Cher	5–10	5–10	4–8	2–4
Farrah Fawcett	5–10	5–10	3–6	2–4

Subject	Value ($)			
	Cover and Feature	**Cover Only**	**Feature Only**	**Cameo**
Cheryl Ladd	4–8	3–6	3–6	2–4
Marilyn Monroe	5–10	5–10	3–5	2–4
Marie Osmond	5–10	5–10	5–10	2–4
Victoria Principal	4–8	3–6	3–6	2–4
Jaclyn Smith	3–6	3–6	3–6	2–4
Suzanne Somers	3–6	3–6	3–6	2–4
Lindsay Wagner	3–6	3–6	3–6	2–4
Raquel Welch	4–8	4–8	3–6	2–4
Brooke Shields	15–30	15–30	5–10	2–5

MOST COLLECTIBLE MALE STARS OF THE SEVENTIES, EIGHTIES, AND NINETIES

Note: There are no outstanding collectible male stars of this period; most issues featuring male movie and/or TV star covers from the seventies, eighties, and nineties sell for $2 to $4 each.

MOST COLLECTIBLE FEMALE STARS OF THE EIGHTIES AND NINETIES

Subject	Value ($)			
	Cover and Feature	**Cover Only**	**Feature Only**	**Cameo**
Cher	4–8	3–6	3–5	2–4
Tyra Banks	5–10	5–10	2–4	2–4
Drew Barrymore	5–15	5–15	3–6	2–4
Christie Brinkley	4–8	4–8	3–5	3–5

	Value ($)			
Subject	Cover and Feature	Cover Only	Feature Only	Cameo
Megan Follows	5–10	5–10	5–10	3–6
Melissa Joan Hart	10–20	10–20	5–10	2–4
Kathy Ireland	3–6	3–6	3–6	3–6
Madonna	5–10	5–10	3–6	2–4
Alyssa Milano	5–15	5–15	3–6	2–4
Lucy Lawless	10–30+	10–20+	3–6	2–4
Demi Moore	3–6	3–5	2–5	2–4
Brooke Shields	10–20	10–20	3–6	2–4

PEOPLE VALUES

People (Weekly)

Year	Issue	Description	Value ($)
1974	March 4	Mia Farrow: The Great Gatsby, Jim Croce, Alice Cooper	15–30
	March 11	Martha Mitchell	5–10
	March 18	J. Paul Getty	5–10
	March 25	Raquel Welch	15–30
	April 1	Garry Ford, Alice Cooper: The Jekyll and Hyde of Glitter Rock, Pat Nixon, Minnie Pearl, Chris Evert	10–20
	April 8	Ted Kennedy and Ted Jr., Stevie Wonder	2–4
	April 15	Lorne Greene	4–8
	April 22	Tatum O'Neal	6–12
	April 29	Joan Baez: New Life, New Songs, Marilyn Monroe, Cheech & Chong, Sally Struthers	5–10
	May 6	George and Cornelia Wallace	2–4

Year	Issue	Description	Value ($)
1974	May 13	Peter Bogdanovich and Cybill Shepherd	2–4
	May 20	E. Howard Hunt	2–4
	May 27	Pat Nixon	2–4
	June 3	Cicely Tyson	2–4
	June 10	The Kissingers	2–4
	June 17	Jack Lemmon	5–10
	June 24	Joan Kennedy: Her Nervous Breakdown, James Earl Jones, Jimmy the Greek, Maria Muldaur: Classic Blues	2–4
	July 1	Telly Savalas	2–4
	July 8	Suzy and Mark Spitz, Gene Kelly, Linda Lovelace	3–6
	July 15	Carol Burnett, Rock Hudson	5–10
	July 22	Larry Csonka	2–4
	July 29	Faye Dunaway	3–6
	August 5	Eagleton	1–2
	August 12	Barbara Walters and Jim Hartz, The Duchess of Windsor at Home, Mia Farrow	1–2
	August 19	Charles Bronson	2–5
	August 26	President Ford	1–2
	September 2	Catherine Deneuve	3–6
	September 9	John and Mo Dean in California, Paul Anka Is on Top Again, Valerie Harper, The Private World of Happy Rockefeller	2–4
	September 16	Joe Namath	1–2
	September 23	Gloria Steinem: Fighting Sexism with New Tactics, Three Sinatras on One Stage, Lauren Bacall	3–7
	September 30	Mary Tyler Moore	5–10
	Octernter 7	Paul Newman	2–4
	Octernter 14	Jackie Onassis	2–4
	Octernter 21	Susan Ford	1–2
	Octernter 28	Burt Reynolds and Dinah Shore	2–4
	November 4	Richard Burton	2–4
	November 11	Prince Charles	3–6

Year	Issue	Description	Value ($)
1974	November 25	Johnny Carson and Wife	2–4
	December 9	Cloris Leachman, Hedy Lamarr, Yul Brynner	2–4
	December 16	Kathy and Bing Crosby	2–4
	December 23	Dustin Hoffman	2–4
	December 30	Double Issue Special	2–4
1975	January 6	25 Most Intriguing People Issue . . . Faye Dunaway, Karen Black, Cher, Linda Ronstadt, Bad Company	3–6
	January 13	Elvis Presley Is 40, Friends of Jack Benny Say Goodbye, Lynn Redgrave: The Happy Hooker	5–10
	January 20	Judge Sirica, Richard Burton, Britt Ekland, Tony Perkins	2–4
	January 27	Liv Ullmann, Tammy Wynette, The Wiz	2–4
	February 3	Chris Evert and Billie Jean King	2–4
	February 10	Cher	10–20
	February 17	Happy Rockefeller, Patricia Neal, Archie Bunker, Susan Blakely	2–4
	February 24	Olivia Newton-John	12–25
	March 3	Onassis	2–4
	March 10	James Caan and Barbra Streisand	2–4
	March 17	Alan Alda	3–6
	March 24	Ann-Margret	3–6
	March 31	Jackie Onassis	4–8
	April 7	The Fondas	3–5
	April 14	Warren Beatty	1–2
	April 21	Paul and Linda McCartney	10–20
	April 28	Ellen Burstyn, Robert Blake	2–4
	May 5	Jimmy Connors	1–2
	May 12	Lauren Hutton	2–4
	May 19	Elizabeth Taylor	3–6
	May 26	Nancy Walker	2–4
	June 2	Clint Eastwood: A Box-Office Killing, Jimmie Walker	5–10

April 29, 1974

June 30, 1975

January 19, 1976

February 23, 1976

May 31, 1976

August 2, 1976

August 23, 1976

March 12, 1984

June 13, 1977

Year	Issue	Description	Value ($)
1975	June 9	Mick Jagger: His Stones Hit the U.S. While Bianca Conquers the Continent, Pat Nixon Reappears, Joe Namath Nixes $5 Million, Ann-Margret at Cannes	5–10
	June 16	Betty in Europe, The Endless Summer of the Beach Boys, Arnold Schwarzenegger, Britt Ekland	3–7
	June 23	Jane Fonda	2–4
	June 30	Bette Midler	3–5
	July 7	Muhammad Ali	5–10
	July 14	Carroll O'Connor	3–6
	July 21	Paul Newman and Joanne Woodward	2–4
	August 8	Peter Sellers	2–4
	August 11	Sonny Bono	10–20
	August 18	Elton John: His New Look . . . Everything's Slimmer but His Wallet, Diane Keaton: Woody Allen's Spacy Star, Tatum O'Neal	7–15
	August 25	Jaws' Roy Scheider, Paul Newman	1–2
	September 1	Grace Kelly	2–4
	September 8	Cher and Gregg Allman	6–12
	September 15	Valerie Harper	2–4
	September 22	Rose Kennedy, David Niven, Phil Spector, Calvin Klein	1–2
	September 29	Howard Cosell	2–4
	October 6	Nancy Kissinger, Patty Hearst, Dennis Weaver, Natalie Cole	1–2
	October 13	Marlon Brando	2–4
	October 20	Julie and David Eisenhower	2–4
	October 27	Robert Redford, Elton John's New Hit Is Neil Sedaka	2–4
	November 3	Gene Hackman, Grand Ole Opry at 50, Gregg Allman	2–4
	November 10	Bob Dylan	5–10
	November 17	Bea Arthur	2–4

Year	Issue	Description	Value ($)
1975	November 24	Jennifer O'Neill	3–6
	December 1	Julia Child	2–4
	December 8	Jack Nicholson	2–4
	December 15	Roger Daltry of The Who	5–10
	December 22	Billy Graham	2–4
1976	January 5	25 Most Intriguing People issue . . . Cher, Dolly Parton, Emmylou Harris, Lindsay Wagner	4–8
	January 12	Liza Minnelli	3–6
	January 19	Lee Majors and Farrah Fawcett	5–10
	January 26	Diana Ross	7–15
	February 9	Mary Tyler Moore in Moscow, Margot Kidder	4–8
	February 16	Chris Evert, Jack Ford	1–2
	February 23	Nancy Reagan, Maud Adams, Bob Dylan and Scarlet Rivera	2–4
	March 1	Michael Caine, Jill Clayburgh	1–2
	March 8	Marisa Berenson	1–2
	March 15	Elizabeth Taylor	2–4
	March 22	Rob Reiner and Penny Marshall, Phoebe Snow, Ginger Rogers	2–4
	March 29	Glen Campbell	2–4
	April 5	The Beatles: Will They Sing Again for $50 Million?	3–6
	April 12	Audrey Hepburn	5–10
	April 19	Telly Savalas, Robert Redford, Linda Blair, David Bowie Busted	2–4
	April 26	Barbra Streisand	2–4
	May 3	Dustin Hoffman, Robert Redford	2–4
	May 10	Truman Capote	1–3
	May 17	Goldie Hawn	3–5
	May 24	The Fonz: His Cult Grows, Fred Astaire, David Rockefeller, Elizabeth Taylor	5–10
	May 31	Frank Sinatra, Expectant Cher, Marilyn Monroe	10–20
	June 7	Paul McCartney: What Will Daddy Do When He Grows	

Year	Issue	Description	Value ($)
1976	June 7	Up? . . . The Wings Tour, Jo-Jo Starbuck	3–6
	June 14	Jerry Brown	1–2
	June 21	Raquel Welch . . . What's New for JUGS, Bob Hope, Bruce Springsteen	10–20
	June 28	Rudolf Nureyev	10–20
	July 5	Louise Lasser . . . Mary Hartman, Jimmy Dean	2–4
	July 12	Celebs of '76 . . . Sonny Bono, Flip Wilson, etc., A Message from Jerry Garcia of The Grateful Dead, Ann-Margret	6–12
	July 19	Jim and Amy Carter, Barney Miller, Stevie Wonder	1–3
	July 26	Lindsay Wagner	10–20
	August 2	The Carpenters	10–20
	August 9	Peter Falk	3–6
	August 16	Carol Burnett	2–4
	August 23	The Beach Boys . . . Still Riding the Crest 15 Hairy Years Later, Diahann Carroll, Sandy Dennis	6–12
	August 30	Princess Caroline	2–4
	September 6	David Bowie	5–10
	September 13	Paul Lynde	2–4
	September 20	Phyllis George	2–4
	September 27	Cher, Gregg Allman, and Children	7–15
	October 4	Woody Allen, Elton John's Songbird Is Kiki Dee	3–6
	October 11	Barbara Walters	2–4
	October 18	The Captain and Tennille	4–8
	October 25	Stevie Wonder: Life Offstage, Bernadette Peters	2–4
	November 1	Lee Radziwill	1–2
	November 8	Tony Randall	3–6
	November 15	Rosalynn Carter, Mel Tillis, Olivia Newton-John, Roger Moore	4–8

Year	Issue	Description	Value ($)
1976	November 22	Marjoe Wallace, Jimmy Connors, Dorothy Hamill the Star, Twiggy	2–4
	November 29	John Travolta	10–20
	December 6	Charlie's Angels . . . Farrah Fawcett, Jaclyn Smith, and Kate Jackson	10–20
	December 13	Robert Wagner and Natalie Wood	5–10
	December 20	Led Zeppelin	5–10
1977	January 3	25 Most Intriguing People of 1976 Issue . . . Farrah Fawcett, King Kong, Robert Redford, Jane Fonda	4–8
	January 10	Barbra Streisand and Kris Kristofferson	3–7
	January 17	Ringo: His Tax Exile, His New Fiancée, His Rap on a Beatles Reunion, The Women in Gary Gilmore's Tormented Life	2–4
	January 24	Claudine Longet	2–3
	January 31	Jessica Lange	3–5
	February 7	George C. Scott and Wife, Trish: A Fifth Marriage Mellows the Brawling Actor, Jerry Lewis's $1.25 Million Broadway Bomb, The Selling of Gary Gilmore, Funky Music's Godfather	2–4
	February 14	Elizabeth Taylor and John Warner	2–4
	February 21	Rod Stewart and Britt Ekland . . . A Sexy Swede Tames the Rascal of Rock, Paul Newman	3–6
	February 28	Ralph Nader, 15 Farrahs in Detroit, The Best Dressed, Lauren Bacall, Lesley Ann Warren	2–4
	March 7	Bjorn Borg, Bob Dylan, Larry Flint, Arnold Schwarzenegger	1–2

Year	Issue	Description	Value ($)
1977	March 14	Julie Andrews, Boston: Rock's Brainiest Band, Grace Jones	3–6
	March 21	David Carradine	10–20
	March 28	Faye Dunaway	2–4
	April 4	Dolly Parton	2–4
	April 11	Bruce Jenner and Chrystie	1–2
	April 18	Jackie Onassis	2–4
	April 25	Sally Field	4–8
	May 5	Bianca Jagger	3–5
	May 9	Alex Haley	1–2
	May 16	Jane Fonda	2–4
	May 23	David Frost and Richard Nixon, Dickey Betts on Cher and Gregg Allman, Yul Brynner	2–4
	May 30	Cindy Williams	5–10
	June 6	Fleetwood Mac	15–20
	June 13	John Travolta	10–20
	June 20	Elizabeth Taylor, Liza Minnelli	2–4
	June 27	Peter Frampton: More Alive Than Ever	4–8
	July 4	Farrah Fawcett and Lee Majors	5–10
	July 11	Linda (Exorcist II) Blair at 18, Michael Learned, Star Wars	10–20
	July 18	Star Wars . . . Talented Folks, Buck Owens	10–20
	July 25	Tom and Nancy Seaver	1–2
	August 1	Jacqueline Bisset, Emerson, Lake & Palmer Tour, Bette Davis	2–4
	August 8	Barry Manilow	4–8
	August 15	David Doyle, Jaclyn Smith	5–10
	August 22	Sissy Spacek	3–6
	August 29	Mary Feldman and Ann-Margret, Miss Universe, The Late Elvis Presley	2–4
	September 5	Dan Rather	1–2
	September 12	Susan Saint James	2–3
	September 19	Robert Blake	2–3
	September 26	Cheryl Ladd	7–15

Year	Issue	Description	Value ($)
1977	October 3	Tony Orlando's Breakdown, Patty Hearst, Kristy McNichol	3–6
	October 10	Remembering Elvis Presley, Bernadette Peters, Wings	2–4
	October 17	O. J. Simpson, Dick Cavett, Debby Boone Lights Up the Pop Charts, Patty Duke and John Astin	2–4
	October 24	Linda Ronstadt: Rock's Hottest Flame, Farrah Fawcett Works Again, Diana Ross, Peter Frampton	5–10
	October 31	Donny and Marie: at 18, She's Sexed Up Her TV Image . . . But All the Osmonds Still Check Out Her Dates, 007's Dazzling New Lady Spook . . . Barbara Bach, Cher, Tatum O'Neal	10–25
	November 7	Suzanne Somers, Joyce DeWitt, and John Ritter	4–8
	November 14	Michelle Phillips	2–4
	November 21	Rolling Stones' Mick and Keith: Jagger's Genius Partner Richards Tells How He Kicked Heroin, but He's Not Off the Hook in a Canadian Court, Susan Dey: Laurie Partridge in a Nude Movie?	5–10
	November 28	Al Pacino and Marthe Keller	2–3
	December 5	Gilda Radner Live, Freddie Mercury of Queen, Arlo Guthrie	2–4
	December 12	Crosby, Stills, and Nash	3–5
	December 19	Marlo Thomas	1–2
1978	January 2	25 Most Intriguing People Issue . . . Diane Keaton, Shaun Cassidy, Goldie Hawn, Stevie Nicks: Fleetwood Mac's Sexiest Symbol, Tony Orlando	6–12
	January 9	John Travolta, Karen Gorney	10–20
	January 16	The New Elton John: He's Given Up Those Nutty Glasses but Not	

Year	Issue	Description	Value ($)
1978	January 16	Lasses, Cocaine in Hollywood, Grizzly Adams's Close Shave, Linda Blair	5–10
	January 23	Helen Reddy: The Woman Roars Softer Now . . . Family Comes First, and She's Got Jerry Brown's Ear, The Uppity Butler on Soap, Benny Goodman, Angela Davis	2–4
	January 30	Penny Marshall, Mike McKean, David L. Lander, and Cindy Williams	2–4
	February 6	The Bee Gees	10–20
	February 13	Clint Eastwood and Sondra Locke	3–6
	February 20	Henry Winkler	3–6
	February 27	Walter Mondale and Wife	1–2
	March 6	Goldie Hawn	2–4
	March 13	Richard Pryor	1–2
	March 20	Geneviève Bujold	1–2
	March 27	Carroll O'Connor, Jean Stapleton, Rob Reiner, and Sally Struthers of All in the Family	5–10
	April 3	Diane Keaton, Anne Bancroft, Shirley MacLaine, Jane Fonda, and Marsha Mason	2–4
	April 10	Cher, Gene Simmons	10–20
	April 17	Pat and Debby Boone	2–4
	April 24	Linda Lavin	3–6
	May 1	Steve Martin	2–4
	May 8	Sylvester Stallone	3–5
	May 15	Shaun Cassidy	3–6
	May 22	John Ritter	2–4
	May 29	Brooke Shields at 12 in Pretty Baby: Child Porn	10–20
	June 5	Loretta Lynn, Crystal Gayle	5–10
	June 12	Ron Howard	3–5
	June 19	Cheryl Tiegs	3–6

Year	Issue	Description	Value ($)
1978	June 26	Jane Fonda, Jon Voight	2–4
	July 3	Princess Caroline and Philippe Junot	2–4
	July 10	Ed Asner	1–2
	July 17	Carly Simon: She's Conquered Her Stage Fright, Paul Newman's Daughter, Alice Faye, Bob Dylan Tours	5–10
	July 24	Ali MacGraw and Kris Kristofferson	2–4
	July 31	Olivia Newton-John, How the Celebs Get Lured into Studio 54, Robert Klein, Bianca Jagger	10–20
	August 7	Joan Kennedy	1–2
	August 14	Carrie Fisher and Darth Vader	5–10
	August 21	The Elvis Presley Legend	2–4
	August 28	Ann-Margret	2–4
	September 4	Margaret Trudeau	1–2
	September 11	Michael Landon, Melissa Gilbert, and Melissa Sue Anderson	10–20
	September 19	Cheryl Ladd	5–10
	September 25	Joe Namath: Scouting Report, The Final Hours of The Who's Keith Moon, Pam Shriver, The Smothers Brothers, Mary Tyler Moore, Farrah Fawcett, Linda Ronstadt	3–5
	October 2	Battlestar Galactica	7–15
	October 9	Jaclyn Smith	5–10
	October 16	Chicago	4–8
	October 23	Elizabeth Taylor and John Warner	2–4
	October 30	Robin Williams and Pam Dawber	5–10
	November 6	Patty Hearst and Bernard Shaw	1–2
	November 13	Jackie Onassis	3–6
	November 20	Kristy McNichol and Jimmy McNichol	3–6
	November 27	Angie Dickinson	2–4
	December 4	Priscilla Presley	2–3

Year	Issue	Description	Value ($)
1978	December 11	Suzanne Somers, John Ritter, and Joyce DeWitt	5–10
	December 18	Ann-Margret	2–4
1979	January 1	25 Most Intriguing People Issue . . . John Travolta, John Belushi, Brooke Shields, Cheryl Tiegs, Meat Loaf, Donna Summer Cleans Up Her Act, Grace Slick, Elton John, Star Trek	3–6
	January 8	Christopher Reeve as Superman	4–8
	January 15	Diana Ross	5–10
	January 22	Neil Diamond, Barbra Streisand	3–6
	January 29	The Women of The Waltons	6–12
	February 5	Rod Stewart, Britt Ekland, Liz Treadwell and Alana Hamilton	4–8
	February 12	Robin Williams, Pam Dawber	5–10
	February 19	Barbra Streisand and Jon Peters	2–4
	February 26	John Denver: The Unsung Story, Roots II, Sondra Locke, Brooke Shields, Phyllis George, Clint Eastwood, Loretta Lynn	10–20
	March 5	Farrah Fawcett: The Most Boring Woman on TV?, Jaclyn Smith: The Most Beautiful, Kiss: Most Disliked?, Billy Joel	4–8
	March 12	Loretta Swit	4–8
	March 19	Billy Joel Rocks Cuba, Blythe Danner, Rock Hudson, Sally Field, Johnny Mathis, Paul McCartney	3–6
	March 26	The New Betty Ford, Miss America on Tour . . . Kylene Baker, Dire Staits: Rock's Sultans of Swing, Bee Gees	2–4
	April 2	Robert De Niro, Warren Beatty, Jon Voight	1–3

Year	Issue	Description	Value ($)
1979	April 9	Donna Pescow, Marvin Gaye, Cheryl Ladd, Mick Jagger	2–4
	April 16	Jane Fonda, Michael Douglas	2–4
	April 23	Burt Reynolds	2–4
	April 30	Linda Ronstadt and Governor Brown, Paul Rogers of Bad Company, Faye Dunaway, Melba Moore, Art Garfunkel	5–10
	May 7	Battle of the Live-In Lovers . . . Lee Marvin, Peter Frampton, Nick Nolte, Keith Richards' Drug Rap Concert in Toronto, Gene Tierney, Cheryl Ladd, Suzanne Somers, Ali MacGraw	2–4
	May 14	Five's Company . . . Suzanne Sommers, etc., Gary Coleman, Eric Clapton, Bob Dylan, Marilyn Monroe, Suzi Quatro, The Bee Gees	5–10
	May 21	Johnny Carson	2–3
	May 28	Morley Safer, Harry Reasoner, and Mike Wallace	1–2
	June 4	Kate Jackson	5–10
	June 11	Mariel Hemingway	3–5
	June 18	Rob Reiner and Father, Carl Reiner	2–4
	June 25	Paul Newman	2–4
	July 2	Ted Kennedy	1–2
	July 9	Olivia Newton-John	7–15
	July 17	Carly Simon and Motherhood, Bette Midler	3–6
	July 23	Sylvester Stallone, Talia Shire	3–6
	July 30	Stan Dragoti, Cheryl Tiegs	2–4
	August 6	Hanging Out with The Bee Gees: A Backstage Look at the Summer's Hottest Tour, the Boat People, Tanya Tucker, Paul and Linda McCartney	10–20

Year	Issue	Description	Value ($)
1979	August 13	Roger Moore, Lois Chiles, and Richard Kiel	3–6
	August 20	Farrah Fawcett	3–6
	August 27	Phil Donahue	1–2
	September 3	Miss Piggy, Erik Estrada, Conway Twitty, Sandy Duncan, Paul Stanley as a Father, Crystal Gayle, Deborah Harry Meets the Real Blondie, Roger Daltrey, Teddy Pendergrass, Kiss	5–10
	September 10	Kenny Rogers, Donna Summer, Paul McCartney, Blondie's Debbie Harry and Peter Frampton	5–10
	September 17	Margot Kidder	2–4
	September 24	Shelley Hack . . . The Classy New Angel, Ethel Merman	5–10
	October 1	Carol Burnett and Daughter, Jim Belushi, Peter Criss of Kiss: His Wife Talks, Debby Boone, Barbara Parkins, Elton John	3–6
	October 8	Nick Nolte, Bruce Springsteen Sparks the No-Nuke Rally, Elvis Presley's Doctor, Patty Duke Astin	2–4
	October 15	Suzanne Somers	3–7
	October 22	Cher	3–6
	October 29	Robin Williams	2–4
	November 6	Jill Clayburgh	2–4
	November 12	Loni Anderson and Howard Hesseman: WKRP, Kate Jackson, ABBA	2–4
	November 19	The 10 Sexiest Bachelors in the World, Estrada, Andy Gibb, Bo Derek and Dudley Moore, Cathy Bach: Dazzling	

Year	Issue	Description	Value ($)
1979	November 19	Duchess of Hazard, The Eagles, Mick and Bianca Jagger, Roger Daltrey	3–6
	November 26	Fleetwood Mac	15–30
	December 3	Dick Van Patten, Grant Goodeve, Adam Rich, and Willie Aames	2–4
	December 10	Kenny Rogers and Marianne Gordon	2–4
	December 17	Those Women of Dallas . . . Linda Gray, Victoria Principal, Charlene Tilton; Anne Murray, the Angels' Charlie, Linda Ronstadt, Farrah Fawcett, Donny and Marie, Crystal Gayle	3–6
	December 24	25 Most Intriguing People Issue . . . Debbie Harry, Bo Derek, Olivia Newton-John, Bob Seger, Ellen Foley	5–10
1980	January 7	Bette Midler	3–6
	January 14	Lee Majors, Farrah Fawcett and Ryan O'Neal	2–4
	January 21	Steve Martin, Suzanne Somers: Why Did She Pose Nude?, The Police: Rock's New Hit Squad, Marilyn Monroe, Janis Joplin, Aerosmith, Natalie Cole, Jane Fonda	2–4
	January 28	Elvis Presley: How Did He Die?, Cybill Shepherd's Blues, Lynda Carter, Pernell Roberts, Butterfly McQueen	2–4
	February 4	Chris Evert Lloyd, Donna Summer: The Flip Side of Music's Bad Girl, Paul McCartney in the Clink, Deborah Harry	3–6
	February 11	Bo and John Derek, Lucille Ball	2–4

Year	Issue	Description	Value ($)
1980	February 18	Robert Redford, Patti Hansen, Liz Taylor, Cliff Richard, John Belushi and the Dead Boys	
	February 25	Liza Minnelli, Goldie Hawn, Jihan Sadat	2–4
	March 3	Lindsay Wagner: The Bionic Woman Comes on Strong in Scruples, Dan Rather, Isaac Hayes, Meryl Streep, Neil Diamond, Jane Fonda	6–12
	March 10	Britt Ekland, Rod Stewart, Peter Sellers, Warren Beatty	
	March 17	Mackenzie Phillips, Bonnie Franklin, Valerie Bertinelli, Jackie Onassis	2–4
	March 24	Bo Derek, Gilda Radner, Bruce Jenner, Dustin Hoffman, Jane Fonda, The Eagles	
	March 31	Tatum O'Neal and Kristy McNichol, Alan King, Anne and Nancy Wilson of Heart: Alive and Well on the Road, The Knack	5–10
	April 7	Richard Gere	1–2
	April 14	Larry Hagman, Susan Anton	2–4
	April 21	Olivia Newton-John and Andy Gibb, Susan Strasberg	10–20
	April 28	Penny Marshall, Erik Estrada and Larry Wilcox	1–2
	May 5	Jacqueline Bisset and Paul Newman, Ursula Andress	2–4
	May 12	The Who: Peter Townshend Talks about Concert Tragedy	3–5
	May 19	Jodie Foster, Loretta Lynn and Sissy Spacek	5–10
	May 26	Mac Davis, Pogo	2–4
	June 2	Valerie Harper, Chuck Barris, Linda Ronstadt, Bernadette Peters	4–8

Year	Issue	Description	Value ($)
1980	June 9	The Empire Strikes Back, Yoda, Gloria Vanderbilt	5–10
	June 16	Soap Opera Stars Special	1–2
	June 23	John Travolta: Urban Cowboy, Bernie Taupin, Dolly Parton	6–12
	June 30	Tanya Roberts and Glen, The Richard Pryor Tragedy, Sean Connery	5–10
	July 7	The Empire's Fab Four . . . Harrison Ford, Billy Dee Williams, Carrie Fisher, and Mark Hamill, Elton John, Tanya Roberts: Charlie's Newest Angel	6–12
	July 14	Larry Hagman	1–2
	July 21	Nancy and Ronald Reagan, the Reagan Kids	3–6
	July 28	Jack Nicholson, Princess Caroline and Philippe Junot	2–3
	August 4	Dan Aykroyd and John Belushi: The Blues Brothers, Joyce DeWitt	5–10
	August 11	Brooke Shields and Chris Atkins, Dan Rather	5–10
	August 18	Kiss with Eric Carr, Ed McMahon	10–20
	August 25	John Davidson	1–2
	September 8	Airplane: The Summer's Stillest Movie, Ron Ely: Me Tarzan, Rachel Sweet: Rock Is Sweet on Rachel, The Rolling Stones' Emotional Rescue, Linda Ronstadt, Tina Turner	1–2
	September 15	Angie Dickinson: Dressed To Kill, Ron Reagan: His 53 Movies, Karen Carpenter's All-Star Wedding, Diana Ross, Elton John	2–4

Year	Issue	Description	Value ($)
1980	September 22	Richard Chamberlain, Cheech and Chong	1–2
	September 29	26 Best and Worst Dressed People . . . Debbie Harry, Cher, etc., Those Marilyn Monroe Years, Elton John, Matt Dillon	4–8
	October 6	Carly Simon Exclusive, Tony Geary, Lesley Ann Warren, Raquel Welch, Carrie Fisher, Bo Derek, Paul Simon	3–6
	October 13	Cathy Lee Crosby	1–2
	October 20	Liz Taylor: Life with Liz, Steve McQueen, Peter Criss: Post Kiss, Keith Richards, Bruce Lee, Ingrid Bergman	2–4
	October 27	Genie Francis, Marilyn Monroe	2–4
	November 3	Paul Simon Still Creative, Jackie Gleason, David Bowie, Carly Simon, Lynda Carter	2–4
	November 10	Linda Gray, John Wayne	2–4
	November 17	Nancy Reagan, Kliban Cat,	
	November 24	Melissa Gilbert as Anne Frank, Dorothy Hamill, Bruce Springsteen	3–6
	December 1	Kenny Rogers, Ingrid Bergman	2–3
	December 8	Mary Crosby, John Denver	2–4
	December 15	Mary Tyler Moore	2–4
	December 22	John Lennon: 1940–1980, a Tribute, Rudolph the Red-Nosed Reindeer, Sheree North, Tatum O'Neal, Rockpile	4–8
1981	January 5	25 Most Intriguing People Issue . . . Brooke Shields, Goldie Hawn, Robert Redford, Pat Benatar Sinks to the Top	

Year	Issue	Description	Value ($)
1981	January 5	of the Rock Pile, Nancy Allen, Farrah Fawcett, Jane Seymour, Stevie Nicks Goes Solo, Barbara Bach, John Travolta, Ursula Andress	5–10
	January 12	Yoko Ono: How She Is Holding Up, Suzanne Somers, Susan Anton	2–4
	January 19	Dolly Parton, Lily Tomlin, Jane Fonda, Charlene Tilton	2–4
	January 26	Charlene Tilton, Truman Capote	1–2
	February 2	Frank Sinatra	5–10
	February 9	Tanya Roberts, Barbara Mandrell	4–8
	February 16	Sally Struthers and Daughter, Jane Seymour	2–3
	February 23	Ringo and Barbara Bach: Ringo Talks Movingly About John, The Reunion That Never Was, and His Saving Love for Barbara Bach, An Update on Paul, George and Yoko, Aretha Franklin Bounces Back, Barbra Streisand, The Blues Brothers, Faye Dunaway, Linda Ronstadt, Carly Simon, Jennifer O'Neill	2–4
	March 2	Mackenzie Phillips and Dad, John Phillips, Jared Martin	2–3
	March 9	Soap Stars Special	1–2
	March 16	Blondie's Debbie Harry: Pop's Sassy Lady Cleans Up Her Act and Aims for Hollywood, Shelley Duvall: Olive Oyl, The Stars Fight L.A. Crime	10–20
	March 23	Jackie Onassis, Loni Anderson	2–4

Year	Issue	Description	Value ($)
1981	March 30	Victoria Principal, Andy Gibb, William Hurt	10–20
	April 4	Cathy Bach, Elizabeth Taylor	2–4
	April 13	Ronald Reagan	1–2
	April 20	Jodie Foster	3–6
	April 27	Danielle Brisebois: Archie's Angel, Fred Astaire at 81, Tanya Tucker, Jessica Lange, Cathy Lee Crosby, Eric Clapton	2–3
	May 4	Tanya Tucker, Glen Campbell	3–6
	May 11	Farrah Fawcett, Ryan O'Neal, Jim Davis	2–4
	May 18	Victoria Principal, Robert Redford, Kenny Rogers, Nancy Reagan, Prince Charles, Barbra Streisand	2–4
	May 25	Billie Jean and Larry King, Barbara Cartland, Big Bird	1–2
	June 1	Phyllis George and Son, Burt Reynolds	1–2
	June 8	Lauren Bacall, Tony Geary	1–2
	June 15	Alan Alda, Jessica Lange	1–2
	June 22	Lady Diana Spencer, John Lennon	5–10
	June 29	Richard Pryor, Pam Dawber, Andy Gibb	4–8
	July 6	Christopher Reeve as Superman: He Beds Lois in His Man of Steel Sequel, But in Film, and Fact, He Shuns Marriage Like Kryptonite, Kim Carnes Eyes Bette Davis, Barbi Benton, Harrison Ford, Liz Taylor	2–4
	July 13	Morgan Fairchild, Doc Severinsen	3–6
	July 20	Harrison Ford and Karen Allen, Joyce Bartle's Legs and Roger Moore	3–6

Year	Issue	Description	Value ($)
1981	July 27	Bo Derek, Miles O'Keefe	2–4
	August 3	Prince Charles and Lady Diana	5–10
	August 10	Brooke Shields, Frank Sinatra	5–10
	August 17	John Travolta and Nancy Allen: Blow Out . . . A Hot-Blooded Hollywood Dream Team Ignites a Diller of a Thriller, Rick Springfield: He's Rockin' General Hospital, Lynn Redgrave, Meat Loaf Toni Tennille, Liza Minnelli, Foreigner, Carly Simon, Jennifer O'Neill	6–12
	August 24	Margot Kidder, James Taylor	2–3
	August 31	Mark Hamill, Elvis Presley	2–4
	September 7	Kris Kristofferson and Daughter, Andy Kaufman	1–2
	September 14	Dudley Moore and Susan Anton, Kim Carnes	2–3
	September 21	The 29 Best and Worst Dressed People . . . Linda Gray, Bo Derek, Broadway's Glowing Goodbye to Elizabeth Taylor	1–2
	September 28	Pat Benatar, Rubik's Cube	5–10
	October 5	Faye Dunaway and Joan Crawford	2–4
	October 12	Justice Sandra Day O'Connor, Mick Jagger, Sorrell Booke	2–3
	October 19	Jaclyn Smith, Jackie Kennedy Onassis	3–6
	October 26	Lindsay Wagner, Princess Caroline	4–8
	November 2	Richard Simmons, Kristy McNichol	1–2
	November 9	Valerie Bertinelli, Henry Fonda	3–6
	November 16	Elizabeth Taylor, Tony Geary and Genie Francis	1–2

Year	Issue	Description	Value ($)
1981	November 23	Princess Diana, Ed Asner	5–10
	November 30	John and Caroline Kennedy	1–2
	December 7	Johnny Carson, Candice Bergen	1–2
	December 14	Cast from Three's Company, Natalie Wood	5–10
	December 21	Larry Hagman, Rod and Alana Stewart	2–3
1982	January 4	Elizabeth Taylor, President Reagan, Mick Jagger, Diana, Tom Selleck, John McEnroe, Barbara Mandrell	1–2
	January 11	Richard Thomas and Triplets	1–2
	January 18	Calvin Klein and Brooke Shields, Elvis Presley	2–4
	January 25	Cher	5–10
	February 1	Patty Hearst: Finally, Her Own Story, Donny Osmond: Tired of Being a Goody Two-Shoes, Peter Sellers's Kids, Liz Taylor, Tanya Tucker, Diana Rigg, Kenny Rogers, Johnny Lee	2–4
	February 8	Timothy Hutton, Barry Manilow	1–2
	February 15	Olivia Newton-John, Sally Field	10–20
	February 22	Daniel Travanti, Veronica Hamel, and Michael Conrad of Hill Street Blues, James Coco	1–2
	March 1	Suzanne Somers, Edward Kennedy	3–6
	March 8	Tom Selleck, Christie Brinkley: Supermodel and Billy Joel, Kate Jackson in Making Love, Janis Joplin, Jack Nicholson	2–4
	March 15	Liz Taylor and Richard Burton, An Osmond Ski Bash, William Shatner	2–4

Year	Issue	Description	Value ($)
1982	March 22	John Belushi: A Dangerous Life . . . A Tragic Death, Carol Burnett, Jane Fonda, Dean Jones, Julie Andrews, James Garner	3–6
	March 29	Kenny Rogers: A Neglectful Father Reforms, The Hollywood Drug Fad That Killed John Belushi, Bianca Jagger, Bernadette Peters, Bob Dylan, Kristy McNichol, Billie Holiday	2–4
	April 5	Princess Grace, Neil Diamond	2–4
	April 12	Henry Fonda, Kate Jackson	2–3
	April 19	Readers' Poll Issue . . . Tom Selleck, Brooke Shields, Stefanie Powers, Sean Connery, Debbie Allen, Lesley Ann Warren	2–4
	April 26	Cheryl Tiegs . . . Fashion's $100 Million Lady, Ingrid Bergman, Those 36 Lost Beatles Tunes, Jessica Lange, Nastassja Kinski, Marie Osmond, Heart's Wilson Sisters, Jodie Foster, Brooke Shields	3–6
	May 3	On Location with Tom Selleck, Shelley Bruce of Annie, Adrienne Barbeau, Ted Nugent, Sting, Catherine Bach, Sigourney Weaver Alarmed by Muslim Threats, Lee Remick	2–4
	May 10	Pamela Sue Martin and John James, Chariots of Fire	4–8
	May 17	Tony Geary, Nastassja Kinski	1–2
	May 24	Jane Fonda and Tom Hayden, Ken Marshall of Marco Polo	1–2

Year	Issue	Description	Value ($)
1982	May 31	Stefanie Powers	1–2
	June 7	Loni Anderson and Burt Reynolds, Pia Zadora, Sophia Loren	3–6
	June 14	Melody Thomas, Tristan Rogers, and Lisa Brown of the Soaps	1–2
	June 21	Sylvester Stallone and Son, Barbara Walters	2–4
	June 28	E.T. and Henry Thomas	1–2
	July 5	Princess Di, Marie Osmond a Bride	2–4
	July 12	Aileen Quinn and Sandy of Annie, Dyan Cannon	1–2
	July 19	Dan Aykroyd on John Belushi, E.T., A Family Reunion for the Rolling Stones, Drew Barrymore, Robert Redford	10–20
	July 26	Richard Simmons and Mickey Mouse, Jane Fonda, Diana Ross, Star Trek's Tempestuous Kirstie Alley, Love Boat's Doc, Ozzy Osbourne Ties the Knot	2–4
	August 2	Dolly Parton Talks, Monty Python, Valerie Bertinelli, The Beatles, Harrison Ford, Jill St. John, Charlton Heston	2–4
	August 9	Hollywood Kids . . . John Ritter and Wife, Paul McCartney: A $3 Million Love Affair?, Led Zep's Robert Plant, The Dukes of Hazzard, Marilyn Monroe Remembered, Eddie Money	2–4
	August 16	Princess Di, Sinatra, Jill St. John, Facts of Life, Joan Collins, REO Speedwagon, Victoria Principal, Andy Gibb, Huey Lewis	6–12

Year	Issue	Description	Value ($)
1982	August 23	All about E.T.: The Untold Story, John Travolta and the Summer Stock Stars, Elton John Salutes Yoko and Sean Lennon, Sly Stallone, Tanya Tucker, Chicago, Elvis Costello, Andy Gibb, Susan Anton	1–3
	August 30	Jill St. John and Robert Wagner, Lucie Arnaz, Richard Harris, Farrah, Morgan Fairchild, Drew Barrymore, Kenny Rogers	3–7
	September 9	Olivia Newton-John, Burt Reynolds and Goldie Hawn, Richard Pryor	7–15
	September 13	Robin Williams, Dolly Parton	2–4
	September 20	The Best and Worst Dressed . . . Brooke Shields, Victoria Principal, Prince Charles, Sophia Loren, Nancy and Ronald Reagan	5–10
	September 27	Princess Grace	2–4
	October 4	Ted Knight, Nancy Dussault and Sitcom Son, Prince Andrew	2–4
	October 11	Scott Baio, Richard Chamberlain/Thorn Birds, Mary Martin, Patty Duke, Tanya Roberts, Carolyn Jones and The Addams Family, John Cougar, Cherry Boone, Brian Eno	3–6
	October 18	Falcon Crest Cast	1–2
	October 25	Why the Famous Date the Famous, Mia Farrow, Liz Taylor, Art Garfunkel, Kim Carnes, Bob Geldof, Richard Thomas	2–4

January 25, 1982

February 28, 1983

July 5, 1982

June 6, 1983

March 28, 1988

May 8, 1989

June 8, 1987

April 25, 1988

May 9, 1994

Year	Issue	Description	Value ($)
1982	November 1	Garfield the Cat, Christie Brinkley	2–4
	November 8	John Delorean and Family,	
1983	February 28	Brooke Shields: The Shock of Araby, Luther Vandross, Sonny Bono, Billy Joel, John Denver, Johnny Carson	6–12
	March 7	Sylvester Stallone and John Travolta, Queen Elizabeth II	5–10
	March 14	Readers' Poll Issue . . . Victoria Principal, Linda Evans, Koo Stark, Dustin Hoffman, Jodie Foster, Linda Ronstadt, The Bee Gees	2–3
	March 21	Bing Crosby, Linda Gray	1–2
	March 28	Richard Chamberlain: The Thorn Birds, Gary Coleman's Troubled Life, Sheena Easton, Margot Kidder	2–3
	April 4	The Oscars, E.T., Paul Newman, Pete Townshend, Shelley Long	1–2
	April 11	Linda Evans, Jon Voight	1–2
	April 18	The Crime of David Soul, Lois Chiles of Dallas, Tom Selleck, An Insider Look at the Beatles, Koo and the Royals	1–2
	April 25	Joan Rivers, Knight Rider, Oak Ridge Boys Feud, Nastassja Kinski, Jack Palance, Liz Taylor	1–2
	May 2	Dena Al-Fassi, Mariette Hartley, The Outsider's Teen Queen, Randy Newman Zings L.A., Mick Jagger, Julian Lennon	1–2
	May 9	Kristy McNichol, Bob Newhart	2–4

Year	Issue	Description	Value ($)
1983	May 16	Helen Reddy, Jamie Farr	2–4
	May 23	Victoria Principal, Adolf Hitler	3–6
	May 30	Mr. T, Richard Gere	1–2
	June 6	Carrie Fisher and Jabba the Hutt	10–20
	June 13	Tony Perkins of Psycho II, David Bowie and Stevie Nicks and a Rockfest Blowout, Genie Francis, Rickie Lee Jones, Lesley Ann Warren, Cher, Goldie Hawn, Connie Chung	6–12
	June 20	Sally Ride, Return of the Jedi, Twiggy, Roger Moore, Elton, Menudo, WarGames's Ally Sheedy	1–3
	June 27	Prince William, Love Boat's All-Star China Cruise, Patricia Neal, Loretta Lynn, Neil Young, Pete Townshend, Elton	1–3
	July 4	Robert Wagner . . . Superdad, John Lennon: The Sellout of Friends and Lovers, Twilight Zone's John Lithgow	1–2
	July 11	Richard Pryor and Eddie Murphy, Princess Daisy	1–2
	July 18	James Bond's Babes . . . Barbara Bach, etc., Spirited Shirley MacLaine, Burt Reynolds, Dolly Parton, Tom Selleck	2–4
	July 25	John Travolta: Two for Travolta, 3-D Movies and Jaws, Billy Joel, Diana Ross, Rod Stewart, Olivia Newton-John, Wendy O. Williams . . . The First Lady of Shock Rock, Kirstie Alley, Elizabeth Taylor	2–4

Year	Issue	Description	Value ($)
1983	August 1	Goldie Hawn, Mick Jagger at 40, Boy George, Styx, John Travolta, Brooke Shields, Cathy Bach	2–4
	August 8	Diana Ross: The Concert Controversy, Michael Jackson, Return of the Jedi: Behind the Magic, Flashdance Chic	3–5
	August 15	Ryan O'Neal and Farrah Fawcett, Griffin O'Neal	2–4
	August 22	Kenny Rogers and Linda Evans, Jamie Lee Curtis, David Bowie, Stevie Nicks, Bruce Springsteen, Jackson Browne	3–5
	August 29	Fall Preview Special, Cher, Olivia Newton-John, Kate Jackson, David Bowie, John Travolta, John Delorean, Martin Sheen, Jamie Farr, Harry Morgan	4–8
	September 5	Princess Grace, Sting	2–4
	September 12	Chevy Chase and Fatherhood, Barry Manilow, Tragedy Revisits Jerry Lee Lewis, Grace Kelly Part II, Liz Taylor, Marilyn Monroe, Marilu Henner, Dottie West	2–3
	September 19	Korean Airline Tragedy, Brooke Shields	2–5
	September 26	The Best and Worst Dressed . . . Princess Diana, Mr. T, John Travolta, Fidel Castro, Christie Brinkley, Donna Mills	2–5
	October 3	Bobby Kennedy Jr., Vanessa Williams	2–3
	October 10	Natalie Wood, Joan Collins	2–4

Year	Issue	Description	Value ($)
1983	October 17	Michael Jackson, Sean Connery and Kim Basinger, MTV	4–7
	October 24	M.A.S.H. Cast and Feature . . . After M.A.S.H.	5–10
	October 31	Pierce Brosnan, The Right Stuff Cast	1–2
	November 7	Jessica Savitch	1–2
	November 11	Princess Di, Brigitte Bardot, Til' Tuesday, Patsy Cline	5–10
	November 14	Paul McCartney, Lindsay Wagner	3–5
	November 21	Karen and Richard Carpenter, Mariel Hemingway	5–10
	November 28	The Kennedys: 20 Years Later, Linda Evans, Diane Keaton, Barry Manilow, Joan Collins, Kenny Rogers	1–2
	December 5	Jane Pauley, Mary Tyler Moore, Dr. Robert Levine	1–2
	December 12	Barbra Streisand	2–4
	December 19	Olivia Newton-John: Will Grease Lightning Strike Again?, Annie Lennox Makes Eurythmics Throb, Al Pacino, Yoko Ono, Jamie Lee Curtis Makes Ant Music with Adam, Mick Jagger Croons for Pregnant Jerry Hall, Linda Evans	10–20
1984	January 2	Year-End Double Issue Special, Richard Chamberlain, Mr. T, Ronald Reagan, Vanessa Williams, Jennifer Beals	2–4
	January 9	Princess Caroline, Keith Richards, Patti Hansen	2–4

Year	Issue	Description	Value ($)
1984	January 16	Dennis Wilson and the Beach Boys, Princess Caroline	3–6
	January 23	Cher, Jaclyn Smith	4–8
	January 30	Mr. T, Lindsay Wagner	2–4
	February 6	Debra Winger and Shirley MacLaine Talk about Mothers and Daughters, The Beatles' U.S. Invasion: The Insider's View, Mia Farrow, Boy George	1–2
	February 13	Michael Jackson, Peter Jennings	2–4
	February 20	John Lennon's Last Songs . . . Yoko's Bittersweet Story, Chris Evert and the Rock Star, Silkwood, Dyan Cannon, Michael Caine, Diane Keaton, Greta Garbo	1–3
	February 27	Bo Derek, Princess Diana	2–4
	March 5	People's First 10 Years . . . Farrah Fawcett: A New Kind of Love Goddess, John Travolta, John Lennon, Jane Fonda	2–3
	March 12	Tom Selleck	2–4
	March 19	Paul Newman	1–2
	March 26	Gary and Lee Hart, Linda Ronstadt	2–3
	April 2	Kevin Bacon, Footloose	1–2
	April 9	Daryl Hannah: Splash	2–4
	April 16	John Delorean and Children	1–2
	April 23	Boy George, Robert Duvall and Meryl Streep	3–5
	May 7	Michael Jackson, The Jackson Brothers	3–5
	May 14	Ethel and David Kennedy	1–2
	May 21	Dolly Parton, Willie Nelson, Kenny Rogers, Loretta Lynn, George Strait, Crystal Gayle	2–4

Year	Issue	Description	Value ($)
1984	May 28	Robert Redford	1–2
	June 4	Griffin O'Neal and Ryan, Andy Kaufman	1–2
	June 11	John Belushi, Michael Jackson	2–4
	June 18	Jackie Onassis, Boy George	2–3
	June 25	Princess Caroline and Son, Prince William	1–2
	July 2	Harrison Ford and Kate Capshaw, Jermaine Jackson	2–4
	July 9	Dolly Parton and Sylvester Stallone, Elizabeth Taylor	2–4
	July 16	People Poll Special . . . Boy George, Mick Jagger, Jerry Hall, Ronald Reagan, Christie Brinkley, Walter Mondale	2–4
	July 23	Michael Jackson: Magic . . . Behind the Scenes, Nastassja Kinski: A New Mom, Neil Diamond Plays for Di	2–4
	July 30	Geraldine Ferraro, Phoebe Cates, Billy Joel, Spinal Tap	1–2
	August 6	Vanessa Williams, Liza Minnelli	2–4
	August 13	Special Comedy Issue . . . David Letterman, Joan Rivers, Eddie Murphy, Bill Murray, Rodney Dangerfield	1–2
	August 20	Richard Burton, Prince: Rock's Reigning Prince . . . Loud, Lewd and #1, Mary Lou Retton	2–3
	August 27	Fall Preview Issue . . . Morgan Fairchild Dolls Up, Christie Brinkley and Billy Joel, Stefanie Powers, Tanya Roberts, etc.	3–5
	September 3	Bruce Springsteen, Bo Derek	2–4
	September 10	Vanessa Williams, Truman Capote	2–4

Year	Issue	Description	Value ($)
1984	September 17	Cyndi Lauper, Elizabeth Taylor	3–5
	September 24	The Best and Worst Dressed . . . Michael Jackson, Goldie Hawn, Geraldine Ferraro, Raquel Welch, Bo Derek, Bill Murray	2–3
	October 1	Princess Diana and Prince Henry, Mary Tyler Moore	1–2
	October 8	Farrah Fawcett, John Delorean	2–4
	October 15	Sally Field, Ryan O'Neal, Farrah Fawcett, Prince, Vanity	2–4
	October 22	Sophia Loren and Son, Barry Manilow	2–4
	October 29	David: The Bubble Boy, Jon-Erik Hexum, Princess Diana	1–2
	November 5	Diane Sawyer, Nick Nolte	1–2
	November 12	Kid Stars . . . Drew Barrymore, Ricky Schroder, and Henry Thomas, Joan Collins, Elton John	5–10
	November 19	Rock's Reclusive Prince: A Rare Look inside the Secret World of His Royal Badness, Princess Stephanie, Richard Burton, Baby Fae	2–4
	November 26	Liza Minnelli, Miss America, Sharlene Wells	1–2
	December 3	Baby Fae and Mother	1–2
	December 10	Joan Rivers and Husband, Bill Cosby and Baby Fae	1–2
	December 17	Linda Evans	1–2
	December 24	Double Issue Special, Mary Lou Retton, Farrah Fawcett, Tina Turner, Bruce Springsteen, Richard Gere	2–4

January 30, 1978

May 29, 1978

June 5, 1978

May 14, 1979

August 6, 1979

August 10, 1981

August 17, 1981

November 23, 1981

December 14, 1981

Year	Issue	Description	Value ($)
1985	January 7	New Brides Special . . . Jamie Lee Curtis, Olivia Newton-John, Mariel Hemingway, Bette Midler, Sally Field	5–10
	January 14	Princess Diana and Prince Harry, Sting	5–10
	January 21	The 30 Hardest Working Celebs . . . Cyndi Lauper, Goldie Hawn, Eddie Murphy, Hall and Oates, etc., Amy Irving, Duran Duran, REO Speedwagon, the Real Charlotte Brontë	2–4
	January 28	Ted Kennedy and Children	1–2
	February 4	Mel Gibson: The Sexiest Man Alive, Meredith Baxter-Birney's Family Ties, Gumby's Back, Clint Eastwood	2–4
	February 11	Cagney & Lacey, Van Halen's David Lee Roth Rocks, Alone, Brash, Bratty Sean Penn, David Bowie in the Snow, Tina Turner, Bob Dylan, Harrison Ford	2–3
	February 18	Teen Suicide . . . Molly Ringwald cover, Christina O and Farrah, Kelly McGillis, Cyndi Lauper, Princess Caroline	2–3
	February 25	The Night Rock Cried . . . for Ethiopia: Michael Jackson, Diana Ross, Bob Dylan, Willie Nelson, Lionel Richie, Bruce Springsteen, Hollywood Wives's Angie Dickinson, Gloria Steinem versus Playboy, Michelle Pfeiffer, The Go-Go's	2–4

Year	Issue	Description	Value ($)
1985	March 4	TV's Rerun Madness . . . I Love Lucy, M.A.S.H., The Mary Tyler Moore Show, Star Trek, etc., Cyndi Lauper, The Who, Bruce Springsteen, Los Lobos, Mick Jagger, Matt Dillon	2–4
	March 11	Madonna, Elizabeth Taylor	5–10
	March 18	Cher and the True Story of Mask, Dynasty's Amanda, Tab Hunter, David Lee Roth, Tanya Tucker	4–8
	March 25	High-Salaried Celebs . . . Are They Worth It?	2–3
	April 1	Jacqueline Bisset and Alexander Godunov	2–3
	April 8	Christie Brinkley and Billy Joel's Wedding, Jackie Smith Shows Off Her Real-Life Angel, Diana Ross, Jimmy Page	2–4
	April 15	Dr. Ruth Westheimer, Princess Stephanie, Hall and Oates	1–2
	April 22	James Garner: The Last Real Man, Wham in China, Annie Lennox: Outrageous Hair, Crystal Gayle, Oliver Reed, Fish Farmer Ian Anderson, The Singing Nun	2–4
	April 29	Rape, Linda Evans, Tina Turner, Tom Selleck, Madonna and Rosanna Arquette, Pia Zadora	2–4
	May 6	Bette Dearest: Bette Davis's Daughter Talks, John Lennon: His Sister's Exclusive Story, Dynasty's Emma Samms	2–4
	May 13	Madonna, Patrick Duffy and Elizabeth Taylor	5–10

Year	Issue	Description	Value ($)
1985	May 20	Charles and Di, Ron and Nancy, Harlem's Apollo: The All-Night Jam, Britt Ekland, Diana Ross, Annie Lennox	5–10
	May 27	Bruce Springsteen and Wife . . . Who's the Boss Now?, Michael Landon, The Pointer Sisters	3–6
	June 3	Sylvester Stallone's Silent Son, Chuck Norris, Bob Hope's Jokebag, Grace Jones Parties, Margaret Hamilton: A Beautiful Woman, Peter Sellers, Boy George, Bianca Jagger	2–4
	June 10	The Story of the Septuplets' Parents, Stacy Keach, John Travolta, Karen Black, Tyrone Power	1–2
	June 17	Von Bulow: A Shattered Family, Bruce Springsteen's Irish Gig, Don Johnson's Summer Job, Cybill Shepherd	2–3
	June 24	Josef Mengele, John Travolta and Jamie Lee Curtis, The Smiths, John Denver	2–4
	July 1	Cyndi Lauper, Warren Beatty, Elton John, Morgan Fairchild	2–4
	July 8	Jack Nicholson: The Strange Sweet Love Story, Can Madonna Get Sean Penn to the Altar? Rambo: America's Avenger, Phil Collins, Laraine Newman, Cher, Morgan Fairchild	3–6
	July 15	Tina Turner, Christina Onassis, Lorenzo Lamas	2–4

Year	Issue	Description	Value ($)
1985	July 22	Malice in the Palace: Forget Shy Di, Duran Duran: A Romp with the Idol Rich, Brigitte Nielsen	2–4
	July 29	Live-Aid Special . . . Mick Jagger, Tina Turner, Madonna, Keith Richards, Ron Wood, Bob Dylan, Hall and Oates	3–4
	August 5	Ali MacGraw, Bob Geldof and Nancy Reagan	1–2
	August 12	The Other Life of Rock Hudson, Michael J. Fox, Ratt, The Monkees, Cyndi Lauper	2–4
	August 19	Ann Jillian Exclusive, Bruce Springsteen: What's Next?	2–4
	August 26	Duran Duran's Simon LeBon: A Brush with Death at Sea	2–4
	September 3	Madonna and Sean Penn	2–4
	September 9	Priscilla Presley Exclusive . . . Life with Elvis, Samantha Smith	2–3
	September 16	Prince/Madonna/David Lee Roth, etc. . . . . Has Rock Gone Too Far?, Priscilla Presley on Elvis Part II	2–4
	September 23	Rock Hudson	1–2
	September 30	Olivia Newton-John and Hubby, Billy Crystal, Princess Stephanie, Cher and Tina Turner, Boy George, Eddie Murphy	2–4
	October 7	Don Johnson, Backstage at Farm Aid, Bob Dylan	2–3
	October 14	Arnold Schwarzenegger, Heather Thomas Kicks Cocaine, Ringo's Grandchild, Aretha Franklin, Cybill Shepherd	2–3

Year	Issue	Description	Value ($)
1985	October 21	Marilyn Monroe and Rock Hudson: Their Last Days, Barbara Eden, John Schneider, Diana Ross Meets New Guy	2–3
	October 28	The Best and Worst Dressed, Princess Stephanie, Madonna, Phillip Michael Thomas	2–3
	November 4	Cybill Shepherd: TV's Sexiest Spitfire, Clarence Clemons, Elvira: Mistress of the Macabre, Hall and Oates, John Cougar, Duran Duran's John Taylor, Bruce Springsteen	2–4
	November 11	What's Diana Worth to Britain?, Brigitte Bardot, Robert Wagner, Sissy Spacek	1–2
	November 18	AIDS: Every Parent's Nightmare, Rae Dawn Chong, Bill Cosby, Exotic Barbara Carrera	2–4
	November 25	Barbara Stanwyck and Linda Evans, Rock Hudson's Last Lover Talks, Mick Jagger, Marla Gibbs, Jerry Hall	2–3
	December 2	Raisa Gorbachev, Joan Rivers and Liz Taylor	.50–1
	December 9	Philip Michael Thomas, Sylvester Stallone, Katharine Hepburn Redefined, Whitney Houston's Big Break	2–4
	December 16	Baryshnikov: Ballet's Russian Romeo, Love Boat's Gopher, Joni Mitchell, Tracy Nelson: Rick's Daughter, Liz Taylor	2–3
	December 23	25 Most Intriguing People Issue . . . Don Johnson, Michael J. Fox, Bruce Springsteen and Wife, Madonna, Bob Geldof	2–3

Year	Issue	Description	Value ($)
1986	January 6	Donna Dixon, Barbi Benton, Madonna, Lindsay Wagner	2–4
	January 13	Ingrid Bergman, Teddy Pendergrass, Michael Douglas, Kathleen Turner	1–2
	January 20	Ricky Nelson, Meryl Streep, Robert Redford	5–10
	January 27	Mark Harmon: The Sexiest Man Alive, Donna Reed: It Was a Good Life	1–2
	February 3	Bette Midler at 40, Liz Taylor and Stevie Wonder, Jessica Lange, Sade, Yoko Ono's Lost Daughter, Cher	2–4
	February 10	Christa McAuliffe, Julian and Sean Lennon, Madonna, Billy Joel, Keith Richards, Elvis, Chuck Berry, James Brown	2–3
	February 17	Diana Ross's Supreme Day, Brooke Shields, Pia Zadora	2–4
	February 24	The Rebel Reagan . . . Patti Davis, Michael J. Fox	1–2
	March 3	Michele Duvalier and Imelda Marcos: The Dragon Ladies, Night Court's Sassy Sidekick, Stevie Wonder	1–2
	March 10	Who Makes What Issue . . . Whoopi, Sade, Kim Basinger, Rosanna Arquette, Debra Winger, Grateful Dead, Phil Collins	2–3
	March 17	Caroline Kennedy, Katharine Hepburn, Clint Eastwood	1–2
	March 24	George Harrison: Madonna's Beatle Boss, Pouty Princess Molly Ringwald, Troy Beyer	2–4

Year	Issue	Description	Value ($)
1986	March 31	Are These Old Maids? . . . Donna Mills, Sharon Gless, Linda Ronstadt, and Diane Sawyer, Estelle Getty, Peter Sellers and Britt Ekland, Sally Field, Jacqueline Bisset, Diane Keaton	2–4
	April 7	Sarah Ferguson, Mr. Mister, Joan Collins, Twisted Sister,	
	April 17	Pia Zadora, Sly Stallone, Al Pacino	2–3
	April 14	Lionel Richie: Pop's #1 Hit Man, Opie and Andy Return to Mayberry, Farewell to James Cagney, Maureen O'Sullivan, Apollonia, Billy Crystal	2–4
	April 21	Ed McMahon and Family, Liz Taylor, Tony Danza, Madonna, Cher, LL Cool J, Mariel Hemingway	2–3
	April 28	Avenging Sergeant Ford, Moonlighting, The Bangles	2–3
	May 5	Dolly Parton: Peppery Talk, The Osmonds, Abbie Hoffman	2–4
	May 12	The Duke and Duchess of Windsor: Their Secret Love Letters, Arnold and Maria Shriver: A Splendid Wedding, Adam West: Batman	2–4
	May 19	Whitney Houston: America's Top New Star, How Sexy Is Cybill Shepherd?	3–5
	May 26	Joan Rivers, Heather Locklear and Her Motley Crue-Man, Neil Diamond, Johnny Carson, Sean Penn	2–4
	June 2	Donna Mills, Tom Cruise: Top Gun	2–4

Year	Issue	Description	Value ($)
1986	June 9	Rock Hudson's Story, Prince's Sneak Preview, Elvis Costello: More Smile, Less Bile, Kathleen Turner, Elle MacPherson, Robert Palmer	2–4
	June 16	The Rock Hudson Story: The Drama of His Final Days, Howie Mandel, Belinda Carlisle, Ozzy Osbourne, Tatum O'Neal	2–4
	June 23	John Kennedy Jr., Bruce Willis, Mikhail Baryshnikov, John James, The New Van Halen, Henry Ford in Love, Tony Bennett, Sammy Hagar	2–4
	June 30	Uncle Sam's Dirty Book, Ralph Macchio's Karate Master, Monika Scharre the Model, Anne Bancroft	1–2
	July 7	Prince William, Janet Jackson Scores High	2–4
	July 14	David Letterman, Tony Danza's Tony Wedding, Kate Collins, The Jets, Tatum O'Neal, Diana Ross, Connie Francis	2–4
	July 21	Prince, Robert Redford and Debra Winger, Boy George	2–3
	July 28	Hollywood Hunks '86 . . . Rodney Dangerfield and Danny DeVito, Christie Brinkley . . . A Salute to the Bikini . . . Joan Collins, Brigitte Bardot, Jayne Mansfield	2–4
	August 4	Caroline Kennedy's Wedding, Dwight Yoakam	1–2
	August 11	Pierce Brosnan . . . Remington Steele, Madonna's Man, Alien's Creator, Eric Clapton, Peter Townshend, Boy George	2–4

Year	Issue	Description	Value ($)
1986	August 18	Infidelity . . . Jack Nicholson, John McEnroe and Tatum O'Neal	2–4
	August 25	Vanna White, Paul Shaffer, Max Headroom, Willard Scott	2–4
	September 1	Farrah Fawcett, Eddie Murphy, Carol Burnett, Lucille Ball, Barbra Streisand, Tina Turner	2–4
	September 8	Priscilla Presley: "I'm Sick of Lies," Elton John, Alien's Sigourney Weaver, Peggy Lipton, Grace Jones	3–5
	September 15	Frank Sinatra: His Life and Loves, Liz Taylor, Diane Sawyer . . . 1963, The Pet Shop Boys, Joey Heatherton, The Monkees, Jan and Dean, Frankie Avalon, Bobby Rydell, Peter Noone	5–10
	September 22	Frank Sinatra and Women Part II . . . Victoria Principal, Natalie Wood, Lauren Bacall, Mia Farrow, etc., Barbra Streisand, Farrah Fawcett	5–10
	September 29	Patrick Duffy/Dallas, David Lee Roth: Rock's Sexy Road Warrior, Debra Winger, Jane Fonda, Tammy Wynette, Sissy Spacek	2–4
	October 6	Elizabeth Taylor and Robert Wagner, Paul Simon, Hollywood on Trial, Princess Di, David Rappaport	2–3
	October 13	Princess Diana and Sarah Ferguson	5–10
	October 20	Charlie's Angels . . . Look Homeward Angels: 10 Years Ago, Paul Hogan, Bruce Springsteen, Humphrey Bogart, John Wayne	5–10

Year	Issue	Description	Value ($)
1986	October 27	Joan Rivers, Ricky Nelson's Kids	2–4
	November 3	Kathleen Turner: Hollywood's Most Wanted Woman, Chuck Berry, The New Monkees, Johnny Cash, Keith Richards	2–4
	November 17	David and Julie Eisenhower, Tom Selleck, Angela Lansbury, Meredith Baxter-Birney, Huey Lewis, Bruce Hornsby, Diana Ross, Jimi Hendrix, Mary Wilson, Gregg Allman, Crosby, Stills, and Nash	2–4
	November 24	Carol Burnett, Troubled Boy George, Rock-Hot Bon Jovi, Anita Baker, Daryl Hannah, Jackson Browne	2–4
	December 1	The Best and Worst Dressed Issue . . . Cher, Cyndi Lauper, Liz Taylor, Cybill Shepherd, Elton John, Eric Clapton, Frank Zappa	2–4
	December 15	Cary Grant, Mae West, Ingrid Bergman, Sophia Loren, Dyan Cannon	1–2
	December 22	25 Most Intriguing People Issue . . . Vanna White, Whitney Houston, Bette Midler, Run DMC, Diana Ross, Michael Jackson	2–4
1987	January 5	Bruce Willis and His Films, The Best of 1986, Cheers, Michael J. Fox, Liz Taylor, Snow White Turns 50, The Beverly Hillbillies, Marla Hanson, Kathleen Turner, Greta Garbo	2–4

Year	Issue	Description	Value ($)
1987	January 12	Oprah Winfrey, Billy Idol, Ellen Greene	1–2
	January 19	Huey Lewis: Rock's Best News, Howard Hesseman, Diane Sawyer, Ron Reagan, Leonard Nimoy	2–4
	January 26	Prince Edward, Shirley MacLaine, Sophia Loren	1–2
	February 2	L.A. Law's Susan Dey and Corbin Bernsen, Basil Rathbone as Sherlock Holmes, Chicago and Their Music, Mick Jagger, Cher	3–6
	February 9	The 100th Birthday of Hollywood . . . Marilyn Monroe, Liz Taylor, Bette Davis, Marlon Brando, The Wizard of Oz, Marlene Dietrich, Molly Ringwald John Wayne, The Beastie Boys	3–6
	February 16	Liberace 1919–1987, Pam Dawber, Fergie, Ann-Margret	2–3
	March 2	My Sister Sam's Pam Dawber Lands the Sexiest Man Alive, Jean Simmons, John Lennon Exclusive Part II	2–4
	March 9	Charlie Sheen, Tom Berenger, Willem Dafoe	1–2
	March 16	Cybill Shepherd and Her Groom: The Wedding Album, Jill Ireland, Suzanne Somers, Goldie Hawn	2–4
	March 23	Mary Beth Whitehead, Elizabeth Stern and Baby	1–2
	March 30	Harry Hamlin: The Sexiest Man	1–2
	April 6	Russia Special	1–2
	April 13	Teen Sex Issue, Jane Fonda, Tina Turner, Paul Newman	1–2

Year	Issue	Description	Value ($)
1987	April 20	Michael J. Fox, The Women of Designing Women	1–2
	April 27	David Crosby: The Confessions of a Coke Addict, Elizabeth Taylor Joins the Dash for the Duchess's Diamonds	2–4
	May 4	Michael Caine, Hill Street Blues, He-Man	1–2
	May 11	Ted Danson, Madonna	1–2
	May 18	Gary Hart and Donna Rice, Sean Penn, Linda Purl	1–3
	May 25	Dustin Hoffman and Warren Beatty, Brigitte Nielsen	1–3
	June 1	Rita Hayworth Exclusive, Joan Rivers Fired, Diana and Charles Party at Cannes, Janis Joplin at 17	2–4
	June 8	Charles and Di, The Beatles, Susanna Hoffs Exclusive, Suzanne Vega	5–10
	June 15	Donna Rice	2–4
	June 22	Celebrating the 60s . . . A Summer of Love, Peter Max, Janis Joplin, Jimi Hendrix, Gurus, The Beatles, etc.	3–6
	June 29	Miss America and Miss Wrong: The Bess Myerson Scandal, Robert De Niro, Peter O'Toole, Jenny Agutter	2–3
	July 6	Fred Astaire 1899–1987, John Travolta, Meat Loaf, Madonna	2–4
	July 13	Jackie Gleason: So Long Pal, Patty Duke, Tom Cruise	2–4
	July 20	Fergie and Di, Patty Duke, Mel Brooks, Howdy Doody	1–2
	July 27	Oliver North, People Poll Special . . . Donna Rice, Eddie Murphy, Ronald Reagan, Jim and Tammy Bakker, Cybill Shepherd	1–2

Year	Issue	Description	Value ($)
1987	August 3	AIDS, Donovan, Annie Pujol, Liz Taylor, Fergie	2–4
	August 10	The Divorce Duels of Brigitte Nielsen and Joan Rivers, Marilyn Monroe: 25 Years Later, Frankie Avalon and Annette Funicello: Back on the Burning Sands	2–4
	August 17	Elvis Presley: 10 Years Later, Carly Simon's Victory Over Paralyzing Stage Fright, Lou Diamond Phillips, Madonna on Tour, Whitney Houston, John Denver	
	August 24	Jackie O, Boy George Back from a $1,000-a-Day Habit, 007's Maryam d'Abo	2–4
	August 31	Joan River's Tragedy, Fall Preview Issue, Dolly Parton, Emily Lloyd, Farrah Fawcett, Cher, The Cars	2–4
	September 7	A Family at War . . . The Nelsons, Carrie Fisher, Mary Hart	1–2
	September 14	Michael Jackson: He's Back and Bad, Lisa Lisa and Cult Jam	3–6
	September 21	Here Comes Fergie, Tom Selleck's Secret Tahoe Wedding, Madonna: A Sentimental Journey, Jump Street's Holly Robinson	2–3
	September 28	Princess Caroline: What Would Grace Say?, Matthew Broderick Faces Prison, Remembering Lorne Greene	1–2
	October 5	Jessica Hahn, Elizabeth Taylor	2–4
	October 12	Michael Jackson Exclusive: Message from Michael	3–6

Year	Issue	Description	Value ($)
1987	October 19	Pat Anthony: A Mother's Love, Valerie Harper Strikes Back, Bruce Springsteen Cutting Loose, A Beatle Coming Back, Jackson Browne, Roy Orbison, Elvis Costello, Jackson Five	2–4
	October 26	Glenn Close and Michael Douglas . . . Real Life Fatal Attractions, Princess Anne in the U.S.A., Karen Carpenter, Spuds	2–4
	November 2	Baby Jessica McClure, Nancy Reagan	1–2
	November 9	Princess Di, Barry Manilow Comeback, Paul Newman	5–10
	November 16	The Best and Worst Dressed . . . Brigitte Nielsen, Elizabeth Taylor, Bruce Willis, Diane Keaton, Madonna, and Others	2–3
	November 23	Don Johnson and Sheena Easton, Staci Keanan, Michael Jackson	2–4
	November 30	Jay Leno, Kirstie Alley, Howdy Doody and Buffalo Bob	3–4
	December 7	Donald Trump, Courteney Cox	1–2
	December 14	Madonna and Sean Penn: The Divorce of Madonna and Sean, Deidre Hall, Lillian Gish, Bette Davis	3–5
	December 21	Cybill Shepherd Exclusive: Cybill and Her Twins, Harry Chapin, Bruce Springsteen	2–4
	December 28	Double Issue Special, Princess Diana, Baby Jessica McClure, Michael Douglas, Oliver North, Brigitte Nielsen	5–10
1988	All issues not listed are $2–4 each		
	January 25	Cher: The Ultimate Liberated Woman, Liz Taylor Part II	3–6

Year	Issue	Description	Value ($)
1988	March 28	Andy Gibb: A Superstar at 19, Prince Charles, Sting, Henry Winkler, Cybill Shepherd, Cher, Ziggy Marley	4–8
	April 25	Princess Diana, Eleanor Mondale	5–10
1989	All issues not listed are $2–4 each.		
	All Princess Di issues $3–6 each		
1990	All issues not listed are $1–2 each.		
	January 29	Drew Barrymore: No Happy Ending, Jodie Foster, Annie II	4–8
	July 2	Madonna and Warren Beatty	3–6
	July 16	Princess Diana, Vanna White	4–8
1991	All issues not listed are $1–2 each		
	February 11	Princess Diana, Caroline Kennedy	4–8
	February 18	Lucille Ball and Desi Arnaz, Gloria Estefan	3–4
	April 15	Madonna and Michael Jackson, Donnie Wahlberg	3–6
	May 6	Michael Landon, Larry Hagman, Princess Diana	2–4
	June 17	Princess Diana, Prince William and Prince Harry, Johnny Carson	4–8
	July 15	Michael Landon	2–4
	July 22	Prince Charles and Princess Diana, Lee Remick	4–8
	September 9	Beverly Hills 90210 Cast, Princess Diana	2–4

1992 to present $1–2 each

US VALUES

Year	Issue	Description	Value ($)
1977	June 28	Kate Jackson, Sylvester Stallone's Own Story, Linda Blair, Debbie Harry/Blondie	5–10

June 28, 1977

May 16, 1978

July 25, 1978

July 29, 1985

December 16, 1985

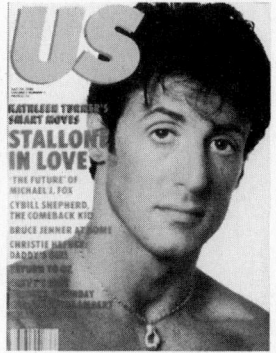

July 29, 1985

April 1993

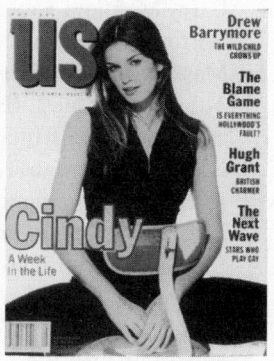

May 5, 1994

July 1996

Year	Issue	Description	Value ($)
1977	July 12	Glen Campbell, Mac Davis ABBA: The Rock Group That Pays 85% of Sweden's Taxes, Marty Feldman, Ann-Margret	5–10
	August 9	Paul Michael Glaser: Alias Starsky, Peter Frampton Talks, Suzanne Somers	5–10
	October 18	Sylvester Stallone: Rock's Back, Lesley Ann Warren's Sexy New Role, Mackenzie Phillips Gets a New Image, Kristy and Jimmy McNichol, Jamie Lee Curtis: A New Curtis Shows Her Petticoat, Keith Richards: Rock's Bad Boy Goes Straight, Bess Myerson	5–10
1978	January 10	Cher and Gregg Allman: The Untold Story of Their Loving Fight to Save a Marriage, Close Encounters' Richard Dreyfuss, Cindy Williams Family Snapshots, The Love Boat's Skipper, Donna Summer: Lust Lady	10–20
	March 7	Suzanne Somers: Sex on TV, Barry Manilow, Richard Burton, Behind Darth Vader's Mask, Madeline Kahn	3–6
	March 21	The Very Private Life of Paul and Linda McCartney, Fantasy Island's Little Man, Loretta Lynn: Her Struggle with Fame and Drugs, Reggie Jackson	3–5
	April 18	Elizabeth Taylor, Parker Stevenson: The Other Hardy Boy, James Taylor, The Gritty Humor of TV's Flo	2–4

Year	Issue	Description	Value ($)
1978	May 30	Olivia Newton-John Photo Special: A Sneak Preview of Grease, The Search for Elvis Look-alikes, The Bee Gees' Kid Brother Fights Bad-Boy Image, John Travolta and Olivia Newton-John Talk, Barbara Walters	10–20
	June 13	Anthony Quinn and Jackie Bisset: The Onassis Rip-Off, Rock's Carly Simon: Why Fans Terrify Me, Those Characters on One Day at a Time, The Man Behind the Dracula Boom, Patti Smith, Joe Namath	3–5
	July 11	TV's Hulk, Johnny Mathis Lucks in Again, Kris Kristofferson	3–5
	August 22	Goldie Hawn, Why Elvis Presley Lives, TV's McNichol Kids, Hard Rock's Boston Blast, Bonnie Tyler	3–6
	September 19	Who's Hot, Who's Not . . . Battlestar Galactica, The Hulk, Wonder Woman, etc., The Who: Rock's Bad Boys Are Back	3–5
	October 3	Mick Jagger: Rock's Menace Is Now Calmer, Kate Jackson Marriage, Rocky Preview	5–10
	November 28	Raquel Welch and the Muppets, John Belushi, Chris Evert, Rod Stewart Makes Music Out of Blond Trouble, Bob Urich, Angie Dickinson: Sexy and Alone, Heart: The Wilson Sisters	6–12

Year	Issue	Description	Value ($)
1979	February 6	Kristy McNichol: TV's All-American Teen, The Bee Gee's Barry Gibb and Drugs, James Arness	2–4
	February 20	Elvis Presley 10-Page Special, Darth Vader, Carpenters	2–4
	March 20	Cher on Her Own, Natalie Wood: Sexy Scenes	5–10
	April 17	Special Oscar Issue, Heaven Can Wait, Jane Fonda, The Deer Hunter	2–3
	May 1	Second Anniversary Issue, Cheryl Tiegs, Farrah Fawcett, The Blues Brothers, John Travolta, Mork and Mindy	2–4
	May 29	Rod Stewart and Alana Hamilton, Dawn of the Dead: The Most Gruesome Movie Ever, Dionne Warwick, Kate Jackson, Suzanne Somers, Jill Clayburgh, Jaclyn Smith	3–6
	June 26	The Village People, Ali MacGraw's Steamy Sex Scenes	5–10
	August 7	Cheryl Ladd, Rock's New Off-Screen Love, Tanya Tucker, Sissy Spacek, Sally Field, Charlie's Angels	5–10
	September 4	John Travolta Comes Out of Hiding, Betty Ford, Marlon Brando on Sex and Money	10–20
	November 27	The Bee Gees: Why They're Breaking Up, Ann-Margret Fights Back After a Near Breakdown, Bo Derek: America's Newest Sex Symbol	15–30
1980	January 8	The Sexy New Star Trek . . . Persis Khambatta, 1980's	

Year	Issue	Description	Value ($)
1980	January 8	Preview Special, The Knack Leads Power Pop, Science Fiction Fashions	5–10
	May 13	Kenny Rogers and Wife, Deborah Raffin, Jane Fonda, Rod Stewart	2–4
	June 10	Sally Field: A Survivor, The Urban Cowboy: John Travolta, Pam Dawber off the Tube, John Derek	2–4
	June 24	Cathy Lee Crosby, Billy Joel: The Bad Boy Is Back for More, The Hulk's New Image, Bo Derek's Kid Sister: Another 10, The Village People, Valerie Perrine and Alan Carr, Jane Fonda	2–4
	July 8	John Schneider: The Dukes of Hazzard, Clint Eastwood: Mr. Macho Reshapes His Image, Rock's Meat Loaf and Debbie Harry Seek Stardom Together, Jan Smithers of WKRP, Cher	2–4
	September 16	Toni Tennille: Blonde and Dynamite, The Rolling Stones Recharged by Emotional Rescue, Hart to Hart's Stefanie Powers, Gary Sandy: WKRP, Maud Adams, Jerry Reed, The Kinks Live On, Dave Davies	2–4
	September 30	The Chips Feud, Larry Hagman, The Who's Roger Daltrey: Inside His Marriage	2–4
	October 28	Barbra Streisand and Barry Gibb, Stevie Nicks: Fleetwood Mac's Rock Sorceress Talks about Men and Music, Paul Michael Glaser, Gregory	

Year	Issue	Description	Value ($)
1980	October 28	Harrison, Melissa Gilbert, David Soul	5–10
	November 11	The New Cher, Horror Flicks: Turning Blood into Bucks, Lynda Carter: Inside Her Million-Dollar Marriage, Loni Anderson as Jayne Mansfield	6–12
	December 23	Special Year-End Issue, Bo Derek, Kenny Rogers, Larry Hagman, The Empire Strikes Back, Cathy Lee Crosby	2–4
1981	January 6	Super Witches of the Soaps, Gutsy Goldie Hawn Goes It Alone, The Bellamy Brothers, Nina Hagen, Dire Straits, Rock's Pat Benatar: She's a Sexy Tinkerbell, Barbara Eden, Dolly Parton, Burt Reynolds	2–4
	January 20	Brooke Shields: Pants Cause Ripples, Kris Kristofferson's Gate Crash, Goldie Hawn Glitters, Cher's Black Rose Withers, Bruce Springsteen Bosses, Jane Fonda, Dolly Parton, Elizabeth Taylor's Daughter	6–12
	February 3	The 50 Hottest Couples, Farrah Fawcett, Tanya Tucker, Marlo Thomas, Kenny Rogers, Dallas, Flash Gordon's Spacy Women, Leo Sayer, Teddy Pendergrass Cleans Up His Act	2–4
	March 17	Dynasty's Darling Linda Evans, Bo Derek, TV's Sexiest Hunks, Suzanne Somers, John Lennon Exclusive, My Secret Life with the Rolling Stones: A Special Feature	2–4

Year	Issue	Description	Value ($)
1981	March 31	Sally Field Hits the Back Roads, Audrey Landers Vamps, The Police: Rock's Most Arresting Group, Todd Rundgren, Kris Kristofferson	3–6
	May 12	Greatest American Hero, Paul McCartney: Getting the Beatles Together, 007, This Is Elvis Presley: Old Home Movies and a New Film Reveal the Presley Nobody Knew	3–6
	June 9	Jaclyn Smith: The Devilish Angel, Dolly Parton, Paul Newman, Slim Whitman, Fantasy Island	5–10
	June 23	Kristy McNichol at 18, Burt Reynolds: What Women Have Taught Me, Foreigner: At Last on Radio, Shocking Chaka Khan, Sheena Easton, Dennis Quaid, Angie Dickinson	2–4
	July 7	Bodies Beautiful Issue . . . Victoria Principal: Red, Hot, and 31, Lois Lane Makes It with Superman, Linda Gray	4–8
	July 21	Eddie Van Halen, Olivia Newton-John, Brooke Shields, Tanya Tucker, Fleetwood Mac	10–20
	August 18	Bo Derek and Tarzan, Brooke Shields Is Tough: Making Endless Love, James Taylor, Britt Ekland	3–6
	September 29	Priscilla Presley Fights for her Daughter's Future, JFK Jr., Mick Jagger: Jagger of the Jungle, Rocky Horror's Shocking Sequel, Meat Loaf Heats Up after His Breakdown,	

Year	Issue	Description	Value ($)
1981	September 29	Bo's Swinging Tarzan, Keith Moon	2–4
	November 10	Mick Jagger: Jagger Says Marriage Turns Him to Stone, John Belushi, TV's Gonzo, Jamie Lee Curtis: Hex, Sex, Creepy, and Weepy	3–6
	December 8	John Lennon and Yoko Ono: Their Struggle against Heroin and Each Other, Judy and Audrey Landers: Growing Up Sexy, Ronnie Milsap, Loni Anderson, Carly Simon, Dr. Hook, The Doors: On Fire, John Entwistle, Chris Atkins, Nastassja Kinski	3–6
1982	February 2	Dolly Parton and Burt Reynolds, Mick Jagger, Farrah Fawcett, Fred Astaire, Connie Francis, Jane Fonda	2–4
	February 16	Tony Geary, Maggie Eastwood: Life without Clint, Jerry Lee Lewis, Diane Keaton, Judy Collins	2–3
	March 2	Tom Selleck, Who's Hot, Who's Not, Olivia Newton-John, An Intimate Look at Elizabeth Taylor	2–4
	April 13	Couples of the Soaps, Joanie and Chachi, Paul McCartney by His Wife Linda, Debbie Harry as a Playboy Bunny	4–8
	April 27	Best and Worst Dressed People Issue . . . Tom Selleck, Suzanne Somers, Liz Taylor, Linda Evans, Burt Reynolds	2–4
	May 11	Charlene Tilton, Lindsay Wagner, Jaclyn Smith, Sissy	

Year	Issue	Description	Value ($)
1982	May 11	Spacek, Julie Andrews, John Belushi's Last Party	2–5
	May 25	Christie Brinkley and Tom Selleck, Who Killed Sal Mineo?, Nastassja Kinski: Cat People's Untamed Sex Kitten, Nick Lowe, Willie Aames	2–4
	June 22	Linda Evans, Star Trek: The Death of Spock, Princess Grace, Johnny Mathis on Friends and Lovers, Charlene Tilton, Road Warrior, Annie, Pia Zadora	2–4
	July 6	Morgan Fairchild, Linda Evans, Sylvester Stallone: Rocky III, Sheena Easton: Sheena Shines, The Clash, Connie Stevens, Jamie Farr	2–4
	November 23	Tom Selleck, Faye Dunaway: Men, Movies, and Me, My Wild Life with David Bowie by His Ex-Wife, Bette Midler, Jodie Foster	2–4
1983	April 25	TV's Super Wives . . . Linda Evans and Linda Gray, Hot Suits Special . . . Shannon Tweed, Bruce Penhall, Tom Selleck	2–4
	May 23	Charlene Tilton, Diana Ross Rejoins the Supremes, Lindsay Wagner, Princess Di, John Schneider	1–2
	June 20	Return of the Jedi, Farrah Fawcett's Two Lovers	5–10
	October 10	Christina Delorean, JFK, Carol Burnett: Serious Talk, Jodie Foster Since Hinkley, Led Zeppelin's Robert Plant Flies Solo	2–4

Year	Issue	Description	Value ($)
1983	October 24	Kate Jackson: Kate's Back, Tom Selleck: The Next James Bond?, MTV's Naughty Nina, John Travolta, Natalie Wood	3–6
1984	January 30	The Odd Couples . . . Caroline Kennedy, Joan Collins, Billy Joel and Christie Brinkley, Goldie Hawn, Adam Ant and Jamie Lee Curtis, Joanna Carson, Shelley Long	2–4
	February 13	Lisa Marie Presley at 16, Donna Mills, The Beatles 20th Anniversary Tribute, Bette Davis: Beating Cancer	2–4
	February 27	The Stars' Biggest Lie . . . Ageless Victoria Principal, Shari Belafonte, Landers Sisters, Veronica Hamel, Nancy Reagan, Joan Collins, David Hasselhoff	2–3
1985	March 25	Farrah Fawcett and Son . . . Love Babies, Charles and Diana, Melissa Gilbert, Lionel Richie, Clint Eastwood, Michelle Pfeiffer, David Lee Roth	2–4
	May 6	Bill Cosby, JFK and the Mafia, Phil Collins's Noisy Bedroom, Nashville Wives, The New Edition	1–2
	July 1	Cher	3–6
	July 15	Jamie Lee Curtis	2–4
	July 29	Sylvester Stallone in Love, The Future of Michael J. Fox, Cybill Shepherd, Bruce Jenner at Home, Christie Hefner, Return to Oz, Prince's Birthday	2–4
	August 12	Tina Turner	3–5

Year	Issue	Description	Value ($)
1985	August 26	Tony Danza, Madonna and Sean: Cool for Marriage, Carly Simon's Home Pleasures, Pee-Wee Herman, Teri Copley	2–3
	September 9	Joan Collins: The U.S. Interview, Robert Blake's Toughest Mission, The Double Life of Jennifer Beals, Bob Hope, Kevin Costner: Silverado Sex Symbol, Mickey Mouse	2–4
	September 23	1985 Fall Preview Special . . . Miami Vice, Dustin Hoffman, Dynasty, Moonlighting, Robert Wagner, Cagney & Lacey	2–3
	October 7	Hollywood Faces AIDS, Elvis's Other Women, Michael Douglas, Madonna's Honeymoon, Tom Selleck	2–3
	October 21	Bill Cosby After Hours, Billy Crystal's Double Play, Jane Seymour's Country Castle, Rachel Ward, Jenilee Harrison	2–3
	November 4	The Irresistible Robert Wagner, Why Rona Barrett Hates Barbara Walters, John and Yoko's TV Bio, Being Brooke Shields, The Last Days of Jon-Erik Hexum, Whitney Houston	2–3
	November 18	Shirley MacLaine: Her Many Lives, Arnold Schwarzenegger, Patrick Swayze, Michele Lee, Morgan Fairchild	1–2
	December 2	John James, Family Ties's Other Fox, Bruce Willis: Moonlighting's Mystery Man, Simon LeBon on Board	1–2

Year	Issue	Description	Value ($)
1985	December 16	Charles and Diana: The Di-namic Duo, Betty White, Mitch Gaylord, Sinatra at His Frankest	10–20
	December 30	Michael Douglas and Danny DeVito, Morgan Fairchild's Mating Call, Barbi Benton, Heather Locklear	1–2
1986	January 13	Cybill Shepherd Rating Men, The Trouble with Saturday Night Live, Whoopi Goldberg, Meet the Equalizer	2–4
	January 27	Michael J. Fox	1–2
	February 10	Barbra Streisand	1–2
	February 24	Robert Redford, Dean Paul Martin, Mary Tyler Moore	1–2
	March 10	Goldie Hawn: Solid Goldie . . . A Wildcat Lands on Her Feet, Stacy Keach, Chuck Norris, Julian Lennon	2–4
	March 26	Oscar Fever, Cher, Donna Reed, Molly Ringwald, Madonna	2–4
	April 4	Clint Eastwood	3–6
	April 21	Don Johnson	1–2
	May 5	Dynasty	1–2
	May 19	Tony Danza, Hands Across America	1–2
	June 6	Alan Alda	1–2
	June 16	Richard Pryor	1–2
	June 30	Tom Cruise Interview, David Bowie: Mr. Cool Warms Up, Down Home with Dolly Parton, Cloris Leachman, Michelle Phillips: The Last Red-Hot Mama	2–4
	July 14	Arnold Schwarzenegger	1–2
	July 28	Bette Midler	1–2
	August 8	Whitney Houston	2–4

Year	Issue	Description	Value ($)
1986	August 25	Bruce Willis	1–2
	September 8	Tina Turner	2–3
	September 22	Cybill Shepherd	2–3
	October 6	Patrick Duffy	1–2
	October 20	The 10 Sexiest Men and Women	2–4
	November 3	Elizabeth Taylor	2–4
	November 17	Loni Anderson	2–4
	December 1	Tom Cruise, Paul Newman	1–2
	December 15	Eddie Murphy	1–2
	December 29	Entertainment Yearbook Double Issue Special	2–4
1987	January 26	Clint Eastwood	2–4
	February 9	Don Johnson and Philip Michael Thomas	2–3
	February 23	Bruce Willis and Cybill Shepherd, 30 Famous Couples Talk, Sophia Loren, Michael Jackson	2–3
	March 9	Valerie Bertinelli	2–4
	March 23	Why We Love Family Ties, Burt Reynolds, Vanna White, Garry Shandling, Kathleen Turner, Christie Brinkley	2–4
	April 6	The Oscars: Who Will Win	1–2
	April 20	The 10 Sexiest and the 10 Richest	1–2
	May 4	Harry Hamlin	1–2
	May 18	Shelley Long . . . Celebrity Moms and Kids	3–5
	June 1	Diana Ross	2–4
	June 15	Summer Sneak Preview Special	1–2
	July 13	10th Anniversary Double Issue Special	1–2
	August 10	The Private Life of Mark Harmon, Jessica Hahn, Madonna	2–4
	August 24	Elvis Presley: The Last Days	2–4
	September 7	Madonna Talks	2–4
	September 21	Cybill Shepherd and Bruce Willis, Fall Preview	2–3

Year	Issue	Description	Value ($)
1987	October 5	Worrying about Whitney Houston	2–4
	October 19	Who's the Sexiest in 1987?	2–3
	November 2	Bruce Willis	1–2
	November 16	Princess Diana	5–10
	November 30	Farrah Fawcett	2–4
	December 14	Tom Selleck	2–4
	December 28	Year-End Double Issue Special	2–3
1988	January 25	Charlie Sheen, The 10 Most Beautiful Women	2–3
	February 8	Who's In and Who's Out Special	1–2
	February 22	Patrick Swayze and Wife, Lisa Niemi	1–2
	March 7	Tom Selleck, Reader's Poll Special	2–3
	March 21	Brigitte Nielsen	2–4
	April 4	Rob Lowe	1–2
	April 18	Michael J. Fox	1–2
	May 2	The 10 Sexiest Bachelors	1–2
	May 16	Demi Moore, Mother's Day Special	3–6
	May 30	Marlee Matlin, The Hottest Couples	2–3
	June 13	Sylvester Stallone	1–2
	June 27	Jane Seymour Gets Personal . . . The Frantic, Romantic World of Jane, Chevy Chase Interview, Gloria Estefan	3–6
	July 11	The Boys of Summer Double Issue Special	1–2
	August 8	Tom Cruise	1–2
	August 22	Julianne Phillips	1–2
	September 5	Jeff Bridges	1–2
	September 19	The 10 Most Stylish Celebs, Fashion Issue Special	2–3
	October 3	Don Johnson on Love, Sexy John Stamos	1–2
	October 17	The 10 Sexiest	2–3

Year	Issue	Description	Value ($)
1988	October 31	Valerie Bertinelli	2–4
	November 14	Kirstie Alley, Whoopi Goldberg	2–4
	November 28	Jason and Justine Bateman, Betty White	2–3
	December 12	Mel Gibson	1–2
	December 26	Year-End Double Issue Special	2–3
1989	January 23	Sexy Talk from Kim Basinger: interview, photos and cover, Melanie Griffith: Working Mom, Cruising with the Bangles, Bianca Jagger, Bette Midler, Anita Baker, Madonna	2–4
	February 6	Who's In and Who's Out	1–2
	February 20	Hollywood's Red-Hot Couples	2–4
	March 6	Suddenly Single . . . Madonna, Julianne Phillips, Robin Givens, Cybill Shepherd, Michelle Pfeiffer, Tom Selleck on Bringing Up Baby	2–4
	March 20	Oprah Winfrey	1–2
	April 3	The 10 Most Beautiful Women	2–3
	April 17	Ken Wahl	1–2
	May 1	Roseanne Barr	1–2
	May 29	Patrick Swayze	1–2
	June 12	Madonna	5–10
	June 26	Johnny Depp	2–3
	July 10	Summer Double Issue Special	2–3
	August 7	Rob Lowe Special	2–3
	August 21	Michael J. Fox	2–3
	September 4	Kevin Costner	1–2
	September 18	Arsenio Hall	1–2
	October 2	Bruce Willis	1–2
	October 16	Those Hollywood Feuds	1–2
	October 30	Candice Bergen, Al Pacino's Comeback, Bon Jovi	2–4
	November 13	The 10 Sexiest	2–3
	November 27	Mick Jagger	3–6
	December 11	Paula Abdul	3–6

Year	Issue	Description	Value ($)
1990	January 8	1989 Yearbook Issue . . . Kim Basinger, Madonna, Paula Abdul, The Stones, The Who, Michelle Pfeiffer, Meg Ryan, Andie MacDowell, Cher, John Travolta, Jack Nicholson	2–4
	January 22	Tom Cruise	1–2
	February 5	Who's In and Who's Out	1–2
	February 19	Paul and Linda McCartney	3–6
	March 5	Janet Jackson	3–6
	March 19	Elvis Presley . . . TV's Portrait, Fashion Issue	3–5
	April 2	Michelle Pfeiffer, New Goddesses	2–4
	April 16	The 10 Sexiest Bachelors	1–2
	April 30	Richard Gere	1–2
	May 14	The 10 Most Beautiful Women	2–4
	May 28	Inside Twin Peaks	3–6
	June 11	Richard Grieco, Judy Belushi	1–2
	June 25	Annual Readers' Poll Special	1–2
	July 9	Summer Double Issue Special	2–3
	August 6	Tom Cruise, Andrew Dice Clay	1–2
	August 20	Harrison Ford	2–4
	September 3	Mel Gibson	1–2
	September 17	Demi Moore	2–4
	October 1	Ken Olin	1–2
	October 15	Arsenio Hall, Madonna: The Struggle to Stay on Top, Backstage with the Hottest Girl Groups . . . Seduction, En Vogue, The Allure of James Dean, Kim Basinger, Paula Abdul	2–4
	October 29	The 10 Sexiest Stars	2–4
	November 12	Patrick Swayze	1–2
	November 26	The US Heavy 100	2–4
	December 10	Dennis Quaid	1–2
1991–present			1–2

TV Guide

⊰✢⊱

To the collector of *TV Guide* magazine, back issues are as treasured as bars of gold, fine paintings, or rare coins. Collectors' dedication for this publication is so widely known that even an episode of *Seinfeld* centered on a collector's obsession with acquiring every issue. Most *TV Guide* collectors, however, are less interested in having complete runs than in purchasing the issues that feature a specific star or show. Why do people collect *TV Guide?* The reasons are varied. For many people, vintage *TV Guide*s evoke happy feelings of the simpler days of youth. They are willing to pay a price to recapture these fond memories. They also hunger for information on television shows not found in reference books and are willing to pay a price for this information. Collectors also want memorabilia from their favorite shows. A *TV Guide* may contain a cover article on the subject, an inside story and photos, a program blurb, *TV Guide* "Close-Up," or a full- or half-page program ad. Video collectors may want the *TV Guide* for a week of shows they have on tape. There are some collectors who are trying to complete an entire run of the magazine. Other collectors may want a full set of Fall Previews; a copy from their birth date each year; only cowboys or one particular star or show; animals; Emmy Award issues; Olympic issues; and so on. The subjects of interest are virtually limitless. The current popular collecting trend is issues of *TV Guide* featuring pop culture show covers. Such shows as *Batman, Superman, The Addams Family, I Love Lucy, I Dream of Jeannie, Xena: Warrior Princess, Buffy, The Vampire Slayer, Seinfeld, The X-Files, Star Trek, Lost in Space, Gilligan's Island,* and *The Brady Bunch* are but a few. Owing to the popularity of cable TV, particularly *TV Land* and *Nick at Nite,* some subjects may be popular one year but actually drop in value the next. For instance, *Route 66* and *Dennis the Menace* issues were very popular when these shows were on Nickelodeon and *Nick at Nite* during the mid 1980s and early 1990s, but are not so popular now.

The history of *TV Guide* magazine actually goes back to before World War II, when TV stations would send out weekly program schedule cards to TV-set owners. As TV programming grew there arose a need for publications that specialized in TV programming listings. The digest size became the norm because of its convenient size. The first of these digest-size TV log magazines was *TV Forecast,* based in Chicago, which began on May 16, 1948. Within a few weeks *Television Guide,* based in New York City, and *Teleguide,* based in the Washington-Baltimore area, began on June 14, 1948. During the next five years, similar publications sprang up in other cities with two or more stations. These included the following:

> *TV Forecast* (later *TV Guide*) of New England
> *Local Television* (later *TV Digest*) of Philadelphia
> *TV Image* of Los Angeles
> *TV Digest* of Pittsburgh
> *TV Digest* of Atlanta
> *TV News* of Indianapolis
> *Tele-Views* (later *TV Forecast*) of Davenport–Rock Island–Moline
> *TV Today* of Michigan–Ohio–Ontario
> *TV Dial* of Cincinnati–Dayton–Columbus
> *TV Life* of Portland, Oregon
> *TV Press* of Louisville, Kentucky
> *TV Preview* of Dallas, Texas
> *TV Showtimes* (later *TV Forecast*) of Minneapolis–St. Paul
> *TV Weekly* of Denver, Colorado
> *TV Review* of St. Louis, Missouri

For the advanced collector, these pre-Lucy's baby issues, called "pre-nationals," are the major focus of interest. In many ways this pre-1953 era is still unexplored, as new titles are discovered each year. One title recently discovered, although not of digest size, is *Phillipp's Television Weekly,* of New York City. This issue is dated January 26, 1948 (Vol.1, #1), which predates the original *TV Forecast* by almost four months. It is still not known how long this publication lasted. The first issue of New York's *Television Guide* and the first issue of Chicago's *TV Forecast* were sent out free to all TV-set owners. *TV Forecast*'s first issue's circulation was 16,000 copies; five years later it had climbed to 192,549. New York City's *Television Guide*'s average circulation in 1948 was just 8,557. In 1949 it was 42,972; in 1950, 157,461; in 1951, 292,341; and in 1952, 359,297. Compare this to 1998's average circulation of just a little over 15,000,000 per issue.

The first "national" *TV Guide* was dated April 3, 1953, and had Lucy's baby on the cover. Lucille Ball had tied the birth of her son to the plot of her popular TV show, and this seemed to be the obvious point to start the national publication. *TV Guide*'s average circulation in 1953 was 1,481,654. Circulation of *TV Guide*s peaked in 1974–1975 at around 19,000,000, and *TV Guide*s from these years are very common. Circulation started to dip after that, to a low of about 15,000,000 by the end of 1998 and into 1999. The person appearing on the most national *TV Guide* covers is Lucille Ball, with twenty-nine covers to her credit.

In 1990 *TV Guide* experimented with different cover layouts on the same issue in different cities. For example, the November 3, 1990, issue out of Chicago had only the *Cheers* cast on the cover, while the western Illinois edition had the cast of *Cheers* and three other subjects on the cover. In 1991 *TV Guide* tested a larger format (7½ by 10 inches) from March 30 to November 30 in only three cities: Nashville; Rochester, New York; and Pittsburgh. Sixteen of these covers were different from the digest's national edition. In 1996 *TV Guide* decided to go with different regional covers extensively. Instead of the usual 52 different covers per year, 1996 had more than 104. In 1997 there were more than 125 and in 1998 there were 125 different covers, not including the weeks of June 27–July 3 (Hanson) and July 4–10 (Matt Lauer) which had more than 50 different cover variations each week, depending upon the edition.

Other rare covers from 1998 would be the Mark McGwires from the week of September 26–October 2. These covers were only sold within a couple hundred miles of St. Louis and had four different covers: Home run numbers one, fifty, sixty, and sixty-one. The same week Sammy Sosa was only on the Chicago edition. The rest of the country got an *Ally McBeal* cover.

In 1998 *TV Guide* merged with the cable weekly *Total TV* to produce a new larger format *TV Guide* edition for various cable outlets. Newspaper TV supplements are also becoming increasingly popular. These are the *TV Guide* look-alikes which come in weekend newspapers. Some titles from the 1950s and 1960s were actually distributed nationally but with local TV listings like *TV Guide*. Many of the covers of these supplements have beautiful color photographs that rival those appearing on and in *TV Guide*.

Related collectibles would include foreign *TV Guide*–type magazines. Australia's *TV Week* and *TV Times* have published many gorgeous covers from the 1960s of *Star Trek, Bonanza, Family Affair, The Partridge Family, Get Smart, The Man From U.N.C.L.E., The Avengers* and *The Saint* not found in the United States. Other collectibles would include the *TV Guide* game published by Trivia, Inc., in 1984; the promotional 45 rpm record *"TV Guide* Presents Elvis Presley" from 1956; *TV Guide* cookbooks, crossword puzzle books, aprons, swizzle sticks, and other items. Another recent collectible is a 1991 *TV Guide* 200th Issue Commemorative Edition with Lucille Ball on the cover.

The value of vintage *TV Guides* is based on a number of variables. Purists would want the cardboard centerfold intact, as it is counted in the page numbering sequence. Crossword puzzles that are filled in, particularly in pen, lower values for some collectors, as do address labels on the covers. In the mid-1950s this was less of a problem because most cities used address labels on the back cover. New York City editions tend to bring higher prices because of their more detailed program listings. It is difficult to find mint copies of early *TV Guides* as most were used for one week and then discarded. Common cover flaws include torn off address label marks, fingerprints, coffee mug marks, rodent damage, staple tears, heavy creases, and water damage. The issues from the 1950s and early 1960s seem to hold up the best because they are printed on heavier paper stock. *TV Guides* are rarely found in mint condition because of the thin paper used for the covers, as well as the excessive handling they receive because of their usefulness as guides. An example of this is the *Green Hornet* cover; dated October 29, 1966, it is virtually impossible to find in near mint to mint condition owing to its inferior cover paper. By contrast, the March 26, 1966, issue with Batman on the cover was printed on a heavier cover paper and with a different printing process, and copies of this issue in the higher grades of condition are not difficult to find. Professionally bound volumes were given to many TV stations in the 1950s and 1960s. Although these volumes contain complete *TV Guides*, often in mint condition, demand for them is surprisingly limited.

Where can vintage *TV Guides* be found? Collectors in Boise, Idaho, or even locales like Miami or Phoenix should know that they are not going to find a "Lucy's Baby" issue at a neighborhood garage sale or local flea market. The original ten cities to carry national *TV Guide* on

April 3, 1953, were Boston, Chicago, Cincinnati–Dayton–Columbus, Davenport–Rock Island–Moline, Los Angeles, Minneapolis–St. Paul, New York City, Philadelphia, Washington-Baltimore, and Wilkes Barre–Scranton-Binghamton. Sources for locating old *TV Guide*s include flea markets, garage sales, estate sales, auctions, the Internet, trade papers, paper collectible shows, back-issue magazine shops, and mail-order dealers. One of the most respected mail-order dealers is TV Guide Specialists, Box 20, Macomb, Illinois 61445 (*www.oldtvguides.com*) e-mail: info@oldtvguides.com.

TV GUIDE VALUES

(Pre-National)

Year	Issue	Number	Description	Value ($)
1948	Volume I			
	June 14–20	#1	Gloria Swanson and Lois Wilson cover	150–300+
	June 21–27	#2		50–100
	June 28	#3	Video Venus	30–60
	July 5–11	#4	Angel (wrestler) and poet cover, Howdy Doody	30–60
	July 12–18	#5	Pixie Playtime	30–60
	July 19–25	#6		30–60
	July 25	#7		30–60
	August 2–8	#8		30–60
	August 9–15	#9		30–60
	August 16–22	#10		25–50
	August 23–29	#11	Harness Racing, Television Facts	25–50
	August 30	#12		25–50
	September 6–12	#13	Dance cover	25–50
	September 13–19	#14	Ed Sullivan's Toast of the Town	25–50
	September 20–26	#15	Football	25–50
	September 27	#16	Gene Autry cover and feature	25–50

Year	Issue	Number	Description	Value ($)
1948	October 2–8	#17	1948 World Series issue	30–60
	October 9–15	#18	Milton Berle cover and feature	25–50
	October 16–22	#19	Eddie Condon Jam Session	25–50
	October 23–29	#20	Fashions on Parade	25–50
	October 30	#21	Nature of Things	25–50
	November 6–12	#22	Bob Howard cover, contains feature story on Bob Smith and Howdy Doody	50–100
	November 13–19	#23	Hockey at the Garden	25–50
	November 20–26	#24	Bert Lytell/Television Playhouse cover	25–50
	November 27	#25	Goldberg by Goldberg	25–50
	December 4–10	#26	Lanny Ross	25–50
	December 11–17	#27	Danny Webb	25–50
	December 18–24	#28	Phil Silvers cover	25–50
	December 25	#29	Christmas issue	25–50
1949	Volume II			
	January 1–7	#1	Happy New Year issue	25–50
	January 8–14	#2	Cliff-hangers issue	25–50
	January 15–21	#3	Baseball at the Garden	25–50
	January 22–28	#4	Arthur Godfrey cover, Sid Caesar, Ed Sullivan	25–50
	January 29	#5	Kyle MacDonnell cover	20–40
	February 5–11	#6	Harry Conover cover	20–40

#52, 1951

#33, 1953

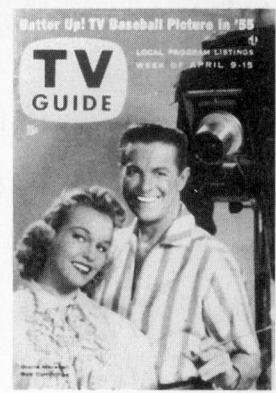

#106, 1955

#112, 1955

#151, 1956

#326, 1959

#522, 1963

#533, 1963

#9, 1953

Year	Issue	Number	Description	Value ($)
1949	February 12–18	#7	Jerry Mahoney cover	20–40
	February 19–25	#8	Morey Amsterdam cover, Ted Mack, Imogene Coca	20–40
	February 26	#9	Howdy Doody's Flub-a-Dub Feature	20–40
	March 5–11	#10	Howdy Doody's Flub-a Dub Feature	20–40
	March 12–18	#11	Joe DiMaggio and Mel Allen cover, Howdy Doody's Flub-a-Dub Feature	50–100
	March 19–25	#12	Manhattan Spotlight	20–40
	March 26	#13	Boxing: Chicago versus New York	20–40
	April 2–8	#14	Mother's Incorporated	20–40
	April 9–15	#15	Douglas Edwards and the News	20–40
	April 16–22	#16	Foodini's Easter Bunny cover	20–40
	April 23–29	#17	Roller Derby cover, Howdy Doody feature	20–40
	April 30	#18	Farmer's Daughter cover	20–40
	May 7–13	#19	TV Mother's Day cover, Boris Karloff: Ford Theater	20–40
	May 14–20	#20	TV Ballet	20–40
	May 21–27	#21	Gigi Durston cover	20–40

Year	Issue	Number	Description	Value ($)
1949	May 28	#22	General Dwight Eisenhower cover, Imogene Coca	20–40
	June 4–10	#23	Morton Downey cover	20–40
	June 11–17	#24	Charlie Chaplin cover	20–40
	June 18–24	#25	First Anniversary issue, The Year in TV	25–50
	June 25	#26	Olsen and Johnson cover	20–40
	July 2–8	#27	Bert Parks cover	20–40
	July 9–15	#28	Mama and Family cover	20–40
	July 16–22	#29	Mary Kay and Johnny cover	20–40
	July 23–29	#30	Peter W. Pixie cover, Ted Mack, Cliff Edwards	25–50
	July 30	#31	The Flying Man and the Helmet	20–40
	August 6–12	#32	Captain Video cover, Candid Camera	200–500+
	August 13–19	#33	Quiz Kids cover	20–40
	August 20–26	#34	Joan Diener cover, TV This Fall	25–50
	August 27	#35	Miss Reingold cover, Ed Sullivan, Art Carney	20–40
	September 3–9	#36	Cover of Kukla, Fran, and Ollie	25–50
	September 10–16	#37	Rita Colton cover	20–40
	September 17–23	#38	TV Football cover	20–40
	September 24–30	#39	Ted Mack cover, women wrestlers	20–40

Year	Issue	Number	Description	Value ($)
1949	October 1–7	#40	Joan Barton cover	20–40
	October 8–14	#41	Frankie Lane cover, Uncle David	15–30
	October 15–21	#42	Perry Como cover	15–30
	October 22–28	#43	Wendy Barrie cover	12–25
	October 29	#44	Bowling cover, Henry Aldrich feature	12–25
	November 5–11	#45	Gregg Sherwood cover, Victor Borge feature	12–25
	November 12–18	#46	Auction-Aire Show cast cover, Ralph Bellamy	12–25
	November 19–25	#47	Jack Carter cover Howdy Doody feature	20–40
	November 26	#48	Ed Wynn cover Chuck Wagon feature	15–30
	December 3–9	#49	The Truex cover	12–25
	December 10–16	#50	Jackie Gleason cover from The Life of Riley	100–300
	December 17–23	#51	Jimmy Powers cover	12–25
	December 24–30	#52	Milton Berle cover	20–40
1950	Volume III			
	January 7–13	#1	Kay Kyser cover	12–25
	January 14–20	#2	Bill Lawrence cover, Oliver Dragon feature	12–25
	January 21–27	#3	Dave Garroway cover	12–25

Year	Issue	Number	Description	Value ($)
1950	January 28	#4	Bert Parks cover, Mr. Magic feature	12–25
	February 4–10	#5	Katharine Hepburn cover, The Lone Ranger feature	50–100
	February 11–17	#6	Ed Sullivan cover, Uncle Fred feature	12–25
	February 18–24	#7	Junior Frolics' Farmer Grey cover	12–25
	February 25	#8	Wrestling on TV cover, The Lone Ranger feature, Dorothy Kilgallen	25–50
	March 4–10	#9	Golden Gloves cover, Magic Cottage feature	12–25
	March 11–17	#10	Morey Amsterdam cover, Howdy Doody feature	15–30
	March 18–24	#11	Pinhead cover, Captain Video feature	25–50
	March 25–31	#12	Eleanor Roosevelt cover, Robert Montgomery feature	12–25
	April 1–7	#13	Sid Caesar cover, Baseball, Mr. I. Magination	12–25
	April 8–14	#14	Happy Easter issue, Molly Goldberg feature	12–25
	April 15–21	#15	Jackie Robinson cover, Bob Hope, Judy Splinters	40–80

Year	Issue	Number	Description	Value ($)
1950	April 22–28	#16	Linda Danson cover, Kukla feature, Alan Young	12–25
	April 29	#17	Women of Wrestling cover, Imogene Coca, Dizzy Dean	12–25
	May 6–12	#18	Hopalong Cassidy cover, Howdy Doody, Henry Aldrich	150–300+
	May 13–19	#19	Milton Berle and his mother cover, Foodini	12–25
	May 20–26	#20	Viera Monkeys cover, Ed Sullivan, Snarky Parker	12–25
	May 27	#21	Roller Derby issue, Wilmethe Pigeon feature	12–25
	June 3–9	#22	Fay Emerson cover, Dennis James feature	12–25
	June 10–16	#23	Sam Renick and the Kentucky Derby cover, Cavalcade of Stars feature, Junior Talent Time	12–25
	June 17–23	#24	Kay Kyser cover, Second Anniversary issue	12–25
	June 24–30	#25	Laraine Day cover, Morey Amsterdam, Children's Hour, Baseball	12–25

Year	Issue	Number	Description	Value ($)
1950	July 1–7	#26	Marion Morgan cover, Happy Felton, Wendy Barrie	12–25
	July 8–14	#27	Ted Williams and Joe DiMaggio cover, Ripley's Believe It or Not, Ted Mack, Alan Young	75–150+
	July 15–21	#28	Magnificent Menasha cover, Mystery Rider, Joan Diener	12–25
	July 22–28	#29	Lynn Bari cover, Gene Autry, Jackie Gleason	12–25
	July 29	#30	Eva Marie Saint cover, Mr. Magic feature	12–25
	August 5–11	#31	Fred Allen and Jack Haley cover, TV Yesterday and Today, Big Top	15–30
	August 12–18	#32	Grace Kelly cover, Captain Video feature, Mama	50–100
	August 19–25	#33	Miss Reingold cover, Captain Video feature	50–100
	August 26	#34	Tennis cover, Rosie the Duck, Bob Emery feature	12–25
	September 2–8	#35	Howdy Doody cover, Ed Sullivan, Time for Beany	100–200+

Year	Issue	Number	Description	Value ($)
1950	September 9–15	#36	Eddie Cantor cover, Fireside Theatre	12–25
	September 16–22	#37	Groucho Marx, Frank Sinatra and Gang cover, TV's Golden Age, Sheriff Bob Dixon feature	35–75
	September 23–29	#38	Baseball issue, Rumpus Room, Edie Adams feature, Zoo Parade	12–25
	September 30	#39	Football issue, Danny Kaye, Bing Crosby	12–25
	October 7–13	#40	Alan Young cover, TV Rodeo, Fred Allen, Gabby Hayes feature	12–25
	October 14–20	#41	Miss TV 1950 cover, Max Liebman, Arthur Godfrey	12–25
	October 21–27	#42	Robert Montgomery cover, Space Cadet feature Leslie Nielsen	15–30
	October 28	#43	Jack Benny cover, Jerry Lester, Ed Herlihy	12–25
	November 4–10	#44	Imogene Coca cover, Sid Caeser, Panhandle Pete	12–25
	November 11–17	#45	Dean Martin and Jerry Lewis cover, Ted Steele, Can	

Year	Issue	Number	Description	Value ($)
1950	November 11–17	#45	You Top This? feature	40–80
	November 18–24	#46	The McCrays cover, Faye Emerson, Sheriff Bob Dixon feature	12–25
	November 25	#47	Howdy Doody and Gang cover, TV Kid Shows, The Merry Mailman feature	50–100+
	December 2–8	#48	Gertrude Berg cover, Break the Bank, Bob Emery	12–25
	December 9–15	#49	Walter Winchell cover, Danny Thomas, Dave Garroway	12–25
	December 16–22	#50	Marguerite Piazza cover, Captain Gleen	10–20
	December 23–29	#51	Jimmy Durante cover, Rosemary Clooney, Frank Sinatra feature	15–30
	Decamber 30	#52	Happy New Year issue, Snooky Lanson, Bill Hayes	10–20
1951	Volume IV			
	January 12	#1	Milton Berle cover, Beat the Clock, Magic Clown	12–25
	January 13–19	#2	Roller Derby issue, Groucho Marx, Dr. Wesley Young feature	12–25

Year	Issue	Number	Description	Value ($)
1951	January 20–26	#3	Sheriff Bob Dixon cover, Jackie Gleason, Charlton Heston	10–20
	January 27	#4	Jerry Lester cover, We the People, The Jolly Roger	10–20
	February 3–9	#5	Leave It to the Girls cast cover, Perry Como	10–20
	February 10–16	#6	Bert Parks cover, Buddy Rogers, Captain Video	20–40
	February 17–23	#7	Lilli Palmer cover, Space Barton, Arlene Francis	12–25
	February 24	#8	Big Town cast cover, Garry Moore, Howdy Doody's Princess Summer Fall Winter Spring feature	20–40
	March 3–9	#9	Jack Carter cover, Art Linkletter feature	10–20
	March 10–16	#10	Sid Caesar cover, How the Lone Ronger Found Silver	25–50
	March 17–23	#11	Jack McCarthy, Buster Crabbe, Hopalong Cassidy	10–20
	March 24–30	#12	Arthur Godfrey cover, Truth or Consequences	10–20
	March 29	#13	Horse Racers' issue, Sam	

Year	Issue	Number	Description	Value ($)
1951	March 29	#13	Levenson, Gene Autry	10–20
	April 7–13	#14	Super Circus's Mary Hartline, Bill Stern	10–20
	April 14–20	#15	Joe DiMaggio and Ted Williams cover, Steve Allen, Fireside Theatre	40–80+
	April 21–27	#16	Eddie Cantor cover, Captain Roots, Arthur Murray	10–20
	April 28	#17	Dagmar and Jerry Lester cover, Buster Crabbe	10–20
	May 5–11	#18	Nature Boy Rogers cover	7–15
	May 12–18	#19	Perry Como cover, Dennis James, John Conte	7–15
	May 19–25	#20	Ken Murray cover, Douglas Edwards, Jerry Mahoney	7–15
	May 26	#21	Frank Sinatra cover, Morton Downey, Roller Derby	30–60
	June 2–8	#22	Ralph Bellamy in Man Against Crime cover, Lady Wrestlers feature, Alan Dale	10–20
	June 9–15	#23	Groucho Marx cover, Amos 'n' Andy feature	25–50

Year	Issue	Number	Description	Value ($)
1951	June 16–22	#24	Milton Berle cover, Third Anniversary special	15–30
	June 23–29	#25	Dean Martin and Jerry Lewis cover, Bob Howard	25–50
	June 30	#26	Judy Raben . . . Miss WNBT cover, Ben Grauer	7–15
	July 7–13	#27	Sid Caesar and Imogene Coca cover, Color TV	12–25
	July 14–20	#28	How to Get a Baby on TV, Sheriff Bob Dixon	7–15
	July 21–27	#29	Roxanne cover, Freddy Martin, Hal Tunis	5–10
	July 28	#30	Bathing Suit cover, Story Theatre	5–10
	August 4–10	#31	My Friend Irma's Marie Wilson cover, Sammy Kaye, Is TV Too Sexy?	10–20
	August 11–17	#32	Kathy Norris cover, Strike It Rich, Star of the Family feature	5–10
	August 18–24	#33	Dagmar cover, Peggy Lee, Mel Torme, The Children's Hour feature	5–10
	August 25	#34	Jerry Lester cover, Captain Video, New TV Shows	7–15

Year	Issue	Number	Description	Value ($)
1951	August 31	#35	Special Kid's Shows cover, Twenty Questions	17–35
	September 7–13	#36	Sid Caesar and Imogene Coca cover, Fall Preview 1951–1952 Season Part I	30–60
	September 14–20	#37	Milton Berle cover, Fall Preview 1951–1952 Season Part II	30–60
	September 21–27	#38	Arthur Godfrey cover, Dennis James, TV Theme Song Titles	10–20
	September 28	#39	Groucho Marx and Red Skelton cover, The Lone Ranger, Somerset Maugham	25–50
	October 5–11	#40	Jimmy Durante as a New York Yankee cover, The Big Top, Herb Shriner	20–40
	October 12–18	#41	Bob Hope, Lucille Ball and Danny Thomas cover, Fall Preview 1951–1952 Season Part III	30–60
	October 19–25	#42	Martin Kane as Private Investigator cover, Lloyd Nolan, Tropical Fish on TV	10–20

Year	Issue	Number	Description	Value ($)
1951	October 26	#43	Bert Parks cover, Hopalong Cassidy's horse	15–30
	November 2–8	#44	Jack Benny, Dean Martin, Jerry Lewis, and others on cover, Laura Weber, Football	25–50
	November 9–15	#45	Jackie Gleason cover, Miss New York City TV	25–50
	November 16–22	#46	Frank Sinatra and Milton Berle cover, Johnny Olsen, Roller Derby	25–50
	November 23–29	#47	Howdy Doody cover, The Birthplace of TV, The 10 Most Exciting Men on TV	50–100+
	November 30	#48	Does TV Think You're Stupid, Bud Palmer	7–15
	December 7–13	#49	Agathon of the Jerry Lester Show cover, Ralph Bellamy feature	7–15
	December 14–20	#50	Cathy Hild cover, Ed Sullivan, Foreign Intrigue	7–15
	December 21–27	#51	Annual Awards Special, Walt Disney feature, the Crime Photographer	17–35
	December 28	#52	Roy Rogers cover, TV's 10 Most Exciting Men	25–50

Year	Issue	Number	Description	Value ($)
1952	Volume V			
	January 4–10	#1	Groucho Marx, Milton Berle, Arthur Godfrey, Sid Caesar, and Ed Sullivan cover, What's My Line	10–20
	January 11–17	#2	Red Skelton cover, Amos 'n' Andy feature	12–25
	January 18–24	#3	My Frient Irma's Marie Wilson, You Asked for It	10–20
	January 25–31	#4	A wonderful cover of Lucille Ball and Desi Arnaz: The Marriage That Fooled Hollywood, Ellery Queen	75–200+
	February 1–7	#5	Molly Goldberg cover, Mike Wallace, Donald O'Connor feature	10–20
	February 8–14	#6	Frances Langford cover, Carl Reiner, Mr. Wizard, Don Ameche	10–20
	February 15–21	#7	Harry Truman and Dwight Eisenhower cover, Bob and Ray, Dragnet	10–20
	February 22–28	#8	Captain Video cover, Tom Corbett, Space Patrol, Morey (George Washington) Amsterdam, Guy	

Year	Issue	Number	Description	Value ($)
1952	February 22–28	#8	Mitchell, great full-page+ advertisement for Beany & Cecil	40–80
	February 29	#9	Sid Caesar cover, Molly Goldberg, Dagmar, Tony Bennett feature	10–20
	March 7–13	#10	Arthur Godfrey cover, Little Ton-Ton	7–15
	March 14–20	#11	Dean Martin and Jerry Lewis cover, Buster Crabbe, TV Crime Shows	20–40
	March 21–27	#12	Bess Myerson cover, Robert Q. Lewis	5–10
	March 28	#13	Video's Dancing Daughters cover, The Whistling Wizard, Daytime Soap Operas	5–10
	April 4–10	#14	Marion Marlowe and Frank Parker cover, The Celanese Theatre, Kukla, Fran, and Ollie	5–10
	April 11–17	#15	Baseball cover, Sky King, Joe DiMaggio, Bishop Sheen Feature	10–20
	April 18–24	#16	Jimmy Durante cover, Kid Shows	10–20
	April 25	#17	Dagmar cover, Elizabeth Montgomery, Sky King	20–40

Year	Issue	Number	Description	Value ($)
1952	May 2–8	#18	Strike It Rich's Warren Hull, Groucho Marx, Bud Collyer, Bill Cullen	10–20
	May 9–15	#19	Peggy Wood of Mama cover, Alan Dale	10–20
	May 16–22	#20	Gene Autry cover, Garry Moore, Foreign Intrigue	50–100
	May 23–29	#21	Milton Berle cover, Martha Raye, Rootie Kazootie	15–30
	May 30	#22	Johnnie Ray cover, Irene Dunne, What's My Line	15–30
	June 6–12	#23	Lucille Ball and Desi Arnaz cover, Allen Funt, Joe Bolton, Arthur Godfrey	100–200+
	June 13–19	#24	Jackie Gleason cover, Robert Stack, Wally Cox, Charles Ruggles	20–40
	June 20–26	#25	Special Fourth Anniversary issue, Gabby Hayes	20–40
	June 27	#26	Jerry Mahoney and Paul Winchell cover, Art Carney	20–40
	July 4–10	#27	Bob Hope cover, Julius LaRosa, Larry Storch, Babe Ruth feature	10–20

Year	Issue	Number	Description	Value ($)
1952	July 11–17	#28	Jerry Lewis and Lou Costello cover, Ozzie and Harriet, Danny Thomas, Willie Mays	15–30
	July 18–24	#29	Groucho Marx cover, Dave Garroway, Jack Barry, the Chordettes	25–50
	July 25–31	#30	Sandra Spence of Pantomime Quiz, Robert Stack, Howdy Doody feature	10–20
	August 1–7	#31	Don Russell and Lee Joyce cover, Quick Trick Magic, Robert Q. Lewis	10–20
	August 8–14	#32	The Cisco Kid, Roy Rogers, and Hopalong Cassidy cover, The Cowboy Hall of Fame special feature, Al Pearce	50–100+
	August 15–21	#33	Cast of What's My Line cover, Special Patrol contest issue, Fred Astaire	10–20
	August 22–28	#34	Perry Como and Dinah Shore cover, Fall Preview Special Part I . . . 1952–1953 season	25–50

Year	Issue	Number	Description	Value ($)
1952	August 29	#35	Dorothy Collins cover, Morey Amsterdam, Space Patrol contest	10–20
	September 5–11	#36	Imogene Coca cover, Fall Preview Special Part II . . . 1952–1953 season	25–50
	September 12–18	#37	Lucille Ball and Milton Berle cover, Fall Preview Special Part III . . . 1952–1953 season	50–100
	September 19–25	#38	Dean Martin and Jerry Lewis, Jackie Gleason and Jimmy Durante cover, Fall Preview Special Part IV . . . 1952–1953 season	25–50
	September 26	#39	Roy Rogers cover, Jack Lemmon, Zoo Parade	50–100
	October 3–9	#40	My Friend Irma's Marie Wilson, Jim McKay, Paul Dixon show	5–10
	October 10–16	#41	Al Capp and his cartoon characters cover, the History of TV Guide, Tallulah Bankhead, Captain Video feature	10–20

Year	Issue	Number	Description	Value ($)
1952	October 17–23	#42	Arthur Godfrey cover, Your Show of Shows, Captain Video feature	10–20
	October 24–30	#43	Ed Sullivan and Walter Winchell cover, Arthur Godfrey, Ted Brown, Gabby Hayes	10–20
	October 29	#44	Marion Marlowe cover, Howdy Doody, Dennis Day	10–20
	November 7–13	#45	Reed Hadley of Racket Squad cover, Irene Wicker, Roller Derby	10–20
	November 14–20	#46	TV detectives cover special, Imogene Coca, Lady Wrestlers	15–30
	November 21–27	#47	Howdy Doody and Rootie Kazootie cover, Uncle David, Bishop Sheen, Groucho Marx	50–100
	November 28	#48	Perry Como, Eddie Fisher, Julius LaRosa and Patti Page, Terry and the Pirates, Italians on TV feature	10–20
	December 5–11	#49	Lucy Knoch cover, Wally Cox,	

Year	Issue	Number	Description	Value ($)
1952	December 5–11	#49	Red Skelton, the heroes of Space Patrol	10–20
	December 12–18	#50	Arthur Godfrey cover, Lucille Ball's baby, Dragnet, Space Patrol feature	10–20
	December 19–25	#51	Special Annual Awards issue, Howdy Doody	10–20
	December 26	#52	Jack Russell cover, Ricky and David Nelson, Gale Storm	20–40
1953	Volume VI			
	January 2–8	#1	Jackie Gleason cover, Carl Reiner, Mr. Wizard, Don Ameche	20–40
	January 9–15	#2	Dinah Shore cover, Joan Davis, Eve Arden, Gene Autry feature	10–20
	January 16–22	#3	Ed Sullivan cover, Abbott and Costello, Milton Berle feature	15–30
	January 23–29	#4	Marilyn Monroe cover	150–300+
	January 30	#5	Mary Hartline of Super Circus, Red Buttons, Bob Cummings, Jack Berry	10–20
	February 6–12	#6	Roxanne cover, the Stars' Most	

Year	Issue	Number	Description	Value ($)
1953	February 6–12	#6	Embarrassing Moments special feature	12–25
	February 13–19	#7	Kukla, Fran, and Ollie cover, John Cameron Swayze	15–30
	February 20–26	#8	Julius LaRosa and Lu Ann Simms cover, Slick Trick Quigley, The Macy's TV Party	7–15
	February 27	#9	Groucho Marx and George Fenneman cover, June Valli, Johnnie Ray, George Jessel	15–30
	March 6–12	#10	Jimmy Durante cover, Daytime Soap Operas, the Women of Space Patrol	15–30
	March 13–19	#11	Janette Davis cover, George Burns and Gracie Allen, Academy Awards	10–20
	March 20–26	#12	I Love Lucy's Fred and Ethel Mertz cover, Joe Bolton feature	50–100
	March 27	#13	John Forsythe cover, Betty Furness, Range Rider	10–20

TV GUIDE VALUES

(National)

Note: First nationwide distribution begins with April 3, 1953, issue.

Year	Issue	Number	Description	Value ($)
1953	April 3–9	#1	Lucille Ball's $50,000,000 Baby	150–300+
	April 10–16	#2	Jack Webb cover, You Asked for It, The Star Theatre	35–75
	April 17–23	#3	Milton Berle, Lucille Ball, Sid Caesar and Imogene Coca cover, See It Now	40–80
	April 24–30	#4	Ralph Edwards cover, Wally Cox and Mr. Peepers, Howdy Doody's Princess Summer Fall Winter Spring	30–60
	April 24–30	#5	Eve Arden cover, The Homicide Squad, Dick Tracy, Lucille Ball	15–30
	May 8–14	#6	Arthur Godfrey cover, Your Hit Parade, Roy Rogers	15–30
	May 14–21	#7	Ricky and David Nelson, The Fireside Theatre	50–100
	May 22–28	#8	Red Buttons cover, Howdy Doody, Ted Mack	25–50
	May 29	#9	England's Queen Elizabeth, Mickey Mantle, Roy	

Year	Issue	Number	Description	Value ($)
1953	May 29	#9	Campanella, Bob Hope: Quick Change Artist, Ralph Edwards, Donald O'Connor: Old-Time Song and Dance Man, Bishop Sheen	20–40
	June 5–11	#10	Dean Martin and Jerry Lewis cover, Beat the Clock	20–40
	June 12–18	#11	Eddie Fisher cover, Bob and Ray	12–25
	June 19–25	#12	Ed Sullivan cover, My Friend Irma, Douglas Edwards	10–20
	June 26	#13	Dinah Shore cover, Dean Martin and Jerry Lewis	15–30
	July 3–9	#14	Perry Como cover, TV Playhouse, Mary Stewart	12–24
	July 10–16	#15	Dave Garroway cover, TV's Oddest Jobs	10–20
	July 17–23	#16	Lucille Ball and Desi Arnaz cover, Kukla, Fran, and Ollie, House Party	35–75
	July 24–30	#17	Groucho Marx cover, The Goldbergs, Hopalong Cassidy	25–50
	July 31	#18	Sid Caesar and Imogene Coca	

Year	Issue	Number	Description	Value ($)
1953	July 31	#18	cover, Gene Autry, TV's top tunes	10–20
	August 7–13	#19	Ray Milland cover, Gale Storm and My Little Margie, Roy Rogers	10–20
	August 14–20	#20	Patti Page cover, Martin Kane, The Range Rider	15–30
	August 21–27	#21	Super Circus cover, Fred Allen, Teresa Brewer, Kit Carson	10–20
	August 28	#22	Jayne and Audrey Meadows cover, Bert Parks, Jimmy Durante, Milton Berle, Bob Hope, Tales of the City	15–30
	September 4–10	#23	Mr. Peepers's Wally Cox cover, Juvenile Jury, The Medallion Theater	10–20
	September 11–17	#24	Joan Caulfield and Ralph Edwards cover, Betty Furness, What's My Line, Marlin Perkins	10–20
	September 18–24	#25	First National Fall Preview issue for 1953–1954 TV season	50–100
	September 25	#26	George Reeves as Superman cover, Bob and Ray	200–400+

Year	Issue	Number	Description	Value ($)
1953	October 2–8	#27	Red Skelton cover, Video Theatre, Gene Autry	10–20
	October 9–15	#28	Bishop Sheen cover, Dorothy Kilgallen, George Jessel	10–20
	October 16–22	#29	Beauty contest winners cover, Dean Martin and Jerry Lewis, Paul Winchell	10–20
	October 23–29	#30	Arthur Godfrey cover, Howdy Doody, David Selznick	15–30
	October 30	#31	Kukla and Buelah Witch cover, Joan Davis and I Married Joan, My Favorite Husband	15–30
	November 6–12	#32	Warren Hull cover, Leo G. Carroll and Topper, The Life of Riley	15–30
	November 13–19	#33	Jimmy Durante cover, Ray Bolger, Mary Martin, Ed Sullivan, Carl Reiner	10–20
	November 20–26	#34	Julius LaRosa and Dorothy McGuire cover, Ted Mack's Amateur Hour, Danny Thomas and Make Room for Daddy	15–30

Year	Issue	Number	Description	Value ($)
1953	November 27	#35	Lugene Sanders as Babs Riley, Julius LaRosa, Natalie Wood	15–30
	December 4–10	#36	Loretta Young cover, The Dave Garroway Show	15–30
	December 11–17	#37	Dragnet's Jack Webb cover, Jungle Jim, Ramar of the Jungle	15–30
	December 18–24	#38	Bob Hope cover, The Jack Paar Show	10–20
	December 25–31	#39	Perry Como, Eddie Fisher and Patti Page Christmas Special, The Big Top, Doctor I.Q.	15–30
1954	January 1–7	#40	Bing Crosby cover, TV forecast for '54, Captain Video: "I'll be down to get you in a space ship, honey," Bing Crosby's TV debut, Jackie Gleason's dancing girls, Ray Bloch, Eddie Fisher	15–30
	January 8–14	#41	Joan Caulfield cover, Foreign Intrigue, Twenty Questions	7–15
	January 15–21	#42	Martha Raye cover, Red	

Year	Issue	Number	Description	Value ($)
1954	January 15–21	#42	Skelton, Hopalong Cassidy, Paul Winchell	7–15
	January 22–28	#43	Jayne Meadows and Joan Bennett cover, Your Show of Shows, Kate Smith	10–20
	January 29	#44	Robert Montgomery cover, Maria Riva, Jack Palance, Elizabeth Montgomery	10–20
	February 5–11	#45	Jack Benny cover, Jack Benny May Quit Radio, The Pied Piper of TV, Rocky Graziano, Brandon De Wilde: TV's Jamie, The Jackie Gleason Show, Perry Como	10–20
	February 12–18	#46	Red Skelton cover, Buick Berle Show, The Lucille Ball/Desi Arnaz Movie	10–20
	February 19–25	#47	Ann Sothern cover, Racket Squad	5–10
	February 26	#48	Liberace cover, I Love Lucy, TV Circus, I Remember Mama	10–20
	March 5–11	#49	Frank Parker and Marion Marlowe	

Year	Issue	Number	Description	Value ($)
1954	March 5–11	#49	cover, Danny Thomas and Make Room for Daddy, Lassie	7–15
	March 12–18	#50	Maria Riva cover, Jack Palance, Ronald Reagan: Death Valley Days, Eve Arden: Our Miss Brooks	10–20
	March 19–25	#51	Groucho Marx cover, The Spike Jones Show	12–25
	March 26	#52	Jackie Gleason cover, Space Cadet	12–25
	April 2–8	#53	Eve Arden cover: Our Miss Brooks, Inner Sanctum, Rocket Rangers	15–30
	April 9–15	#54	Milton Berle and Charie Applewhite cover, Private Secretary	7–15
	April 16–22	#55	TV Guide awards annual, Duffy's Tavern	10–20
	April 23–29	#56	Lucille Ball cover, Arnold Stang, Milton Berle, Arlene Francis, Public Defender	25–50
	May 7–13	#58	Ozzie and Harriet, Ricky and David Nelson cover, Annie Oakley	30–60
	May 14–20	#59	Frank Sinatra cover, Your Show	

Year	Issue	Number	Description	Value ($)
1954	May 14–20	#59	of Shows, Jonathan Winters	12–25
	May 21–27	#60	Wally Cox and Patricia Benoit cover, Martin Manulis, Mr. and Mrs. North	10–20
	May 28	#61	My Little Margie's Gale Storm cover, Wally Cox and Mr. Peepers, Imogene Coca	15–30
	June 4–10	#62	Arthur Godfrey cover, Topper, Gene Autry	7–15
	June 11–17	#63	Allen Young and Ben Blue cover, The Roy Rogers Show, Douglas Fairbanks, Jr.	7–15
	June 18–24	#64	Ed Sullivan and Rise Stevens cover, Bud Abbott and Lou Costello	10–20
	June 27	#65	Buffalo Bob and Howdy Doody cover, You Asked for It, Mr. District Attorney	30–60
	July 2–8	#66	I Married Joan's Jim Backus and Joan Davis Cover, The Joe Palooka Story, Pat Brady	15–30
	July 9–16	#67	Arlene Francis cover, Mr. District Attorney, Ray Bolger	10–20

Year	Issue	Number	Description	Value ($)
1954	July 17–23	#68	Roy Rogers cover, The Big Top, Horror Shows on TV	30–60
	July 24–30	#69	Jack Webb and Ann Robinson cover, Jack Paar, Pinky Lee	5–10
	July 31	#70	Life of Riley's William Bendix cover, I Love Lucy, Merv Griffin	15–30
	August 7–13	#71	Perry Como cover, Elizabeth Montgomery, Jackie Gleason, Jimmy and Tommy Dorsey	15–30
	August 14–20	#72	Dean Martin and Jerry Lewis cover, Laurel and Hardy, Bud Abbott and Lou Costello	25–50
	August 21–27	#73	Steve Allen and Jayne Meadows cover, Jack Paar, Dorothy McGuire	15–30
	August 28	#74	Roxanne cover, Red Skelton, Liberace	10–20
	September 4–10	#75	Eddie Fisher cover, Dragnet, Mickey Rooney	10–20
	September 11–17	#76	Betty Hutton cover, Wrestling	5–10
	September 18–24	#77	Liberace cover, TV Westerns, Private Secretary	10–20

Year	Issue	Number	Description	Value ($)
1954	September 25	#78	Special Fall Preview Issue	30–60
	October 2–8	#79	Dick Powell and Teresa Wright cover, Polly Bergen	5–10
	October 9–15	#80	Lucille Ball cover, Richard Boone, Private Secretary	20–40
	October 16–22	#81	Red Buttons cover, Meet Corliss Archer, Ginger Rogers	10–20
	October 23–29	#82	Walt Disney and his creations cover: Why Walt Disney Changed His Mind About TV, Peter Lawford	20–40
	October 30	#83	Joan Caulfield and Barry Nelson, Anne Francis, Grace Kelly	15–30
	November 6–12	#84	George Burns and Gracie Allen cover, Marilyn Monroe, People Are Funny	15–30
	November 13–19	#85	Liberace and Joanne Rio cover, Captain Video, Space Patrol	10–20
	November 20–26	#86	This Is Your Life's Ralph Edwards cover, Vivian Vance, Father Knows Best	7–15

Year	Issue	Number	Description	Value ($)
1954	November 27	#87	Peter Lawford cover, Lassie, Steve Allen	5–10
	December 4–10	#88	George Gobel cover, December Bride, Walt Disney, Howdy Doody	15–30
	December 11–17	#89	Marion Marlowe cover, December Bride, Ronald Reagan	5–10
	December 18–24	#90	Imogene Coca cover, Joyce Randolph, Sherlock Holmes	10–20
	December 25–31	#91	Ozzie and Harriet, David and Ricky Nelson Christmas Cover, Lucille Ball, Space Patrol, Elizabeth Montgomery	25–50
1955	January 1–7	#92	Loretta Young cover, Jackie Gleason, Disneyland	10–20
	January 8–14	#93	Arthur Godfrey cover, George Gobel, Disneyland	10–20
	January 15–21	#94	I've Got a Secret cast cover, Johnny Carson, Disneyland	10–20
	January 22–28	#95	Ed Sullivan cover, Disneyland	10–20
	January 29	#96	Martha Raye cover, Sherlock Holmes	7–15

Year	Issue	Number	Description	Value ($)
1955	February 5–11	#97	Edward R. Murrow cover, Milton Berle, Vampira	7–15
	February 12–18	#98	Your Hit Parade cast cover, Tennessee Ernie Ford, Dagmar	7–15
	February 19–25	#99	Sid Caesar cover, Faye Emerson, Make Room for Daddy	7–15
	February 26	#100	Steve Allen and Judy Holliday cover, Rin Tin Tin	10–20
	March 5–11	#101	Liberace cover, Lucille Ball, Mary Martin, Disneyland	10–20
	March 12–18	#102	Dinah Shore cover, Bob Cummings, Henry Fonda	10–20
	March 19–25	#103	The Honeymooners' Ed Norton (Art Carney) cover, Tennessee Ernie Ford, Richard Boone, Ozzie and Harriet, David and Ricky Nelson	30–60+
	March 26	#104	Eve Arden and Gale Gordon cover, The Millionaire, Rin Tin Tin	10–20
	April 2–8	#105	Tony Martin cover, Marilyn	

Year	Issue	Number	Description	Value ($)
1955	April 2–8	#105	Monroe, Lone Wolf	15–30
	April 9–15	#106	Bob Cummings and Gloria Marshall cover, Donald O'Connor, Eddie Cantor	5–10
	April 16–22	#107	Garry Moore cover, I Love Lucy, Walt Disney's Mickey Mouse	12–25
	April 23–29	#108	My Little Margie's Gale Storm cover, Liberace, Stan Laurel and Oliver Hardy	12–25
	April 30	#109	Walt Disney's Davy Crockett, Fess Parker cover, Lucille Ball, Harpo Marx, June Lockhart	25–50
	May 7–13	#110	Peggy Wood cover, Captain Midnight, Captain Gallant	7–15
	May 14–20	#111	Perry Como cover, The Little Rascals, Steve Allen	12–25
	May 21–27	#112	Jackie Gleason and Audrey Meadows cover, Jayne and Audrey Meadows	25–50
	May 28	#113	Ralph Edwards cover, Dean	

Year	Issue	Number	Description	Value ($)
1955	May 28	#113	Martin and Jerry Lewis, Humphrey Bogart	10–20
	June 4–10	#114	Eddie Fisher cover, Roy Rogers	10–20
	June 11–17	#115	Annie Oakley's Gail Davis cover, Liberace	10–20
	June 18–24	#116	Danny Thomas cover and story	10–20
	June 25	#117	Sid Caesar cover, Gale Storm, the Whiting Sisters	10–20
	July 2–8	#118	Lassie and Rin Tin Tin cover, Soldiers of Fortune	12–25
	July 9–15	#119	Patti Page cover, Captain Gallant, Desi Arnaz	10–20
	July 16–22	#120	Julius LaRosa cover, Marilyn Monroe	12–25
	July 23–29	#121	Jack Webb and Janet Leigh cover, Ed Sullivan, Make Room for Daddy	12–25
	July 30	#122	Lucille Ball and Desi Arnaz cover, Wally Cox: Mr. Peepers, Tony Randall	15–30
	August 6–12	#123	House Party's Art Linkletter cover, Julius LaRosa, Buddy Ebsen	10–20
	August 13–19	#124	Bud Collyer cover, Mel Blanc, The Cisco Kid	5–10

Year	Issue	Number	Description	Value ($)
1955	August 20–26	#125	The $64,000 Question's Hal March cover, Hopalong Cassidy, Johnny Carson	5–10
	August 27	#126	Groucho Marx cover, Jack Benny's Rochester	15–30
	September 3–9	#127	Johnny Carson cover, Father Knows Best, My Little Margie	10–20
	September 10–16	#128	Arthur Godfrey cover, Patti Page, Garry Moore, The Ames Brothers	10–20
	September 17–23	#129	Milton Berle and Esther Williams cover, Frank Sinatra, Judy Garland	10–20
	September 24–30	#130	1955–1956 Fall Preview special, Andy Devine: Andy's Gang, Jackie Gleason and The Honeymooners	25–50
	October 1–7	#131	Mickey Mouse Club cover, The Honeymooners, December Bride	25–50
	October 8–14	#132	George Burns and Gracie Allen cover . . . How Gracie Allen Gets That Way, Ed Murrow Comes to Call, The younger	

Year	Issue	Number	Description	Value ($)
1955	October 8–14	#132	set loves TV . . . TV toys: Howdy Doody, Davy Crockett, Superman, Pinky Lee, and others	15–30
	October 15–21	#133	The Medic's Richard Boone cover, The Honeymooners, Pinky Lee	10–20
	October 22–28	#134	George Gobel cover, Mary Martin, Jackie Gleason, Perry Como, Milton Berle	10–20
	October 29	#135	Sergeant Bilko's Phil Silvers cover, The Millionaire, Robin Hood	12–25
	November 5–11	#136	Nanette Fabray cover, Jack Paar	5–10
	November 12–18	#137	Liberace cover, Phil Silvers: Sergeant Bilko, Our Miss Brooks: Eve Arden	5–10
	November 19–25	#138	Jack Benny cover, The $64,000 Question, Peggy King	7–15
	November 26	#139	Martha Raye cover, I Love Lucy, Gunsmoke	6–12
	December 3–9	#140	Peter Lind Hayes and Mary Healy cover, Alfred	

Year	Issue	Number	Description	Value ($)
1955	December 3–9	#140	Hitchcock Presents, TV's horses	5–10
	December 10–16	#141	Lucille Ball cover, The Ding Dong School	10–20
	December 17–23	#142	Robert Montgomery cover, Sheena of the Jungle	5–10
	December 24–30	#143	Special Christmas issue, Ricky and David Nelson, Disneyland	12–25
	December 31	#144	The People's Choice's Dog, Cleo cover, Lassie	6–12
1956	January 7–13	#145	Arthur Godfrey cover, Long John Silver, The Mickey Mouse Club	6–12
	January 14–20	#146	Loretta Young cover, Dragnet, Highway Patrol	6–12
	January 21–27	#147	Lawrence Welk cover, Tony Randall, Wyatt Earp	5–10
	January 28	#148	Janis Paige cover, Disney animation	5–10
	February 4–10	#149	Ed Sullivan and Judy Tyler cover, Sergeant Preston of the Yukon	5–10
	February 11–17	#150	Perry Como cover, The Honeymooners	10–20

Year	Issue	Number	Description	Value ($)
1956	February 18–24	#151	Jimmy Durante cover, Fireside Theatre, Death Valley Days	5–10
	February 25	#152	Gisele Mackenzie cover, Liberace, Sergeant Bilko	5–10
	March 3–9	#153	Hal March and Lynn Dollar cover, Ann Sothern, Eve Arden: Our Miss Brooks	5–10
	March 10–16	#154	Spring Byington and Frances Rafferty cover, Julius LaRosa, Super Circus	5–10
	March 17–23	#155	Lilli Palmer and Maurice Evans cover, Captain Kangaroo, Meet the Press	5–10
	March 24–30	#156	Dave Garroway cover, Brave Eagle, Ernie Kovacs	5–10
	March 31	#157	Arlene Francis and John Daly cover, Wyatt Earp, Dragnet, Beat the Clock Show	5–10
	April 7–13	#158	Garry Moore and Jayne Meadows cover, Groucho Marx, Lassie, Rin Tin Tin, Sid Caesar	5–10

Year	Issue	Number	Description	Value ($)
1956	April 14–20	#159	Grace Kelly, Princess of Monaco cover, Alfred Hitchcock, Sheena of the Jungle	12–25
	April 21–27	#160	Nanette Fabray cover, Fred Allen, I Love Lucy, Lawrence Welk	5–10
	April 28	#161	Red Skelton cover, Annie Oakley, Our Miss Brooks	5–10
	May 4–11	#162	Mitzi Gaynor and George Gobel cover, Ernie Kovacs, You Asked for It	5–10
	May 12–18	#163	Robin Hood's Richard Green cover, Oscar Levant	5–10
	May 19–25	#164	Sergeant Bilko's Phil Silvers cover, Your Hit Parade, Death Valley Days	10–20
	May 26	#165	Lawrence Welk and Alice Lon cover, Sergeant Preston of the Yukon, Liberace	5–10
	June 2–8	#166	Sid Caesar and Janet Blair cover, The Mickey Mouse Club, Annie Oakley	5–10

Year	Issue	Number	Description	Value ($)
1956	June 9–15	#167	Patti Page cover, Your Hit Parade, Ernie Kovacs, Disneyland	10–20
	June 16–22	#168	Father Knows Best cast cover, Sheena of the Jungle	15–30
	June 23–29	#169	Steve Allen cover, Jayne Mansfield, Roy Rogers	10–20
	June 30	#170	Love That Bob's Robert Cummings cover, The Lone Ranger	10–20
	July 7–13	#171	Lassie cover, Robin Hood, Elvis Presley feature	15–30
	July 14–20	#172	Sheila MacRae cover, Johnny Carson	5–10
	July 21–27	#173	Bill Lundigan and Mary Costa, Mickey Dolenz: Circus Boy, Red Skelton, Groucho Marx	10–20
	July 28	#174	Annie Oakley's Gail Davis cover, Cheyenne, Super Circus	10–20
	August 4–10	#175	The People's Choice's Jackie Cooper and Cleo cover, Milton Berle	6–12
	August 11–17	#176	The 1956 Democratic	

Year	Issue	Number	Description	Value ($)
1956	August 11–17	#176	Convention special	5–10
	August 18–24	#177	The 1956 Republican Convention special	5–10
	August 25–31	#178	Esther Williams cover, George Burns and Gracie Allen, I Love Lucy, Tennessee Ernie Ford	10–20
	September 1–7	#179	Alice Lon cover, Rosemary DeCamp, Wyatt Earp	5–10
	September 8–14	#180	Elvis Presley cover, Elvis in the Army, Ernie Kovacs	50–100+
	September 15–21	#181	1956–1957 Fall Preview special	20–40
	September 22–28	#182	Hal March cover, Elvis Presley Part II, Child Actors special feature	25–50
	September 29	#183	Jackie Gleason cover, The Lone Ranger, Elvis Presley in the Army Part III	25–50
	October 6–12	#184	My Little Margie's Gale Storm cover, The NBC Bandstand, Harry Morgan	10–20
	October 13–19	#185	Ozzie and Harriet, David and Ricky	

Year	Issue	Number	Description	Value ($)
1956	October 13–19	#185	Nelson cover, I Love Lucy	25–50
	October 20–26	#186	Perry Como and Phyllis Goodkind cover, Cheyenne, Private Secretary	5–10
	October 27	#187	Alfred Hitchcock cover, Arlene Francis, Mary Martin	10–20
	November 3–9	#188	Edward R. Murrow cover, Hit Parade, Clint Walker	5–10
	November 10–16	#189	Loretta Young cover, Lucille Ball, Milton Berle	5–10
	November 17–23	#190	Buddy Hackett cover, Sir Lancelot	5–10
	November 24–30	#191	Nanette Fabray cover, Phil Silvers: Sergeant Bilko, Mickey Dolenz: Circus Boy, Lawrence Welk	15–20
	December 1–7	#192	George Burns and Gracie Allen cover, The Mickey Mouse Club, Broken Arrow	10–20
	December 8–14	#193	Victor Borge cover, Dobie Gillis: Dwayne Hickman, Bob Cummings: Love That Bob	6–12

Year	Issue	Number	Description	Value ($)
1956	December 15–21	#194	Dinah Shore cover, Joan Caulfield, The 77th Bengal Lancers	6–12
	December 22–28	#195	Christmas special, Groucho Marx	6–12
	December 29	#196	Jeannie Carson cover, Sir Lancelot, The Life of Riley	6–12
1957	January 5–11	#197	Arthur Godfrey cover, My Little Margie's Gale Storm, Loretta Young Theatre	6–12
	January 12–18	#198	Lucille Ball cover, The 77th Bengal Lancers	10–20
	January 19–25	#199	Jerry Lewis cover, The Buccaneers, Sergeant Bilko	10–20
	January 26	#200	Bob Hope cover, Mickey Dolenz: Circus Boy, Cheyenne	12–25
	February 2–8	#201	Jane Wyman cover, Groucho Marx, Phil Silvers: Sergeant Bilko, Buddy Hackett	5–10
	February 9–15	#202	Wyatt Earp's Hugh O'Brian cover, Broken Arrow, Douglas Fairbanks Jr. feature	12–25

Year	Issue	Number	Description	Value ($)
1957	February 16–22	#203	Father Knows Best's Jane Wyatt and Robert Young cover, You Bet Your Life, Captain Gallant	12–25
	February 23	#204	Charles Van Doren cover, Mike Wallace	5–10
	March 2–8	#205	Dorothy Collins and Gisele Mackenzie cover, Broken Arrow, Sir Lancelot	5–10
	March 9–15	#206	Pat Boone and Arthur Godfrey cover, Zane Grey, Jim Bowie	10–20
	March 16–22	#207	The Emmy Awards special, Barbara Hale	5–10
	March 23–29	#208	Tennessee Ernie Ford cover, Sergeant Bilko, Superman, Dragnet	5–10
	March 30	#209	Julie Andrews cover, Jonathan Winters, Broken Arrow	10–20
	April 6–12	#210	Lawrence Welk cover, Sergeant Preston of the Yukon	5–10
	April 13–19	#211	Nanette Fabray cover, Dean Martin, Ronald Reagan	5–10

Year	Issue	Number	Description	Value ($)
1957	April 20–26	#212	Loretta Young cover, Ida Lupino, Tommy Sands	5–10
	April 27	#213	Groucho Marx cover, Highway Patrol	5–10
	May 4–10	#214	Hal March and Robert Strom cover, Tales of Wells Fargo, Andy Devine	5–10
	May 11–17	#215	Gunsmoke's James Arness cover, Rod Serling	15–30
	May 18–24	#216	Esther Williams cover, Sal Mineo, Ronald Reagan	5–10
	May 25–31	#217	Sid Caesar cover, Spike Jones, The Lone Ranger	6–12
	June 1–7	#218	Ida Lupino and Howard Duff cover, The Mickey Mouse Club, Judy Garland	7–15
	June 8–14	#219	Lassie cover, Elvis Presley, Debra Paget	10–20
	June 15–21	#220	Red Skelton cover, Jackie Gleason, Nina Foch	5–10
	June 22–28	#221	Queen for a Day's Jack Bailey, Maverick, Ed Sullivan, Jack Palance	5–10

Year	Issue	Number	Description	Value ($)
1957	June 29	#222	Oh Susanna's Gale Storm, The Whirlybirds, Jane Wyman, Wyatt Earp	5–10
	July 6–12	#223	What's My Line's cast cover, June Havoc	5–10
	July 13–19	#224	Annie Oakley's Gail Davis cover, Ida Lupino, Vincent Price	10–20
	July 20–26	#225	Julius LaRosa cover, Ann Sothern, Tales of Wells Fargo, Blondie	5–10
	July 27	#226	Garry Moore cover, Shirley MacLaine, Lassie	5–10
	August 3–9	#227	The People's Choice's Cleo cover, Jackie Cooper, Rita Moreno	5–10
	August 10–16	#228	Bob Cummings cover, The Restless Gun, Spike Jones	5–10
	August 17–23	#229	Phil Silvers cover, Jim Bowie	10–20
	August 24–30	#230	Danny Thomas and Marjorie Lord cover, Jack Paar	6–12
	August 31	#231	Cheyenne's Clint Walker cover, Ed Wynn, Vic Damone, The Whiting Sisters	10–20

Year	Issue	Number	Description	Value ($)
1957	September 7–13	#232	Arthur Godfrey and Janette Davis cover, Nat King Cole, Betty White	10–20
	September 14–20	#233	1957–1958 Fall Preview special	20–40
	September 21–27	#234	Pat Boone cover	5–10
	September 28	#235	George Burns and Gracie Allen cover, Dick Clark and American Bandstand	12–25
	October 5–11	#236	Joan Caulfield cover, Broken Arrow, John Cassavetes	5–10
	October 12–18	#237	Richard Boone: Have Gun Will Travel, Louis Nye	5–10
	October 19–25	#238	Loretta Young cover, Rin Tin Tin, Dick Clark and American Bandstand	12–25
	October 26	#239	Phyllis Kirk and Peter Lawford cover, Wagon Train, Hit Parade	5–10
	November 2–8	#240	Lucille Ball cover, Tony Curtis, Robin Hood	15–30
	November 9–15	#241	Maverick's James Garner cover, You Asked for It, Robin Hood	15–30
	November 16–22	#242	Patti Page cover Barbara Eden, Steve Allen	15–30

Year	Issue	Number	Description	Value ($)
1957	November 23–29	#243	Mary Martin cover, Captain Kangaroo's Mr. Green Jeans, Eddie Fisher	5–10
	November 30	#244	Alfred Hitchcock cover, Eve Arden	5–10
	December 7–13	#245	Dinah Shore cover, Tallulah Bankhead, Steve Allen	5–10
	December 14–20	#246	Walt Disney and his creations cover, Horror Pictures on Television, Broken Arrow	7–15
	December 21–27	#247	Christmas special, Peter Lawford, Jack Lemmon	5–10
	December 28	#248	Ricky Nelson cover, Howdy Doody, Eve Arden	25–50
1958	January 4–10	#249	Lawrence Welk cover, Guy Williams: Zorro, Cochise, Woody Woodpecker	10–20
	January 11–17	#250	Gisele Mackenzie cover, Shirley Temple, Boris Karloff	10–20
	January 18–24	#251	The Restless Gun's John Payne cover, Wild Bill Hickok	10–20
	January 25–31	#252	Sid Caesar and Imogene Coca	

Year	Issue	Number	Description	Value ($)
1958	January 25–31	#252	cover, Dennis Weaver	6–12
	February 1–7	#253	Walter Winchell cover, Leave It to Beaver's Jerry Mathers, Perry Mason	10–20
	February 8–16	#254	Tab Hunter and Peggy King cover, Frank Sinatra	10–20
	February 17–21	#255	Walter Brennan, Jerry Lewis	6–12
	February 22–28	#256	Rosemary Clooney cover, The Millionaire, Perry Mason	5–10
	March 1–7	#257	Lassie cover, E. G. Marshall, Sugarfoot	6–12
	March 8–14	#258	Arthur Godfrey cover, Richard Boone and Have Gun Will Travel, William Bendix: The Life of Riley	6–12
	March 15–21	#259	Gunsmoke's James Arness and Amanda Blake cover, The Pat Boone Show, Dick Clark	10–20
	March 22–28	#260	Perry Como cover, TV Westerns, Claude Rains	5–10
	March 29	#261	Tennessee Ernie Ford cover, Rin Tin Tin, Horror shows	6–12

Year	Issue	Number	Description	Value ($)
1958	April 5–11	#262	Gale Storm cover, Where Westerns Are Made	6–12
	April 12–18	#263	Wyatt Earp's Hugh O'Brian cover, Barbara Eden, Wagon Train	12–25
	April 19–25	#264	Polly Bergen cover, Howdy Doody, Richard Diamond	5–10
	April 26	#265	Zorro's Guy Williams cover, Have Gun Will Travel, Gunsmoke	15–30
	May 3–9	#266	Shirley Temple cover, Liberace, Playhouse 90	15–30
	May 10–16	#267	Have Gun Will Travel's Richard Boone, Alfred Hitchcock Presents	15–30
	May 17–23	#268	Make Room for Daddy's Danny Thomas and cast cover, Maverick	15–30
	May 24–30	#269	American Bandstand's Dick Clark cover, Lassie, Annette Funicello	25–50
	May 31	#270	The Thin Man's Phyllis Kirk cover, John Forsythe, Bette Davis	6–12

Year	Issue	Number	Description	Value ($)
1958	June 7–13	#271	Pat Boone cover, Maverick	6–12
	June 14–20	#272	Father Knows Best's Robert Young and Jane Wyatt cover, George Burns and Gracie Allen, Wagon Train's Ward Bond	10–20
	June 21–27	#273	Ed Sullivan cover, Rod Cameron, Perry Mason	5–10
	June 28	#274	Leave It to Beaver's Jerry Mathers cover, Wayde Preston	25–50
	July 5–11	#275	The Price Is Right's Bill Cullen cover, Sky King, Lee Marvin, Barbara Hale	3–6
	July 12–18	#276	Lucille Ball cover, Peter Lawford, John Russell	10–20
	July 19–25	#277	Tales of Wells Fargo's Dale Robertson cover, Polly Bergen, Doris Day	10–20
	July 26	#278	The Millionaire's Marvin Miller cover, Groucho Marx, Clint Walker, TV Westerns	10–20
	August 2–8	#279	The Real McCoys' Walter	

Year	Issue	Number	Description	Value ($)
1958	August 2–8	#279	Brennan cover, Wyatt Earp, Richard Nixon, Benny Goodman	10–20
	August 9–15	#280	Steve Lawrence and Eydie Gorme cover, Guy Williams: Zorro, Lassie, Shirley Temple	10–20
	August 16–22	#281	Wagon Train's cast cover, Harpo Marx, John Forsythe	10–20
	August 23–29	#282	Edie Adams and Janet Blair cover, Jayne Meadows, Bill Cullen	3–6
	August 30	#283	To Tell the Truth cast cover, Lloyd Bridges: Sea Hunt, Gray Ghost	3–6
	September 6–12	#284	Arthur Godfrey cover, Perry Mason, Cheyenne, Milton Berle	3–6
	September 13–19	#285	The Lennon Sisters cover, Spike Jones	5–10
	September 20–26	#286	Fall Preview special	15–30
	September 27	#287	Garry Moore cover, Sea Hunt's Lloyd Bridges, The Rifleman's Chuck Connors	7–15
	October 4–10	#288	American Bandstand's Dick Clark cover, Guy	

Year	Issue	Number	Description	Value ($)
1958	October 4–10	#288	Williams: Zorro, Robert Culp	15–30
	October 11–17	#289	Fred Astaire and Barrie Chase cover, Naked City, Liberace	5–10
	October 18–24	#290	Perry Como cover, Like Elvis, Ann Sothern, Clayton Moore: The Lone Ranger, Amanda Blake	5–10
	October 25–31	#291	George Burns cover, The Texan, Barbara Eden	9–18
	November 1–7	#292	Jack Paar cover, Lou Costello Plays It Straight, Robert Horton, TV studios	6–12
	November 8–14	#293	Loretta Young cover, Western heroes . . . John Wayne, Tom Mix, and others, Anne Francis, TV Wives	6–12
	November 15–21	#294	The Lineup's cast cover, Walt Disney's Westerns, Bob Hope, Davy Crockett	5–10
	November 22–28	#295	Ronald and Nancy Reagan cover, 77 Sunset Strip, Barbara Stanwyck	5–10
	November 29	#296	Victor Borge cover, Ellery Queen, Dobie	

Year	Issue	Number	Description	Value ($)
1958	November 29	#296	Gillis's Tuesday Weld	7–15
	December 6–12	#297	Gunsmoke's James Arness cover, Gale Storm, Monster Makeup, Swiss Family Robinson, Shari Lewis	10–20
	December 13–19	#298	Danny Thomas cover, Donna Reed, Fred Astaire, Barrie Chase, George Fenneman	5–10
	December 20–26	#299	Christmas issue special, Ed Wynn, Shirley Temple	10–20
	December 27	#300	David and Ricky Nelson cover, TV Cowboys special, Garry Moore	25–50
1959	January 3–9	#301	Peter Gunn cast cover, George Burns and Carol Channing, Julia Meade, Jimmy Durante, Steve Canyon	5–10
	January 10–16	#302	Milton Berle cover, Hanna-Barbera's Huckleberry Hound, Jack Webb	5–10
	January 17–23	#303	Maverick's James Garner and Jack Kelly cover,	

Year	Issue	Number	Description	Value ($)
1959	January 17–23	#303	Lucille Ball and Desi Arnaz, Captain Kangaroo, Hit Parade	7–15
	January 24–30	#304	Red Skelton cover, Have Gun Will Travel, Cimarron City, Playhouse 90	6–12
	January 31	#305	George Gobel cover, Gunsmoke's Doc Adams, Carl Reiner, Rory Calhoun	6–12
	February 7–13	#306	The Rifleman's Chuck Connors and Johnny Crawford cover, Naked City	12–25
	February 14–20	#307	Alfred Hitchcock cover, The Donna Reed Show, Tony Randall	6–12
	February 21–27	#308	Perry Mason's Raymond Burr and Barbara Hale cover, Annette Funicello, Bat Masterson, Northwest Passage	10–20
	February 28	#309	Have Gun Will Travel's Richard Boone cover, The Lawman, Bing Crosby, Bachelor Father, The Peter Lind Hayes Show	10–20

Year	Issue	Number	Description	Value ($)
1959	March 7–13	#310	The Real McCoys' Walter Brennan cover, The Restless Gun, The Marx Brothers	10–20
	March 14–20	#311	Arthur Godfrey cover, Ann Sothern, Yancy Derringer, Wyatt Earp, Spring Byington	3–6
	March 21–27	#312	Ann Sothern cover, The Three Stooges, Tales of Wells Fargo, Western sets	10–20
	March 28	#313	Tennessee Ernie Ford cover, Patricia Barry, Lloyd Bridges, Naked City, TV Females, Mary Martin Special: Peter Pan, Dodge City	15–30
	April 4–10	#314	77 Sunset Strip cover, Tombstone Territory, Hugh Downs	5–10
	April 11–17	#315	Wagon Train's Ward Bond cover, The Thin Man	7–15
	April 18–24	#316	Dinah Shore cover, Charley Weaver, Rawhide	7–15
	April 25	#317	Dick Powell cover, Steve	

Year	Issue	Number	Description	Value ($)
1959	April 25	#317	McQueen, Cheyenne, June Lockhart	5–10
	May 2–8	#318	Wyatt Earp's Hugh O'Brian cover, The Lawman, Jack Webb, Barbara Stanwyck	5–10
	May 9–15	#319	77 Sunset Strip's Edd "Kookie" Byrnes cover, The Rifleman's Johnny Crawford, Gunsmoke	10–20
	May 16–22	#320	Loretta Young cover, Sergeant Bilko, Naked City	7–15
	May 23–29	#321	Bob Hope cover, You Asked for It	5–10
	May 30	#322	Steve McQueen cover, Mary Tyler Moore, Tony Dow of Leave It to Beaver	7–15
	June 6–12	#323	Gale Storm cover, Female Western Stars	5–10
	June 13–19	#324	Pat Boone cover	7–15
	June 20–26	#325	Robert Young and Lauren Chapin cover, Connie Stevens, Annette Funicello, The Three Stooges	20–40
	June 27	#326	Sea Hunt's Lloyd Bridges, The Death of TV's	

Year	Issue	Number	Description	Value ($)
1959	June 27	#326	Superman George Reeves, Piper Laurie, Patty McCormack, U.S. Marshal	20–40
	July 4–10	#327	Jon Provost and Lassie cover, Connie Francis	7–15
	July 11–17	#328	Peter Gunn cast, Father Knows Best	5–10
	July 18–24	#329	Janet Blair cover, Perry Mason, Leave It to Beaver	5–10
	July 25–31	#330	The Lawman's John Russell cover, Jayne Meadows, Faye Emerson	5–10
	August 1–7	#331	Dave Garroway cover, Maverick, June Lockhart, The Real McCoys	5–10
	August 8–14	#332	Donna Reed cover, Gene Autry and Roy Rogers, 77 Sunset Strip, Diane Ladd	5–10
	August 15–21	#333	Lawrence Welk cover, Clint Eastwood-Rawhide, Mary Tyler Moore	7–15
	August 22–28	#334	I've Got a Secret cast cover, Jerry Mathers of Leave It to Beaver, Johnny Carson	5–10

Year	Issue	Number	Description	Value ($)
1959	August 29	#335	Dick Clark cover, Jerry Lewis, Broderick Crawford	10–20
	September 5–11	#336	Maverick's James Garner and Jack Kelly cover, Clint Eastwood, Bachelor Father	10–20
	September 12–18	#337	Arthur Godfrey cover, Gunsmoke	5–10
	September 19–25	#338	Fall Preview special	20–40
	September 26	#339	Hennesey cast cover, Dobie Gillis, Men into Space	5–10
	October 3–9	#340	June Allyson cover, Dick Clark: American Bandstand	7–15
	October 10–16	#341	The Detectives' Robert Taylor cast cover, Dobie Gillis, Bette Davis	5–10
	October 17–23	#342	Ingrid Bergman cover, The Rifleman, Sid Caesar	5–10
	October 24–30	#343	Dennis the Menace's Jay North cover, Groucho Marx, Tales of Wells Fargo	15–30
	October 31	#344	Fred Astaire cover, Rawhide	5–10
	November 7–13	#345	Jack Benny cover, The Twilight	

Year	Issue	Number	Description	Value ($)
1959	November 7–13	#345	Zone, Bonanza	10–20
	November 14–20	#346	Perry Como cover, Gunsmoke, Maverick	5–10
	November 21–27	#347	Cheyenne's Clint Walker cover, Dobie Gillis	10–20
	November 28	#348	Art Carney cover, Johnny Cash	25–50
	December 5–11	#349	Dobie Gillis's cast cover, Robert Stack: The Untouchables	12–25
	December 12–18	#350	Danny Thomas cover, The Wizard of Oz	10–20
	December 19–25	#351	Christmas issue special, Ernie Kovacs, Wagon Train, Art Carney	6–12
	December 26	#352	Loretta Young cover, Charley Weaver, Bobby Darin	7–15
1960	January 2–8	#353	Gunsmoke cast cover, Tales of the Vikings	10–20
	January 9–15	#354	Father Knows Best's Jane Wyatt and Elinor Donahue cover, Tuesday Weld, Maverick	7–15
	January 16–22	#355	Charley Weaver cover, The Rebel's Nick Adams	7–15

Year	Issue	Number	Description	Value ($)
1960	January 23–29	#356	The Real McCoys cover, The Deputy, Men into Space	10–20
	January 30	#357	Garry Moore cover, Tony Randall	5–10
	February 6–12	#358	Paladin's Richard Boone cover, Fred MacMurray: My Three Sons, Connie Stevens	7–15
	February 13–19	#359	Peter Gunn cast cover, Hawaiian Eye, The Texans	5–10
	February 20–26	#360	Red Skelton cover, Bob Denver: Dobie Gillis, Dennis the Menace	5–10
	February 27	#361	The Untouchables' Robert Stack cover, The Twilight Zone, Milburn Stone	5–10
	March 5–11	#362	Dennis the Menace's Jay North cover, Bonanza's Dan Blocker	7–15
	March 12–18	#363	The Rifleman's Chuck Connors cover	10–12
	March 19–25	#364	Perry Mason cast cover, Nick Adams: The	

Year	Issue	Number	Description	Value ($)
1960	March 19–25	#364	Rebel, Bob Cummings	5–10
	March 26	#365	Donna Reed cover, The Untouchables, Lee Marvin	5–10
	April 2–8	#366	Tennessee Ernie Ford cover, Robert Conrad	4–8
	April 9–15	#367	77 Sunset Strip's Efrem Zimbalist Jr., Ed Wynn, Eva Gabor	5–10
	April 16–22	#368	Ann Sothern cover, Shelley Fabares: The Donna Reed Show	10–20
	April 23–29	#369	Laramie cast cover, Tony Randall, Groucho Marx	5–10
	April 30	#370	Lassie and June Lockhart cover, Broken Arrow, Jackie Gleason, Arthur Godfrey	7–15
	May 7–13	#371	Elvis Presley and Frank Sinatra cover, Steve Allen, Westerns on TV	20–40
	May 14–20	#372	Ernie Kovacs and Edie Adams cover, What's My Line, Carl Reiner	5–10
	May 21–27	#373	Bat Masterson's Gene Barry cover, The Untouchables, Ross Martin	10–20

Year	Issue	Number	Description	Value ($)
1960	May 28	#374	Hawaiian Eye's Connie Stevens cover, Father Knows Best	5–10
	June 4–10	#375	Riverboat's Darren McGavin cover, The Lawman	4–8
	June 11–17	#376	Bachelor Father cast cover, The Alaskans, Roger Moore	4–8
	June 18–24	#377	Adventures in Paradise cover, Rod Serling: The Twilight Zone, The Deputy, Shelley Fabares	7–15
	June 25	#378	Bonanza cast cover, Annette Funicello, Fabian, Bob Denver	20–40
	July 2–8	#379	Lawrence Welk cover, Johnny Ringo	4–8
	July 9–15	#380	David Brinkley and Chet Huntley cover, The Untouchables	4–8
	July 16–22	#381	Lucille Ball cover, The Untouchables, Connie Stevens	10–20
	July 23–29	#382	John Charles Daly cover, Richard Nixon	4–8
	July 30	#383	Tightrope's Mike Connors cover, Tuesday Weld, Howdy Doody	7–15

Year	Issue	Number	Description	Value ($)
1960	August 6–12	#384	Esther Williams cover, Bert Parks	3–6
	August 13–19	#385	The Rebel's Nick Adams cover, 77 Sunset Strip	15–30
	August 20–26	#386	Betsy Palmer cover, Merv Griffin	3–6
	August 27	#387	77 Sunset Strip cast cover, Popeye, Bob Denver, Spike Jones	5–10
	September 3–9	#388	Arlene Francis cover, The Lawman	3–6
	September 10–16	#389	American Bandstand's Dick Clark cover, Tom Poston, Rawhide	12–25
	September 17–23	#390	Dick Powell and June Allyson cover, Bonanza's Pernell Roberts, Charlie Chaplin	4–8
	September 24–30	#391	Fall Preview special	20–40
	October 1–7	#392	Dinah Shore cover, The Andy Griffith Show	5–10
	October 8–14	#393	Arthur Godfrey cover, Leave It to Beaver, Maverick	5–10
	October 15–21	#394	Carol Burnett and Marion Lorne cover, Dobie Gillis, Boris Karloff: Thriller	5–10

Year	Issue	Number	Description	Value ($)
1960	October 22–28	#395	Debbie Reynolds cover, The Untouchables, Gail Davis	5–10
	October 29	#396	Danny Kaye cover, Thriller, Tab Hunter, Route 66	5–10
	November 5–11	#397	Loretta Young cover, The Twilight Zone	5–10
	November 12–18	#398	Fred MacMurray cover, Jack Benny, Death Valley Days	5–10
	November 19–25	#399	Wagon Train's Ward Bond cover, Dina Merrill	5–10
	November 26	#400	Abby Dalton cover, Tab Hunter, James Garner: Maverick	5–10
	December 3–9	#401	Shirley Temple cover, Perry Como	10–20
	December 10–16	#402	Gunsmoke's James Arness and Amanda Blake cover, James Garner	10–20
	December 17–23	#403	Checkmate cast cover, Harpo Marx, Walt Disney	3–6
	December 26–30	#404	Christmas issue special, June Allyson	3–6
	December 31	#405	The Roaring Twenties' Dorothy	

Year	Issue	Number	Description	Value ($)
1960	December 31	#405	Provine cover, Perry Mason, The Aquanauts	3–6
1961	January 7–13	#406	Richard Boone cover, The Islanders	3–6
	January 14–20	#407	Perry Como cover, Have Gun Will Travel's Richard Boone	3–6
	January 21–27	#408	Barbara Stanwyck cover, Shirley Temple	3–6
	January 28	#409	Andy Griffith and Ronnie Howard (Opie) cover, Adventures in Paradise	10–20
	February 4–10	#410	Clint Eastwood cover, The Andy Griffith Show	10–20
	February 11–17	#411	Peter Gunn cast cover, Wally Cox, Disneyland	3–6
	February 18–24	#412	Nanette Fabray cover, Jackie Gleason, Route 66	3–6
	February 25	#413	Allen Funt and the cast of Candid Camera cover, The Tall Man, Leave It to Beaver	5–10
	March 4–10	#414	Perry Mason's Raymond Burr cover, Danny Thomas: Make Room for Daddy, The Roaring Twenties	3–6

Year	Issue	Number	Description	Value ($)
1961	March 11–17	#415	The Untouchables' Robert Stack cover, Lee Remick, Raymond Burr: Perry Mason	3–6
	March 18–24	#416	The Danny Thomas Show's Marjorie Lord, The Flintstones, Loretta Young, Jane Wyatt	3–6
	March 25–31	#417	Alfred Hitchcock cover, The Untouchables, Maverick	3–6
	April 1–7	#418	77 Sunset Strip's Roger Smith cover, Sea Hunt's Lloyd Bridges, Tarzan Through the Years	3–6
	April 8–14	#419	National Velvet cast cover, The Naked City, 77 Sunset Strip	3–6
	April 15–31	#420	Mitch Miller cover, Surfside Six	3–6
	April 22–28	#421	Garry Moore cover, Perry Como, George Burns	3–6
	April 29	#422	Hong Kong's Rod Taylor cover, Garry Moore	3–6
	May 6–12	#423	Donna Reed cover, Mr. Ed,	

Year	Issue	Number	Description	Value ($)
1961	May 6–12	#423	Boris Karloff: Thriller	3–6
	May 13–19	#424	Bonanza's Ben Cartwright cover, Walt Disney	10–20
	May 20–26	#425	The Real McCoys cover, Walt Disney, Andy Williams	5–10
	May 27	#426	Ronald Reagan and Dorothy Malone cover, Walt Disney, Jim Backus	5–10
	June 3–9	#427	The Naked City's cast cover, Perry Mason	3–6
	June 10–16	#428	Efrem Zimbalist Jr. cover, The Naked City	3–6
	June 17–23	#429	Lawrence Welk cover, Bonanza's Michael Landon	10–20
	June 24–30	#430	Wagon Train cast cover, Nanette Fabray	3–6
	July 1–7	#431	The Flintstones cover, Colt .45, Peggy Lee	12–25
	July 8–14	#432	Harry Morgan and Cara Williams cover, Peter Gunn	3–6
	July 15–21	#433	Gardner McKay cover, Julie London, Dennis the Menace	3–6
	July 22–28	#434	Route 66 cast cover, Donna	

Year	Issue	Number	Description	Value ($)
1961	July 22–28	#434	Reed's Paul Petersen	5–10
	July 29	#435	Captain Kangaroo cover, Ozzie and Harriet and Boys	10–20
	August 5–11	#436	My Three Sons cast cover, Captain Kangaroo, Adventures in Paradise	5–10
	August 12–18	#437	Soap Opera special, Bob Cummings	3–6
	August 19–25	#438	Troy Donahue cover, Elizabeth Montgomery, The Untouchables	7–15
	August 26	#439	Hugh Downs cover, My Three Sons, Charley Weaver	3–6
	September 2–8	#440	Dobie Gillis's Dwayne Hickman and Bob Denver cover, Clint Eastwood: Rawhide, Perry Mason	12–25
	September 9–15	#441	Checkmate cast cover, Robert Fuller, Shari Lewis	3–6
	September 16–22	#442	Fall Preview special	20–40
	September 23–29	#443	Mitch Miller cover, Jack Benny, Mary Tyler Moore	3–6

Year	Issue	Number	Description	Value ($)
1961	September 30	#444	Carol Burnett cover, Mickey Spillane	3–6
	October 7–13	#445	Walter Cronkite and President Eisenhower cover, Candid Camera's Allen Funt, 77 Sunset Strip, Hazel	3–6
	October 14–20	#446	Red Skelton cover, Michael Rennie	3–6
	October 21–27	#447	Car 54 Where Are You cast cover, Red Skelton, 77 Sunset Strip	15–30
	October 28	#448	The Twilight Zone, Alfred Hitchcock Presents	5–10
	November 4–10	#449	Dorothy Provine cover, The Defenders, Perry Mason's Raymond Burr	3–6
	November 11–17	#450	Robert Stack and Wife cover, Sid Caesar, Anne Baxter	3–6
	November 18–24	#451	Garry Moore and Durward Kirby cover, Howdy Doody	3–6
	November 25	#452	Gunsmoke's James Arness and Amanda Blake, Adventures in Paradise	7–10

Year	Issue	Number	Description	Value ($)
1961	December 2–8	#453	Joey Bishop cover, National Velvet, Gunsmoke's Dennis Weaver	3–6
	December 9–15	#454	Dick Van Dyke and Mary Tyler Moore cover, Gloria Swanson	10–20
	December 16–22	#455	Dr. Kildare's Richard Chamberlain and Raymond Massey cover, 77 Sunset Strip	3–6
	December 23–29	#456	Christmas issue special, Fabian, Car 54 Where Are You?	5–10
	December 30	#457	Cynthia Pepper cover, Checkmate	3–6
1962	January 6–12	#458	American Bandstand's Dick Clark cover, Bonanza's Michael Landon	10–20
	January 13–19	#459	Hazel cast cover, Sex on TV, Robert Young	3–6
	January 20–26	#460	The Rifleman's Chuck Connors cover, Dr. Kildare's Richard Chamberlain, Rocky & Bullwinkle, Robert Young	12–25
	January 27	#461	Myrna Fahey cover, Leave It to

Year	Issue	Number	Description	Value ($)
1962	January 27	#461	Beaver's Jerry Mathers, The Dick Van Dyke Show	6–12
	February 3–9	#462	Mark Richmond cover, 77 Sunset Strip's Connie Stevens	3–6
	February 10–16	#463	Jackie Kennedy cover, Gunsmoke's Amanda Blake, Route 66	3–6
	February 17–23	#464	Danny Thomas cover, The 87th Precinct	3–6
	February 24	#465	Troy Donahue cover, Johnny Carson, Ben Casey, Huckleberry Hound	3–6
	March 3–9	#466	Perry Mason cast cover, Danny Thomas, Surfside Six	3–6
	March 10–16	#467	Jack Paar cover, Zorro's Guy Williams, Rawhide's Clint Eastwood	6–12
	March 17–23	#468	The Defenders cast cover, Dobie Gillis, Maverick's James Garner	4–8
	March 24–30	#469	Dick Powell cover, Leave It to Beaver's Jerry Mathers, Johnny Carson	6–12

Year	Issue	Number	Description	Value ($)
1962	March 31	#470	Mr. Ed and Wilbur (Alan Young) cover, Bachelor Father, Inger Stevens: The Farmer's Daughter	12–25
	April 7–13	#471	Wagon Train's John McIntire cover, The Real McCoys, Dick Powell	5–10
	April 14–20	#472	Route 66 cast cover, Dr. Kildare	3–6
	April 21–27	#473	Connie Stevens cover, The Twilight Zone's Rod Serling, Route 66	3–6
	April 28	#474	The 87th Precinct cast cover, Don Adams	3–6
	May 5–11	#475	Dobie Gillis cast cover, Abby Dalton, The Law and Mr. Jones	10–20
	May 12–18	#476	The Andy Griffith Show's Don Knotts, Candid Camera's Allen Funt, The Danny Thomas Show's Marjorie Lord	10–20
	May 19–25	#477	The Naked City's Paul Burke cover, Dr. Kildare, Password, Marlo Thomas	3–6
	May 26	#478	My Three Sons' Fred MacMurray,	

Year	Issue	Number	Description	Value ($)
1962	May 26	#478	Bud Collyer, Hazel	3–6
	June 2–8	#479	Mary Tyler Moore cover, Maverick, The Corruptors	5–10
	June 9–15	#480	77 Sunset Strip's Efrem Zimbalist Jr. cover, Julie Andrews, Bob Newhart	3–6
	June 16–22	#481	Dr. Kildare's Dick Chamberlain and Raymond Massey cover, Paul Anka	5–10
	June 23–29	#482	Arlene Francis cover, Ed Sullivan, Mr. Ed, Bonanza	5–10
	June 30	#483	Mitch Miller cover, The Twilight Zone	5–10
	July 7–13	#484	David Brinkley cover, Dobie Gillis's Tuesday Weld	5–10
	July 14–20	#485	Checkmate cast cover, Jackie Cooper, Gunsmoke's Dennis Weaver	3–6
	July 21–27	#486	Donna Reed cover, Perry Mason, Bonanza	5–10
	July 28	#487	The Price Is Right's Bill Cullen cover, Adventures in Paradise	3–6

Year	Issue	Number	Description	Value ($)
1962	August 4–10	#488	Dennis the Menace cast cover, Ann-Margret, Clint Walker	10–20
	August 11–17	#489	The Untouchables' Robert Stack cover, Sid Caesar, Bullwinkle	5–10
	August 18–24	#490	I've Got a Secret cast cover, Ozzie and Harriet, Robert Conrad	3–6
	August 25–31	#491	Lawrence Welk cover, Beverly Garland	3–6
	September 1–7	#492	Troy Donahue and Connie Stevens cover	3–6
	September 8–14	#493	Bonanza cast cover, Dr. Kildare Meets Ben Casey, Inger Stevens	17–35
	September 15–21	#494	Fall Preview special	20–40
	September 22–28	#495	Ben Casey's Vince Edwards cover, My Three Sons	3–6
	September 29	#496	Lucille Ball cover, The Untouchables	10–20
	October 6–12	#497	Hazel cast cover, Danny Thomas, Mr. Ed	3–6
	October 13–19	#498	Jackie Gleason cover, Dinah Shore, Merv Griffin	3–6

Year	Issue	Number	Description	Value ($)
1962	October 20–26	#499	Loretta Young cover, Jackie Gleason	3–6
	October 27	#500	Sam Benedict cast cover, Fred Astaire, The Virginian	3–6
	November 3–9	#501	Our Man Higgins cover, Charles Boyer, The Virginian	3–6
	November 10–16	#502	The Beverly Hillbillies cast cover, Car 54, The Rifleman, Stoney Burke	25–50
	November 17–23	#503	Stoney Burke's Jack Lord cover, The Eleventh Hour, Bob Hope	3–6
	November 24–30	#504	Jackie Kennedy cover, Milburn Stone	3–6
	December 1–7	#505	I'm Dickens, He's Fenster cover, Jackie Gleason, Clint Eastwood	3–6
	December 8–14	#506	Dick Van Dyke cover, The Virginian, Roy Rogers	3–6
	December 15–21	#507	The Nurses cast cover, The Beverly Hillbillies, Route 66	5–10
	December 22–28	#508	Christmas issue special, Judy Carnes	3–6

Year	Issue	Number	Description	Value ($)
1962	December 29	#509	Edie Adams cover, Shari Lewis, The Naked City	3–6
1963	January 5–11	#510	Ben Casey cast cover, Terry Moore, Leave It to Beaver, Our Man Higgins	3–6
	January 12–18	#511	Arnold Palmer cover, Perry Como, Marjorie Lord	3–6
	January 19–25	#512	Car 54 Where Are You? cast cover, Leave It to Beaver's Tony Dow, It's a Man's World	15–30
	January 26	#513	Route 66 cast cover, The Alfred Hitchcock Hour, Bette Davis on Perry Mason	5–10
	February 2–8	#514	Jack Webb cover, Yogi Bear, Julie Newmar	5–10
	February 9–15	#515	McHale's Navy's Ernest Borgnine cover, Vivian Vance Off Camera	1–20
	February 16–22	#516	Princess Grace (Kelly), cover, Pebbles on The Flintstones, Sid Caesar	10–20
	February 23	#517	Carol Burnett cover, Sid Caesar, Mary Tyler Moore	3–6

Year	Issue	Number	Description	Value ($)
1963	March 2–8	#518	The Eleventh Hour cast cover, The Lucy Show, Lloyd Bridges	3–6
	March 9–15	#519	The Beverly Hillbillies' Donna Douglas and Buddy Ebsen cover, Car 54 Where Are You?, Cyd Charisse	10–20
	March 16–22	#520	Richard Chamberlain cover, Phil Silvers, Judy Garland, Hazel, Ed Sullivan	3–6
	March 23–29	#521	Andy Williams cover, Charles Bronson of Empire, Jack Benny, Hope Lange	3–6
	March 30	#522	Bonanza cast cover	17–35
	April 6–12	#523	Lucille Ball cover, The Dakotas, anniversary issue	10–20
	April 13–19	#524	Empire's Richard Egan cover, Garry Moore	2–4
	April 20–26	#525	Red Skelton cover, George Gobel, Dinah Shore	2–4
	April 27	#526	Perry Mason cover, Liz Taylor, Mary Tyler Moore	2–4

Year	Issue	Number	Description	Value ($)
1963	May 4–10	#527	The Virginian cast cover, President Kennedy	2–4
	May 11–17	#528	The Andy Griffith Show's Don Knotts and Ron Howard cover, special color pages on Ann-Margret, Stoney Burke	10–20
	May 18–24	#529	The Defenders cast cover, Dr. Kildare	2–4
	May 25–31	#530	Lawrence Welk cover, Burt Reynolds of Gunsmoke, Ben Casey	2–4
	June 1–7	#531	Garry Moore and Dorothy Loudon cover, Barbara Bain, Combat	3–6
	June 8–14	#532	Johnny Carson cover, The Naked City	3–6
	June 15–21	#533	Combat cast cover, Mary Tyler Moore, Jerry Lewis	15–30
	June 22–28	#534	Candid Camera's Allen Funt and Durward Kirby cover, Route 66	10–20
	June 29	#535	Donna Reed and Carl Betz cover, Cloris Leachman	2–4
	July 6–12	#536	Route 66 cast cover, The Beverly Hillbillies	5–10

Year	Issue	Number	Description	Value ($)
1963	July 13–19	#537	The Lively Ones cast cover, McHale's Navy, The Andy Griffith Show's Ronnie Howard	2–4
	July 20–26	#538	Gunsmoke's James Arness and Dennis Weaver cover, Ben Casey's Vince Edwards	7–15
	July 27	#539	Game show issue	2–4
	August 3–9	#540	Morey Amsterdam cover, The New York Mets, Combat	2–4
	August 10–16	#541	I've Got a Secret cast cover, Johnny Carson	2–4
	August 17–23	#542	My Three Sons' Fred MacMurray cover, Mickey Rooney	3–6
	August 24–30	#543	Lassie cast cover, Jack Lemmon, Carol Burnett	5–10
	August 31	#544	Have Gun Will Travel's Richard Boone, Joey Heatherton	5–10
	September 7–13	#545	The Beverly Hillbillies' Donna Douglas and Irene Ryan cover, Ann-Margret	10–20
	September 14–20	#546	Fall Preview special	20–40

Year	Issue	Number	Description	Value ($)
1963	September 21–27	#547	Dr. Kildare's Richard Chamberlain cover, Edie Adams, Ozzie and Harriet	4–8
	September 28	#548	Inger Stevens cover, Ben Casey, Lucille Ball	3–6
	October 5–11	#549	Phil Silvers cover, Willie Mays, Elizabeth Taylor	2–4
	October 12–18	#550	Chuck Connors and Ben Gazzara cover, Jayne Mansfield, Phil Silvers	10–20
	October 19–25	#551	Judy Garland cover, McHale's Navy's Tim Conway, The Rifleman's Johnny Crawford	7–15
	October 26	#552	The Virginian cover, Breaking Point	2–4
	November 2–8	#553	My Favorite Martian cast cover, The Fugitive	25–50
	November 9–15	#554	Carol Burnett cover, The Jerry Lewis Show	2–4
	November 16–22	#555	Mr. Novak cast cover, The Beverly Hillbillies, My Favorite Martian, Meredith MacRae	6–12

Year	Issue	Number	Description	Value ($)
1963	November 23–29	#556	Burke's Law's Gene Barry cover, David Susskind	2–4
	November 30	#557	George C. Scott cover, Danny Kaye, The Twilight Zone, Jack Palance, The Greatest Show on Earth	3–6
	December 7–13	#558	Wagon Train cast cover, Yvette Mimieux, Dr. Kildare	5–10
	December 14–20	#559	Bing Crosby, Frank Sinatra, and Dean Martin cover, The Outer Limits, Jerry Lewis	10–20
	December 21–27	#560	Christmas issue special, Lassie, Arthur Godfrey	2–4
	December 28	#561	Patty Duke cover, Inger Stevens, Lassie	10–20
1964	January 4–10	#562	The Dick Van Dyke Show cast cover, Petticoat Junction, Gunsmoke	5–10
	January 11–17	#563	June Lockhart and other women of TV cover, Jeffrey Hunter, Ripcord, The Fugitive	3–6
	January 18–24	#564	Bonanza's Pernell Roberts cover,	

Year	Issue	Number	Description	Value ($)
1964	January 18–24	#564	The Patty Duke Show, The Andy Griffith Show's Don Knotts, Burke's Law	10–20
	January 25–31	#565	Assassination of President Kennedy special	5–10
	February 1–7	#566	Danny Kaye cover, Combat, My Favorite Martian's Bill Bixby	10–20
	February 8–14	#567	Petticoat Junction's leading young females cover, Jonathan Winters	10–20
	February 15–21	#568	Andy Williams cover, The Dick Van Dyke Show, Bess Myerson	2–4
	February 22–28	#569	The Fugitive's David Janssen cover, The Outer Limits, Alfred Hitchcock, Red Skelton	15–30
	February 29	#570	The Nurses cast cover, Mae West, Mr. Ed	2–4
	March 7–13	#571	Dr. Kildare's Richard Chamberlain cover, Animals on TV	2–4
	March 14–20	#572	The Beverly Hillbillies cast	

Year	Issue	Number	Description	Value ($)
1964	March 14–20	#572	cover, Gunsmoke, Bonanza, Have Gun Will Travel, Joseph Cotten	15–30
	March 21–27	#573	The Andy Griffith Show cast cover, Judy Garland, The Outer Limits	15–30
	March 28	#574	Lawrence Welk cover, color photos of The Beverly Hillbillies' Donna Douglas, George C. Scott, Petticoat Junction	10–20
	April 4–10	#575	Ben Casey's Vince Edwards cover, The Farmer's Daughter, Inger Stevens	2–4
	April 11–17	#576	My Favorite Martian cast cover, Bob Hope, Burt Reynolds, Suzy Parker	12–25
	April 18–24	#577	Mr. Novak cast cover, The Beatles on The Ed Sullivan Show-The Beatles back in Britain	5–10
	April 25	#578	Danny Thomas cover, Shari Lewis, Jack Palance	2–4
	May 2–8	#579	The Farmer's Daughter cast	

Year	Issue	Number	Description	Value ($)
1964	May 2–8	#579	cover, Angie Dickinson, Judy Garland	2–4
	May 9–15	#580	Combat cast cover, The Avengers, Jack Benny	12–25
	May 16–22	#581	Alfred Hitchcock cover, McHale's Navy, Carol Burnett	2–4
	May 23–29	#582	Mary Tyler Moore cover, Judy Garland	2–4
	May 30	#583	McHale's Navy cast cover, Petticoat Junction	5–10
	June 6–12	#584	Gunsmoke's Amanda Blake cover, Milton Berle, Steve Allen, The Fugitive, Ozzie and Harriet	2–4
	June 13–19	#585	The Flintstones cover, Candid Camera	7–15
	June 20–26	#586	The Donna Reed Show cover, McHale's Navy	2–4
	June 27	#587	Johnny Carson and wife cover, The Farmer's Daughter, Inger Stevens, Barbara Bain, Gunsmoke	2–4
	July 4–10	#588	Perry Mason cover, Mr. Novak	2–4

Year	Issue	Number	Description	Value ($)
1964	July 11–17	#589	Walter Cronkite and other TV anchormen cover, Red Skelton	2–4
	July 18–24	#590	The Virginian cover, George C. Scott	2–4
	July 25–31	#591	My Three Sons cover, Eva Marie Saint	5–10
	August 1–7	#592	Today cast cover, The Beverly Hillbillies, Donna Reed	4–8
	August 8–14	#593	Burke's Law cast cover, Mike Wallace, Anna Maria Alberghetti	2–4
	August 15–21	#594	Wagon Train cast cover, Perry Mason	2–4
	August 22–28	#595	The Defenders cover, Rudy Vallee, General Hospital	2–4
	August 29	#596	Patty Duke Show cover, Carol Lynley, Fred Astaire	10–20
	September 5–11	#597	Lucille Ball cover, Peter Lawford	4–8
	September 12–18	#598	The Fugitive cover, Bonanza's Ben Cartwright, Gypsy Rose Lee	10–20
	September 19–25	#599	Fall Preview special	20–40
	September 26	#600	Bonanza's Dan Blocker cover,	

Year	Issue	Number	Description	Value ($)
1964	September 26	#600	Gomer Pyle, Sophia Loren	10–20
	October 3–9	#601	Peyton Place's Mia Farrow, Jill St. John	2–4
	October 10–16	#602	The Rogues cast cover, My Favorite Martian, Combat	5–10
	October 17–23	#603	Lassie cover, The Man from U.N.C.L.E., The Patty Duke Show	7–15
	October 24–30	#604	The Man from U.N.C.L.E. cover, Bewitched, Gunsmoke	25–50
	October 31	#605	Addams Family's Gomez and Morticia cover, The Smothers Brothers, Gilligan's Island	25–50+
	November 7–13	#606	Dr. Kildare's Richard Chamberlain cover, Wagon Train, Leslie Caron	2–4
	November 14–20	#607	Cara Williams cover, Petticoat Junction, Tony Franciosa	2–4
	November 21–27	#608	Gomer Pyle U.S.M.C. cover, Margaret Rutherford	5–10
	November 28	#609	Bewitched's Elizabeth	

Year	Issue	Number	Description	Value ($)
1964	November 28	#609	Montgomery cover, Lauren Bacall, Winston Churchill, The Addams Family	10–20
	December 5–11	#610	No Time for Sergeants cover, Tina Louise, Gomer Pyle	2–4
	December 12–18	#611	My Living Doll's Julie Newmar cover, Bing Crosby	5–10
	December 19–25	#612	Christmas issue special, The Munsters	10–20
	December 26	#613	Juliet Prowse cover, Fess Parker, Jack Klugman	2–4
1965	January 2–8	#614	The Munsters cast cover, The Mickey Mouse Club, Rawhide	30–60+
	January 9–15	#615	Broadside cast cover, Carol Burnett, Danny Kaye	2–4
	January 16–22	#616	Bob Hope cover, The Man from U.N.C.L.E., Peyton Place	5–10
	January 23–29	#617	Chuck Connors cover, Everything from Cinderella to Peyton Place	3–6
	January 30	#618	Inger Stevens cover, Voyage to	

Year	Issue	Number	Description	Value ($)
1965	January 30	#618	the Bottom of the Sea	10–20
	February 6–12	#619	Jackie Gleason cover, Bing Crosby, The Man from U.N.C.L.E.	5–10
	February 13–19	#620	Andy Williams cover, Popeye, Ben Casey, Harry Belafonte, Jim Backus	2–4
	February 20–26	#621	Mr. Novak cast cover, The Addams Family	10–20
	February 27	#622	The Beverly Hillbillies cover, Mae West, Flipper, The Fugitive	15–30
	March 6–12	#623	The Fugitive cover, Three Stooges, Johnny Carson	10–20
	March 13–19	#624	Bonanza cast cover, Ron Howard	10–20
	March 20–26	#625	Peyton Place cover, Anne Bancroft, Petticoat Junction, Mitch Miller	2–4
	March 27	#626	Dick Van Dyke Show cover, The Munsters, Carol Burnett	10–20
	April 3–9	#627	Ben Casey's Vince Edwards cover, The King Family	2–4

Year	Issue	Number	Description	Value ($)
1965	April 10–16	#628	The Tycoon's Walter Brennan cover, The Fugitive's One-Armed Man	3–6
	April 17–23	#629	The Man from U.N.C.L.E. cover, Sally Kellerman	15–30
	April 24–30	#630	The Andy Griffith Show cover, June Lockhart, Barbra Streisand, Gilligan's Island	5–10
	May 1–7	#631	Wendy and Me's Connie Stevens cover, Voyage to the Bottom of the Sea, George Burns	6–12
	May 8–14	#632	Gilligan's Island's Bob Denver cover, The Man from U.N.C.L.E.	10–20
	May 15–21	#633	Twelve O'Clock High's Robert Lansing cover, The Man from U.N.C.L.E.'s David McCallum, Chuck Connors: Branded, Gilligan's Island	5–10
	May 22–28	#634	Julie Andrews cover, Voyage to the Bottom of the Sea: The making of the Seaview, Harvey Korman, The Beverly Hillbillies	10–15

Year	Issue	Number	Description	Value ($)
1965	May 29	#635	Bewitched's Elizabeth Montgomery and Dick York cover, Dick Van Dyke	12–22
	June 5–11	#636	Flipper cover, Gardner McKay, The Fugitive	6–12
	June 12–18	#637	Gunsmoke's Amanda Blake and Milburn Stone cover, The Rogues, Janet Margolin	4–6
	June 19–25	#628	Voyage to the Bottom of the Sea cover, Bonanza	25–45
	June 26	#629	Hullabaloo cover, Gomer Pyle, TV dog actors	3–6
	July 3–9	#640	Jimmy Dean cover, Shelley Winters	3–6
	July 10–16	#641	The Munsters' Yvonne DeCarlo and Fred Gwynne cover, Julie Newmar, The King Family	20–35+
	July 17–23	#642	McHale's Navy cast cover, Gilligan's Island, Bewitched, Walt Disney	12–22
	July 24–30	#643	Raymond Burr cover, The Munsters, I Spy, Daniel Boone, Jimmy Dean	12–22

Year	Issue	Number	Description	Value ($)
1965	July 31	#644	My Three Sons cast cover, The Man from U.N.C.L.E., Barbara Eden: I Dream of Jeannie	10–15
	August 7–13	#645	Burke's Law cover, Daniel Boone, Hazel, Al Hirt	3–5
	August 14–20	#646	Lassie cover, Sally Field, The Lennon Sisters, Hazel's Shirley Booth	3–5
	August 21–27	#647	Daniel Boone's Fess Parker cover, Eileen Fulton, Discover, Mel Blanc	3–5
	August 28	#648	Lucille Ball cover, Jack Benny, Peyton Place, The Virginian	3–6
	September 4–10	#649	Bonanza cast cover, Lawrence Welk, The Addams Family's Lurch	12–22
	September 11–17	#650	Fall Preview special	20–40
	September 18–24	#651	Honey West's Anne Francis cover, Dawn Wells	12–22
	September 25	#652	Jackie Gleason cover, Tony Curtis: Run for	

Year	Issue	Number	Description	Value ($)
1965	September 25	#652	Your Life, The Flintstones	3–5
	October 2–8	#653	Get Smart's Don Adams and Barbara Feldon cover, Rawhide, Combat	12–25
	October 9–15	#654	Honey West's Anne Francis cover, My Three Sons, I Spy, Soupy Sales	10–20
	October 16–22	#655	Red Skelton cover, Juliet Prowse, Trials of O'Brian, Roaring Chicken	3–6
	October 23–29	#656	Branded's Chuck Connors cover, Honey West, Gunsmoke, I Spy's Bill Cosby	10–15
	October 30	#657	Addams Family cover, Get Smart	20–40+
	November 6–12	#658	Lost in Space cover, Jackie Cooper	40–80+
	November 13–19	#659	Joey Heatherton cover, Richard Crenna, Frank Sinatra	6–12
	November 20–26	#660	The F.B.I. cover, F Troop, Rod Serling	3–6
	November 27	#661	Hogan's Heroes' Bob Crane cover, Liza Minnelli, Green Acres	10–20

Year	Issue	Number	Description	Value ($)
1965	December 4–10	#662	Juliet Prowse cover, The Wild, Wild West, My Mother the Car	6–12
	December 11–17	#663	F-Troop cover, Peter Falk, Gidget	7–15
	December 18–24	#664	Gomer Pyle, U.S.M.C. cover, Mr. Ed	6–10
	December 25–31	#665	Christmas issue special, Bewitched, Hogan's Heroes	5–10
1966	January 1–7	#666	Carol Channing cover, The F.B.I., Ben Casey	3–5
	January 8–14	#667	Green Acres' Eva Gabor and Eddie Albert cover, Petticoat Junction, Gilligan's Island	5–10
	January 15–21	#668	I Spy's Robert Culp and Bill Cosby cover, The Loner	10–20
	January 22–28	#669	The Fugitive's David Janssen cover, Hogan's Heroes' Werner Klemperer	10–20
	January 29	#670	Please Don't Eat the Daisies cast cover, Get Smart, Mr. Roberts, Garry Moore	2–5
	February 5–11	#671	I Dream of Jeannie's Barbara Eden and Larry	

Year	Issue	Number	Description	Value ($)
1966	February 5–11	#671	Hagman cover, Lost in Space, The Smothers Brothers	15–25
	February 12–18	#672	Peyton Place's Barbara Parkins and Ryan O'Neal cover, The Virginian, Batman, Jacques Cousteau	3–6
	February 19–25	#673	Run for Your Life's Ben Gazzara, The Big Valley's Lee Majors, Dr. Kildare	3–5
	February 26	#674	The Big Valley's Barbara Stanwyck cover, The Dick Van Dyke Show	7–15
	March 5–11	#675	Get Smart's Barbara Feldon cover, My Favorite Martian, Andy Warhol	10–20
	March 12–18	#676	Beverly Hillbillies cast cover, I Dream of Jeannie	10–20
	March 19–25	#677	The Man from U.N.C.L.E.'s David McCallum and Robert Vaughn cover, The Donna Reed Show's last episode	12–25
	March 26	#678	Batman's Adam West cover,	

Year	Issue	Number	Description	Value ($)
1966	March 26	#678	Flipper, Secret Agent	20–40
	April 2–8	#679	Dean Martin cover, Honey West, The Man U.N.C.L.E., Get Smart	7–15
	April 9–15	#680	The Long Hot Summer's Roy Thinnes cover, My Mother the Car	2–5
	April 16–22	#681	Petticoat Junction cover, The Wild, Wild West	10–20
	April 23–29	#682	Andy Williams cover, Wide World of Sports, Barbara McNair	2–5
	April 30	#683	Lucille Ball cover, My Mother the Car, Jesse James	2–5
	May 7–13	#684	President Johnson cover, My Three Sons	2–5
	May 14–20	#685	Frank Sinatra cover and special, The Avengers	5–10
	May 21–27	#686	The Wild, Wild West's Robert Conrad and Ross Martin cover, Get Smart, The Dick Van Dyke Show's last episode	15–30
	May 28	#687	Gidget's Sally Field cover, Red Skelton	5–10

Year	Issue	Number	Description	Value ($)
1966	June 4–10	#688	Mayberry's Andy Griffith, The Man from U.N.C.L.E., Batman	5–10
	June 11–17	#689	Gilligan's Island cast cover, Dragnet	10–20
	June 18–24	#690	Bewitched cast cover, Arlene Francis, Willie Mays	10–20
	June 25	#691	Laredo cast cover, Batman's Batmobile	5–10
	July 2–8	#692	Walter Cronkite cover, Sarah: Napoleon Solo's secretary from The Man from U.N.C.L.E.	5–10
	July 9–15	#693	Flipper cover, The Soupy Sales Show, Sammy Davis, Jr.	5–10
	July 16–22	#694	My Three Sons' Fred MacMurray and William Demarest cover, Voyage to the Bottom of the Sea's David Hedison, The Fugitive	6–12
	July 23–29	#695	The F.B.I. cover, Laredo, The Munsters	5–10
	July 30	#696	Johnny Carson cover, The Beatles, Bette	

Year	Issue	Number	Description	Value ($)
1966	July 30	#696	Davis	5–10
	August 6–12	#697	Daktari cover, "No One Ever Upsets the Star"	15–30
	October 22–28	#708	Lucille Ball in London cover and special, Bewitched, Bozo the Clown	5–10
	October 29	#709	Green Hornet cast cover, The Time Tunnel	35–75
	November 5–11	#710	The Man from U.N.C.L.E. cast cover, The Bell Telephone Hour	15–30
	November 12–18	#711	That Girl's Marlo Thomas cover, Gene Arthur, Mission Impossible, Roger Miller	2–5
	November 19–25	#712	Hogan's Heroes cover, The Monkees, Merv Griffin	10–20
	November 26	#713	Tarzan's Ron Ely cover, Frank Sinatra	2–5
	December 3–9	#714	Rat Patrol cast cover, Dark Shadows	15–30
	December 10–16	#715	Gunsmoke's James Arness cover, Mickey Rooney, Milton Berle, The Rat Patrol	4–8

Year	Issue	Number	Description	Value ($)
1966	December 17–23	#716	Occasional Wife cover, Tina Louise, The Girl from U.N.C.L.E., David Carradine	4–8
	December 24–30	#717	Christmas issue special, Linda Evans in 1966, Pistols and Petticoats, The Wild, Wild West's Robert Conrad, Disney	7–15
	December 31	#718	The Girl from U.N.C.L.E.'s Stefanie Powers cover, Larry Hagman	10–20
1967	January 7–13	#719	Run for Your Life's Ben Gazzara cover, The Avengers' Diana Rigg, Love on a Rooftop	5–10
	January 14–20	#720	Art Carney cover, Dom DeLuise, Pistols and Petticoats	2–5
	January 21–27	#721	The Avengers' Diana Rigg and Patrick Macnee cover, Petula Clark, The Iron Horse	20–40
	January 28	#722	The Monkees cover, Jackie Gleason	15–30
	February 4–10	#723	The Iron Horse's	

#658, 1965

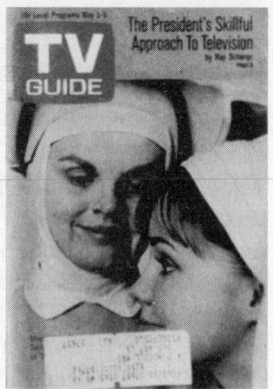

#840, 1969

#678, 1966

#709, 1966

#721, 1967

#727, 1967

#760, 1967

#763, 1967

#774, 1968

Year	Issue	Number	Description	Value ($)
1967	February 4–10	#723	Dale Robertson cover, Candid Camera, Lauren Bacall, Captain Nice	2–5
	February 11–17	#724	Mission Impossible's Barbara Bain and Martin Landau cover, Mr. Terrific, Captain Nice, TV cartoons, Batman, The Girl from U.N.C.L.E.	10–20
	February 18–24	#725	Dean Martin cover, Lana Wood, Diahann Carroll, The Invaders	4–8
	February 25	#726	Phyllis Diller cover, Laredo, Alan King	2–5
	March 4–10	#727	Star Trek's William Shatner and Leonard Nimoy cover, The Road West, Ingrid Bergman	25–50+
	March 11–17	#728	Dorothy Malone cover, The Girl from U.N.C.L.E.'s Noel Harrison, Jane Fonda, Daniel Boone	4–8
	March 18–24	#729	Jackie Gleason cover, Sea Hunt, Dragnet	4–8
	March 25–31	#730	I Spy's Robert Culp and Bill	

Year	Issue	Number	Description	Value ($)
1967	March 25–31	#730	Cosby cover, Star Trek, Batman's Robin, The Boy Wonder	10–20
	April 1–7	#731	Daktari cover, Rango's Tim Conway, T.H.E. Cat	2–4
	April 8–14	#732	Dick Van Dyke cover, The Girl from U.N.C.L.E., Phil Silvers	3–6
	April 15–21	#733	The Starlet 1967 cover and special, The Beverly Hillbillies' Irene Ryan, The Felony Squad	3–6
	April 22–28	#734	Family Affair cast cover, Lucille Ball, Tijuana Brass, Smothers Brothers	5–10
	April 29	#735	Lawrence Welk cover, Star Trek's Mr. Spock, The Avengers	10–20
	May 6–12	#736	Dragnet's Jack Webb and Harry Morgan cover, Jack Banner	4–8
	May 13–19	#737	Bewitched's Elizabeth Montgomery cover, Greg Morris	6–10
	May 20–26	#738	Andy Griffith cover, Gilligan's	

Year	Issue	Number	Description	Value ($)
1967	May 20–26	#738	Island's Dawn Wells	4–8
	May 27	#739	F-Troop cast cover, T.H.E. Cat, Mr. Terrific	6–12
	June 3–9	#740	The Felony Squad's Howard Duff cover, The Emmy Awards, Vic Damone	2–4
	June 10–16	#741	The Smothers Brothers cover The Avengers' Diana Rigg and the Emma Peeler, The Time Tunnel	10–20
	June 17–23	#742	Ed Sullivan cover, Tim Conway, What's My Line's last show	2–4
	June 24–30	#743	Get Smart's Barbara Feldon and Don Adams cover, Disney	10–20
	July 1–7	#744	David Brinkley and Chet Huntley cover, The Man from U.N.C.L.E., Hillbillies, Tarzan	3–6
	September 23–29	#756	The Monkees cover, I Dream of Jeannie's Barbara Eden, Rock Hudson	12–25
	September 30	#757	The Flying Nun's Sally Field cover, The Time Tunnel, The Man from U.N.C.L.E.	10–20

Year	Issue	Number	Description	Value ($)
1967	October 7–13	#758	He and She's Jack Cassidy cover, Cimarron Strip, Marlo Thomas	2–4
	October 14–20	#759	Johnny Carson cover, Star Trek's Androids, Daktari	10–20
	October 21–27	#760	Mia Farrow cover, Don Knotts, The High Chaparral	2–4
	October 28	#761	Who Killed Hollywood special, John Wayne, Henry Fonda, Paula Prentiss, Carol Burnett	2–4
	November 4–10	#762	Cimarron Strip cover, Batman's Batgirl . . . Yvonne Craig	10–20
	November 11–17	#763	Yvette Mimieux cover, TV specials, Mothers-in-law, Harry Reasoner	3–6
	November 18–24	#764	Star Trek's William Shatner and Leonard Nimoy cover, Ironside, Hippies	25–50+
	November 25	#765	Garrison's Gorillas cover, Mel Blanc, Who Killed Hollywood	10–20
	December 2–8	#766	Danny and Marlo Thomas cover, Barbara Stanwyck, Jack Paar	2–4

Year	Issue	Number	Description	Value ($)
1967	December 9–15	#767	The Mothers-in-law's Eve Arden cover, Gomer Pyle's Frank Sutton, Carol Burnett	2–4
	December 16–22	#768	Sebastian Cabot cover, Pat Paulsen, Ed McMahon	2–4
	December 23–29	#769	Christmas issue special, Bonanza, Hogan's Heroes' Richard Dawson	4–8
	December 30	#770	Carol Burnett cover, Lynn Redgrave, Cousteau	2–4
1968	January 6–12	#771	The Wild, Wild West's Robert Conrad cover	15–30
	January 13–19	#772	Bob Hope cover, Marlo Thomas, Mannix, The High Chaparral	2–4
	January 20–26	#773	High Chaparral cover, Garrison's Gorillas, Mission Impossible	5–10
	January 27	#774	Bewitched's Elizabeth Montgomery cover, Cowboy in Africa's Chuck Connors	7–15
	February 3–9	#775	Run for Your Life's Ben Gazzara cover,	

Year	Issue	Number	Description	Value ($)
1968	February 3–9	#775	N.Y.P.D., Winter Olympics	2–4
	February 10–16	#776	The Smothers Brothers cover	3–5
	February 17–23	#777	The F.B.I. Cover, My Three Sons, Jonathan Winters	3–5
	February 24	#778	Joey Bishop cover, It Takes a Thief, The Man from U.N.C.L.E.'s Robert, Vaughn	4–8
	March 2–8	#779	Bonanza's Lorne Greene and David Canary cover, The Avengers, The Newlywed Game	10–15
	March 9–15	#780	Jackie Gleason cover, Lucille Ball, The Dating Game, Jack Benny	4–8
	March 16–22	#781	The Flying Nun's Sally Field cover, Don Rickles, Bill Cosby, Mannix	15–20+
	March 23–29	#782	I Spy's Robert Culp and Bill Cosby cover, Zsa Zsa Gabor, Laugh-In, Petticoat Junction	10–15
	March 30	#783	Lucille Ball cover, Ed Ames, Walter Brennan	3–5
	April 6–12	#784	Ironside cover, Daktari, Tarzan	4–8
	April 13–19	#785	Carl Betz cover, Angie Dickinson photos	4–8

Year	Issue	Number	Description	Value ($)
1968	April 20–26	#786	Get Smart's Barbara Feldon cover, The Jerry Lewis Show, Beverly Hillbillies' Irene Ryan	15–25
	April 27	#787	Leslie Uggams cover, The High Chaparral's Cameron Mitchell	5–10
	May 4–10	#788	Mission Impossible cast cover, Vicki Lawrence	8–12
	May 11–17	#789	Daniel Boone's Fess Parker cover, Dragnet	3–6
	May 18–24	#790	Mannix's Mike Connors cover, Lucille Ball, Vivian Vance	3–6
	May 25–31	#791	Peyton Place's Diana Hyland cover, Raquel Welch, The Prisoner	9–20
	June 1–7	#792	Ed Sullivan cover, Richard Burton and Elizabeth Taylor, The Wild, Wild West	8–12
	June 8–14	#793	Hugh Downs cover, Salvador Dali on TV	3–6
	June 15–21	#794	High Chaparral cover, Glen Campbell, Abby Dalton	4–8

Year	Issue	Number	Description	Value ($)
1968	June 22–28	#795	Toni Helfer cover, Star Trek's William Shatner	15–30
	June 29	#796	It Takes a Thief's Robert Wagner cover, Goldie Hawn, Gunsmoke	8–12
	July 6–12	#797	I Dream of Jeannie's Barbara Eden cover, Johnny Carson	15–25
	July 13–19	#798	Andy Griffith, Don Knotts, and Jim Nabors cover, Hawaii Five-0	8–12
	July 20–26	#799	The Big Valley cast cover, Laugh-In's Kaye Ballard, Andy Griffith	15–20
	July 27	#800	Frank Sinatra Jr. and Joey Heatherton cover, Cher, Dom DeLuise	8–12
	August 3–9	#801	TV Anchormen cover, Hogan's Heroes' Bob Crane, The Avengers' Diana Rigg	8–12
	August 10–16	#802	Gentle Ben cast cover, Mannix, Joan Rivers	4–8
	August 17–23	#803	Gunsmoke cast cover, Frank Gifford, Merv Griffin	8–12
	August 24–30	#804	Star Trek cast cover, Edd	

Year	Issue	Number	Description	Value ($)
1968	August 24–30	#804	Byrnes, Clint Eastwood	30–50+
	August 31	#805	Johnny Carson cover, The Prisoner	8–12
	September 7–13	#806	Family Affair cast cover	8–12
	September 14–20	#807	Fall Preview special	20–40+
	September 21–27	#808	Laugh-In's Rowan and Martin cover, Art Carney, Anthony Quinn	8–12
	September 28	#809	Dean Martin cover, Peyton Place, Lee Marvin	3–6
	October 5–11	#810	My Three Sons cast cover, Dragnet, Carol Burnett, The Mod Squad	8–12
	October 12–18	#811	Olympics cover, Tiny Tim, Raymond Burr, TV monsters	8–12
	October 19–25	#812	Jim Nabors cover, Charlie Brown, The Ghost and Mrs. Muir, Mannix, Dragnet	4–8
	October 26	#813	The Ghost and Mrs. Muir's Hope Lange, Gomer Pyle, Jay Silverheels	8–12
	November 2–8	#814	The Mod Squad cover, Jackie Gleason, The High Chaparral	10–20

Year	Issue	Number	Description	Value ($)
1968	November 9–15	#815	Special Get Smart wedding cover and feature, Johnny Carson, James Garner	15–30
	November 16–22	#816	The Good Guys cast cover, Patrick Macnee	8–12
	November 23–29	#817	Frank Sinatra cover, Woody Allen, Peggy Fleming	4–8
	November 30	#818	Ann-Margret cover, Brigitte Bardot, Elvis Presley	8–12
	December 7–13	#819	That's Life cover, Diana Ross, Hawaii Five-0	8–12
	December 14–20	#820	Diahann Carroll cover, Green Acres' Arnold the Pig, John Wayne, Adam 12	8–12
	December 21–27	#821	Christmas issue special, Mayberry R.F.D., Walt Disney's Mickey Mouse	8–12
	December 28	#822	Doris Day cover, Michael Caine	4–8
1969	January 4–10	#823	Here Come the Brides' Bobby Sherman and cast cover, Hawaii Five-0	15–25
	January 11–17	#824	Bob Hope cover, Cousteau, Peyton Place	3–6

Year	Issue	Number	Description	Value ($)
1969	January 18–24	#825	The Outsider's Darren McGavin cover, The Prisoner, The Land of the Giants	15–25
	January 25–31	#826	Land of the Giants cast cover, 60 Minutes, Judy Carnes	25–45+
	February 1–7	#827	High Chaparral cover, David McCallum, Dark Shadows	8–12
	February 8–14	#828	Mission Impossible cast cover, Stella Stevens	10–20
	February 15–21	#829	Ironside's Raymond Burr cover, Land of the Giants, Jimmy Durante	8–12
	February 22–28	#830	Lancer cast cover, Land of the Giants	8–12
	March 1–7	#831	Lucille Ball and her children cover, The Outcasts, Dean Martin	4–8
	March 8–14	#832	Laugh-In cast cover, Jonathan Winters	8–12
	March 15–21	#833	Mayberry R.F.D. cover, Tom Jones, Hawaii Five-0, Lancer	8–12
	March 22–28	#834	Bewitched's Elizabeth Montgomery cover, Isaac	

Year	Issue	Number	Description	Value ($)
1969	March 22–28	#834	Asimov, Mission Impossible	15–25
	March 29	#835	The Name of the Game cast cover, Get Smart's Don Adams, The Felony Squad	8–12
	April 5–11	#836	The Smothers Brothers cover, Kate Smith, I Dream of Jeannie	8–12
	April 12–18	#837	Mary Tyler Moore cover, Dick Van Dyke, Goldie Hawn	8–12
	April 19–25	#838	Lawrence Welk cover, Joan Blondell, The Beatles	4–8
	April 26	#839	Jack Paar cover, Pierre Salinger, The F.B.I.	3–6
	May 3–9	#840	The Flying Nun's Sally Field cover, Ray Bradbury	15–25
	May 10–16	#841	Space special, Richard Chamberlain	3–6
	May 17–23	#842	Marlo Thomas cover, Wayne Newton, Pogo, The Ghost and Mrs. Muir	4–8
	May 24–30	#843	Today cast cover, Tom Jones, Mayberry R.F.D.	3–6
	May 31	#844	Family Affair cast cover, Walter Brennan	10–15

Year	Issue	Number	Description	Value ($)
1969	June 7–13	#845	The Hollywood Dancers cover, Robert Mitchum	3–6
	June 14–20	#846	Glen Campbell cover, Playboy After Dark, Green Acres	8–12
	June 21–27	#847	Jackie Gleason cover, TV's Soap As the World Turns	4–8
	June 28	#848	Julia cast cover, Joyce Van Patten	4–8
	July 5–11	#849	Adam 12 cast cover, Rosemary DeCamp, That Girl	8–12
	July 12–18	#850	Mod Squad cast cover, Petticoat Junction, Frank Sinatra	10–20
	July 19–25	#851	Apollo 11 cover and special moon telecast, Paul Lynde	6–12
	July 26	#852	Petticoat Junction cast cover, Carol Burnett, Lucille Ball	10–15
	August 2–8	#853	Lancer cover, Mission Impossible's Peter Graves, Laugh-In's Ruth Buzzi	8–12
	August 9–15	#854	Sports cover and feature, The Mod Squad's Peggy Lipton, Liberace, Don Murray	8–12

Year	Issue	Number	Description	Value ($)
1969	August 16–22	#855	Merv Griffin cover, Night Gallery, Robert Culp	8–12
	August 23–29	#856	High Chaparral cover, The Beverly Hillbillies, Lassie	8–12
	August 30	#857	Johnny Cash cover, Bing Crosby, Lassie, Milton Berle	4–8
	September 6–12	#858	Green Acres cover, The King Family	5–10
	September 13–19	#859	Fall issue special	15–30+
	September 20–26	#860	Jim Nabors cover, Room 222, Lassie	4–8
	September 27	#861	Marcus Welby, M.D., cover, Gina Lollobrigida	4–8
	October 4–10	#862	Bill Cosby cover, Sesame Street, Bill Bixby	3–6
	October 11–17	#863	TV and children special issue, Buddy Ebsen, Then Came Bronson	3–6
	October 18–24	#864	Mission Impossible cast cover, Richard Burton	8–12
	October 25–31	#865	My World and Welcome to It cover, Walt Disney, Land of the Giants, Room 222	8–12

#808, 1968

#809, 1968

#856, 1969

#556, 1969

#963, 1971

#501, 1972

#539, 1973

#1071, 1973

#1086, 1974

Year	Issue	Number	Description	Value ($)
1969	November 1–7	#866	Room 222 cast cover, Marcus Welby, Ann-Margret	4–8
	November 8–14	#867	Andy Williams cover, Leslie Uggams, Bill Cosby	3–6
	November 15–21	#868	The Governor and J.J. cover, Star Trek's William Shatner	8–12
	November 22–28	#869	I Dream of Jeannie special marriage issue . . . Barbara Eden on cover wearing wedding gown, Medical Center, The Mod Squad	15–20+
	November 29	#870	Bonanza cast cover, The Ghost and Mrs. Muir	15–25
	December 6–12	#871	Doris Day cover, Bracken's World, Mission Impossible	4–8
	December 13–19	#872	Then Came Bronson cover, David Frost, Simon and Garfunkel	4–8
	December 20–26	#873	Christmas issue special, The Courtship of Eddie's Father, Julia	4–8
	December 27	#874	Remembering 1969 special issue,	

Year	Issue	Number	Description	Value ($)
1969	December 27	#874	The Avengers' Diana Rigg, Adam 12	8–12
1970	January 3–9	#875	TV in the Seventies special issue, My World and Welcome to It	4–8
	January 10–16	#876	My Three Sons cover, Susan Saint James, Henry Fonda, Land of the Giants	8–12
	January 17–23	#877	Ironside cover, Flip Wilson, Jack Benny	3–6
	January 24–30	#878	Tom Jones cover, Bette Davis, Ricardo Montalban	3–6
	January 31	#879	Debbie Reynolds cover, John Wayne, The Bold Ones, Room 222	3–6
	February 7–13	#880	Bewitched cover, The Brady Bunch, Bobby Sherman	9–15
	February 14–20	#881	Bracken's World cover, Soap Operas, Dick Clark, John Wayne	3–6
	February 21–27	#882	Medical Center cast cover, Hee Haw, Room 222	3–6
	February 28	#883	Mod Squad cast cover, Jimmy Durante, Engelbert Humperdinck	8–12

Year	Issue	Number	Description	Value ($)
1970	March 7–13	#884	Hee Haw cover, Pat Paulsen	3–6
	March 14–20	#885	Diahann Carroll cover, Tim Conway, The Wizard of Oz	3–6
	March 21–27	#886	Jackie Gleason cover, Ringo Starr, Bill Cosby, Harry Belafonte, and Lena Horne	3–6
	March 28	#887	Rowan and Martin cover, Ringo on Laugh-In	3–6
	April 4–10	#888	The Brady Bunch cast cover, Laugh-In, Green Acres	15–25
	April 11–17	#889	Carol Burnett cover, Robert Wagner, Fred Astaire	3–6
	April 18–24	#890	The Bold Ones cover, Burl Ives, Lawrence Welk, Art Linkletter, Dean Martin	3–6
	April 25	#891	John Wayne and Raquel Welch cover and special, Leonard Nimoy, Terry-Thomas	8–12
	May 2–8	#892	Glen Campbell cover, Love American Style, The Nelsons, Isaac Asimov	3–6
	May 9–15	#893	David Frost cover, The Avengers' Diana Rigg, Robert Vaughn	8–12

Year	Issue	Number	Description	Value ($)
1970	May 16–22	#894	Vice President Agnew cover, James Stewart, Muppets	3–6
	May 23–29	#895	Tricia Nixon cover and her tour of the White House special with Mike Wallace, The Lennon Sisters, Liberace, Lancer	3–6
	May 30	#896	The Governor and J.J. cover, The Forsythe Saga	3–6
	June 6–12	#897	Robert Young cover, Doc Severinsen, Captain Kangaroo	3–6
	June 13–19	#898	Johnny Cash cover, The Forsythe Saga, Laugh-In	4–8
	June 20–26	#899	To Rome with Love cover, The Lone Ranger, Room 222	3–6
	June 27	#900	Liza Minnelli cover and special, The Hollywood Squares	3–6
	July 4–10	#901	The Courtship of Eddie's Father cover, Bill Bixby, Carol Burnett	3–6
	July 11–17	#902	The Beverly Hillbillies cover, Sesame Street, Bewitched	8–12

Year	Issue	Number	Description	Value ($)
1970	July 18–24	#903	The Golddiggers cover, Peter Graves, Gunsmoke's James Arness	8–12
	July 25–31	#904	Mayberry R.F.D. cast cover, Juliet Mills, Love American Style	3–6
	August 1–7	#905	Chet Huntley cover, The Odd Couple, Laugh-In	3–6
	August 8–14	#906	That Girl cover, Hogan's Heroes	3–6
	August 15–21	#907	Johnny Carson cover, Female stars, General Hospital	3–6
	August 22–28	#908	Gunsmoke cover, Jo Anne Worley, Mae West	4–8
	August 29	#909	Green Acres' Eddie Albert cover, Barefoot in the Park, Joel Grey	8–12
	September 5–11	#910	Lucille Ball and Liz Taylor cover, Miss America	15–20
	September 12–18	#911	Fall issue special	10–15
	September 19–25	#912	Mary Tyler Moore cover, The Young Lawyers, Chad Everett	4–8
	September 26	#913	Room 222 cast cover, The Partridge Family	8–12
	October 3–9	#914	Red Skelton cover, Lesley Ann	

Year	Issue	Number	Description	Value ($)
1970	October 3–9	#914	Warren, Dinah Shore	3–6
	October 10–16	#915	Arnie cover, Anne Francis, Flip Wilson	3–6
	October 17–23	#916	The Partridge Family cover, Arnie	15–25
	October 24–30	#917	Don Knotts cover, Hee Haw, Tim Conway	3–6
	October 31	#918	Mannix cover, Robert Stack, Dark Shadows	8–12
	November 7–13	#919	Nancy cast cover, Buck Owens	3–6
	November 14–20	#920	The Immortals cover, Christopher George, Lily Tomlin, The Odd Couple	3–6
	November 21–27	#921	Sally Marr cover, The Cisco Kid, Laugh-In	3–6
	November 28	#922	John Wayne cover and special, Yvette Mimieux	8–12
	December 5–11	#923	Dick Cavett cover, John Wayne, Mannix	4–8
	December 12–18	#924	Ed Sullivan and the Muppets cover, McCloud, The Mary Tyler Moore Show	4–8
	December 19–25	#925	Christmas issue special, Stewart Granger, Green Acres' Eva Gabor	3–6

Year	Issue	Number	Description	Value ($)
1970	December 26	#926	Julia cast cover, Yvette Mimieux, The Interns	4–8
1971	January 2–8	#927	Remember 1970 special, The Odd Couple's Tony Randall, The Partridge Family	8–12
	January 9–15	#928	Andy Griffith cover, Pinky Lee	3–6
	January 16–22	#929	Johnny Cash and June Carter cover, Make Room for Daddy, Green Acres' Arnold the Pig	3–6
	January 23–29	#930	Flip Wilson cover, Lassie, Dark Shadows	8–12
	January 30	#931	Gunsmoke's James Arness cover, Loretta Swit	4–8
	February 6–12	#932	The Odd Couple cover and feature	6–12
	February 13–19	#933	Goldie Hawn cover, The Immortals	4–8
	February 20–26	#934	Doris Day cover, The Interns, Hawaii Five-0, Carol Burnett	3–6
	February 27	#935	Hal Holbrook cover, All in the Family	3–6
	March 6–12	#936	The Interns' Broderick Crawford cover,	

Year	Issue	Number	Description	Value ($)
1971	March 6–12	#936	Alias Smith and Jones, Dinah Shore	8–12
	March 13–19	#937	The Name of the Game cover, Secret Storm	3–6
	March 20–26	#938	Harry Reasoner cover, The Interns, George C. Scott	3–6
	March 27	#939	Bonanza cast cover, The Partridge Family, Pearl Bailey	8–12
	April 3–9	#940	Cable TV special feature, Lee Meriwether, Firing Line	3–6
	April 10–16	#941	Bob Hope cover, Merv Griffin	3–6
	April 17–23	#942	Paul Newman cover, The Young Lawyers, Allan Sherman	3–6
	April 24–30	#943	Marcus Welby, M.D., cover, Mission Impossible, Lesley Ann Warren, The Beverly Hillbillies	4–8
	May 1–7	#944	Mary Tyler Moore cover, Lloyd Bridges, Tony Randall	6–10
	May 8–14	#945	Henry Fonda cover, The Smith Family, High Chaparral	3–6
	May 15–21	#946	TV Journalism special, Alias	

Year	Issue	Number	Description	Value ($)
1971	May 15–21	#946	Smith and Jones's Peter Duel	15–20
	May 22–28	#947	The Partridge Family's David Cassidy cover and feature . . . David's Teenage World, The Mary Tyler Moore Show's Ed Asner, Stiller and Meara	15–20
	May 29	#948	All in the Family cast cover, James Komack, American TV in China	8–12
	June 5–11	#949	Rowan and Martin cover, All My Children, Isaac Asimov	3–6
	June 12–18	#950	Lucille Ball cover, The Hollywood Squares	3–6
	June 19–25	#951	The Courtship of Eddie's Father cover, Dark Shadows	8–12
	June 26	#952	Adam 12 cover, Christine Crawford, Annie, Laugh-In	3–6
	July 3–9	#953	The Mod Squad cast cover, Old-Time Radio	15–20
	July 10–16	#954	Sesame Street's Cookie Monster cover, All in the Family's Sally	

Year	Issue	Number	Description	Value ($)
1971	July 10–16	#954	Struthers, Mel Torme	4–8
	July 17–23	#955	Medical Center's Chad Everett cover, Dick Cavett	3–6
	July 24–30	#956	Walt Disney's Dingaling Lynx cover, Arthur Fiedler	3–6
	July 31	#957	Henry the VIII on TV cover and special, Mr. Ed's Alan Young	4–8
	August 7–13	#958	As the World Turns cast cover, Mary Tyler Moore Show's Ted Knight, Gene Wilder	3–6
	August 14–20	#959	Bonanza cover, The Carpenters, Bewitched	8–12
	August 21–27	#960	Henry Fonda cover, Public TV, Connie Stevens, The Mod Squad	4–8
	August 28	#961	Announcers of Monday Night Football cover, Walter Cronkite	3–6
	September 4–10	#962	Hawaii Five-O's Jack Lord cover, Robert Morley, Ed Sullivan	10–18
	September 11–17	#963	Fall Preview special	8–12
	September 18–24	#964	Sandy Duncan cover, Funny	

Year	Issue	Number	Description	Value ($)
1971	September 18–24	#964	Face, Bearcats, Howdy Doody	4–8
	September 25	#965	Shirley MacLaine cover, Richard Boone, Cher	3–6
	October 2–8	#966	James Stewart cover, Mission Impossible's Barbara Bain, Rex Humbard	4–8
	October 9–15	#967	Dick Van Dyke and Hope Lange cover, Bonanza, Sandy Duncan	4–8
	October 16–22	#968	Mia Farrow cover and special . . . Then and Now, John Wayne, Sesame Street, The Partridge Family, Gidget	8–12
	October 23–29	#969	Longstreet's James Franciscus cover, Rod Taylor, Bearcats, Lynda Day George	3–6
	October 30	#970	The Good Life's Larry Hagman cover, Glen Campbell, Longstreet	3–6
	November 6–12	#971	Cannon's William Conrad cover, Anthony Eisley	3–6
	November 13–19	#972	The Partners' Don Adams cover, Sue Ane Langdon, Ann-Margret	3–6

Year	Issue	Number	Description	Value ($)
1971	November 20–26	#973	All in the Family cast cover, Funny Face, Nichols	8–12
	November 27	#974	Joanne Woodward cover, Modern-Day Monster Makers, Night Gallery	8–12
	December 4–10	#975	Special issue . . . John Wayne, Bob Hope, Julie Andrews, and Carol Burnett cover and feature, Dick Van Dyke, George Kennedy	4–8
	December 11–17	#976	James Garner cover, Hope Lange, Cannon, TV Wrestling	4–8
	December 18–24	#977	The Partridge Family cast cover, Patricia Neal, McCloud	15–20
	December 25–31	#978	Christmas issue special, Bobby Sherman, Lucille Ball	4–8
1972	January 1–7	#979	1971 Remembered, McMillan and Wife	3–6
	January 8–14	#980	Flip Wilson cover, McMillan and Wife	2–5
	January 15–21	#981	European TV, John Wayne, Bette Davis	2–4

Year	Issue	Number	Description	Value ($)
1972	January 22–28	#982	Mission Impossible cast cover, Nichols, Raymond Burr	5–10
	January 29	#983	David Janssen cover, Columbo	2–4
	February 5–11	#984	Ironside cast cover, Buddy Ebsen, Night Gallery	6–10
	February 12–18	#985	Owen Marshall Attorney at Law cover, Marilyn Monroe, Sonny and Cher	4–8
	February 19–25	#986	TV Journalism special, Alias Smith and Jones, Don Rickles	8–12
	February 26	#987	Mary Tyler Moore cover, Susan Hayward, Sanford and Son	5–10
	March 4–10	#988	Johnny Carson cover, Vera Miles, Alex Karras	2–4
	March 11–17	#989	Marcus Welby, M.D., cast cover, Morris the Cat	2–4
	March 18–24	#990	Sonny and Cher cover, Gunsmoke's James Garner	6–12
	March 25–31	#991	Columbo's Peter Falk cover, Star Trek	6–12
	April 1–7	#992	Glenn Ford cover, Julie Adams, Emergency	2–4

Year	Issue	Number	Description	Value ($)
1972	April 8–14	#993	TV Political Coverage special, Jerry Lewis, Roger Moore, The Story of the Oscar	2–4
	April 15–21	#994	Moon Spectacular special, All in the Family's Rob Reiner, David Frost	3–6
	April 22–28	#995	Don Rickles cover, Hope Lange, The Muppets, Hank Aaron	3–6

Note: April 29–May 5 issue begins *TV Guide*'s change in issue numbering.

Year	Issue	Number	Description	Value ($)
1972	April 29	#496 (#996)	McMillan and Wife cover, Longstreet, TV's Golddiggers	3–6
	May 6–12	#497 (#997)	Funny Face's Sandy Duncan cover, Peter Marshall, General Hospital	2–4
	May 13–19	#498 (#998)	Sanford and Son cover, Janet Blair, Jennifer O'Neill	4–8
	May 20–26	#499 (#999)	F.B.I. cover, Brenda Vaccaro, Gary Collins	
	May 27	#500 (#1000)	All in the Family cast cover, The Future of Bonanza, Lloyd Bridges	6–12

Year	Issue	Number	Description	Value ($)
1972	June 3–9	#501 (#1001)	Night Gallery's Rod Serling cover, Ruth Buzzi, Carroll O'Connor	15–20
	June 10–16	#502 (#1002)	Doris Day cover, Susan Hampshire, Lassie, Mel Blanc, Dr. Who	3–6
	June 17–23	#503 (#1003)	Emergency's Julie London cover, Melba Moore, Marty Feldman	3–5
	June 24–30	#504 (#1004)	Mannix's Mike Connors cover, Sherry Bain, Mary Tyler Moore	3–6
	July 1–7	#505 (#1005)	Carol Burnett cover, Room 222	3–6
	July 8–14	#506 (#1006)	Merv Griffin cover, Susan Sullivan, Lucille Ball	2–5
	July 15–21	#507 (#1007)	The Partridge Family's David Cassidy cover, Curt Gowdy, British TV	12–22
	July 22–28	#508 (#1008)	Adam 12 cast cover, Phil Donahue	3–6
	July 29	#509 (#1009)	Love American Style cover, Emergency, Sandy Duncan	3–6
	August 5–11	#510 (#1010)	War and Peace on TV special, William Shatner, David Steinberg	6–12

Year	Issue	Number	Description	Value ($)
1972	August 12–18	#511 (#1011)	Leonardo da Vinci TV special, Alan King	2–4
	August 19–25	#512 (#1012)	Medical Center's Chad Everett cover, As the World Turns	2–4
	August 26	#513 (#1013)	Olympics issue special, Bobby Darin	3–5
	September 2–8	#514 (#1014)	The Odd Couple cover, Liza Minnelli, David Niven	6–12
	September 9–15	#515 (#1015)	Fall Preview special	15–20
	September 16–22	#516 (#1016)	Yul Brynner, The King and I cover, Laugh-In's Goldie Hawn	3–6
	September 23–29	#517 (#1017)	Banacek's George Peppard cover, Ed McMahon, Dr. Joyce Brothers	2–4
	September 30	#518 (#1018)	Bridget Loves Bernie cover, Doctor in the House, Bill Cosby	3–5
	October 7–13	#519 (#1019)	Bonanza cast cover, Mission Impossible, Groucho Marx	10–15
	October 14–20	#520 (#1020)	Assignment Vienna's Robert Conrad cover, The Protectors, The Mod Squad	6–12
	October 21–27	#521 (#1021)	Carroll O'Connor and Cloris	

Year	Issue	Number	Description	Value ($)
1972	October 21–27	#521 (#1021)	Leachman in Of Thee I Sing cover and special, Lee Majors, The Rookies	3–5
	October 28	#522 (#1022)	Charlie Brown cover and special, Julie Andrews, Jacqueline Scott	6–12
	November 4–10	#523 (#1023)	John Wayne cover, The Little People, President Richard Nixon	3–5
	November 11–17	#524 (#1024)	America's Alistair Cooke cover, Patton, David Carradine	3–5
	November 18–24	#525 (#1025)	Maude's Bea Arthur cover, James Caan, The Waltons, Henry Mancini	3–5
	November 25	#526 (#1026)	Search cast cover, Orson Welles, Lassie, Paul Lynde	2–4
	December 2–8	#527 (#1027)	Mike Douglas cover, Banacek	2–4
	December 9–15	#528 (#1028)	Julie Andrews cover, Ghost Story, Alice Cooper	6–12
	December 16–22	#529 (#1029)	The Duke and Duchess of Windsor cover and special, Bridget Loves Bernie	4–8

Year	Issue	Number	Description	Value ($)
1972	December 23–29	#530 (#1030)	Christmas issue special, The Partridge Family, Gavin MacLeod	6–12
	December 30	#531 (#1031)	Barbara Walters cover, Isaac Asimov, Assignment Vienna	2–4
1973	January 6–12	#532 (#1032)	1972 Reviewed, Shelley Winters	2–3
	January 13–19	#533 (#1033)	China special, Susan Dey, Robert Vaughn	12–22
	January 20–26	#534 (#1034)	Bob Newhart Show cast cover, Dr. Kildare	5–10
	January 27	#535 (#1035)	The Rookies cast cover, The Waltons, Mission Impossible	5–10
	February 3–9	#536 (#1036)	Bill Cosby cover, Elizabeth Taylor: The Burtons, Hawaii Five-0	3–5
	February 10–16	#537 (#1037)	The Paul Lynde Show cover, Maude's Adrienne Barbeau, M.A.S.H.	6–12
	February 17–23	#538 (#1038)	McMillan and Wife's Susan Saint James and Rock Hudson cover, Diana Rigg, Larry Hagman	6–12
	February 24	#539 (#1039)	M.A.S.H. cast cover, John	

Year	Issue	Number	Description	Value ($)
1973	February 24	#539 (#1039)	Wayne, Kate Jackson	6–12
	March 3–9	#540 (#1040)	Cannon's William Conrad cover, Dr. Jekyll and Mr. Hyde, Kung Fu	3–5
	March 10–16	#541 (#1041)	Marlo Thomas cover and special, Gene Wilder	3–5
	March 17–23	#542 (#1042)	Sanford and Son cover, Mission Impossible	6–12
	March 24–30	#543 (#1043)	Ann-Margret cover and special, Admiral Perry, M.A.S.H., Bette Davis	6–12
	March 31	#544 (#1044)	Lucille Ball and Desi Arnaz Jr. cover and special	6–12
	April 7–13	#545 (#1045)	Children's TV special, The Partridge Family, Kim Novak	6–12
	April 14–20	#546 (#1046)	The Little People's Shelley Fabares and Brian Keith cover, Barnaby Jones	6–12
	April 21–27	#547 (#1047)	Raymond Burr as Pope John cover and special, Bobby Darin	3–5
	April 28	#548 (#1048)	The Waltons cast cover, TV Western plots, Cleavon Little	6–12

Year	Issue	Number	Description	Value ($)
1973	May 5–11	#549 (#1049)	Columbo's Peter Falk cover, Paul Lynde, Star Trek	6–12
	May 12–18	#550 (#1050)	Shirley Booth cover, Skylab, Peyton Place, Jayne Kennedy	2–4
	May 19–25	#551 (#1051)	Mary Tyler Moore cover, The Brady Bunch, Isaac Asimov	6–12
	May 26	#552 (#1052)	Streets of San Francisco cover, Jimmy Breslin, Kung Fu	3–5
	June 2–8	#553 (#1053)	All in the Family cover, Fannie Flagg, Mark Spitz	5–10
	June 9–15	#554 (#1054)	Madigan's Richard Widmark cover, The Bob Newhart Show, Lee Meriwether	3–5
	June 16–22	#555 (#1055)	Maude cast cover, American Bandstand, M.A.S.H.	3–5
	June 23–29	#556 (#1056)	Kung Fu's David Carradine cover, Lola Falana	12–22
	June 30	#557 (#1057)	McCloud's Dennis Weaver cover, Bridget Loves Bernie	3–5
	July 7–13	#558 (#1058)	Dick Cavett cover, Jacqueline Susann	2–4
	July 14–20	#559 (#1059)	Sonny and Cher cover, Michael Tilson-Thomas	6–12

Year	Issue	Number	Description	Value ($)
1973	July 21–27	#560 (#1060)	Marcus Welby and Medical Center cover, Helen Reddy, Peter Graves	3–5
	July 28	#561 (#1061)	TV sex movies special, Monty Hall, General Hospital	3–5
	August 4–10	#562 (#1062)	Adam 12 cover, Julie Harris	3–5
	August 11–17	#563 (#1063)	Hee Haw's Roy Clark cover, Anne Meara, Hank Aaron	3–5
	August 18–24	#564 (#1064)	Emergency's Robert Fuller cover, Bill Cosby, Mary Tyler Moore	3–5
	August 25–31	#565 (#1065)	Barnaby Jones's Buddy Ebsen cover, Secret Storm	3–5
	September 1–7	#566 (#1066)	Miss America contest special, Bert Parks	2–4
	September 8–14	#567 (#1067)	Fall Preview Special	12–22

Note: Beginning with the September 15–21 issue, *TV Guide* returns to the original issue numbering.

Year	Issue	Number	Description	Value ($)
1973	September 15–21	#1068	Football special	2–4
	September 22–28	#1069	Hawaii Five-0 cover, Paul Winchell, Peter Pan	6–12
	September 29	#1070	Vietnam War special issue,	

Year	Issue	Number	Description	Value ($)
1973	September 29	#1070	Diana Rigg, Gunsmoke, The Waltons	6–12
	October 6–12	#1071	Diana's Diana Rigg, Wolfman Jack, Bilko	6–12
	October 13–19	#1072	TV's Limits special, Sally Field, Burt Reynolds	3–5
	October 20–26	#1073	Kojak's Telly Savalas cover, 60 Minutes, Randy Mantooth	3–5
	October 27	#1074	Adam's Rib cover, Barbra Streisand, Steve McQueen	3–5
	November 3–9	#1075	Needles and Pins cover, Alfred Hitchcock	2–4
	November 10–16	#1076	A Week of Specials, Adam's Rib, Sammy Davis Jr.	2–4
	November 17–23	#1077	Frank Sinatra cover, Natalie Wood, My Fair Lady	3–5
	November 24–30	#1078	Cousteau cover and Antarctica special, Milton Berle, The Waltons, Frankenstein	3–5
	December 1–7	#1079	The Magician's Bill Bixby cover, Perry Mason	3–5

Year	Issue	Number	Description	Value ($)
1973	December 8–14	#1080	Mary Tyler Moore cast cover, Buck Taylor, The Magician	3–5
	December 15–21	#1081	Katharine Hepburn cover, 3-D TV, Darren McGavin	2–5
	December 22–28	#1082	Christmas issue special, The Rockefellers, Susan Strasberg	3–5
	December 29	#1083	Mason Reese cover, Miss World, The Guiding Light	3–5
1974	January 5–11	#1084	Reviewing 1973, Richard Chamberlain	2–4
	January 12–18	#1085	Maude cast cover	2–4
	January 19–25	#1086	Bob Hope cover, Larry Hagman	2–4
	January 26	#1087	Kung Fu's David Carradine cover, W. C. Fields, The Diary of Jane Pittman	9–17
	February 2–8	#1088	Lotsa Luck's Dom DeLuise cover, Jason Robards, The Magician, Isaac Asimov	2–4
	February 9–15	#1089	M.A.S.H. cast cover	6–12
	February 16–22	#1090	The Streets of San Francisco cast cover	3–5

Year	Issue	Number	Description	Value ($)
1974	February 23	#1091	Hec Ramsey's Richard Boone cover, Gloria Swanson, Upstairs, Downstairs	2–4
	March 2–8	#1092	Hawkins's James Stewart cover, Alice Cooper, Lloyd Bridges	6–12
	March 9–15	#1093	TV news and show-biz special, Martin Sheen, Shirley Jones	5–10
	March 16–22	#1094	Carol Burnett and Vicki Lawrence cover, The Six Million Dollar Man, Upstairs, Downstairs	4–8
	March 23–29	#1095	Doc Elliot cover, Oscar Wild, Carl Sagan, Gunsmoke	2–4
	March 30	#1096	Toma cast cover, The Oscar, Happy Days	3–5
	April 6–12	#1097	Norman Lear, Redd Foxx, and Carroll O'Connor cover, Good Times, Tarzan	3–5
	April 13–19	#1098	The Waltons cast cover, The Odd Couple, Sally Field	6–12
	April 20–26	#1099	Columbo's Peter Falk cover, Richard	

Year	Issue	Number	Description	Value ($)
1974	April 20–26	#1099	Roundtree, Isaac Asimov, Andy Griffith	3–5
	April 27	#1100	QB VII cover, Liza Minnelli	2–4
	May 4–10	#1101	The Rookies cast cover, Firehouse, Isaac Asimov	4–6
	May 11–17	#1102	The Bob Newhart Show cover, Nova	4–6
	May 18–24	#1103	The Six Million Dollar Man's Lee Majors cover, Johnny Carson	6–12
	May 25–31	#1104	McCloud cast cover, Soul Train, Robert Morley	3–5
	June 1–7	#1105	Sonny and Cher cover, Carl Sagan	6–12
	June 8–14	#1106	KQED TV San Francisco cover, John Davidson, Columbo	2–4
	June 15–21	#1107	Happy Days' Ron Howard and Kathy O'Dare cover, All in the Family	5–10
	June 22–28	#1108	John Chancellor cover, Japanese TV, Nancy Walker	2–4
	June 29	#1109	Good Times cover, The Six Million Dollar Man	5–10
	July 6–12	#1110	Lucille Ball cover, Japanese TV	3–5

Year	Issue	Number	Description	Value ($)
1974	July 13–19	#1111	Johnny Carson cover, Cannon, Mannix, Barnaby Jones	3–5
	July 20–26	#1112	Made-for-TV Films special, Betty White, Mac Davis	2–4
	July 27	#1113	Apple's Way cover, Sherlock Holmes, Columbo	2–4
	August 3–9	#1114	Emergency cast cover, The Hudson Brothers	3–5
	August 10–16	#1115	TV Game shows, M.A.S.H.	3–5
	August 17–23	#1116	Police Story cover, Good Times, Johnny Carson	2–4
	August 24–30	#1117	Susan Blakely cover, Tom Snyder, M.A.S.H.	3–5
	August 31	#1118	Kojak's Telly Savalas cover, Evel Knievel, Henry Fonda	3–5
	September 7–13	#1119	Fall Preview special	6–12
	September 14–20	#1120	New Show winners special, Connie Stevens, O. J. Simpson	3–5
	September 21–27	#1121	Football 1974 special, Barbara Walters	2–4
	September 28	#1122	Friends and Lovers cover, Bill Cosby, Shazam	2–4

Year	Issue	Number	Description	Value ($)
1974	October 5–11	#1123	Sanford and Son cover, Demond Wilson	4–8
	October 12–18	#1124	Rhoda's Valerie Harper cover, James Earl Jones, That's My Mama	4–8
	October 19–25	#1125	Chico and the Man's Freddie Prinze cover, Born Free, Robert Culp	6–12
	October 26	#1126	The Waltons cast cover, Columbo, Elvis Presley	6–12
	November 2–8	#1127	M.A.S.H. cast cover, Clint Eastwood, Born Free, The Jeffersons	6–12
	November 9–15	#1128	Sophia Loren cover, Lucas Tanner, Isaac Asimov	3–5
	November 16–22	#1129	The Godfather on TV special, Marlon Brando, Jodie Foster	4–6
	November 23–29	#1130	What a Week special, Chico and the Man	4–6
	November 30	#1131	Get Christie Love's Teresa Graves cover, Paul Newman, John Denver, Police Woman	4–6
	December 7–13	#1132	Little House on the Prairie's	

Year	Issue	Number	Description	Value ($)
1974	December 7–13	#1132	Michael Landon cover, The Planet of the Apes	6–12
	December 14–20	#1133	Good Times cast cover, Harry-O	3–5
	December 21–27	#1134	Christmas issue special, The Rockford Files	3–5
	December 28	#1135	TV Bowling special, Upstairs, Downstairs, Citizen Kane	2–4
1975	January 4–10	#1136	Police Woman's Angie Dickinson cover, Richard Chamberlain, Little House on the Prairie	6–12
	January 11–17	#1137	Harry-O's David Janssen cover, Little House on the Prairie	3–5
	January 18–24	#1138	That's My Mama cast cover, Maureen Stapleton	3–5
	January 25–31	#1139	Today cover, Upstairs, Downstairs, Tony Orlando	3–5
	February 1–7	#1140	The Rockford Files' James Garner cover, TV's Old Shows, Mac Davis	6–12
	February 8–14	#1141	Bob Newhart cover, Linda Blair, Another World	6–12

Year	Issue	Number	Description	Value ($)
1975	February 15–21	#1142	The Rookies cast cover, Superman	6–12
	February 22–28	#1143	Kojak's Telly Savalas cover, The Jeffersons, Isaac Asimov	3–5
	March 1–7	#1144	Chico and the Man cover, The Smothers Brothers, Karen Black (Note: This issue is dated March 1–8 on the cover.)	4–8
	March 8–14	#1145	Medical Center's Chad Everett cover, David McCallum	3–5
	March 15–21	#1146	Karen Valentine cover, TV Hockey	3–5
	March 22–28	#1147	Streets of San Francisco cast cover, Arnold Palmer	3–5
	March 29	#1148	Maude cover, The Gong Show, Baretta, Medical Center	4–8
	April 5–11	#1149	TV Baseball special, Cher, Stacy Keach	4–8
	April 12–18	#1150	Cher cover, Barney Miller	6–12
	April 19–25	#1151	Movin' On cast cover, Nevada Smith, Connie Chung	3–5
	April 26	#1152	McCloud cover, Animation special, Karen	4–6

Year	Issue	Number	Description	Value ($)
1975	May 3–9	#1153	Rhoda cast cover, S.W.A.T.	3–5
	May 10–16	#1154	Muhammad Ali cover, The Untouchables, Dinah Shore, Baretta	3–5
	May 17–23	#1155	Petrocelli cover, Monty Python, The Lawyers	2–4
	May 24–30	#1156	Jason Robards and Colleen Dewhurst cover, A Moon for the Misbegotten, 25 years of What's My Line, Sanford and Son	6–12
	May 31	#1157	The Bob Newhart Show cast cover, The Smothers Brothers, William Conrad	6–12
	June 7–13	#1158	Little House on the Prairie cast cover, Cloris Leachman: Sooner, S.W.A.T.	6–12
	June 14–20	#1159	TV Violence issue special, Isaac Asimov	2–4
	June 21–27	#1160	The Jeffersons cast cover, TV Shows of the Fifties, Mickey Mouse Club, 1976 Olympics	5–9
	June 28	#1161	Bicentennial issue special, M.A.S.H.	2–4

Year	Issue	Number	Description	Value ($)
1975	July 5–11	#1162	Tony Orlando and Dawn cover, The new faces of Space 1999, Aliens, Lucy, Lassie	6–12
	July 12–18	#1163	Apollo/Soyuz space mission special, Gladys Knight, Stacy Keach	3–5
	July 19–25	#1164	Barney Miller cast cover, Good Times, Rod Serling death story	4–8
	July 26	#1165	Howard K. Smith and Harry Reasoner cover, Pay TV	2–4
	August 2–8	#1166	Mike Douglas cover, Pat Finley, The Bob Newhart Show	3–5
	August 9–15	#1167	Buddy Ebsen cover, Liza Minnelli, Emergency	3–5
	August 16–22	#1168	Emergency cast cover, M.A.S.H.'s Loretta Swit, McCloud, The Waltons	4–6
	August 23–29	#1169	The Waltons cast cover, Gunsmoke's Chester, The Beverly Hillbillies' Donna Douglas	6–12

Year	Issue	Number	Description	Value ($)
1975	August 30	#1170	Carroll O'Connor cover, Isaac Asimov, M.A.S.H.	2–4
	September 6–12	#1171	Fall Preview special	6–12
	September 13–19	#1172	NFL Winners special, Gene Shalit	2–4
	September 20–26	#1173	Barbara Walters cover, Beacon Hill	2–4
	September 27	#1174	Howard Cosell cover, M.A.S.H.'s Jamie Farr	2–4
	October 4–10	#1175	Jennie's Lee Remick cover	2–4
	October 11–17	#1176	The Family Holvak cover, Far-Out Space Nuts, Marcus Welby, Ellery Queen	2–4
	October 18–24	#1177	TV's sex crisis special, The Bionic Woman, Cher	4–8
	October 25–31	#1178	Cloris Leachman cover, Martin Sheen, Barbary Coast	3–5
	November 1–7	#1179	Lloyd Bridges cover, The Crash Experts, Morgan Fairchild	4–8
	November 8–14	#1180	Rhoda cover, James Arness, All in the Family	4–8
	November 15–21	#1181	Starsky and Hutch cast cover, Trekkies	6–12

Year	Issue	Number	Description	Value ($)

Note: The following four issues of *TV Guide* were printed with improper issue numbering.

1975	November 22–28	#1181	A Week of Specials, Doctors' Hospital, Matt Helm	2–4
	November 29	#1182	Tony Curtis cover, To Tell the Truth, Ellery Queen	2–4
	December 6–12	#1183	Family Viewing special, John Denver, Harry-0, Welcome Back Kotter	2–4
	December 13–19	#1184	Switch cover, When Things Were Rotten	2–4

Note: Issue numbering returns to proper sequence.

1975	December 20–26	#1186	Christmas issue special, Andy Williams, Switch	2–4
	December 27	#1187	Baretta's Robert Blake cover, Mickey Mouse, Starsky and Hutch	3–5
1976	January 3–9	#1188	Kojak's Telly Savalas cover, Saturday Night Live, Bob Barker	3–5
	January 10–16	#1189	Happy Days cover, Medical Center	4–8
	January 17–23	#1190	Police Woman cover, The Super Bowl, The Adams Chronicles	6–12

Year	Issue	Number	Description	Value ($)
1976	January 24–30	#1191	M.A.S.H. cover, Louis Armstrong, The Honeymooners	5–10
	January 31	#1192	S.W.A.T. cover, Desi Arnaz Remembers Part I	4–6
	February 7–13	#1193	Barney Miller cover, Desi Arnaz Remembers Part 11	4–6
	February 14–20	#1194	Sanford and Son's Redd Foxx cover, The Waltons	4–6
	February 21–27	#1195	Cannon's William Conrad cover, Redd Foxx, One Day at a Time	2–4
	February 28	#1196	Bob Hope cover, The Addams Family, Space 1999	6–12
	March 6–12	#1197	The Rockford Files' James Garner cover, Johnny Carson	4–8
	March 13–19	#1198	Chico and the Man cover, The Batmobile, The Bionic Woman	5–10
	March 20–26	#1199	Danny Thomas cover, Laverne & Shirley, Harry-O	2–4
	March 27	#1200	Bronk's Jack Palance cover, Donny and Marie	2–4
	April 3–9	#1201	Baseball 1976 special	1–2
	April 10–16	#1202	Police Story cover, Russian TV	2–4

Year	Issue	Number	Description	Value ($)
1976	April 17–23	#1203	Welcome Back Kotter cover, The Jeffersons	2–4
	April 24–30	#1204	Maude cover, Rich Little, Cousteau and the Calypso	3–5
	May 1–7	#1205	The Blue Knight's George Kennedy cover, Mary Hartman, Mary Hartman, Happy Days' Marion Ross	3–5
	May 8–14	#1206	The Bionic Woman's Lindsay Wagner cover, Sonny and Cher, Tom Snyder	12–22
	May 15–21	#1207	On the Rocks cover, Peter Ustinov and Zero Mostel, British TV	2–4
	May 22–28	#1208	Laverne & Shirley cover, Soap Opera Queens	4–8
	May 29	#1209	Little House on the Prairie cast cover, Saturday Night Live	6–12
	June 5–11	#1210	Sonny and Cher cover, The Donny and Marie Show	6–12
	June 12–18	#1211	Harry-O cover, Gail Christian	3–5
	June 19–25	#1212	Mary Hartman, Mary Hartman	

Year	Issue	Number	Description	Value ($)
1976	June 19–25	#1212	cover, Sylvia Chase	2–4
	June 26	#1213	Mary Tyler Moore and her Moscow special cover, Rich Little	6–12
	July 3–9	#1214	Bicentennial special, TV from Mars	2–4
	July 10–16	#1215	Convention special, Jimmie Walker, Wayne Rogers	2–4
	July 17–23	#1216	The Olympics special, Welcome Back Kotter	2–4
	July 24–30	#1217	One Day at a Time's Bonnie Franklin cover, Mary Tyler Moore, Isaac Asimov	3–5
	July 31	#1218	Terrorism on TV, The Beach Boys, Maude's Adrienne Barbeau	6–12
	August 7–13	#1219	Donny and Marie Osmond cover, Female boxing	12–22
	August 14–20	#1220	Columbo cover, TV in South Africa, The Muppets	3–5
	August 21–27	#1221	The Waltons cast cover, Frankie Avalon, Lily Tomlin	6–12
	August 28	#1222	The Bionic Woman cover, M.A.S.H.	6–12

Year	Issue	Number	Description	Value ($)
1976	September 4–10	#1223	Annual Football Predictions issue, Neil Sedaka	2–4
	September 11–17	#1224	Bob Dylan cover and feature: Bob Dylan Today, British TV	6–12
	September 18–24	#1225	Fall Preview special	6–12
	September 25	#1226	Charlie's Angels cover, Barney Miller	12–22
	October 2–8	#1227	Serpico's David Birney cover, Paul Michael Glaser	2–4
	October 9–15	#1228	All's Fair's Bernadette Peters cover, The Gong Show	3–5
	October 16–22	#1229	World Series issue special, Cher, Sherlock Holmes	3–5
	October 23–29	#1230	Alice's Linda Lavin cover, Isis, TV Wrestling	3–5
	October 30	#1231	The Election special, M.A.S.H.'s helicopter pilot, The Jeffersons	3–5
	November 6–12	#1232	Gone with the Wind cover and special first TV showing, The Six Million Dollar Man, The Bionic Woman	6–12
	November 13–19	#1233	Dorothy Hamill cover, John	

#1203, 1976

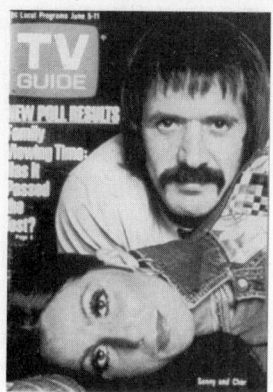

#1210, 1976

#1221, 1976

#1251, 1977

#1271, 1977

#1285, 1977

#1295, 1978

#1284, 1977

#1299, 1978

#1098, 1974

#1874, 1989

#1107, 1974

#1124, 1974

#1134, 1974

#1158, 1975

#1170, 1975

#1171, 1975

#1181, 1975

Year	Issue	Number	Description	Value ($)
1976	November 13–19	#1233	Denver, Happy Days' Tom Bosley, Charlie's Angels	4–8
	November 20–26	#1234	NBC's 50th Birthday special, Kojak, Carol Burnett	2–4
	November 27	#1235	Starsky and Hutch cover, George C. Scott, Rhoda	6–12
	December 4–10	#1236	Tony Randall cover, Chico and the Man, Nancy Walker	3–5
	December 11–17	#1237	Rhoda's Valerie Harper cover, Peter Pan, The Streets of San Francisco	4–6
	December 18–24	#1238	John Chancellor and David Brinkley cover, Alice, Rich Man, Poor Man Part 11	2–4
	December 25–31	#1239	Christmas issue special, Dick Van Dyke, General Hospital	2–4
1977	January 1–7	#1240	John Travolta cover, The Captain and Tennille	4–6
	January 8–14	#1241	Super Bowl special, Lesley-Anne Down	3–5
	January 15–21	#1242	Jimmy Carter special, Dinah	

Year	Issue	Number	Description	Value ($)
1977	January 15–21	#1242	Shore, Charlie's Angels	3–5
	January 22–28	#1243	Roots cover, Robert Stack, Dolly Parton	2–4
	January 29	#1244	Wonder Woman cover, Tony Randall	6–12
	February 5–11	#1245	Barbara Walters cover, James Arness, Phil Donahue, Roots	2–4
	February 12–18	#1246	Kojak cast cover, Barbara Walters, Bob Hope, Roots	3–5
	February 19–25	#1247	Nancy Walker cover, Grammy Awards, What's Happening, Roots	2–4
	February 26	#1248	McMillan and Wife cover, Welcome Back Kotter, Baa Baa Black Sheep	4–8
	March 5–11	#1249	Liv Ullmann cover, The Rockford Files	3–5
	March 12–18	#1250	Lauren Hutton cover, Rich Man, Poor Man	3–5
	March 19–25	#1251	Mary Tyler Moore cover, The Wizard of Oz, Catherine Schell of Space 1999, The Hobbit	6–12
	March 26	#1252	Quincy's Jack Klugman cover, Happy Days'	

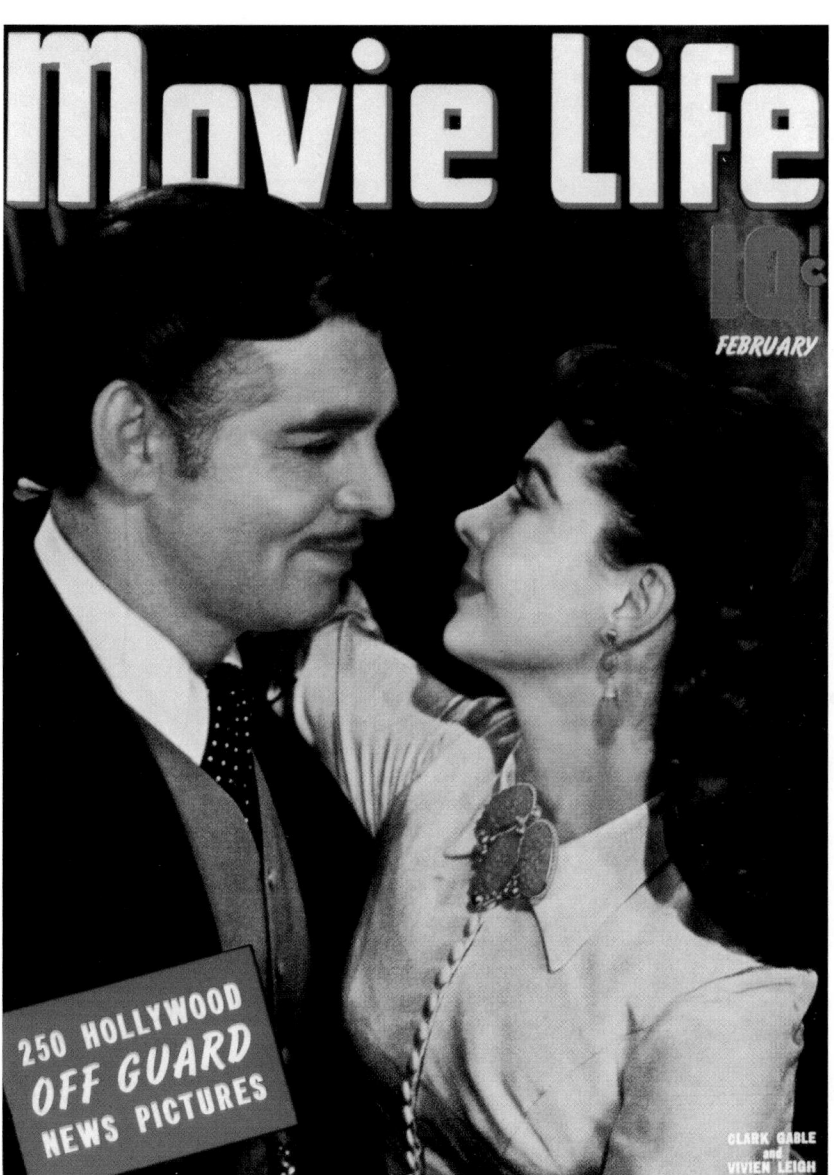

Movie Life

Family Circle

Photoplay

PHOTOPLAY

MARCH
25 CENTS

TRAGIC
TRUTH
ABOUT
JOHN
GILBERT'S
DEATH

by Adela
Rogers
St. Johns

SHIRLEY
TEMPLE

GOD'S INCOME TAX ON HOLLYWOOD
By Channing Pollock

**THE CONFIDENTIAL HISTORY OF
BILL POWELL** By Frederick L. Collins

Photoplay

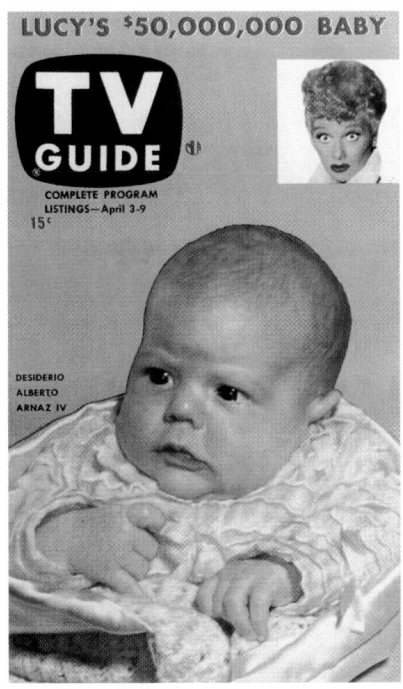

TV Guide

TV Guide

Weird

Kiss

See

Year	Issue	Number	Description	Value ($)
1977	March 26	#1252	Erin Moran, TV Comics	4–8
	April 2–8	#1253	Dinah Shore cover, Hee Haw, Fred Berry	2–4
	April 9–15	#1254	Baseball special, Fish, Ernie Kovacs	2–4
	April 16–22	#1255	Frank Sinatra cover, Fantastic Journey	2–5
	April 23–29	#1256	60 Minutes cover, Baa Baa Black Sheep, Charlie's Angels	4–6
	April 30	#1257	David Frost and Richard Nixon cover, Barbara Parkins, Stefanie Powers, Chevy Chase	4–6
	May 7–13	#1258	One Day at a Time cast cover	3–5
	May 14–20	#1259	Today's Tom Brokaw cover, The New Mickey Mouse Club	3–5
	May 21–28	#1260	Charlie's Angels' Farrah Fawcett cover, Quincy	6–12
	May 29	#1261	Baretta's Robert Blake cover, All in the Family, Roots, Grizzly Adams	4–6
	June 4–10	#1262	M.A.S.H.'s Alan Alda cover, Queen Elizabeth	4–6

Year	Issue	Number	Description	Value ($)
1977	June 11–17	#1263	Grizzly Adams cover, Fish, The Hardy Boys, Nancy Drew	4–8
	June 18–24	#1264	Laverne & Shirley cover, TV News	4–8
	June 25	#1265	The Waltons cast cover, David Brenner, Charlie's Angels' Farrah Fawcett	6–12
	July 2–8	#1266	Alice cover, Star Trek, Mushroom Magic	6–12
	July 9–15	#1267	C.P.O. Sharkey cover, Fernwood 2-Night	2–4
	July 16–22	#1268	Barney Miller cast cover, Victor Hugo	3–5
	July 23–29	#1269	Public TV special, TV's Money Movies, King Kong	3–5
	July 30	#1270	Johnny Carson cover, Daniel Boone, Soap	3–5
	August 6–12	#1271	The Muppets cover and feature: Behind the Scenes on the Muppet Show, Jackie Robinson	3–5
	August 13–19	#1272	Starsky & Hutch's David Soul cover, TV Boxing	6–12
	August 20–26	#1273	The Rockford Files cover, Ed Bradley	5–10

Year	Issue	Number	Description	Value ($)
1977	August 27	#1274	Hollywood Fights Back . . . Sex & Violence, Jane Pauley	3–5
	September 3–9	#1275	Jason Robards and Andy Griffith cover and feature: Washington, Behind Closed Doors, Laugh-In '77, Charlie's Angels	4–6
	September 10–16	#1276	Fall Preview special	6–12
	September 17–23	#1277	Football issue special, John Wayne, M.A.S.H., Patrick McGoohan	3–6
	September 24–30	#1278	The Betty White Show cover, Rhoda, Soap	3–5
	October 1–7	#1279	Rosetti and Ryan cover, Isaac Asimov	2–3
	October 8–14	#1280	Donny and Marie Osmond cover, Hee Haw, X-rated Pay TV, Soap	12–22
	October 15–21	#1281	Lou Grant's Ed Asner cover, The Love Boat, Little House on the Prairie, CHiPs	3–5
	October 22–28	#1282	Welcome Back Kotter cast cover, Rafferty	3–5
	October 29	#1283	We've Got Each Other cover, Space Academy, Mark Hamill	3–5
	November 5–11	#1284	The Hardy Boys cover, Happy	

Year	Issue	Number	Description	Value ($)
1977	November 5–11	#1284	Days, On Our Own, The Addams Family Cartoon Show	6–12
	November 12–18	#1285	The Godfather on TV special, All in the Family, I Claudius, Soap	3–5
	November 19–25	#1286	Frank Sinatra cover, Charlie's Angels, Betty White	3–5
	November 26	#1287	Soap cast cover, Doonesbury	2–4
	December 3–9	#1288	Man from Atlantis's Patrick Duffy cover, Happy Days, Bette Midler, The Love Boat	6–12
	December 10–16	#1289	The Censors special, Marlo Thomas, The World of Magic, The Man from Atlantis	4–6
	December 17–23	#1290	One Day at a Time cast cover, We've Got Each Other, The Grand Ole Opry	5–10
	December 24–30	#1291	Christmas issue special, Kristy McNichol, Star Wars and Star Trek, Isaac Asimov	6–12
	December 31	#1292	Kojak cover, I Claudius, Julia Child, Soap	3–5

Year	Issue	Number	Description	Value ($)
1978	January 7–13	#1293	Happy Days cover and feature	3–5
	January 14–20	#1294	Super Bowl cover by Charles Addams	2–4
	January 21–27	#1295	Cast of Family cover and feature	3–5
	January 28	#1296	Life and Times of Grizzly Adams	3–5
	February 4–10	#1297	The Love Boat	3–5
	February 11–17	#1298	Jack Klugman: Quincy	3–5
	February 18–24	#1299	Charlie's Angels	4–8
	February 25	#1300	Cast of M.A.S.H. cover and feature	
	March 4–10	#1301	On Our Own cover and feature	2–4
	March 11–17	#1302	Carter Country	2–4
	March 18–24	#1303	Lindsay Wagner of The Bionic Woman cover and feature	4–8
	March 25–31	#1304	Mary Tyler Moore and Walter Cronkite	3–5
	April 1–7	#1305	Baseball	2–4
	April 8–14	#1306	Alice cast cover	3–5
	April 15–21	#1307	Holocaust	2–4
	April 22–28	#1308	Changing the Shape of Television	2–4
	April 29	#1309	Laverne & Shirley cast cover	3–5
	May 6–12	#1310	Barnaby Jones's Buddy Ebsen cover and feature	2–4
	May 13–19	#1311	Little House on the Prairie cast cover and feature	4–8

Year	Issue	Number	Description	Value ($)
1978	May 20–26	#1312	Three's Company cast cover	3–5
	May 27	#1313	Phil Donahue	2–4
	June 3–9	#1314	Starsky and Hutch	3–5
	June 10–16	#1315	UFOs on TV	2–4
	June 17–23	#1316	Rhoda's Valerie Harper	2–4
	June 24–30	#1317	Can You Believe the Ratings	2–4
	July 1–7	#1318	Fantasy Island cast cover	3–5
	July 8–14	#1319	The Young and the Restless cast cover	2–4
	July 15–21	#1320	Black Sheep Squadron's Robert Conrad cover	4–8
	July 22–28	#1321	Love Boat's Gavin MacLeod	3–5
	July 29	#1322	Saturday Night Live cast cover	4–8
	August 5–11	#1323	The Jeffersons cast cover	4–6
	August 12–18	#1324	Good Morning America's David Hartman	2–4
	August 19–25	#1325	Sport on TV	2–4
	August 26	#1326	Charlie's Angels' Cheryl Ladd	6–12
	September 2–8	#1327	Pro Football 1978	2–4
	September 9–15	#1328	Fall Preview special	3–5
	September 16–22	#1329	Battlestar Galactica cast cover	6–12
	September 23–29	#1330	Mary Tyler Moore	3–5
	September 30	#1331	Centennial cast cover	2–4

#1260, 1977

#1335, 1978

#1382, 1979

#1416, 1980

#1421, 1980

#1419, 1980

#1564, 1983

#1482, 1981

#1569, 1983

Year	Issue	Number	Description	Value ($)
1978	October 7–13	#1332	World Series	2–4
	October 14–20	#1333	Robert Urich of Vegas	2–4
	October 21–27	#1334	WKRP cast cover	3–5
	October 28	#1335	Mork & Mindy	3–5
	November 4–10	#1336	Welcome Back Kotter's John Travolta	3–5
	November 11–17	#1337	Ron Leibman of Kaz	2–4
	November 18–24	#1338	Foreign lobbyists and TV	2–4
	November 25	#1339	Suzanne Somers cover and feature	3–6
	December 2–8	#1340	Benji	2–4
	December 9–15	#1341	Lou Grant	2–4
	December 16–22	#1342	Eight Is Enough cast cover	3–5
	December 23–29	#1343	Christmas issue special	2–4
	December 30	#1344	Dick Clark	2–4
1979	January 6–12	#1345	All in the Family by Hirschfeld	3–6
	January 13–19	#1346	Network News Chiefs	2–4
	January 20–26	#1347	Super Bowl XIII	2–4
	January 27	#1348	Katharine Hepburn	3–5
	February 3–9	#1349	CHiPs cast cover	2–4
	February 10–16	#1350	William Shakespeare	2–4
	February 17–23	#1351	Roots II	2–4
	February 24	#1352	James Arness	3–5
	March 3–9	#1353	Gary Coleman	2–4
	March 10–16	#1354	60 Minutes cast cover	2–4
	March 17–23	#1355	M.A.S.H.	3–6
	March 24–30	#1356	Fantasy Island	3–5

Year	Issue	Number	Description	Value ($)
1979	March 31	#1357	Baseball '79	2–4
	April 7–13	#1358	Battlestar Galactica's Maren Jensen	6–12
	April 14–20	#1359	Quincy cast cover	3–5
	April 21–27	#1360	Walter Cronkite	2–4
	April 28	#1361	Taxi	3–5
	May 5–11	#1362	Paper Chase	2–4
	May 12–18	#1363	What Viewers Hate About TV	2–4
	May 19–25	#1364	Laverne & Shirley cast cover	3–5
	May 26	#1365	Ken Howard of White Shadow	2–4
	June 2–8	#1366	Rockford Files' James Garner	3–5
	June 9–15	#1367	Donna Pescow of Angie	2–4
	June 16–22	#1368	Dallas	3–5
	June 23–29	#1369	Johnny Carson	2–4
	June 30	#1370	Dukes of Hazzard	3–5
	July 7–13	#1371	Barney Miller	3–5
	July 14–20	#1372	Little House on the Prairie cast cover	4–8
	July 21–27	#1373	B.J. and the Bear	2–4
	July 28	#1374	The Incredible Hulk	4–8
	August 4–10	#1375	Joyce DeWitt of Three's Company	3–5
	August 11–17	#1376	Soap idol Rod Arrants	2–4
	August 18–24	#1377	Lou Grant cast cover	3–5
	August 25–31	#1378	Pro Football '79	2–4
	September 1–7	#1379	Miss America	2–4
	September 8–14	#1380	Fall Preview special	3–6

Year	Issue	Number	Description	Value ($)
1979	September 15–21	#1381	Benson	2–4
	September 22–28	#1382	Carroll O'Connor	3–5
	September 29	#1383	Pope John Paul II	2–4
	October 6–12	#1384	World Series	2–4
	October 13–19	#1385	Tom Snyder	2–4
	October 20–26	#1386	WKRP cast cover	3–5
	October 27	#1387	Muhammad Ali in Freedom Road	2–4
	November 3–9	#1388	Hart to Hart	3–5
	November 10–16	#1389	The Bee Gees	6–12
	November 17–23	#1390	The Associates cast cover	2–4
	November 24–30	#1391	Trapper John	3–5
	December 1–7	#1392	Barbara Walters	2–4
	December 8–14	#1393	Talk show hosts	2–4
	December 15–21	#1394	The Fonz	2–4
	December 22–28	#1395	Christmas issue special	2–4
	December 29	#1396	Charlie's Angels cast cover	5–8
1980	January 5–11	#1397	M.A.S.H. cast cover	3–6
	January 12–18	#1398	CHiPs	2–4
	January 19–25	#1399	Super Bowl '80	2–4
	January 26	#1400	Soap	2–3
	February 2–8	#1401	Diff'rent Strokes cast cover	3–5
	February 9–15	#1402	Olympics	2–3
	February 16–22	#1403	Barnaby Jones cast cover	3–5
	February 23–29	#1404	Campaign '80	2–3
	March 1–7	#1405	Fantasy Island cover by Hirschfeld	3–5
	March 8–14	#1406	Dallas	3–5
	March 15–21	#1407	Family cast cover	2–4
	March 22–28	#1408	Misadventures of Sheriff Lobo	2–3

Year	Issue	Number	Description	Value ($)
1980	March 28	#1409	Archie Bunker's Place	3–5
	April 5–11	#1410	1980 Baseball	2–3
	April 12–18	#1411	Olivia Newton-John	6–12
	April 19–25	#1412	Alice cast cover	3–5
	April 26	#1413	United States	2–3
	May 3–9	#1414	Mork & Mindy	3–5
	May 10–16	#1415	One Day at a Time cast cover	3–5
	May 17–23	#1416	The Jeffersons cast cover	3–5
	May 24–30	#1417	Situation Comedies	1–3
	May 31	#1418	Vegas cast cover	1–3
	June 7–13	#1419	Knots Landing	2–4
	June 14–20	#1420	House Call's Lynn Redgrave	2–3
	June 21–27	#1421	Hart to Hart cast cover	2–4
	June 28	#1422	Trapper John, M.D., cast cover	3–4
	July 5–11	#1423	Little House on the Prairie cast cover	4–7
	July 12–18	#1424	Dukes of Hazzard cast cover	3–6
	July 19–25	#1425	The Love Boat cast cover	3–5
	July 26	#1426	Taxi	2–4
	August 2–8	#1427	Real People	1–3
	August 9–15	#1428	Children's TV	1–3
	August 16–22	#1429	TV's Hunks	1–4
	August 23–29	#1430	General Hospital's Genie Francis	3–4
	August 30	#1431	Pro Football '80	1–3
	September 6–12	#1432	Richard Chamberlain of Shogun	2–4

Year	Issue	Number	Description	Value ($)
1980	September 13–19	#1433	Fall Preview special	3–5
	September 20–26	#1434	Priscilla Presley	3–5
	September 27	#1435	Cosmos	2–4
	October 4–10	#1436	Lou Grant	2–4
	October 11–17	#1437	World Series	2–4
	October 18–24	#1438	Sophia Loren	2–4
	October 25–31	#1439	Barney Miller cover by Hirschfeld	2–4
	November 1–7	#1440	Reagan, Carter, and Anderson cover	2–4
	November 8–14	#1441	Flo's Polly Holliday	2–4
	November 15–21	#1442	Dallas's Larry Hagman	3–5
	November 22–28	#1443	Mork & Mindy's Paw Dawber	3–5
	November 29	#1444	Monday Night Football	2–4
	December 6–12	#1445	Diff'rent Strokes	3–5
	December 13–19	#1446	I'm a Big Girl Now	2–4
	December 20–26	#1447	Christmas issue special	3–5
	December 27	#1448	Magnum, P.I.	3–6
1981	January 3–9	#1449	Too Close for Comfort	2–5
	January 10–16	#1450	Good Morning America	2–4
	January 17–23	#1451	Ronald Reagan	2–4
	January 24–30	#1452	Super Bowl '81	2–4
	January 31	#1453	Johnny Carson, Bob Hope, and George Burns cover	2–4
	February 7–13	#1454	Jane Seymour of East of Eden	3–5

Year	Issue	Number	Description	Value ($)
1981	February 14–20	#1455	WKRP	3–5
	February 21–27	#1456	Faye Dunaway as Eva Peron	3–5
	February 28	#1457	Hollywood's Cocaine Connection	2–4
	March 7–13	#1458	Dukes of Hazzard cast cover	3–5
	March 14–20	#1459	Suzanne Somers cover and feature	3–5
	March 21–27	#1460	House Calls	2–4
	March 28	#1461	Johnny Carson cover by Amsel	2–4
	April 4–10	#1462	Baseball 1981	2–4
	April 11–17	#1463	Ed Asner of Lou Grant	2–4
	April 18–24	#1464	Ted Koppel of ABC News	2–4
	April 25	#1465	Alan Alda cover by Hirschfeld	3–5
	May 2–8	#1466	That's Incredible	2–4
	May 9–15	#1467	Dallas	3–5
	May 16–22	#1468	Hart to Hart cast cover	2–4
	May 23–29	#1469	Harper Valley P.T.A.'s Barbara Eden	3–6
	May 30	#1470	Dan Rather	2–4
	June 6–12	#1471	Taxi	3–5
	June 13–19	#1472	Trapper John, M.D.	3–5
	June 20–26	#1473	Real People hosts cover	2–4
	June 27	#1474	Linda Evans of Dynasty	3–5
	July 4–10	#1475	Diff'rent Strokes' Dana Plato and Gary Coleman	3–6

Year	Issue	Number	Description	Value ($)
1981	July 11–17	#1476	Prime Time Vixens	3–6
	July 18–24	#1477	B.J. and the Bear	3–6
	July 25–31	#1478	Prince Charles and Diana Spencer	2–4
	August 1–7	#1479	Miss Piggy	2–4
	August 8–14	#1480	Carroll O'Connor	3–5
	August 15–21	#1481	The Day Elvis Died	3–6
	August 22–28	#1482	Ann Jillian of It's a Living	3–6
	August 29	#1483	Pro Football '81	2–4
	September 5–11	#1484	Backstage with Miss America	2–4
	September 12–18	#1485	Fall Preview special issue	3–5
	September 19–25	#1486	Kate Mulgrew as Rachel Manion	2–4
	September 26	#1487	The Battle for Northern Ireland	2–4
	October 3–9	#1488	Valerie Bertinelli of One Day at a Time	3–6
	October 10–16	#1489	Jaclyn Smith as Jacqueline Kennedy	2–5
	October 17–23	#1490	World Series	2–4
	October 24–30	#1491	Middle East News Coverage	2–4
	October 31	#1492	Hill Street Blues cast cover	2–4
	November 7–13	#1493	The Two of Us	2–4
	November 14–20	#1494	Loretta Lynn	3–6
	November 21–27	#1495	John Lennon cover and feature	5–10
	November 28	#1496	Merlin Olsen of Father Murphy	3–5
	December 5–11	#1497	Private Benjamin	2–4

Year	Issue	Number	Description	Value ($)
1981	December 12–18	#1498	Video Games	2–4
	December 19–25	#1499	Christmas issue special	2–4
	December 26	#1500	Henry Fonda	3–5
1982	January 2–8	#1501	Magnum, P.I.	3–5
	January 9–15	#1502	Michael Landon	4–7
	January 16–22	#1503	Bending the Rules in Hollywood	2–4
	January 23–29	#1504	Football Issue	2–4
	January 30	#1505	CHiPs	3–5
	February 6–12	#1506	The Jeffersons	3–5
	February 13–19	#1507	TV's Holocaust Films	1–3
	February 20–26	#1508	60 Minutes cast cover	1–3
	February 27	#1509	Dynasty cast cover	2–4
	March 6–12	#1510	Love, Sidney cast cover	1–3
	March 13–19	#1511	Three's Company cast cover	3–6
	March 20–26	#1512	President Reagan	2–4
	March 27	#1513	Dallas's Larry Hagman	2–5
	April 3–9	#1514	Baseball	1–3
	April 10–16	#1515	Today's Tom Brokaw	1–3
	April 17–23	#1516	Happy Days cast cover	4–7
	April 24–30	#1517	Ingrid Bergman as Golda Meir	1–3
	May 1–7	#1518	Dukes of Hazzard cast cover	2–4
	May 8–14	#1519	Goldie Hawn	3–4
	May 15–21	#1520	Marco Polo	1–3
	May 22–28	#1521	Falcon Crest	1–3
	May 29	#1522	Anatomy of a Smear	1–3

Year	Issue	Number	Description	Value ($)
1982	June 5–11	#1523	Love Boat	2–5
	June 12–18	#1524	Foreign Disinformation on U. S. TV	1–2
	June 19–25	#1525	Hill Street Blues	1–4
	June 26	#1526	Knots Landing's Michele Lee	2–5
	July 3–9	#1527	Too Close for Comfort	3–5
	July 10–16	#1528	Facts of Life cast cover	2–5
	July 17–23	#1529	Rick Springfield of General Hospital	3–5
	July 24–30	#1530	Greatest American Hero	3–5
	July 31	#1531	Father Murphy cast cover	3–4
	August 7–13	#1532	Archie Bunker's Place cast cover	2–4
	August 14–20	#1533	T. J. Hooker's William Shatner	3–5
	August 21–27	#1534	Gimme a Break	2–4
	August 28	#1535	Laverne & Shirley	3–5
	September 4–10	#1536	Almost Miss America	4–6
	September 11–17	#1537	Fall issue special	3–5
	September 18–24	#1538	Victoria Principal	3–5
	September 25	#1539	Ratings of TV newspeople	2–4
	October 2–8	#1540	Genie Francis	3–5
	October 9–15	#1541	World Series	2–4
	October 16–22	#1542	Honey Boy	2–4
	October 23–29	#1543	Dynasty	3–5
	October 30	#1544	Trapper John, M.D.	2–4
	November 6–12	#1545	Fame	2–4
	November 13–19	#1546	The Blue and the Gray	3–5

Year	Issue	Number	Description	Value ($)
1982	November 20–26	#1547	Three's Company cast cover	3–6
	November 27	#1548	Family Ties' Meredith Baxter-Birney	3–5
	December 4–10	#1549	1982's Best Video Games	2–4
	December 11–17	#1550	Sally Struthers and daughter	2–4
	December 18–24	#1551	Too Close for Comfort cast cover	3–5
	December 25–31	#1552	Christmas issue special	2–4
1983	January 1–7	#1553	Bob Newhart and Mary Frann	4–6
	January 8–14	#1554	John Madden	2–4
	January 15–21	#1555	Nine to Five cast cover	2–4
	January 22–28	#1556	TV's Investigative Reporters	2–4
	January 29	#1557	The Winds of War	3–5
	February 5–11	#1558	Cheryl Ladd as Grace Kelly	4–8
	February 12–18	#1559	The final M.A.S.H. episode issue	4–8
	February 19–25	#1560	Jaclyn Smith and Ken Howard	2–4
	February 26	#1561	All My Children cast cover	2–4
	March 5–11	#1562	Valerie Bertinelli	3–6
	March 12–18	#1563	Hill Street Blues	2–4
	March 19–25	#1564	Gary Coleman and Nancy Reagan	2–4
	March 26	#1565	Thorn Birds	5–10
	April 2–8	#1566	Donna Mills of Knots Landing	4–6
	April 9–15	#1567	Elvis Presley	4–8

Year	Issue	Number	Description	Value ($)
1983	April 16–22	#1568	60 Minutes cast cover	3–5
	April 23–29	#1569	Happy Days	4–8
	April 30	#1570	Tom Selleck	4–6
	May 7–13	#1571	Silver Spoons cast cover	4–6
	May 14–20	#1572	Dynasty	3–5
	May 21–27	#1573	Bob Hope	2–4
	May 28	#1574	Dallas	3–5
	June 4–10	#1575	The Fall Guy cast cover	3–6
	June 11–17	#1576	Alan Alda, Linda Evans, Valerie Bertinelli	3–5
	June 18–24	#1577	Simon & Simon cast cover	4–8
	June 25	#1578	Knight Rider	4–8
	July 2–8	#1579	M.A.S.H., Dynasty, Thorn Birds	2–4
	July 9–15	#1580	Falcon Crest cast cover	3–5
	July 16–22	#1581	TV's Hunks	2–4
	July 23–29	#1582	Knots Landing cast cover	4–6
	July 30	#1583	The Jeffersons	3–5
	August 6–12	#1584	Network Newswomen	2–4
	August 13–19	#1585	Days of Our Lives	2–4
	August 20–26	#1586	Hart to Hart	3–5
	August 27	#1587	White House News Coverage	2–4
	September 3–9	#1588	All in the Family final episode	5–10
	September 10–16	#1589	Fall Preview special	4–6
	September 17–23	#1590	Miss America Pageant	3–5
	September 24–30	#1591	Three's Company cast cover	4–6

Year	Issue	Number	Description	Value ($)
1983	October 1–7	#1592	Gregory Harrison	2–4
	October 8–14	#1593	Willie Nelson and Anne Murray	5–10
	October 15–21	#1594	Larry Hagman and Joan Collins	4–6
	October 22–28	#1595	Mr. Smith	2–4
	October 29	#1596	Hotel cast cover	2–4
	November 5–11	#1597	Princess Daisy	2–4
	November 12–18	#1598	President Kennedy	3–5
	November 19–25	#1599	The Day After	2–4
	November 26	#1600	Linda Evans and Kenny Rogers cover	4–6
	December 3–9	#1601	Johnny Carson and Barbara Walters cover	3–5
	December 10–16	#1602	Tom Selleck	3–5
	December 17–23	#1603	Silver Spoons' Erin Gray	4–6
	December 24–30	#1604	The Love Boat cast cover	4–6
	December 31	#1605	Farrah Fawcett	4–8
1984	January 7–13	#1606	After M.A.S.H. cast cover	3–5
	January 14–20	#1607	Emmanuel Lewis	2–4
	January 21–27	#1608	TV Game Show Hosts	2–4
	January 28	#1609	Cybill Shepherd	4–6
	February 4–10	#1610	Winter Olympics	2–4
	February 11–17	#1611	Scarecrow and Mrs. King	4–8
	February 18–24	#1612	Cheers cast cover	4–7
	February 25	#1613	60 Minutes cast cover	3–4
	March 3–9	#1614	Ann-Margret and Treat Williams	3–6
	March 10–16	#1615	The A-Team cast cover	4–7

Year	Issue	Number	Description	Value ($)
1984	March 17–23	#1616	Priscilla Presley	4–6
	March 24–30	#1617	Hill Street Blues	3–5
	March 31	#1618	Teri Copley	3–5
	April 7–13	#1619	George Washington	2–4
	April 14–20	#1620	Knight Rider	4–7
	April 21–27	#1621	The Far Pavilions	1–4
	April 28	#1622	Happy Days 1974–1984	4–7
	May 5–11	#1623	Lesley-Anne Down	3–5
	May 12–18	#1624	Crystal Gayle	4–8
	May 19–25	#1625	Morgan Fairchild	4–6
	May 26	#1626	Hardcastle & McCormick	4–7
	June 2–8	#1627	Victoria Principal	4–6
	June 9–15	#1628	Remington Steele cast cover	3–6
	June 16–22	#1629	Larry Hagman, Joan Collins	3–5
	June 23–29	#1630	Connie Sellecca	3–5
	June 30	#1631	Review of 1983–1984 Season	3–5
	July 7–13	#1632	Valerie Bertinelli	4–6
	July 14–20	#1633	Johnny Carson	2–4
	July 21–27	#1634	Knots Landing cast cover	3–5
	July 28	#1635	Olympics	2–4
	August 4–10	#1636	Simon & Simon	4–7
	August 11–17	#1637	Call to Glory cast cover	2–4
	August 18–24	#1638	Jane Pauley	2–3
	August 25–31	#1639	Mike Hammer	2–3
	September 1–7	#1640	Who Shot Dallas's Bobby?	3–5
	September 8–14	#1641	Fall Preview special	4–8
	September 15–21	#1642	George Burns and Catherine Bach	3–5

Year	Issue	Number	Description	Value ($)
1984	September 22–28	#1643	Mistral's Daughter	2–3
	September 29	#1644	Heartsounds	1–3
	October 6–12	#1645	Paper Dolls	1–3
	October 13–19	#1646	Cosby Show	1–3
	October 20–26	#1647	Aurora by Night	2–4
	October 27	#1648	Brooke Shields	4–6
	November 3–9	#1649	Election Night Drama	2–4
	November 10–16	#1650	Dynasty	2–4
	November 17–23	#1651	Top Models	2–4
	November 24–30	#1652	Kate & Allie	4–6
	December 1–7	#1653	Hotel	2–4
	December 8–14	#1654	Falcon Crest	2–4
	December 15–21	#1655	Connie Sellecca, Priscilla Presley, Jaclyn Smith	3–5
	December 22–28	#1656	Webster cast cover	3–5
	December 29	#1657	Dallas	3–5
1985	January 5–11	#1658	Elvis Presley	4–8
	January 12–18	#1659	Knots Landing	3–5
	January 19–25	#1660	President Reagan	2–4
	January 26	#1661	Riptide	2–4
	February 2–8	#1662	Cagney & Lacey cover by Amsel	5–10
	February 9–15	#1663	Night Court	3–5
	February 16–22	#1664	Hollywood Wives cast cover	2–4
	February 23	#1665	Bruce Springsteen, Prince, Michael Jackson	5–10
	March 2–8	#1666	Michael Landon	4–8
	March 9–15	#1667	Angela Lansbury	3–5
	March 16–22	#1668	Lauren Tewes	2–4
	March 23–29	#1669	Dynasty's Diahann Carroll	3–5
	March 30	#1670	A.D. cast cover	2–4
	April 6–12	#1671	Richard	

Year	Issue	Number	Description	Value ($)
1985	April 6–12	#1671	Chamberlain	2–4
	April 13–19	#1672	Space cast cover	2–4
	April 20–26	#1673	Dallas's Deborah Shelton	2–4
	April 27	#1674	Family Ties cast cover	4–8
	May 4–10	#1675	Phoebe Cates in Lace II	4–8
	May 11–17	#1676	Cheryl Ladd	4–8
	May 18–24	#1677	Christopher Columbus	2–4
	May 25–31	#1678	Cover Up	2–4
	June 1–7	#1679	Hill Street Blues	3–5
	June 8–14	#1680	Simon & Simon	4–8
	June 15–21	#1681	Summer TV Surprises	2–4
	June 22–28	#1682	Nancy Reagan	2–4
	June 29	#1683	The Best and Worst We Saw	2–4
	July 6–12	#1684	Cheers cast cover	4–8
	July 13–19	#1685	The Fall Guy's Heather Thomas	4–8
	July 20–26	#1686	Hottest Soap Couples	2–4
	July 27	#1687	Miami Vice	4–6
	August 3–9	#1688	Romance on the Set	2–4
	August 10–16	#1689	Madonna	4–8
	August 17–23	#1690	Real Men versus the Wimps	2–4
	August 24–30	#1691	Knots Landing	2–4
	August 31	#1692	The A-Team	3–6
	September 7–13	#1693	The Cosby Show	2–4
	September 14–20	#1694	Fall Preview special	5–10
	September 21–27	#1695	Michael J. Fox	4–6
	September 28	#1696	Howard Cosell	2–4
	October 5–11	#1697	Don Johnson and Cybill Shepherd	3–5

Year	Issue	Number	Description	Value ($)
1985	October 12–18	#1698	Victoria Principal	3–5
	October 19–25	#1699	Golden Girls cast cover	3–5
	October 26	#1700	Network Newscasters	2–4
	November 2–8	#1701	North and South cast cover	2–4
	November 9–15	#1702	Prince Charles and Princess Diana	2–4
	November 16–22	#1703	Dynasty II . . . The Colbys	2–4
	November 23–29	#1704	Who's the Boss cast cover	3–5
	November 30	#1705	Is Knots Landing Better?	2–4
	December 7–13	#1706	Cybill Shephard	3–5
	December 14–20	#1707	Hell Town's Robert Blake	3–4
	December 21–27	#1708	Highway to Heaven cast cover	4–8
	December 28	#1709	Crazy Like a Fox	2–3
1986	January 4–10	#1710	Connie Sellecca	3–4
	January 11–17	#1711	Scarecrow and Mrs. King	3–4
	January 18–24	#1712	Night Court cast cover	3–4
	January 25–31	#1713	Joan Collins	3–5
	February 1–7	#1714	Peter the Great	2–3
	February 8–14	#1715	Hollywood Love Scenes	3–4
	February 15–21	#1716	Angela Lansbury	3–5
	February 22–28	#1717	Crossings	3–5
	March 1–7	#1718	Dynasty's Linda Evans	3–5
	March 8–14	#1719	Miami Vice	3–5
	March 15–21	#1720	If Tomorrow Comes	2–3
	March 22–28	#1721	Bill Cosby	1–3

Year	Issue	Number	Description	Value ($)
1986	March 29	#1722	Sexual Harassment	2–3
	April 5–11	#1723	Family Ties cast cover	3–5
	April 12–18	#1724	Dream West	2–3
	April 19–25	#1725	10 Most Attractive Men on TV	3–5
	April 26	#1726	Kate & Allie cast cover	3–5
	May 3–9	#1727	Del Stranger versus North and South	2–3
	May 10–16	#1728	Cheers cast cover	4–6
	May 17–23	#1729	Burt Lancaster	2–5
	May 24–30	#1730	Larry Hagman	2–4
	May 31	#1731	MacGyver	3–5
	June 7–13	#1732	10 Most Talented TV Stars	3–5
	June 14–20	#1733	Webster	2–4
	June 21–27	#1734	Knots Landing's Teri Austin	3–5
	June 28	#1735	Ronald and Nancy Reagan	2–4
	July 5–11	#1736	The Goodwill Games	2–4
	July 12–18	#1737	The Worst and Best on TV	3–5
	July 19–25	#1738	Spenser: For Hire cast cover	3–5
	July 26	#1739	TV's Top Moneymakers	3–5
	August 2–8	#1740	TV's Macho Man	3–5
	August 9–15	#1741	Growing Pains cast cover	3–5
	August 16–22	#1742	Suzanne Somers	3–5
	August 23–29	#1743	Valerie Harper	3–5
	August 30	#1744	Dallas . . . The Mystery of Bobby's Return	3–5

Year	Issue	Number	Description	Value ($)
1986	September 6–12	#1745	Miss America, NFL Football	2–4
	September 13–19	#1746	Fall Preview special	4–8
	September 20–26	#1747	George Washington	2–4
	September 27	#1748	Perfect Strangers	2–4
	October 4–10	#1749	Lucille Ball and Andy Griffith	5–10+
	October 11–17	#1750	L.A. Law cast cover	4–6
	October 18–24	#1751	Family Ties	4–6
	October 25–31	#1752	Falcon Crest	3–5
	November 1–7	#1753	Rage of Angels	2–4
	November 8–14	#1754	Joan Collins and George Hamilton	3–5
	November 15–21	#1755	Fresno cast cover	2–4
	November 22–28	#1756	Farrah Fawcett	4–8
	November 29	#1757	Jack and Mike	2–4
	December 6–12	#1758	Designing Women's Delta Burke	3–5
	December 13–19	#1759	Promise	2–4
	December 20–26	#1760	Our House cast cover	3–5
	December 27	#1761	Dynasty's Heather Locklear	4–6
1987	January 3–9	#1762	Angela Lansbury	3–5
	January 10–16	#1763	Nightline's Ted Koppel	2–4
	January 17–23	#1764	Amen	3–5
	January 24–30	#1765	Knots Landing	2–4
	January 31	#1766	Golden Girls cast cover	3–5
	February 7–13	#1767	Ann-Margret	3–5
	February 14–20	#1768	Controversy over Amerika	2–4

#1603, 1983

#1602, 1983

#1846, 1988

#1875, 1989

#2245, 1996

#2273, 1996

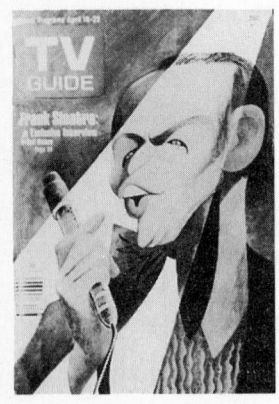

#1255, 1997

#2258, 1996

#2316, 1997

Year	Issue	Number	Description	Value ($)
1987	February 21–27	#1769	Tom Selleck and Frank Sinatra	3–5
	February 28	#1770	Valerie Bertinelli	3–5
	March 7–13	#1771	Justine Bateman and Michael J. Fox	4–6
	March 14–20	#1772	Dallas's Victoria Principal	3–5
	March 21–27	#1773	Miami Vice	3–5
	March 28	#1774	Growing Pains	3–5
	April 4–10	#1775	L.A. Law	3–5
	April 11–17	#1776	Bob Newhart cast cover	3–5
	April 18–24	#1777	Who's the Boss's Tony Danza	3–5
	April 25	#1778	Hunter	2–4
	May 2–8	#1779	Cheers cast cover	4–6
	May 9–15	#1780	My Sister Sam	3–5
	May 16–22	#1781	Head of the Class cast cover	3–5
	May 23–29	#1782	The Equalizer	4–8
	May 30	#1783	Moonlighting's Cybill Shepherd	3–5
	June 6–12	#1784	Grading TV's Child Stars	3–5
	June 13–19	#1785	Cagney & Lacey	3–5
	June 20–26	#1786	Night Court's Markie Post	3–5
	June 27	#1787	The Best and Worst We Saw	3–5
	July 4–10	#1788	Barbara Walters	2–4
	July 11–17	#1789	Cosby Show	2–4
	July 18–24	#1790	Kate Jackson, Victoria Principal, Oprah Winfrey	3–5
	July 25–31	#1791	Molly Dodd	2–4
	August 1–7	#1792	The Young and the Restless	2–4
	August 8–14	#1793	Is TV Getting Bolder?	2–4

Year	Issue	Number	Description	Value ($)
1987	August 15–21	#1794	Alf	4–6
	August 22–28	#1795	Soviet Bloc Nations' TV	2–4
	August 29	#1796	Amen	2–4
	September 5–11	#1797	Dynasty's Terri Garber	3–5
	September 12–18	#1798	Fall Preview special	4–8
	September 19–25	#1799	Brooke Shields	4–9
	September 26	#1800	L.A. Law	3–5
	October 3–9	#1801	Victoria Principal	3–5
	October 10–16	#1802	TV's Best and Worst Sitcoms	3–5
	October 17–23	#1803	Dolly Parton	4–6
	October 24–30	#1804	Moonlighting cast cover	3–5
	October 31	#1805	Family Ties	3–5
	November 7–13	#1806	Napoleon	3–5
	November 14–20	#1807	Cheers	3–5
	November 21–27	#1808	Gambler	2–4
	November 28	#1809	David and Meredith Baxter-Birney	3–5
	December 5–11	#1810	Connie Sellecca	3–5
	December 12–18	#1811	Hooperman's John Ritter	2–4
	December 19–25	#1812	Keshia Knight Pulliam	2–4
	December 26	#1813	A Year in the Life cast cover, Star Trek	4–8
1988	January 2–8	#1814	Falcon Crest cast cover	3–5
	January 9–15	#1815	Emma Samms	4–6
	January 16–22	#1816	Cagney & Lacey cast cover	4–6
	January 23–29	#1817	Campaign '88	2–4
	January 30	#1818	Elvis and Priscilla Presley	3–6

Year	Issue	Number	Description	Value ($)
1988	February 6–12	#1819	Jaclyn Smith and Robert Wagner	3–5
	February 13–19	#1820	Winter Olympics	2–4
	February 20–26	#1821	Noble House	2–4
	February 27	#1822	Cheryl Ladd	3–5
	March 5–11	#1823	Oprah Winfrey	2–4
	March 12–18	#1824	Is TV Getting Better or Worse?	2–4
	March 19–25	#1825	Miami Vice	3–5
	March 26	#1826	Sheree J. Wilson	2–4
	April 2–8	#1827	Growing Pains	3–5
	April 9–15	#1828	Harry Hamlin	2–4
	April 16–22	#1829	Frank's Place	2–4
	April 23–29	#1830	Jason Bateman	2–4
	April 30	#1831	Dr. Ruth, Golden Girls	3–5
	May 7–13	#1832	Richard Chamberlain, Jaclyn Smith	3–5
	May 14–20	#1833	Meet the Press	2–4
	May 21–27	#1834	Prince Charles and Princess Diana	2–4
	May 28	#1835	Family Ties	3–5
	June 4–10	#1836	ABC Sports	2–4
	June 11–17	#1837	Thirtysomething cast cover	3–5
	June 18–24	#1838	1988 Network News All-Stars	2–4
	June 25	#1839	The Best and the Worst	3–5
	July 2–8	#1840	Designing Women cast cover	3–5
	July 9–15	#1841	Head of the Class cast cover	3–5
	July 16–22	#1842	The Six Most Beautiful Women	3–5
	July 23–29	#1843	TV and the American Family	2–4

Year	Issue	Number	Description	Value ($)
1988	July 30	#1844	Leann Hunley	2–4
	August 6–12	#1845	The Best Daytime Soaps	2–4
	August 13–19	#1846	The Alfer	3–5
	August 20–26	#1847	21 Jump Street	3–5
	August 27	#1848	Mariel Hemingway	4–6
	September 3–9	#1849	Fall Survivor's Guide	2–4
	September 10–16	#1850	Kaye Lani	2–4
	September 17–23	#1851	Olympics	2–4
	September 24–30	#1852	Cosby Show cast cover	2–4
	October 1–7	#1853	Fall Preview special	4–8
	October 8–14	#1854	Brandon Tartikoff and Stars	2–4
	October 15–21	#1855	Bull Durham	2–4
	October 22–28	#1856	The AIDS Scare	2–4
	October 29	#1857	Harry Hamlin, Linda Kozlowski	2–4
	November 5–11	#1858	Election	2–4
	November 12–18	#1859	War and Remembrance cast cover	2–4
	November 19–25	#1860	Remembering JFK	2–4
	November 26	#1861	Barbara Walters' Specials	2–4
	December 3–9	#1862	Guide to Holiday Specials	2–4
	December 10–16	#1863	Empty Nest cast cover	2–4
	December 17–23	#1864	Kramer, Wilson, Belafonte	2–4
	December 24–30	#1865	Angela Lansbury	3–5
	December 31	#1866	Sandy Duncan, Jason Bateman	3–5
1989	January 7–13	#1867	8th Annual J. Fred Muggs Awards	2–4

Year	Issue	Number	Description	Value ($)
1989	January 14–20	#1868	Moonlighting cast cover	3–5
	January 21–27	#1869	Elvis Presley	4–6
	January 28	#1870	Roseanne cast cover	3–5
	February 4–10	#1871	Hot February	2–4
	February 11–17	#1872	Junior on the Couch	2–4
	February 18–24	#1873	The Best Children's Shows	2–4
	February 25	#1874	Victoria Principal	3–5
	March 4–10	#1875	Vanna White	3–5
	March 11–17	#1876	What's In	2–4
	March 18–24	#1877	Oprah, Jackie, Robin Givens	2–4
	March 25–31	#1878	Oscars	2–4
	April 1–7	#1879	Women of L.A. Law	3–5
	April 8–14	#1880	The Busy Person's TV Guide	2–4
	April 15–21	#1881	Joan Collins	2–4
	April 22–28	#1882	Jason Bateman, Kirk Cameron	3–5
	April 29	#1883	May Is Bustin' Out	2–4
	May 6–12	#1884	TV Is 50	2–4
	May 13–19	#1885	Dynasty's Tracy Scoggins	2–4
	May 20–26	#1886	Roseanne's Roseanne Barr	3–5
	May 27	#1887	Cheers' Kirstie Alley	3–5
	June 3–9	#1888	Oprah Winfrey	2–4
	June 10–16	#1889	Fred Savage	2–4
	June 17–23	#1890	Knots Landing's Donna Mills	3–5
	June 24–30	#1891	Soap Couples	2–4
	July 1–7	#1892	TV Stars in the Movies	2–4

Year	Issue	Number	Description	Value ($)
1989	July 8–14	#1893	The Best and the Worst	2–4
	July 15–21	#1894	Network News All-Stars	2–4
	July 22–28	#1895	Roseanne Barr, Nicollette Sheridan	2–4
	July 29	#1896	Married with Children cast cover	3–5
	August 5–11	#1897	Tabloid TV	2–4
	August 12–18	#1898	TV's News Queens	2–4
	August 19–25	#1899	Hollywood's Drug Scene	2–4
	August 26	#1900	Oprah Winfrey's Head on Ann-Margret's Body cover	5–10
	September 2–8	#1901	Miss America, Football	2–4
	September 9–15	#1902	Fall Preview special	4–6
	September 16–22	#1903	Roseanne Barr, Bill Cosby	2–4
	September 23–29	#1904	Foster, Haje, Tyson	2–4
	September 30	#1905	Elizabeth Taylor, Mark Harmon	2–4
	October 7–13	#1906	Delta Burke and Gerald McRaney	2–4
	October 14–20	#1907	World Series	2–4
	October 21–27	#1908	Anything But Love's Jamie Lee Curtis	3–5
	October 28	#1909	The Final Days	2–4
	November 4–10	#1910	Farrah, Bateman, Bertinelli	3–5

Year	Issue	Number	Description	Value ($)
1989	November 11–17	#1911	Richard Chamberlain	2–4
	November 18–24	#1912	Courteney Cox, Barry Bostwick	2–4
	November 25	#1913	Victoria Principal	3–5
	December 2–8	#1914	Holiday special	2–4
	December 9–15	#1915	The '80's	2–4
	December 16–22	#1916	Doogie Howser	2–4
	December 23–29	#1917	Murphy Brown's Candice Bergen	3–5
	December 30	#1918	Julia Duffy, Jean Smart	3–5
1990	January 6–12	#1919	Rock Hudson	3–5
	January 13–19	#1920	Roseanne	2–4
	January 20–26	#1921	Arsenio Hall, Dana Delany	2–4
	January 27	#1922	Super Bowl, Indiana Jones	3–5
	February 3–9	#1923	Lesley Ann Warren	2–4
	February 10–16	#1924	The Hottest TV Couples	2–4
	February 17–23	#1925	Elvis Presley	3–5
	February 24	#1926	Challenger Disaster	3–5
	March 3–9	#1927	Children's TV	2–4
	March 10–16	#1928	L.A. Law cast cover	3–5
	March 17–23	#1929	The Simpsons	3–5
	March 24–30	#1930	Oscar Night, Billy Crystal	2–4
	March 31	#1931	America's Funniest Videos	2–4
	April 7–13	#1932	Valerie Bertinelli, Carol Burnett	2–4
	April 14–20	#1933	What's In/What's Out	1–3

Year	Issue	Number	Description	Value ($)
1990	April 21–27	#1934	Arnold Schwarzenegger	2–4
	April 28	#1935	May Sweeps	1–3
	May 5–11	#1936	Oprah Winfrey	1–3
	May 12–18	#1937	Growing Pains cast cover	2–4
	May 19–25	#1938	Carol Burnett cover by Hirschfeld	2–4
	May 26	#1939	TV Goes to the Movies	1–3
	June 2–8	#1940	Steve Bond, Barbara Crampton	1–3
	June 9–15	#1941	Bart Simpson, Ninja Turtles	2–4
	June 16–22	#1942	Dana Delany	1–3
	June 23–29	#1943	Arsenio Hall	2–4
	June 30	#1944	Summer Survival Guide	1–3
	July 7–13	#1945	The Best and the Worst	1–3
	July 14–20	#1946	A Different World	1–3
	July 21–27	#1947	TV's Top Teen Stars	3–5
	July 29	#1948	Guide to New Home Video	1–3
	August 4–10	#1949	Candice Bergen, Kirstie Alley, Nicollette Sheridan	2–4
	August 11–17	#1950	TV Sports and Money	1–3
	August 18–24	#1951	Designing Women cast cover	2–4
	August 25–31	#1952	Delany, Smith, Sheridan	1–3
	September 1–7	#1953	Madonna, Paula Abdul, Janet Jackson	3–5

Year	Issue	Number	Description	Value ($)
1990	September 8–14	#1954	The Women of Twin Peaks	3–5
	September 15–21	#1955	Fall Preview special	4–8
	September 22–28	#1956	Fall Preview special II	2–4
	September 29	#1957	Fall Preview special III	2–4
	October 6–12	#1958	Fall Preview special IV	2–4
	October 13–19	#1959	New Teen Shows	2–4
	October 20–26	#1960	The Best and Worst Dressed	1–3
	October 27	#1961	Horror on TV	2–4
	November 3–9	#1962	November to Remember	1–3
	November 10–16	#1963	Susan Lucci	2–4
	November 17–23	#1964	The Muppets	1–3
	November 24–30	#1965	Linda Evans	2–4
	December 1–7	#1966	Guide to the Holidays	1–3
	December 8–14	#1967	Full House cast cover	1–3
	December 15–21	#1968	Designing Women's Dixie Carter	1–3
	December 22–28	#1969	Batman, The Flash, Dick Tracy	2–4
	December 29	#1970	Murphy Brown cast cover	2–4
1991	January 5–11	#1971	Jane Pauley	2–4
	January 12–18	#1972	Farrah Fawcett and Ryan O'Neal	2–4
	January 19–25	#1973	The Best Stories of 60 Minutes	1–3
	January 26	#1974	Cybill Shepherd	2–4
	February 2–8	#1975	Julia Roberts, MC Hammer, Gary Cole	2–4

Year	Issue	Number	Description	Value ($)
1991	February 9–15	#1976	Lucy and Desi	2–4
	February 16–22	#1977	Watching the War	1–3
	February 23	#1978	Roseanne, War News, Mr. Rogers	1–3
	March 2–8	#1979	Jaleel White of Family Matters	1–3
	March 9–15	#1980	Empty Nest	1–3
	March 16–22	#1981	Teenage Mutant Ninja Turtles	3–5
	March 23–29	#1982	Kevin Costner, Whoopi Goldberg, Julia Roberts	2–4
	March 30	#1983	Cheryl Ladd, Whitney Houston	3–5
	April 6–12	#1984	Baseball TV Preview	1–3
	April 13–19	#1985	Designing Women's Delta Burke	2–4
	April 20–26	#1986	Burt Reynolds and Marilu Henner	2–4
	April 27	#1987	Dinosaurs	2–4
	May 4–10	#1988	Larry Hagman: Adios Dallas	2–4
	May 11–17	#1989	L.A. Law cast cover	2–4
	May 18–24	#1990	Murphy Brown cast cover	2–4
	May 25–31	#1991	Julia Roberts, Arnold Schwarzennegger	2–4
	June 1–7	#1992	A Different World	1–3
	June 8–14	#1993	Michael Landon	3–5
	June 15–21	#1994	The Wizard of Oz, 50 Best Videos	2–4
	June 22–28	#1995	Gerald McRaney and Delta Burke	1–3

Year	Issue	Number	Description	Value ($)
1991	June 29	#1996	The Battle for Johnny Carson's Crown	1–3
	July 6–12	#1997	The Best and the Worst	1–3
	July 13–19	#1998	Michael Landon	3–5
	July 20–26	#1999	Michael Landon	3–5
	July 27	#2000	2,000 Issue Special	2–4
	August 3–9	#2001	Madonna: MTV's 10th Anniversary	3–5
	August 10–16	#2002	TV's Most Beautiful Women	1–3
	August 17–23	#2003	Kevin Costner, Macauley Culkin	1–3
	August 24–30	#2004	Beverly Hills 90210's Shannen Doherty	3–5
	August 31	#2005	Star Trek: Kirk versus Picard	3–5
	September 7–13	#2006	Northern Exposure's Janine Turner	2–4
	September 14–20	#2007	Fall Preview special	5–7
	September 21–27	#2008	Jan Hooks and Julia Duffy	2–4
	September 28	#2009	Parent's Guide to New Kids' Shows	1–3
	October 5–11	#2010	Best and Worst Dressed	1–3
	October 12–18	#2011	Jacqueline Kennedy	1–3
	October 19–25	#2012	Dynasty's Linda Evans and Joan Collins	2–4
	October 26	#2013	Joan Rivers	1–3
	November 2–8	#2014	Michael Landon	3–5

Year	Issue	Number	Description	Value ($)
1991	November 9–15	#2015	Is Network News Crumbling?	1–3
	November 16–22	#2016	Valerie Bertinelli	2–4
	November 23–29	#2017	Madonna	3–5
	November 30	#2018	The Judds	3–4
	December 7–13	#2019	Holiday Viewing Guide	1–3
	December 14–20	#2020	Beverly Hills 90210	1–3
	December 21–27	#2021	Northern Exposure	2–4
	December 28	#2022	John Goodman	2–4
1992	January 4–10	#2023	Roseanne	3–6
	January 11–17	#2024	Jane and Henry Fonda	3–6
	January 18–24	#2025	Empty Nest's Dreyfuss	3–6
	January 25–31	#2026	Superbowl XXVI	3–6
	February 1–7	#2027	Jessica Lange	3–6
	February 8–14	#2028	Winter Olympics Issue	4–7
	February 15–21	#2029	Regis Philbin and Kathie Lee Gifford	4–7
	February 22–28	#2030	Fake News	4–7
	February 29	#2031	Young Indiana Jones	4–7
	March 7–13	#2032	Macauley Culkin	3–6
	March 14–20	#2033	Jane Pauley	3–6
	March 21–27	#2034	Magic Johnson	3–6
	March 28	#2035	Disney's Beast/ Oscars	3–6
	April 4–10	#2036	Moss/Lang of Bold & Beautiful	3–6
	April 11–17	#2037	S.O.S.-Save Our Show	3–6
	April 18–24	#2038	cast of Home Improvement	4–7
	April 25	#2039	Burt Reynolds	4–7
	May 2–8	#2040	Woody Harrelson and Jackie Swanson	4–7

Year	Issue	Number	Description	Value ($)
1992	May 9–15	#2041	Goodby-y-y-y-y-e Johnny	5–9
	May 16–22	#2042	Oprah	5–9
	May 22–29	#2043	Seinfeld	5–9
	May 30	#2044	Cast of Wonder Years	5–9
	June 6–12	#2045	Grant Show of Melrose Place	3–6
	June 13–19	#2046	Bob Saget of Full House	3–6
	June 20–26	#2047	Year's Best & Worst	3–6
	June 27	#2048	Phil Donahue	3–6
	July 4–10	#2049	Delta Burke	3–6
	July 11–17	#2050	Luke Perry and Shannen Doherty	5–9
	July 18–24	#2051	Cindy Crawford Patrick Stewart	10–20
	July 25–31	#2052	Summer Olympics Guide	2–5
	August 1–7	#2053	David Letterman Dana Carvey	2–5 2–5
	August 8–14	#2054	Di vs Chuck: The Soap Opera	10–15
	August 15–21	#2055	Roseanne, Whoopi, Koppel: Zapping	3–6
	August 22–28	#2056	TV Violence Battering Our Kids?	3–6
	August 29	#2057	Roseanne: The Emmys	3–6
	September 5–11	#2058	Joan Lunden	2–4
	September 12–18	#2059	Special Fall Preview Issue	5–10
	September 19–25	#2060	Candice Bergen of Murphy Brown	2–5
	September 26	#2061	Billy Ray Cyrus & Reba McEntire	2–5
	October 3–9	#2062	Bob Newhart of Bob	2–5

Year	Issue	Number	Description	Value ($)
1992	October 10–16	#2063	Give Up TV for $1 Million?	2–5
	October 17–23	#2064	Leeza Gibbons, Jay Leno, Best Dressed	2–5
	October 24–30	#2065	Goofy, Max of Goof Troop— Kids TV	3–6
	October 31	#2066	J. Roberts, Peter Falk, Jaclyn Smith	4–6
	November 7–13	#2067	Frank Sinatra	4–6
	November 14–20	#2068	Michael Jackson	4–6
	November 21–27	#2069	Diane Sawyer	2–4
	November 28	#2070	Bart and Maggie Simpson	4–8
	December 5–11	#2071	Stamos, Blake, Dylan of Full House	2–4
	December 12–18	#2072	Katey Sagal of Married with Children	3–6
	December 19–25	#2073	Toon Boom	2–5
	December 26	#2074	Year in Cheers and Jeers	2–4
1993	January 2–8	#2075	Sci-Fi Issue	5–10
	January 9–15	#2076	Bill and Hillary Clinton	2–5
	January 16–22	#2077	Dana Carvey and Phil Hartman	2–5
	January 23–29	#2078	Fresh Prince's Will Smith	2–5
	January 30	#2079	Coach's Craig T. Nelson	2–5
	February 6–12	#2080	Katie Couric	2–5
	February 13–19	#2081	Billy Ray Cyrus	5–10
	February 20–26	#2082	Jane Seymour of Dr. Quinn	2–4
	February 27	#2083	Jane Pauley and Barney	2–4
	March 6–12	#2084	Cher, Regis Philbin	3–5

Year	Issue	Number	Description	Value ($)
1993	March 13–19	#2085	Mary Tyler Moore	3–5
	March 20–26	#2086	Hunter Tylo and Antonio Sabato Jr.	2–4
	March 27	#2087	Billy Crystal and Oscars	2–4
	April 3–9	#2088	Heather Locklear of Melrose Place	5–10
	April 10–16	#2089	Ted Danson	2–4
	April 17–23	#2090	40th Anniversary Issue	3–6
	April 24–30	#2091	Cast of Home Improvement	5–10
	May 1–7	#2092	Knots Landing Ending	3–6
	May 8–14	#2093	Arsenio Hall, Tori Spelling	2–4
	May 15–21	#2094	Closing Time at Cheers	2–4
	May 22–28	#2095	Linda Ellerbee	2–4
	May 29	#2096	Richard Simmons, Best and Worst TV	2–4
	June 5–11	#2097	Connie Chung	2–4
	June 12–18	#2098	Blossom's Joey Lawrence	3–5
	June 19–25	#2099	Cast of Little House, A Martinez	2–4
	June 26	#2100	Cindy Crawford, Naomi Campbell, Beverly Johnson	5–10
	July 3–9	#2101	Vanna White	4–8
	July 10–16	#2102	Larry Hagman of Staying Afloat	2–4
	July 17–23	#2103	Julia Roberts—Hot Blooded Hollywood	3–6
	July 24–30	#2104	Summer Sci-Fi Issue	5–10
	July 31	#2105	Patrick Stewart of Star Trek: The Next Generation	5–10

Year	Issue	Number	Description	Value ($)
1993	August 7–13	#2106	Full House's Mary-Kate and Ashley Olsen	3–5
	August 14–20	#2107	Furor over R-rate, Network TV	3–5
	August 21–27	#2108	Loni Anderson	3–5
	August 28	#2109	Letterman, Leno, Chase, Arsenio, Koppel	2–4
	September 4–10	#2110	William Shatner: Star Trek Memories	5–10
	September 11–17	#2111	Kelsey Grammer of Frasier	4–8
	September 18–24	#2112	Special Fall Preview issue	6–12
	September 25	#2113a	Raymond Burr	6–12
	September 25	#2113b	Wynonna and Clint	6–12
	October 2–8	#2114	Victoria Principal	4–8
	October 9–15	#2115	Harry Anderson, John Larroquette	3–6
	October 16–22	#2116	Tony Geary, Genie Francis of General Hospital	3–6
	October 23–29	#2117	Faye Dunaway, Paula Poundstone, Jason Alexander	3–6
	October 30	#2118	Kid's TV (Bert and Ernie)	3–6
	November 6–12	#2119	Mike Wallace: Inside 60 Minutes	5–10
	November 13–19	#2120	Hillary Clinton and Big Bird	2–4
	November 20–26	#2121	Waltons Come Home Again	3–6
	November 27	#2122	Dolly Parton	3–6
	December 4–10	#2123	James Stewart, Donna Reed, Fresh	5–10
	December 11–17	#2124	Bette Midler, Prince Jennie Garth	3–6

Year	Issue	Number	Description	Value ($)
1993	December 18–24	#2125	Batman, Spock, Lucy, Get Smart	5–10
	December 25	#2126	Johnny Carson	2–4
1994	January 1–7	#2127	Tim Allen	4–8
	January 8–14	#2128	David Caruso of NYPD Blue	2–4
	January 15–21	#2129	Avery Brooks of Deep Space 9	5–10
	January 22–28	#2130	Ellen DeGeneres, Tim Reid, Henry Winkler	3–5
	January 29	#2131	Valerie Bertinelli, Football	3–6
	February 5–11	#2132	Heather Locklear, Fabio, Courtney Thorne-Smith	4–8
	February 12–18	#2133	Winter Olympics, Nancy Kerrigan	2–4
	February 19–25	#2134	Olympics, Cybill Shepherd	2–4
	February 26	#2135	Whitney Houston	5–10
	March 5–11	#2136	Dennis Franz of NYPD Blue	3–6
	March 12–18	#2137	Kid's TV, Erin Davis	3–5
	March 19–25	#2138	Oscars, Barbara Walters, Whoopi Goldberg	3–5
	March 26	#2139	Diane Sawyer	3–5
	April 2–8	#2140	Loni Anderson	3–5
	April 9–15	#2141	Kirstie Alley	3–5
	April 16–22	#2142	Nicollette Sheridan	3–5
	April 23–29	#2143	Jason Alexander of Seinfeld	4–6
	April 30	#2144	Garth Brooks	3–5
	May 7–13	#2145	Rob Lowe of The Stand	5–7
	May 14–20	#2146	Star Trek: The Next Generation Collector's Edition	10–20

Year	Issue	Number	Description	Value ($)
1994	May 21–27	#2147	Farrah Fawcett	4–6
	May 28	#2148	Andrew Shue of Melrose Place	3–5
	June 4–10	#2149	Elizabeth Taylor	5–7
	June 11–17	#2150	Madonna, Brett Butler, Laura Leighton	6–8
	June 18–24	#2151	TV's Top Dogs	5–7
	June 25	#2152	Tim Allen, Jay Leno, Jane Seymour	5–7
	July 2–8	#2153	Reba McIntire	5–10
	July 9–15	#2154	Go, Go, Power Rangers!	4–7
	July 16–22	#2155	Cindy Crawford	3–5
	July 23–29	#2156	Oprah	3–5
	July 30	#2157	O. J. Simpson	3–5
	August 6–12	#2158	Paul Reiser, Mad About You	5–7
	August 13–19	#2159	Cast of Baywatch	4–7
	August 20–26	#2160	Barbra Streisand by Hirschfeld	5–8
	August 27	#2161	David Letterman	10–15
	September 3–9	#2162	John Madden	6–8
	September 10–16	#2163	Tim Allen, David Caruso, Emmys	6–8
	September 17–23	#2164	Special Fall Preview issue	12–16
	September 24–30	#2165	Cast of Frasier	7–9
	October 1–7	#2166	Christie Brinkley	5–7
	October 8–14	#2167	Kate Mulgrew of Star Trek: Voyager	8–10
	October 15–21	#2168	Melissa Gilbert	3–5
	October 22–28	#2169	Suzanne Somers, Jay Leno	5–7
	October 29	#2170	Power Rangers, Kids' TV	5–7
	November 5–11	#2171	Shannen Doherty	6–8
	November 12–18	#2172	Cast of Scarlett	6–8
	November 19–25	#2173	Cast of E.R.	3–5

Year	Issue	Number	Description	Value ($)
1994	November 26	#2174	Ellen DeGeneres	7–9
	December 3–9	#2175	Crystal Bernard of Wings	3–5
	December 10–16	#2176	Jane Pauley, Matthew Fox, Steven Wolf	4–7
	December 17–23	#2177	Kathie Lee Gifford	3–5
	December 24–30	#2178	Year in Cheers and Jeers	5–7
	December 31	#2179	Bear's Collins, Phillips	10–14
1995	January 7–13	#2180	Oprah	2–4
	January 14–20	#2181	Cast of Voyager, John Leguizamo	4–8
	January 21–28	#2182	Shawn and Marlon Wayans, Delta Burke	2–4
	January 29	#2183	Super Bowl XXIX	2–5
	February 4–10	#2184	Jerry Seinfeld, Roseanne	3–6
	February 11–17	#2185	Heather Locklear	5–10
	February 18–24	#2186	Sally Field	3–6
	February 25	#2187	George Clooney	4–8
	March 4–10	#2188	Power Rangers	4–8
	March 11–17	#2189	David Duchovny and Gillian Anderson of the X-Files	6–12
	March 18–24	#2190	Roseanne, Tim Allen, Seinfeld	4–8
	March 25–31	#2191	David Letterman	2–4
	April 1–7	#2192	Talk Shows out of Control?	2–4
	April 8–14	#2193	Jennie Garth	2–4
	April 15–21	#2194	Fran Drescher of The Nanny	3–6
	April 22–28	#2195	Susan Lucci	3–5
	April 29	#2196	Kate Mulgrew	4–8
	May 6–12	#2197	Jane Seymour, Joe Lando	4–8

Year	Issue	Number	Description	Value ($)
1995	May 13–19	#2198	The Judds	3–6
	May 20–26	#2199	NYPD Blue's Gail O'Grady	3–5
	May 27	#2200	Pamela Anderson	3–6
	June 3–9	#2201	Larry King, Connie Chung	2–4
	June 10–16	#2202	Michael Jackson and Lisa Marie Presley, George Clooney, Pocahontas	3–6
	June 17–23	#2203	Brett Butler, Bryant Gumbel	3–5
	June 24–30	#2204	White Power Ranger	3–5
	July 1–7	#2205	Victoria Principal	3–6
	July 8–14	#2206	Cal Ripkin Jr., Seinfeld	3–6
	July 15–21	#2207	Kes and Neelix of Voyager	10–20
	July 22–28	#2208	Dean Cain of Superman	4–8
	July 29	#2209	Josie Bissett	3–5
	August 5–11	#2210	Tom Selleck	3–6
	August 12–18	#2211	Cybill Shepherd, Jimmy Smits	2–4
	August 19–25	#2212	Regis Philbin	2–4
	August 26	#2213	Brian Austin Green, Tiffany-Amber Thiessen	2–4
	September 2–8	#2214	Chris Zorich	4–8
	September 9–15	#2215	Paul Reiser, Kelsey Grammer, Gary Shandling	3–6
	September 16–22	#2216	Fall Preview issue	3–6
	September 23–29	#2217	Cast of Friends	3–6
	September 30	#2218	Cast of Murder One	2–5
	October 7–13	#2219	Worf, Michael Dorn	3–6
	October 14–20	#2220	George Clooney, Julianna Margulies	2–4
	October 21–27	#2221	Andy, Matt, and Joey Lawrence	4–6

Year	Issue	Number	Description	Value ($)
1995	October 28	#2222	Fergie	2–4
	November 4–10	#2223	Brooke Shields	4–8
	November 11–17	#2224	Oprah	3–6
	November 18–24	#2225	Beatles 1995	5–10
	November 25	#2226	Jane Seymour	4–8
	December 2–8	#2227	Tea Leoni	2–4
	December 9–15	#2228	Cast of Party of Five	3–6
	December 16–22	#2229	Kathie Lee, Cody, Cassidy Gifford	2–4
	December 23–29	#2230	Lisa Kudrow, Heather Locklear	2–5
	December 30	#2231a*	Eddie George, Peyton Manning	4–8
	December 30	#2231b*	Northwestern's Barnett	6–8
1996	January 6–12	#2232	Seinfeld	3–6
	January 13–20	#2233	Morgan Fairchild	2–4
	January 21–26	#2234	Xena and Hercules, Sci-Fi and Fantasy issue	5–10
	January 27	#2235a*	Troy Aikman Super Bowl XXX	3–6
	January 27	#2235b*	Steelers' QB Neil O'Donnell	6–12
	January 27	#2235c*	Troy Aikman of the Dallas Cowboys	15–25
	February 3–9	#2236	Ted Danson, Mary Steenburgen	2–4
	February 10–16	#2237	David Schwimmer, Jennifer Aniston of Friends	3–6
	February 17–23	#2238	John De Lancie, Kate Mulgrew of Voyager	3–6
	February 24	#2239	Tori Spelling	2–5
	March 2–8	#2240	Jimmy Smits, Dennis Franz of NYPD Blue	3–6
	March 9–15	#2241	50 Great Things about TV Now	2–4

*Not distributed nationwide.

Year	Issue	Number	Description	Value ($)
1996	March 16–22	#2242	Billy Crystal	2–4
	March 23–29	#2243		2–4
	March 30	#2244	Joan Lunden	2–4
	April 6–12	#2245	Gillian Anderson and David Duchovny of The X-Files	5–10
	April 13–19	#2246a*	Anthony Edwards of E.R.	3–6
	April 13–19	#2246b*	Steve Yzerman of the Redwings	10–25
	April 20–26	#2247	Cybill Shepherd	2–4
	April 27	#2248	Cast of 60 Minutes	2–4
	May 4–10	#2249	Whitney Houston	3–6
	May 11–17	#2250	Tom Selleck, Courteney Cox	3–5
	May 18–24	#2251	Candice Bergen	2–4
	May 25–31	#2252	Heather Locklear	3–6
	June 1–7	#2253	Jerry Seinfeld	4–8
	June 8–14	#2254	Jenny McCarthy—Summer Preview	2–4
	June 15–21	#2255	Teri Hatcher	4–8
	June 22–28	#2256a*	Conan O'Brien	10–15
	June 22–28	#2256b*	Nascar's Jeff Gordon	15–25
	June 29	#2257	100 Most Memorable Moments on TV special issue	3–6
	July 6–12	#2258	Gillian Anderson of the X-Files	5–10
	July 13–19	#2259	Jerry Mathers	2–4
	July 20–26	#2260	Summer Olympics issue	2–4
	July 27	#2261	U.S. Women's Basketball, Big Summer Sci-Fi Spread	6–12
	August 3–9	#2262	Dean Cain, Jennie Garth	2–4

*Not distributed nationwide.

Year	Issue	Number	Description	Value ($)
1996	August 10–16	#2263		2–4
	August 17–23	#2264	Matthew Perry of Friends	2–4
	August 24–30	#2265a	William Shatner, Star Trek Turns 30	5–15
	August 24–30	#2265b	Patrick Stewart	5–15
	August 24–30	#2265c	Kate Mulgrew	5–15
	August 24–30	#2265d	Avery Brooks	5–15
	August 31	#2266†	Aikman and Smith	2–4
	August 31	#2266a†	Drew Carey	10–12
	September 7–13	#2267	Helen Hunt, Paul Reiser, Mad about You	3–6
	September 14–20	#2268	Special Fall Preview issue	3–6
	September 21–27	#2269	Cybill, X-Files, Friends	5–10
	September 28	#2270a*	Michael J. Fox	4–8
	September 28	#2270b*	Baseball Playoff Preview	10–15
	September 28	#2270c*	" "	10–15
	September 28	#2270d*	" "	10–15
	September 28	#2270e*	" "	10–15
	September 28	#2270f*	" "	10–15
	September 28	#2270g*	" "	12–50
	September 28	#2270h*	" "	25–75
	September 28	#2270i*	" "	20–50
	September 28	#2270j*	" "	15–20
	September 28	#2270k*	" "	40–80
	October 5–11	#2271	Jay Leno	3–6
	October 12–18	#2272	Women of Savannah	5–10
	October 19–25	#2273*	Brooke Shields	5–10
	October 26	#2274*	Cast of Rugrats	3–6
	November 2–8	#2275	Michael Jordan	2–4
	November 9–15	#2276	Robert Urich	2–4
	November 16–22	#2277	Lance Henriksen of Millennium	3–6

*Not distributed nationwide.
†Several different issue covers for August 31, 1996; from #2266b through #2266z are all football-related team covers and run $8–$12 each.

Year	Issue	Number	Description	Value ($)
1996	November 23–29	#2278	Carey Lowell and Kyle Chandler	2–4
	November 30	#2279	Roma Downey of Touched by an Angel	4–8
	December 7–13	#2280*	Drew Carey, Kathy Kinney	2–5
	December 14–20	#2281	Michael Landon, Lassie,	2–4
	December 21–27	#2282a	David Duchovny of The X-Files	5–10
	December 21–27	#2282b	Fox Mulder, X-Files	5–10
	December 28	#2283*	Homicide: Life on the Street	4–8
	December 28	#2283a*	Wildcats' Barnett and Fitzgerald	4–8
	December 28	#2283b*	Cougars' Sarkisian	3–6
	December 28	#2283d*	Seminoles' Bowden	3–6
	December 28	#2283e*	Lions' Paterno	3–6
	December 28	#2283f*	Sun Devils' Plummer	3–5
1997	January 4–10	#2284	Oprah	2–4
	January 11–17	#2285	Dilbert	2–4
	January 18–24	#2286	Winter Preview	2–4
	January 25–31	#2287a	Super Bowl XXXI	3–6
	January 25–31	#2287b*	Green Bay's Brett Favre	5–10
	January 25–31	#2287c*		5–10
	January 25–31	#2287d*		5–10
	January 25–31	#2287e*		5–10
	January 25–31	#2287f*		5–10
	January 25–31	#2287g*		5–10
	February 1–7	#2288	Kevin Sorbo as Hercules	4–8
	February 8–14	#2289	Neve Campbell	2–4
	February 15–21	#2290a*	David Letterman and Showgirls	6–12
	February 15–21	#2290b*	Nascar's Dale Earnhardt	4–8

*Not distributed nationwide.

Year	Issue	Number	Description	Value ($)
1997	February 15–21	#2290c*	Nascar's Jeff Gordon	4–8
	February 15–21	#2290d*	Nascar's Dale Jarrett	4–8
	February 15–21	#2290e*	Nascar's Terry Labonte	4–8
	February 22–28	#2291	Chuck Norris Kicks Butt	3–6
	March 1–7	#2292	3rd Rock from the Sun cast cover	3–6
	March 8–14	#2293a*	Skater Ekaterina Gordeeva	2–5
	March 8–14	#2293b*	Howard Stern	15–30
	March 15–21	#2294	Elmo, Kristin Scott Thomas	2–5
	March 22–28	#2295	Tom Cruise, Woody Harrelson, Barbara Hershey	3–5
	March 29	#2296	God and TV	3–5
	April 5–11	#2297a*	Rosie O'Donnell	3–6
	April 5–11	#2297b*	Flyers' Eric Lindros	5–10
	April 5–11	#2297c*	Panthers' John Vanbiesbrouck	5–10
	April 5–11	#2297d*		5–10
	April 5–11	#2297e*		5–10
	April 5–11	#2297f*		5–8
	April 12–18	#2298	Michael Jordan	2–4
	April 19–25	#2299	Jenny McCarthy	2–4
	April 26	#2300a*	Stephen King	5–10
	April 26	#2300b*	Tom Hanks	3–6
	May 3–9	#2301a*	Lucy Lawless as Xena	10–15
	May 3–9	#2301b*	Kentucky Derby Special	3–6
	May 3–9	#2301c*		3–6
	May 10–16	#2302a*	Kate Mulgrew and Borg	5–10
	May 10–16	#2302b*	Chicago Hope cast	3–6
	May 17–23	#2303	X-Files cast	5–10
	May 24–30	#2304	Kim Delaney	2–4

*Not distributed nationwide.

#2326, 1997

#2331, 1997

#2385, 1998

#2357, 1998

March 12, 1954

January 29, 1954

January 15, 1954

November 13, 1953

July 24, 1953

Year	Issue	Number	Description	Value ($)
1997	May 31	#2305	Michael Richards as Kramer	3–6
	June 7–13	#2306a*	Farrah at 50	10–15
	June 7–13	#2306b*	Leann Rimes	2–4
	June 7–13	#2306c*	Flyers' Rod Brind	4–8
	June 7–13	#2306d*		5–10
	June 14–20	#2307	Caroline in the City's Lea Thompson	3–6
	June 21–27	#2308	Joan Lunden	2–4
	June 28	#2309	100 Greatest Episodes of All Time	3–6
	July 5–11	#2310	Babylon 5 cast, Sci-Fi special	5–10
	July 12–18	#2311		2–4
	July 19–25	#2312	Kathie Lee Gifford	2–4
	July 26	#2313	Jennifer Aniston	2–4
	August 2–8	#2314a*	Buffy the Vampire Slayer	10–15
	August 2–8	#2314b*		3–5
	August 9–15	#2315	French Stewart	2–4
	August 16–22	#2316a	Blue Hawaii Elvis	5–10
	August 16–22	#2316b	Smiling Elvis	5–10
	August 16–22	#2316c	Leather Elvis	5–10
	August 16–22	#2316d	Vegas Elvis	5–10
	August 23–29	#2317a	Miss America, Madison Michele	2–5
	August 23–29	#2317b	Marilyn Monroe	5–10
	August 30	#2318aa		6–12
	August 30	#2318ab		6–12
	August 30	#2318ac		6–12
	September 6–12	#2319	X-Files	3–6
	September 13–19	#2320	Special Fall Preview	3–6
	September 20–26	#2321	Princess Diana	3–6
	September 27	#2322a*	Drew Carey	5–10
	September 27	#2322b*	Astros' Craig Biggio	5–10

*Not distributed nationwide.
†Several different issue covers for August 30, 1997; from #2318a through #2318z are all football-related team covers and run $8–$12 each.

Year	Issue	Number	Description	Value ($)
1997	September 27	#2322c*		5–10
	September 27	#2322d*		5–10
	September 27	#2322e*		5–10
	October 4–10	#2323	Gregory Hines	2–4
	October 11–17	#2324	Ellen DeGeneres	3–5
	October 18–24	#2325	Sabrina the Teenage Witch	5–10
	October 25–31	#2326a*		2–4
	October 25–31	#2326b*		5–15
	October 25–31	#2326c*		5–15
	October 25–31	#2326d*		5–15
	October 25–31	#2326e*		5–15
	October 25–31	#2326f*		5–15
	October 25–31	#2326g		5–15
	November 1–7	#2327	Brandy, Whitney Houston, Cinderella	3–6
	November 8–14	#2328a	Jeri Ryan of Voyager	4–8
	November 8–14	#2328b	Terry Farrell of Deep Space 9	5–10
	November 15–21	#2329	X-Files cast	5–10
	November 22–28	#2330	Jenna Elfman, Dharma and Greg	2–4
	November 29	#2331	Brook Shields	5–10
	December 6–12	#2332	Roma Downey, Touched by an Angel	3–6
	December 13–19	#2333		2–4
	December 20–26	#2334	Best of '97	2–4
	December 27	#2335a*		2–4

1998 to present

Issues featuring covers from: Xena: Warrior Princess, Charmed, Buffy the Vampire Slayer, Sabrina the Teenage Witch, and The X-Files, $7–15+

Issues from 1998, 1999 to present featuring covers from: Star Trek: The Next Generation, Star Trek: Deep Space Nine, Hercules, and Star Wars: Episode 1, $5–10+

*Not distributed nationwide.

Adult Magazines

Any magazine that features nudity (male and/or female) and articles of a sexual nature is classified as an adult magazine. These magazines are for collectors eighteen or older. When collected they should at all times be kept well out of reach and sight of minors.

Adult magazines, at present, are a very large segment of the magazine collecting world. The reasons they are collected are many, but primarily it is for the photos, artwork, and stories. Many well-known female celebrities posed nude early in their careers, and issues containing these nude photos are very much in demand. Artists such as Bode had their work published in such adult magazines as *Gallery*. *Playboy* and other similar adult magazines published stories by renowned authors of both fiction and nonfiction. They also offered exclusive interviews by such legends as Lenny Bruce and Jim Morrison. Many of these stories and interviews are only accessible to the fan or researcher in the pages of specific back issue adult magazines.

Buying Adult Magazines

In today's adult magazine marketplace the buyer has several options. The most economical source for acquiring adult magazines (especially *Playboy, Penthouse, Oui, Hustler,* and other mass market magazines) is the local garage sale, want ad or penny-saver advertisement, and flea markets. While shopping at these sites it is not uncommon to purchase both common and rare issues at a fraction of their true value—generally at prices between $.25 to just a few dollars per issue. When flea-marketing or garage-saling, keep a sharp eye out for adult magazines. Most sellers, although wishing to sell their old issues, will be very conservative in displaying them. The best, most reliable way to buy adult magazines is by mail order. Many dealers will advertise in trade papers and will offer their catalog, usually for a small fee. The better mail order catalogs will list the titles, issues, and contents of each specific issue along with the set asking price. If a customer is ordering for the first time, the mail order dealer will require from the buyer some form of proof of age (eighteen or older only). This proof is generally supplied by the customer with a photocopy of the buyer's driver's license or birth certificate. Back issue magazine stores are also a good source, but with today's high cost of commercial rent and local laws on the sale of adult material, these stores are quickly becoming a thing of the past . . . so enjoy their musty atmosphere while you can. One of the most exciting ways to find a special adult magazine for your collection is by checking out the many Internet auction sites. If you are collecting rare or top name female personalities, don't expect to win your bid at a modest price; you are competing on this venue with collectors from all over the world, who in most cases are willing to pay fantastic prices. It is not uncommon for rarer issues to sell at auction for as much as five to ten times their guide value. On the other hand, if you are collecting issues that are not so much in demand, real bargains can be had.

Selling Adult Magazines

When you have made the decision to sell your adult magazines you will have to choose which venue is right for you. If you wish to sell them the easiest and quickest way, then take out an inexpensive ad (usually $.10 to $.20 per word) in your local want ad press or penny-saver publication, offer them at a garage sale, or drive your unwanted issues down to the flea market. If you sell through these sources, you cannot expect to match either the high or low guide value for your magazines. The average flea marketer and garage saler will expect to purchase these issues at a fraction of their collector value. Generally, issues will sell for $.25 to $1.50. In large metropolitan areas, where the supply is plentiful, back issues will sell at the lowest prices. There are exceptions, however. Rarer *Playboys* (1950s) can sell for up to the low value given in the guide. It is also important that, while planning to sell at a flea market or garage sale, the seller check with the market's and local city or county's regulations on selling adult magazines. In general, flea markets' rules are to keep all adult magazines out of the reach and sight of minors. Displaying them from behind your table, in a manner in which only the title of the magazine can be seen, is the best way. The experienced collector will spot them. Never sell adult magazines to a minor; when in doubt of age, ask for proper identification. If still in doubt do not make the sale. Always be sure that minors are not browsing through your issues, and do not sell any magazine that features nude photos of children or models under eighteen—it is illegal throughout the entire United States and in most other countries.

Selling adult magazines to back issue magazine stores will usually lead to a quick sale. The selling price should be roughly 10 percent of their retail value (the price the dealer is asking for issues in his shop, or guide value) for common issues and up to 60 percent for rarer issues. Many back issue magazine shops will offer the seller a combination of cash and trade value. These offers are generally beneficial to a collector who wishes to unload unwanted and/or duplicate issues and at the same time pick up issues that are needed for his or her collection. Dealers will, at most times, offer a much higher trade value than a cash value.

Selling to a mail order dealer will take much more time. The seller must first compile a list of titles, issues, any special highlights within a specific issue, and condition of each magazine being offered. When sending this list to the mail order dealer, the seller may state his asking price outright or ask the dealer to make an offer. The seller may also wish to sell his issues directly to collectors via the mail. After compiling your list, offer it through a classified ad in a trade paper (cost is usually between $.10 and $.20 per word for classified). It may be wise to ask a small fee for this list, so as to eliminate browsers. When selling adult magazines through the mail, the seller must insist on proof of age by the purchaser (eighteen or older only). A photocopy of the buyer's driver's license or birth certificate will do.

The most exciting, adventurous, and definitely most profitable means of selling your adult magazines is offering them on the many Internet auction sites. Choose a site that you have heard good things about and that you feel comfortable with. Adult magazines that sell best on the Internet auction are those magazines that are rarer, in fine or better condition, and in one form or another contain the most desirable female personalities. For example an issue of *Rogue* with Bettie Page or June

Wilkinson on the cover, with inside nude photos, is an excellent candidate for the Internet auction. Before listing your magazine, search the auction for the title of your magazine and for the major feature of interest in the magazine (i.e., Bettie Page, Marilyn Monroe, June Wilkinson, Julie Newmar, Elvira, Vanessa Del Rio, Shauna Grant, and so on). If your search shows a site with a great deal of activity (40 percent or more of items up for auction have bids on them) then list your item on that site. It is not uncommon, when a bidding war begins between competitive buyers, for a magazine to sell for as much as five to ten times the listed guide price. With high prices like these, it would appear that this is the most profitable way to sell off your unwanted adult magazines.

Adult Magazine Values

The specific female or females who appear in an issue of an adult magazine generally dictate its value. Early issues of *High Society's Celebrity Skin* and issues of *Celebrity Sleuth* can sell for as high as $50 each, which is because these issues contain many, many nude photos of prominent female TV and movie stars and also because the demand greatly outweighs the supply. Newer issues of *Playboy* will have a higher value than an issue twenty years its senior because it features nude photos of a star who is currently very popular. We have listed below basic values for adult magazines for common issues for each decade. Common issues are issues that do not feature the current most collectible female models or stars. Values for these more collectible females will then follow.

COMMON ADULT MAGAZINE VALUES

Issues From	Value ($)
1930–1939	10–20
1940–1949	5–10
1950–1955	4–8
1956–1959	3–7
1960–1965	3–6

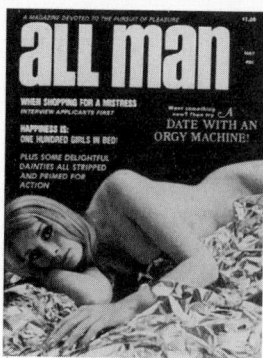

May 1971

May 1970

May 1974

August 1960

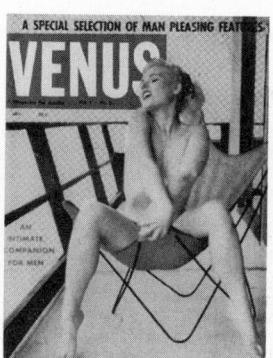

#5, 1958

May 1957

June #3, 1957

October 1957

May 1957

October 1973

August 1957

November 1973

January 1959

April 1957

January 1958

August 1992

May 1995

September 1996

Issues From	Value ($)
1966–1969	3–5
1970–1977	2–4
1978–1985	2–3
1986–1989	2–4
1990 to present	2–3

CURRENT MOST COLLECTIBLE FEMALES APPEARING IN ADULT MAGAZINES

	Value ($)	
Subject	Cover and Pictorial	Cover Only
Pamela Anderson	4–15	2–5
Drew Barrymore	5–10	5–10
Linda Blair	15–30	5–10
Cindy Crawford	8–15	5–10
Vanessa Del Rio	10–20	5–10
Samantha Fox (British singer) (pre-1988)	10–25	6–12
Samantha Fox (1989–present)	8–8	3–5
Shauna Grant	10–30	10–20
Debbie Harry	15–30	10–20
Mai Lin	10–30	10–15
Traci Lords (pre-1988)	20–50	15–30
Traci Lords (1989–present)	5–10	3–5
Amber Lynn	4–10	4–8
Ginger Lynn	10–20	10–15
Madonna	10–20	5–10
Jenny McCarthy	7–15	5–10
Kitten Natividad	5–10	4–10
Susan Nero	10–25	10–20
Bettie Page (pre-1960)	35–75+	20–40+
Bettie Page (pre-1970)	12–25	10–20
Bettie Page (1971–present)	10–20	10–15
Christine Petersen (Elvira) (pre-1980)	15–30	10–20
Christine Petersen (1981–1988)	10–20	7–15
Christine Petersen (1989–present)	7–12	5–8
Claudia Schiffer	5–10	4–8

Subject	Value ($) Cover and Pictorial	Cover Only
S*ports Illustrated*'s Models	5–10	3–6
Julie Strain	5–10	5–10
TV or movie star(s)—any	5–10	3–6
Diane Weber	15–30	10–20
Raquel Welch	10–20	10–20
June Wilkinson	20–50	20–50

Note: For values for issues containing Marilyn Monroe, Jayne Mansfield and other specific female stars, refer to our Movie Magazine Selection.

Important: To help the collector be absolutely sure of the value of their issues, this guide offers "The Official Collectors Hotline," 201-641-7212. Call between normal business hours only, please (EST).

PENTHOUSE VALUES

Year	Issue	Description	Value ($)
1969	September	#1	30–60
	October	#2	15–25
	November	#3	15–20
	December	#4	15–20
1976	March	Priscilla Barnes cover and Pet of the Month centerfold and pictorial	10–20
1977	August	The Nude Women of James Bond	5–10
1980	February	Debbie Harry cover and feature	5–10
1982	October	Morgan Fairchild cover and feature	4–8
1984	September	Vanessa Williams and Traci Lords	25–50
	November	More Vanessa Williams	10–25
1985	September	Madonna cover and nude photos	20–40
1986	January	Madonna Poster	10–20

October 1990

May 1984

July 1991

February 1966

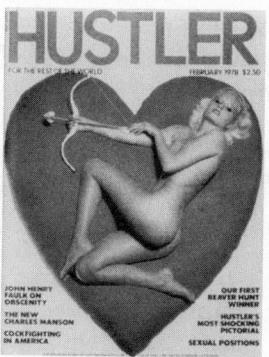

February 1978

June 1985

June 1964

August 1957

December 1957

1987	June	Samantha Fox cover and feature	20–40
	September	Madonna cover and feature	10–20
		Issues with Julie Strain on the cover and/or pictorials	5–10
		All other issues	2–4

PLAYBOY VALUES

Notes:

1. *Playboy* issues are listed by Playmate of the Month first, followed by cover subject and/or pictorial(s) and major feature(s).

2. Most issues of *Playboy* from 1960 on up will not only have a value range, but also a price in parentheses ( ). This is the retail price *Playboy* magazine sells that particular issue for. If there is no price in parentheses, *Playboy* does not have that issue in stock. If (N/A, not available) appears, *Playboy* offered that issue recently but no longer has it in stock.

3. Even though issues of *Playboy* can be acquired for much less, it is important to be aware of the prices being asked and being received by the publisher of *Playboy*.

Year	Issue	Description	Value ($)
1953	December	#1—Marilyn Monroe: Playmate and cover, An Open Letter from California pictorial	1,000–2,500+
1954	January	#2—Margie Harrison, At Home with Dienes, *Playboy* Goes to Art Bell	1,000–2,500+
	February	#3—Margaret Scott, Yvone Menard, Frankie and Johnnie, Paris Hot Spots featuring Yvonne Menard	500–1,200+
	March	#4—Dolores Del Monte, Joanne Arnold cover and pictorial: Sex Sells a Shirt	250–600+
	April	#5—Marilyn Waltz, *Playboy*'s Eyeful	250–500+
	May	#6—Joanne Arnold, Nudes by Weegee	250–500+

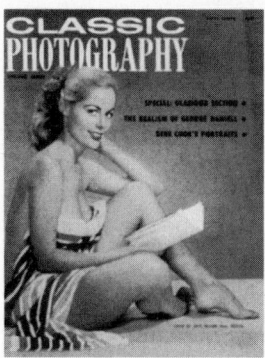

#3, 1957

#1, 1960

February 1995

October 1974

April 1990

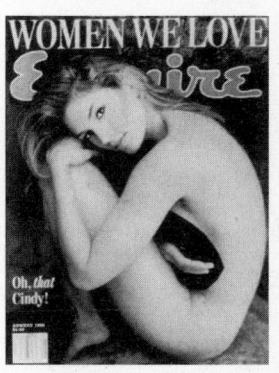

August 1995

April 1996

July 1990

May 1967

Year	Issue	Description	Value ($)
1954	June	#7—Margie Harrison, Outside with Dienes	250–400+
	July	#8—Neva Gilbert, Simone Silva, The Evolution of the Bathing Suit	200–350+
	August	#9—Arline Hunter, A Bump, a Grind and a Gimmick: Yvette Dare, Lilly St. Cyr and Evelyn West	200–350+
	September	#10—Jackie Rainbow, Gina Lollabrigida pictorial	150–250+
	October	#11—Madeline Castle, Nudity in the Foreign Film	100–200+
	November	#12—Diane Hunter, Paris Round the World, The Motoring Playboy	100–200+
	December	#13—Terry Ryan, Photographing a Playmate Pictorial, featuring Terry Ryan, Marlene Dietrich and Terry Moore; The Las Vegas Skin Game	100–225+
1955	January	Bettie Page, Santa Baby: Eartha Kitt, Babylon U.S.A.	100–225+
	February	Jayne Mansfield, Leigh Lewin and Arlene Kieta, Nejla Ates: Broadway's Turkish Delight, Voluptua	100–175+

Note: No issue published for March 1955

	April	Marilyn Waltz, Leigh Lewin, Nude Advertising	100–175+
	May	Marguerite Empey, Bunny Yeager, Terry Shaw and Bettie Page pictorial	100–175+
	June	Eve Myer, Donna Kime, Eve pictorial	100–150+

Year	Issue	Description	Value ($)
1955	July	Janet Pilgram Playmate and cover, Tempest in a C-cup: Tempest Storm	100–150+
	August	Pat Lawler, Gowland's Cool Pool: Joanne Arnold	100–150+
	September	Anne Fleming, Marilyn Monroe pictorial	100–150+
	October	Jean Moorehead, Marilyn McClintock, A Stripper Goes to College, Two Playmates for the Price of One: Jean Moorehead and Johnnie Nicely, Anita Ekberg	100–150+
	November	Barbara Cameron Playmate and cover, West Coast Strippers, Gina Lollabrigida	100–150+
	December	Janet Pilgram Playmate and cover, Burlesque in Tokyo	100–175+
1956	January	Lynn Tutner, The First Two Dozen Playmates	35–75+
	February	Marguerite Empey, Chuckles with Your Cocktails, Jayne Mansfield pictorial	35–75+
	March	Marian Stafford Playmate and cover, Eve Meyer	30–60+
	April	Rusty Fisher, DD in 3D: Diana Dors pictorial	30–60+
	May	Marion Scott, Dolores Taylor, The Lynx with the Lusty Larynx: Meg Myles	30–60+
	June	Gloria Walker, Champagne Flight to Texas: Sally Todd	30–60+
	July	Alice Denham, Peek-a-Boo Pants: Marla English	30–60+
	August	Johnnie Nicely, The Ekberg Bronze: Anita Ekberg	30–60+
	September	Elsa Sorense, Diane Harmsen, Filming the Follies-Bergere	30–60+

June 1958

July 1959

#3, 1993

May 1979

November 1987

December 1989

December 12, 1990

March 1991

November 1991

Summer 1951

October 1941

October 1953

September 1942

May 1942

October 1955

July 1952

Summer 1953

July 1945

Year	Issue	Description	Value ($)
1956	October	Janet Pilgram, How to Bathe a Poodle, Joan Bradshaw	30–60+
	November	Betty Blue	25–50+
	December	Lisa Winters Playmate and cover, Tallulah's Follies	30–60+
1957	January	June Blair, Playmate Review	25–50
	February	Sally Todd, Jayne Mansfield cover and pictorial	25–50
	March	Sandra Edwards, Zsa Zsa in Las Vegas	15–25
	April	Gloria Windsor, Elaine Conte	15–25
	May	Dawn Richard, Li'l Abner's Gals: Julie Newmar, Tina Louise, Carmen Alvarez and Edith Adams	17–25
	June	Carrie Radison, Most Popular Playmate 1956: Lisa Winters, The Back: Vikki Dougan	15–30
	July	Jean Jani, *Playboy*'s Yacht Party	15–25
	August	Dolores Donlon Playmate and cover, View from a Penthouse	15–30
	September	Jacquelyn Prescott, Westerns Are Better Than Ever: Jana Davi	15–30
	October	Colleen Farrington, Latin Quarter Lovelies	15–30
	November	Marlene Callahan, Sophia Loren and Jayne Mansfield pictorial	20–40
	December	Linda Varga, Alone with Lisa: Lisa Winters	15–30
1958	January	Elizabeth Ann Roberts, Playmate Review	20–40

Year	Issue	Description	Value ($)
1958	February	Cheryl Kubert, The Nude Jane Mansfield	15–30
	March	Zahra Norbo, Michilo Hamamura, Brigitte Bardot	15–30
	April	Felicia Atkins, Minsky in Vegas	15–30
	May	Lari Laine, *Playboy*'s Little Acre; Tina Louise, Elga Anderson	15–30
	June	Judy Lee Tomerlin Playmate and cover, Photographing Your Own Playmate	15–30
	July	Linne Nanette Ahlstrand, Joyce Nizzari, Agnes Laurent	15–30
	August	Myrna Weber	15–30
	September	Teri Hope, The Bosom: June Wilkinson	15–30
	October	Mara Corday and Pat Sheehan, Les Girls: Girls of Las Vegas	20–30
	November	Joan Staley, Peekaboo Brigitte: Brigitte Bardot	20–30
	December	Joyce Nizzari, *Playboy*'s Most Popular Playmates: Barbara Cameraon, Jayne Mansfield, Elizabeth Ann Roberts, Janet Pilgram and Lisa Winters, *Playboy*'s 5th Anniversary Scrapbook	25–40
1959	January	Virginia Gordon, Playmate Review	20–40
	February	Eleanor Bradley, Girls in Their Lairs	15–30
	March	Audrey Daston, The Classic Figure: June Blair	15–30
	April	Nancy Crawford, Tina Louise, Marguerite Empey	15–30

Year	Issue	Description	Value ($)
1959	May	Cindy Fuller, *Playboy*'s House Party: Cindy Fuller, Bonnie Harrington, Fran Stacy, Dottie Sykes and Mary Jane Ralston	15–30
	June	Marilyn Hanold, Oriental Sex pictorial	15–30
	July	Yvette Vickers, Making a Splash: Tania Velia	15–30
	August	Clayre Peters, The Bosom in Hollywood: June Wilkinson	15–30
	September	Marianne Gaba, Bunny's Honeys: Lisa Winters, Bunny Yeager, Bonnie Harrington, Myrna Weber, Mary Jane Ralston, Cindy Fuller and Joyce Nizzari	15–30
	October	Elaine Reynolds, Sultry Miss Stewart: Elaine Stewart, Kim Novak pictorial	15–30
	November	Donna Lynn, Hollywood Goes European: Linda Cristal	15–30
	December	Ellen Stratton, Building a Better Brigitte (Bardot)	20–40
1960	January	Stella Stevens, Playmate Review	15–30
	February	Susie Scott, Jayne Mansfield pictorial	25–45
	March	Sally Sarell	12–20
	April	Linda Gamble, Isabel Sarlis pictorial	12–20
	May	Ginger Young	12–20
	June	Delores Welles, Playmate of the Year: Ellen Stratton	12–25
	July	Teddi Smith, Marie Renfro: The Nude Look	12–20

Year	Issue	Description	Value ($)
1960	August	Elaine Paul, Sophia Loren pictorial, Playboy Club Bunnies: Marie Renfro, Annette Prescott, June Wilkinson, Joyce Nizzari and Cynthia Maddox	12–20
	September	Anne Davie, Marie Renfro	12–20
	October	Kathy Douglas, The Girls of Hollywood: Tuesday Weld, June Wilkinson, Tina Louise,Abby Dalton and Yvette Mimieux	12–20
	November	Joni Mathis, June Wilkinson pictorial	15–30
	December	Carol Eden, Teddi Smith, Marilyn Monroe pictorial, Janet Pilgram, Lisa Williams, Linda Vargas, Joyce Nizzari, Ellen Stratton	(125) 25–45
1961	January	Connie Cooper	12–20
	February	Barbara Ann Lawford, The Girls of New York	(100; N/A) 15–30
	March	Tonya Crews, The Nude Wave in Hollywood	(150; N/A) 15–30
	April	Nancy Nielsen, Playmate of the Year: Linda Gamble	15–30
	May	Susan Kelly, The Girls of Sweden	(175; N/A) 15–30
	June	Heidi Becker, Ann Richards pictorial	15–30
	July	Sheralee Connors, Le Crazy Horse pictorial	15–30
	August	Karen Thompson, The Girls of Hawaii	15–30
	September	Christa Speck, The Miami Playboy Club	15–30
	October	Jean Connors, Anthology of Pros pictorial	12–20

Year	Issue	Description	Value ($)
1961	November	Dianne Danford, Anita Ekberg pictorial	15–30
	December	Lyn Larrol, *Playboy*'s Playmate Holiday House Party	15–30
1962	January	Merle Pertile, Playmate Review	15–30
	February	Kari Knudsen, Cynthia Maddox Covergirl, The Girls of Rome pictorial	(125; N/A) 15–30
	March	Pamela Anne Gordon, New Orleans Playboy Club	(125; N/A) 15–30
	April	Roberta Lane, Playmate of the Year: Christa Speck	(125; N/A) 15–30
	May	Marya Carter, The Villian Still Pursues Her: A Pictorial, Cynthia Maddox	15–30
	June	Merissa Mathes, Toast to Bikinis and Scuba Gear and Scuba Dear pictorials	(125; N/A) 15–30
	July	Unne Terjesen, Janet Pilgram pictorial	(75; N/A) 15–30
	August	Jan Roberts, Return to Rome: Gesa Meiken	(75; N/A) 15–30
	September	Mickey Winters	15–30
	October	Laura Young, Bonnie Jo Halpin cover, Girls of London pictorial	(150; N/A) 20–40
	November	Avis Kimble, Playmates of History	15–30
	December	June Cochran, Sheralee Connors cover, Arlene Dahl pictorial, *Playboy*'s Other Girlfriends: Tina Louise, Anita Ekberg, Jill St. John, Sophia Loren, Ann Richards, Elga Anderson, Abby Dalton, Kim Novak, Elaine Stewart,	

Year	Issue	Description	Value ($)
1962	December	Tania Velia and June Wilkinson	(100; N/A) 20–40
1963	January	Judi Montery, Elizabeth Taylor/Cleopatra pictorial	20–40
	February	Toni Ann Thomas, Cheryl Lamphey cover, The Chicks of Cleopatra, The Playmate Pillow Fight: Teddi Smith, Christa Speck, Delores Wells and Carrie Radison	15–30
	March	Adrienne Moreau, Cynthia Maddox cover, Playmate of the Year Run-Off: June Cochran, Avis Kimble and Laura Young	(200; N/A) 15–30
	April	Sandra Settani, Kelly Collins cover, The Girls of Africa, The New York Playboy Club	(125; N/A) 15–30
	May	Sharon Cintron, Playmate of the Year: June Cochran, The Femlin Comes to Life	15–30
	June	Connie Mason, Jayne Mansfield cover and pictorial	15–30
	July	Carrie Enwright, Judy Newton cover, The Bunnies pictorial, Christa Speck, Pam Gordon, Linda Gamble, Carrie Radison, Joyce Nizzari and June Cochran	(125; N/A) 25–50
	August	Phyllis Sherwood, Nancy Perry cover, African Queen: Gillian Tanner Pictorial	(75; N/A) 15–30
	September	Victoria Valentino, Joey Thorpe cover, Europe's New Sex Sirens: Elke Sommer, Sylvia Koscina, Shirley Ann Field, Dany Saval, Sarah Miles, June	

Year	Issue	Description	Value ($)
1963	September	Ritchie, Claudia Cardinale, Catherine Deneuve and others	(125; N/A) 15–30
	October	Christine Williams, Teddi Smith cover, Playboy Clubs: Disneyland for Adults, Elsa Martinelli pictorial	(125; N/A) 15–30
	November	Terre Tucker, Sharon Rogers cover, The Girls of Canada, Cleopatra, Italian Style: Pacale Petit	(100; N/A) 15–30
	December	Donna Michele, Susan Strasberg and Kim Novak pictorial, The Editors' Choice: Lisa Winters, Janet Pilgram, Heidi Becker, Ellen Stratton, Joyce Nizzari, Christa Speck, Avis Kimble, Connie Mason, Donna Michelle, Christine Williams	(200; N/A) 20–40
1964	January	Sharon Rogers, Marilyn Monroe pictorial	25–50
	February	Nancy Jo Hopper, Cynthia Maddox cover, In Bed with Beckett: Mamie Van Doren and Veronique Vendell, 1954 Playmates	10–20
1964	March	Nancy Scott, Olgo Schoberova cover, The Girls of Russia, 1955 Playmates Revisited	10–20
	April	Ashlyn Martin, Karen Lynn and Peter Sellers cover, Peter Sellers Mimes the Movie Lovers, 1956 Playmates Revisited	10–20
	May	Donna Michelle Playmate and cover, 1957 Playmates Revisited	10–20

Year	Issue	Description	Value ($)
1964	June	Lori Winston, Mamie Van Doren cover and pictorial: The Nudest Mamie Van Doren, Susannah York pictorial, 1958 Playmates revisited	10–20
	July	Melba Ogle, Cynthia Maddox cover, The Sex Kitten Grows Up: Brigitte Bardot, 1959 Playmates Revisited	10–20
	August	China Lee, Barbara Reeves cover, The Bunnies of Chicago, 1960 Playmates Revisited	10–20
	September	Astrid Schulz, Heather Hewitt cover, Playboy in Jamaica, Elke Sommer pictorial, 1961 Playmates Revisited	12–25
	October	Rosemary Hillcrest, Judy Newton cover, 1962 Playmates Revisited, Marco Polo's Spices pictorial	10–20
	November	Kai Brendinger, Maria Hoff cover, The Girls of Germany, 1963 Playmate Revisited	(100; N/A) 10–20
	December	Jo Collins, Ian Fleming interview, Carol Baker pictorial, The Readers' Choice Top Ten Playmates: Connie Mason, Laura Young, June Cochran, Christa Speck, Janet Pilgram, Toni Ann Thomas, Joyce Nizzari, Lisa Winters, Heidi Becker and Donna Michelle	10–20

Year	Issue	Description	Value ($)
1965	January	Sally Duberson, Ustinov's Harems pictorial	10–20
	February	Jessica St. George, Teddi Smith cover, The Beatles Interview, Donna Michelle and Kim Novak pictorials	(200; N/A) 20–40
	March	Jennifer Jackson, Carol Lynley pictorial, The Unsinkable Fanny Hill Picture Essay	(175; N/A) 20–40
	April	Sue Williams, Lannie Balcom cover, The Playboy Bed, The Playboy Play-Off, Jo Collins, China Lee and Astrid Schulz	10–20
	May	Maria McBane, The Kiss: Barbara Bouchet, Stella Stevens pictorial	12–25
	June	Hedy Scott, Turid Lundberg cover, The Big Bunny Hop Picture Essay, Ursula Andress pictorial	10–20
	July	Gay Collier, Joey Thorpe cover, The Girls of the Riviera	(125; N/A) 10–20
	August	Lannie Balcom, Jo Collins cover and Playmate of the Year pictorial, Ursula Andress	10–20
	September	Patti Reynolds, Teddi Smith cover, Saturday Night with Genghis Khan pictorial, Jeanne Moreau	(100; N/A) 10–20
	October	Allison Parks, Penny James cover, Catherine Deneuve pictorial, The Bunnies of Miami	10–20

Year	Issue	Description	Value ($)
1965	November	Pat Russo, Beth Hyatt cover, James Bond's Girls pictorial, The Nude Look	(125; N/A) 15–30
	December	Dinah Willis, Allison Parks cover, The *Playboy* Portfolio of Sex Stars: Brigitte Bardot, Ursula Andress, Arlene Dahl, Carroll Baker, Sophia Loren, Tina Louise, Elizabeth Taylor, Jayne Mansfield, Elsa Marinella, Kim Novak, Mamie Van Doren and Carol Lynley	(125; N/A) 15–30
1966	January	Judy Tyler, The Playboy Mansion pictorial, Princess Grace (Kelly) Interview	12–25
	February	Melinda Windsor, The Girls of Rio	(80; N/A) 10–20
	March	Priscilla Wright, Trio Con Brio: Rossana Podesta, Christiana Schmidtmer, Shirley Anne Field, Bob Dylan interview	(125) 10–20
	April	Karia Conway, Cynthia Maddox cover, The *Playboy* Story, History of Sex in the Cinema Featuring the Jean Harlow Nudes, Mae West, Greta Garbo, Marlene Dietrich and Hedy Lamarr	(75; N/A) 10–20
	May	Dolly Read, Allison Parks cover and Playmate of the Year pictorial, Jo Collins in Vietnam pictorial	(80; N/A) 10–20
	June	Kelly Burke, Mary Warren cover, The Girls of Texas	(55) 10–20

Year	Issue	Description	Value ($)
1966	July	Tish Howard, Patti Reynolds, Penny James, Joann Russell, Barbara Shaw and Joey Thorpe cover, Sean Connery Strikes Again: Sue Ann Langdon and Jean Seaberg, Ursula Andress	(125) 10–20
	August	Susan Denberg, Jane Fonda pictorial, The Bunnies of Dixie	(70; N/A) 10–20
	September	Dianne Chandler Playmate and cover, Topless pictorial, Jocelyn Lane	(125) 10–20
	October	Linda Moon, Penny James cover, Ann-Margaret as Art Nude pictorial	(100; N/A) 12–25
	November	Lisa Baker, Sue Bachelor cover, See-Through and Micro Female Fashions, Ingrid Weber, Francisca Gedzek and Uta Levika	(55) 9–18
	December	Sue Bernard, Nancy Gould cover, The Girls of Tahiti, London: Playboy on the Town	(55) 10–20
1967	January	Surrey Marshe, The Playmates of Fine Art, Sex in the Cinema: Sex Stars of the Fifties	(70; N/A) 10–20
	February	Kim Faber, Helen Kirk cover, The girls of Casino Royale pictorial with Woody Allen and Joanna Pettet	(70; N/A) 10–20
	March	Fran Gerard, Nancy Chamberlain cover, The Tate Gallery: Sharon Tate pictorial, The Bunnies of Missouri	(50; N/A) 7–15

Year	Issue	Description	Value ($)
1967	April	Gwen Wong, Cheryl Shrobe cover, Playmate Play-Off pictorial: Lisa Baker, Susan Denberg and Tish Howard	(50; N/A) 7–15
	May	Anne Randall, Beth Hyatt, Sylvia Koscina pictorial, Woody Allen interview	(50; N/A) 6–12
	June	Joey Gibson, Sharon Kristie cover, You Only Live Twice: 007's Oriental Eyefuls pictorial	(55; N/A) 10–20
	July	Heather Ryan, Venita Wolf cover, The Girls of Paris pictorial, Michael Caine interview	(50; N/A) 6–12
	August	Dede Lind, Lisa Baker cover, Sherry Jackson pictorial, Playmate of the Year Lisa Baker	(75; N/A) 10–20
	September	Angela Dorian, Bo Bussmann cover, The Trip: Mara Sykes pictorial	(50) 7–15
	October	Reagan Wilson, The Fox: Anne Heywood and Sandy Dennis pictorials	(50) 6–12
	November	Kaya Christian, Beth Hyatt cover, *Playboy*'s Charter Yacht Party	(50) 6–12
	December	Lynn Winchell Playmate and Cover, Elke Sommer pictorial, The Bunnies of Hollywood	(50) 10–20
1968	January	Connie Kreski, Stella Stevens pictorial	(150; N/A) 15–30
	February	Nancy Harwood, Paulette Lindberg cover, The Lady in Blue: Joanna Pettet, The	

Year	Issue	Description	Value ($)
1968	February	Miss Nude Universe Contest	(55) 6–12
	March	Michelle Hamilton, Sharon Kristie cover, The Bizarre Beauties of Barbarella: Jane Fonda and others, Brush-On Fashions pictorial	(55) 10–20
	April	Gaye Rennie, Dolly Read cover and pictorial	(55) 6–12
	May	Elizabeth Jordon, Angela Dorian cover and Playmate of the Year pictorial, Julie Newmar	(55) 10–20
	June	Britt Fredriksen, Jeannie Wallace cover, The Girls of Scandinavia pictorial	(55) 6–12
	July	Melodye Prentiss, Lynn Hahn cover, Leicia pictorial, Sex in the Cinema	(40) 5–10
	August	Gale Olson, Aino Korva cover, Carroll Baker pictorial	(75) 5–10
	September	Dru Hart, Erika Toth cover, Student Body pictorial featuring Vicky Drake, The Girls of "Funny Girl"	(55) 5–10
	October	Majiken Haugedal, Dale Fahey cover, Barbara McNair	(55) 5–10
	November	Paige Young, Theatre of the Nude	(55) 5–10
	December	Cynthia Myers Playmate and cover, The Girls of the Orient, Erotica	(NA) 10–20
1969	January	Leslie Bianchini, Fifteenth Anniversary Issue, Sex Stars of the Sixties: Natalie Wood, Stella Stevens, Sharon Tate, Carol Lynley	(120; N/A) 15–30

Year	Issue	Description	Value ($)
1969	February	Lorrie Menconi, Nancy Chamberlain cover, Pamela Tiffin pictorial	(55; N/A) 5–10
	March	Kathy MacDonald, Penny James cover, Connie Kreski, Joan Collins, Marie Lijedahl	(55) 6–12
	April	Lorna Hopper, Sharon Kristie cover, The Language of Legs pictorial, Brigitte Bardot, Vanessa Redgrave	(55) 5–10
	May	Sally Sheffield, Paulette Lindberg cover, Camille 2000 pictorial with Danielle Gaubert, Lake Geneva Playboy Club, Auto Erotica	(55) 5–10
	June	Helena Antonaccio, Connie Kreski cover and Playmate of the Year pictorial, De Sade	(100) 7–15
	July	Nancy McNeil, Barbara Klein cover: Barbi Benton Before Name Change, Tina Aumont pictorial	(55) 10–20
	August	Debbie Hooper, Penny James cover, The Bunnies of Detroit, Paula Kelly pictorial	(55) 5–10
	September	Shay Knuth Playmate and cover, Julie Newmar pictorial, The Girls of Australia	(75; N/A) 10–20
	October	Jean Bell, Paulette Lindberg cover, "Oh Calcutta" movie pictorial, War Games pictorial	(55) 5–10
	November	Claudia Jennings	(55) 5–10
	December	Gloria Root, Jorja Beck cover, The Girls of "Hair"	

Year	Issue	Description	Value ($)
1969	December	pictorial, Homage to Toulouse-Lautrec	(55) 5–10
1970	January	Jill Taylor, The Beauty Trap featuring Jeanne Rejaunier, Vargas Revisited, Raquel Welch interview	(125; N/A) 12–25
	February	Linda Forsythe, Norma Bauer cover, Bibi Anderson and Barbara Parkins pictorial	(75) 5–10
	March	Chris Koren, Barbi Benton cover and pictorial, Bunny of the Year: Gina Byrams, The Girls of Julius Ceasar	(75) 10–20
	April	Barbara Hillary, Pamela Nystul cover, Bunny Myra: Myra Van Heck pictorial, The Girls of Israel	(100) 5–10
	May	Jennifer Liano, Phyllis Babila cover, Bedsprings Eternal pictorial, Susanne Benton	(75) 5–10
	June	Elaine Morton, Claudia Jennings cover and Playmate of the Year pictorial, Lola Falana, "Tropic of Cancer" movie pictorial, Tiny Tim interview	(55; N/A) 5–10
	July	Carol Willis, Janet Wolf cover, The Dolls of "Beyond the Valley of the Dolls" pictorial featuring Dolly Read and Cynthia Myers, Shaping Up for "Oh Calcutta"	(75) 5–10
	August	Sharon Clark, Linda Donnelly cover, Raquel Welch and Mae West in	

Year	Issue	Description	Value ($)
1970	August	Myra Goes Hollywood pictorial, The Bunnies of 1970	(75) 5–10
	September	Debbie Ellison, Jackie Ray cover, The No-Bra Look, Elke Sommer, Posterotica	(75) 5–10
	October	Mary and Madeleine Collinson Playmates and cover, Paula Prentiss, Laine Kazan, Pornography and the Unmelancholy Danes	(40; N/A) 5–10
	November	Avis Miller, Crystal Smith cover, Gallo's Girls, Jane Birkin pictorial	(125) 5–10
	December	Carol Imhoh, Shay Knuth cover, Paula Pritchett, The Classic Woman	(75) 5–10
1971	January	Liv Lindeland, Stalking the Wild Veruscka pictorial, Playmate Review, The Act of Love, Mae West interview	(100; N/A) 10–20
	February	Willy Rey, Fran Jeffries pictorial, The Bejeweled Body, The Statue	(55) 5–10
	March	Cynthia Hall, Peggy Smith cover, The Girls of Holland, Alex in Wonderland: Cherie Latimer	(40) 5–10
	April	Chris Cranston, Simone Hammerst, Lana Wood pictorial, Pretty Maides	(40; N/A) 5–10
	May	Janice Pennington, Diane Davies cover, The Bunnies of New York, Sarah Kennedy	(40; N/A) 5–10
	June	Lieko Englins, Sharon Clark cover, The Nude Theatre, Premier Playmates	

Year	Issue	Description	Value ($)
1971	June	Revisited: 1960–1970, Playmate of the Year Pictorial: Sharon Clark	(55) 5–10
	July	Heather Van Every, Kay Sutton York cover, Blooming Beauty: Linda Evans pictorial	(100) 6–12
	August	Cathy Rowland, Christy Miller cover, The Age of Awakening, The Bunnies of 1971	(55) 5–10
	September	Crystal Smith Playmate and cover, "McCabe and Mrs. Miller" pictorial featuring Julie Christie, Girls of the Golden West, Sureal Ladies	(40; N/A) 5–10
	October	Clare Rambbeau, Darine Stern cover, The Porno Girls Picture Essay, Marisa Berenson pictorial	(40; N/A) 4–8
	November	Danielle DeVabre, Debbie Hanlon cover, The Life and Times of Henry Miller, Retiring Personalities pictorial, Sex in the Cinema	(100) 4–8
	December	Karen Christy, "Diamonds Are Forever": Vegas Comes Up 007, Personal Views of the Erotic	(75) 4–8
1972	January	Marilyn Cole, "A Clockwork Orange"	(50) 4–8
	February	P. J. Lansing, Barbara Carrera cover, The Making of MacBeth picture essay, Angel Tomkins pictorial, Signs of Love	(40) 4–8

Year	Issue	Description	Value ($)
1972	March	Ellen Michaels, "Savages" pictorial, The Shirt Off Her Back, Dominique Sanda pictorial	(40) 4–8
	April	Vicki Peters, Pop's Girls, Tiffany Bolling pictorial	(40) 4–8
	May	Deanna Baker, Barbi Benton cover, Monday's Child, Valeris Perrine pictorial	(40; N/A) 5–10
	June	Debbie Davis, Liv Lindeland cover and Playmate of the Year pictorial, Those Sexy French Literary Ladies, Sissy Spacek	(40; N/A) 5–10
	July	Carol O'Neal, Paula Pritchett and Paula Kelly pictorial	(40) 4–8
	August	Linda Summers, Carole Vitale cover, "Box Car Bertha" featuring Barbara Hershey, The Girls of Munich	(40) 4–8
	September	Susan Miller, Sandra Jozefski cover, Student Bodies, "M.A.S.H." 's Karen Phillip pictorial, Skinetic Art	(40) 4–8
	October	Sharon Johansen, Lynn Myers cover, Black and White: Brenda Sykes and Stella Stevens, The Bunnies of 1972, Body Work	(40) 4–8
	November	Lenna Sjooblom, Pamela Rawlings cover, Gwen Welles pictorial	(40) 4–8
	December	Mercy Rooney, Women Eternal, Nancy Robinson,	

Year	Issue	Description	Value ($)
1972	December	Sex Stars of 1972: Victoria Principal, Barbara Hersey, Ali McGraw and others	(100) 4–8
1973	January	Miki Garcia, Peter Turner's Turn-Ons, Playmate Review	(50; N/A) 5–10
	February	Cyndi Wood, Jeanette Larson cover, The Ziegfeld Girls featuring Susan Clark, "Last Tango in Paris" star, Maria Schneider pictorial, In Search of Love's Sure Thing	(40; N/A) 4–8
	March	Bonnie Large, Mercy Rooney cover, Edy Williams pictorial, "A Name for Evil" featuring Samantha Eggar and Sheila Sullivan, Legends in Their Own Time	(40) 4–8
	April	Julie Woodson, Lenna Sjooblom cover, Linda Lovelace, Women with a Twist, Ballerina Dayle Haddon pictorial	(40; N/A) 3–6
	May	Anulka Dziubinska, Bernie Becker cover, Barbara Leigh pictorial as "The Indian," Sex and the Automobile	(40) 7–20
	June	Ruthy Ross, Marilyn Cole cover and Playmate of the Year pictorial, Women's Work	(100) 5–10
	July	Martha Smith, Karen Christy cover, Tisa Farrow pictorial, The Sainted Bond: Jane Seymour and Gloria Hendry, Summer of '72	(40) 5–10
	August	Phyllis Coleman, Cyndi Wood cover, The Tender	

Year	Issue	Description	Value ($)
1973	August	Trap featuring Heather Menzies, Porno Chic	(40) 4–8
	September	Geri Glass, A Star Is Made featuring Lee Meredith, "The Naked Ape" star Victoria Principal pictorial	(75; N/A) 10–20
	October	Valerie Lane, Sheila Ryan cover, The Bunnies of 1973, Sacheen Littlefeather pictorial	(40) 4–7
	November	Monica Tidwell, Anne Randall cover, Ursula Andress pictorial	(40) 3–6
	December	Christine Maddox, Bonita Lou Rossi cover, Barbi Benton pictorial, Pinups, Sex Stars of 1973	(40; N/A) 5–12
1974	January	Nancy Cameron, Cyndi Wood cover, Twentieth Anniversary Special, Twenty Years of *Playboy,* Painted Lady featuring Veruscka	(150; N/A) 10–20
	February	Francine Parks, Karen Christy cover, Butterfly Girl featuring Ratna Assan, Alexandra Hay, The Girls of Skiing, Candice Bergen	(50) 3–6
	March	Pamela Zinszar, Debbie Shelton cover, The Don's Daughter-in-Law featuring Simonetta Stefanneli, Sean Connery in "Zardoz" Movie Photos, The Loving Touch	(50) 4–8
	April	Marlene Marrow, Carron June Sliger cover, Donna Michele pictorial, Sex, Soap and Success: Marilyn Chambers Foreplay	(75) 3–6

Year	Issue	Description	Value ($)
1974	May	Marilyn Lange, Marsha Kay cover, The Devil and the Flesh, Sheer Delights	(50; N/A) 3–6
	June	Sandy Johnson, Cyndi Wood cover and Playmate of the Year pictorial, Hindsight	(125) 5–10
	July	Carole Vitale, Christine Maddox, "Let My People Come," Isela Vega, Ladies in Hats pictorial	(40) 4–8
	August	Jean Manson, Lynnda Kimball cover, Brown Sugar featuring Claudia Lennear, Here Comes the Bride	(40) 3–6
	September	Kristine Hanson, Model Zoya cover, Jane Lubeck: Sis, Boom, Ah!	(40) 3–5
	October	Ester, Cordet, Suzann Shery cover, Lepke's Lady featuring Mary Wilcox, The Bunnies of 1974	(75) 3–6
	November	Bebe Buel, Claudia Jennings cover, Sex in the Cinema, Spec-Tacular	(40) 5–10
	December	Janice Raymond, Robyn Douglas cover, The Erotic World of Salvador Dali, Claudia Jennings pictorial, Sex Stars of 1974: Candice Bergen, Raquel Welch and others	(50) 12–25
1975	January	Lynnda Kimball, Brigitte Bardot pictorial, Playboy Mansion West featuring Barbi Benton, Playmate Review	(125) 8–15

Year	Issue	Description	Value ($)
1975	February	Laura Misch Playmate and cover, Linda Lovelace pictorial, The French Maid	(125) 5–10
	March	Ingeborg Sorenson, Eva Maria, Margot Kidder pictorial, Shaping Up, Ripped-Off	(40) 5–10
	April	Victoria Cunningham, Cyndi Wood cover, Bed and Board, Valerie Perrine pictorial, Donyale Luna	(55) 4–8
	May	Bridgitte Rollins, Carol Christie cover, The Splendor of Gwen: Gwen Welles pictorial, T-shirts	(55) 3–5
	June	Azizi Johari, Marilyn Lange cover and Playmate of the Year pictorial	(75; N/A) 4–8
	July	Lynn Schiller Playmate and cover, Super Surfer: Laura Blears Ching, A Long Look at Legs	(50) 3–5
	August	Lillian Muller Playmate and cover, The Department Store, The Girl from *Playboy*: Kim Komar pictorial	(75) 3–6
	September	Mesina Miller, Amy Arnold cover, Put It On pictorial	(50) 3–6
	October	Jill DeVries, Agneta Eckemyr and Zoe Z cover, Sappho Lisztomania, Fiona Lewis pictorial, Cher	(100) 3–6
	November	Janet Lupo, Patricia McClain cover, The Bunnies of 1975	(50; N/A) 3–7
	December	Nancy Li Brandi, Lillian Muller cover, The Story of O: Corine Clery, Peep	

Year	Issue	Description	Value ($)
1975	December	Show pictorial, Susan Sarandon and Margot Kidder	(50; N/A) 3–5
1976	January	Daina House, Playmates of 1975 cover, Fegley pictorial, Woman, Elton John interview, Playmate Review	(75) 5–10
	February	Laura Lyons, Jill DeVries cover, Kubrick's Countess: Marisa Berenson, Funderwear pictorial	(55; N/A) 3–5
	March	Ann Pennington, Vicki Cunningham cover and pictorial: Fire Belle, Sylvia Kristel: Encore Emmanuelle	(75; N/A) 4–7
	April	Denise Michele, Kristine Del Bell cover, Ursula Andress pictorial, Nanci Li Brandi	(75) 3–6
	May	Patricia McClain, Nancy Cameron cover, Barbara Parkins pictorial, Suze Randall	(55) 4–8
	June	Debra Peterson, Lillian Muller cover and Playmate of the Year pictorial, Women at Work	(55) 4–8
	July	Deborah Borkman, Cyndi Wood cover, Jayne Mansfield's Daughter pictorial: Jayne Marie Mansfield, Sarah Miles	(75; N/A) 4–8
	August	Linda Beatty, Sex in the Great Outdoors, Kristine DeBell	(40) 3–6
	September	Whitney Kine, The Girls of Washington, D.C., Newton's Physiques	(55) 3–5

Year	Issue	Description	Value ($)
1976	October	Hope Olson, Karen Hafter cover, Melanie Griffith Collector's Item pictorial, The Bunnies of 1976	(100) 10–20
	November	Patti McGuire Playmate and cover, Misty Rowe pictorial	(50; N/A) 5–10
	December	Karen Hafter, Deborah Borkman cover, Pompeo Pasar Portfolio featuring over a dozen women, Fellini's Casanova, Karen Black, Sarah Miles, David Bowie	(75) 3–6
1977	January	Susan Lynn Kiger, Barbara Leigh pictorial, Spermula, Playmate Review	(75; N/A) 5–10
	February	Star Stowe, Lena Kansbod cover, The Year in Sex, Playmate Preview, Love Feast pictorial	(40; N/A) 3–6
	March	Nicki Thomas, Susan Kiger cover, Comeback for Casanova pictorial featuring Lillian Muller	(40; N/A) 3–6
	April	Lisa Sohn Playmate and cover, The Girls of the New South, Jennifer Edi	(50) 3–6
	May	Sheila Mullen, Lillian Muller cover, Bewitched by Older Women, Patti D'Arbanville, Kellie Everts	(75) 3–6
	June	Virve Reed, Patti McGuire cover and Playmate of the Year pictorial, Barbara Bach Bondage pictorial	(75; N/A) 6–15
	July	Sondra Theodore, Pamela Serpe cover, Barbara Carrera	

Year	Issue	Description	Value ($)
1977	July	pictorial, The New Girls of Porn	(75; N/A) 6–15
	August	Julia Lyndon, Karen Christy, *Playboy*'s Playmate Photo Contest, Riverboat Gamblers pictorial featuring Patti McGuire, Hope Olson and Cindy Russell, "Madame Claude"	(75) 4–8
	September	Debra Jo Fondren, Denise Michele, Hope Olson and Lisa Sohm cover, Girls of the Big Ten, Jean Manson	(100; N/A) 4–8
	October	Kristine Winder, Barbra Streisand cover and interview, Nureyev's Valentino featuring Michele Phillips, A Masked Ball	(75) 3–6
	November	Rita Lee, Susan Kiger cover, The Bunnies of 1977, Sex in the Cinema 1977	(75) 3–6
	December	Ashley Cox, Sondra Theodore cover, *Playboy*'s Playmate House Party, Swingers' Scrapbook, Melanie Griffith Nude, Kiss in Japan, John Denver interview, Barbara Bach	(N/A) 7–15
1978	January	Debra Jenssen, Rita Lee cover, The Year in Sex: Farrah Fawcett, Cheryl Ladd and Others, 15 page playmate review, Erotic Fantasies pictorial	(40; N/A) 10–20
	February	Janis Schmitt, Hope Olson cover, Close Encounters of the Fourth Kind, Playmates	

Year	Issue	Description	Value ($)
1978	February	International: Foreign Edition pictorial	(75; N/A) 3–6
	March	Christina Smith, Debra Jensen cover, "Pretty Baby" featuring Brooke Shields, Sex on Wheels, Bob Dylan interview	(75; N/A) 6–12
	April	Pamela Jean Bryant, Susan and Patty Kiger cover, Sisters pictorial, The Girls of Crazy Horse	(40; N/A) 3–6
	May	Kathryn Morrison, Debra Peterson cover, "Chameleon" featuring Anita Russel pictorial	(50) 3–6
	June	Gail Stanton, Debra Jo Fondren cover and Playmate of the Year pictorial, Moons in June: Debra Jo Fondren, Rita Lee, Bebe Buel, Cyndi Wood and others	(75; N/A) 7–15
	July	Karen Morton, Pamela Sue Martin cover and pictorial, Call of the Wild pictorial featuring Susan Jensen	(40; N/A) 10–20
	August	Vicki Witt, Nicki Thomas cover, "Eyes of Laura Mars" featuring Faye Dunaway, The Girls in the Office/ Secretaries	(40; N/A) 4–8
	September	Rosanne Katon, Sue Paul cover, The Girls of the PAC 10, Simone Boisseree/ Stunt Girl pictorial	(40; N/A) 4–8
	October	Marcy Hanson, Dolly Parton cover and interview, Girl on a Dolphin pictorial featuring Denice Creedon, Girls of	

Year	Issue	Description	Value ($)
1978	October	the PAC 10: Part II, "Older Women" featuring Karen Black, Alexandra Stewart and Helen Shaver, Cheryl Tiegs	(40; N/A) 5–10
	November	Monique St. Pierre Playmate and cover, The Bunnie of 1978, Sex in the Cinema	(40; N/A) 3–6
	December	Janet Quist, Farrah Fawcett cover, interview and pictorial, Cheerleaders pictorial, Viva Vargas	8–15
1979	January	Candy Loving, The Great Playmate Hunt, Grin and Bare It, *Playboy*'s 25 Beautiful Years: Marilyn Monroe, Jayne Mansfield and others, 25th Anniversary Issue	(125; N/A) 12–25
	February	Lee Ann Michelle, Candy Collins cover, The Girls of Las Vegas, Lexi Vogel: Father Knows Best, The Year in Sex	(40; N/A) 4–8
	March	Denise McConnell, Debra Jensen cover, Naked Cheerleaders, Denise Crosby pictorial	(75; N/A) 6–12
	April	Missy Cleveland, Rita Lee cover, Debra Jo Fondren pictorial, Grace Jones, Disco Queens, 25 Years of Rock 'N Roll featuring Elvis Presley and others	(50; N/A) 5–10
	May	Michele Drake, Cheryle Larsen, Foreign Sex Stars, The Secret Life of Marilyn	

June 1955

#7, 1960

December 1986

January 1957

January 1977

October 1986

May 1990

February 1996

September 1987

July 1995

August 1995

September 1973

September 1978

February 1979

January 1980

January 1981

March 1983

April #2, 1957

Year	Issue	Description	Value ($)
1979	May	Monroe . . . with rare photos, Ken Marcus photo pictorial featuring Janet Quist, Hope Olson, Martha Smith, Lillian Muller and others	(75; N/A) 4–8
	June	Louann Fernald, Monique St. Pierre cover and Playmate of the Year pictorial, *Playboy*'s Past Playmates of the Year: featuring all 19, Dance-Hall Demoiselles	(40; N/A) 4–8
	July	Dorothy Mays, Denise Gauthier cover, The Girls of "Moonraker" pictorial, Patti McGuire pictorial	(75) 5–10
	August	Dorothy Stratten, Candy Loving cover and pictorial, Nastassja Kinski, Monique St. Pierre, Marilyn Cole, Bunny Anika Pavel and Gail Stanton	(100; N/A) 12–25
	September	Vick McCay Playmate and cover, Claudia Jennings pictorial, Ivy League Coeds	(40) 4–8
	October	Ursula Buchfellner, Gig Gangel cover, The Bunnies of 1979, Bunny Costumes, Linda Beatty Carpenter and Cyndi Wook pictures from "Apocalypse Now"	(40) 3–6
	November	Sylvie Garant, Phyllis McCreary cover, Colleen Donovan pictorial, Carnival Knowledge, Sex in the Cinema	(40) 3–6
	December	Candy Collins, Raquel Welch cover and pictorial,	

Year	Issue	Description	Value ($)
1979	December	Playmates Forever featuring Connie Kreski, Lisa Baker, Jo Collins, Sharon Johansen, Liv Lindeland, Nancy Scott, Jean Bell, Heidi Becker, Dede Lind and others, Sex Stars	(50; N/A) 10–20
1980	January	Gig Gangel, Amy Miller and Michele Drake with Steve Martin, N.F.L. Cheerleaders pictorial, *Playboy* Pajama Party, Star Trek's Enterprising Return	(100; N/A) 1–20
	February	Sandy Cagle, Candice Collins cover, The Year in Sex, Suzanne Somers Playmate Test pictorial	(100; N/A) 7–15
	March	Henriette Allais, Bo Derek cover and pictorial, All Fosse, Melonie Haller	(100; N/A) 5–10
	April	Liz Glazowski, Shari Shattuck cover, Women of the Armed Services, *Playboy*'s Playmate Reunion featuring 136 playmates, Linda Ronstadt interview	(100; N/A) 5–10
	May	Martha Thomsen, Teri Welles cover, Flight Attendants pictorial, Silvana Suarez: The Real Miss World	(100; N/A) 4–8
	June	Ola Ray, Dorothy Stratten cover and Playmate of the Year pictorial, Fellini's Feminist Fantasy	(150; N/A) 15–30
	July	Teri Peterson, Sandra Dumas cover, Ten Ways to Find the Perfect 10 pictorial	(55) 4–8

Year	Issue	Description	Value ($)
1980	August	Victoria Cooke, Bo Derek cover and pictorial, The Girls of Hawaii	(125; N/A) 5–10
	September	Lisa Welch, Rita Lee cover, Girls of the Southwest Conference, New Girls on Campus pictorial, Evelyn Guerrero	(100; N/A) 5–10
	October	Mardi Jacquet, S. J. Fellowes cover, The Girls of Canada, Lisa Lyon: Body Beautiful	(75) 5–10
	November	Jeana Tomasino, Mardi Jacquet cover, The Women of the U.S. Government, Sex in the Cinema: Brooke Shields, Bo Derek and others	(125; N/A) 6–12
	December	Terri Welles, An Erotic Portfolio, The Twenty Year pictorial, Sex Stars of 1980, Lesley Anne Down, Misty Rowe, Dorothy Stratten, Linda Kerridge pictorial	(150; N/A) 8–15
1981	January	Karn Price, Barbara Bach cover and pictorial, Honky Tonk Angels, John and Yoko	(150; N/A) 8–15
	February	Vicki Lasseter, Candy Loving, Sandra Theodore and Terri Welles cover and Playmate Roommates pictorial, The Year in Sex, The Girl Next Door	(50; N/A) 5–10
	March	Kimberly Herrin, Cybil and Tricia Barnstable cover and featured in Twins pictorial, Jo Penny	(125; N/A) 6–12

Year	Issue	Description	Value ($)
1981	April	Lorraine Michaels, Liz Wickersham cover; The Girls of Kokomo, Indiana; Rita Jenrette	(75; N/A) 4–8
	May	Gina Goldberg, Gabriella Brum cover and pictorial, Girls of the Adriatic Coast, The Dorothy Stratten Story	(125; N/A) 5–10
	June	Cathy Larmouth, Terri Welles cover and Playmate of the Year pictorial, The Ladies of "You Only Live Twice"	(100; N/A) 5–10
	July	Heidi Sorenson, Jayne Kennedy cover and pictorial, Tender Cousins	(125; N/A) 6–12
	August	Debbie Boostrom, Valerie Perrine cover and pictorial	(N/A) 6–12
	September	Susan Smith, Bo Derek cover and pictorial, Girls of the Southeastern Conference	(75; N/A) 5–10
	October	Kelly Ann Tough, Cathy St. George cover, Maud Adams pictorial, Terri Garr interview, Girls of the Southeastern Conference Part II	(50; N/A) 6–12
	November	Shannon Tweed, Teri Petersen cover, Vikki Lamotta pictorial, Jamie Lee Curtis interview	(75; N/A) 5–10
	December	Patricia Farinelli, Bernadette Peters cover and pictorial, Captured Women, Cheryl Tiegs, and the Playmates Sing	(50; N/A) 4–8
1982	January	Kimberly McArthur, Natalie Levy Bencheton cover, John Derek's Wives pictorial	

Year	Issue	Description	Value ($)
1982	January	featuring Ursula Andress, Linda Evans and Bo Derek, Soap Stars pictorial	(N/A) 4–8
	February	Anne-Marie Fox, Kimberly McArthur cover, The Year in Sex, Sylvia Kristel, Susan Smith	(50) 5–10
	March	Karen Witter, Barbara Carrera cover and pictorial, Pia Zadora, Melani Martin	(40; N/A) 5–10
	April	Linda Rhys Vaughn, Mariel Hemmingway cover and pictorial, Henriette Alais	(40; N/A) 3–6
	May	Kym Main, Vickie Reigle, Beauty and the Badge: Barbara Schantz pictorial, Rae Dawn Chong	(40; N/A) 3–6
	June	Lourdes Ann Kananimanu Estores, Shannon Tweed cover and Playmate of the Year pictorial	(100) 5–10
	July	Lynda Wesmeier Playmate and cover, The Girls of Ma Bell, Dreams pictorial featuring Debra Jo Fodren Lillian Muller and Rita Lee	(50; N/A) 5–10
	August	Cathy St. George, Vicki McCarthy, Marilyn Michaels pictorial, Summer Sex '82, California Girls	(40; N/A) 3–6
	September	Connie Brighton, Kym Herrin cover, The Girls of the Big Eight, Fran Jeffries pictorial	(75) 4–8
	October	Marianne Gravatte, Tanya Roberts cover and pictorial, The Girls of Japan	(40; N/A) 12–20
	November	Marlene Janssen, Lorraine Michaels, The Women of Braniff	(75) 3–6

Year	Issue	Description	Value ($)
1982	December	Charlotte Kemp, Marcy Hanson cover, Sydne Rome pictorial, The Women of *Playboy,* Brooke Shields	(40; N/A) 5–10
1983	January	Lonny Chin, Audrey and Judy Landers cover and pictorial, *Playboy's* Playmate Review, Provocative Period Pieces	(40; N/A) 4–8
	February	Melinda Myers, Kim Bassinger cover and pictorial, The Women of Aspen	(50; N/A) 12–20
	March	Alana Soares, Kim McArthur, Kelly Tough and Karen Witter, Marina Verola: Taking Stock of Marina, The First Playmate Play-Offs	(35; N/A) 4–8
1983	April	Christina Ferguson, Carry Lee cover, Ladies of Spain, Pamela Bellwood pictorial: Going Ape	(75) 3–6
	May	Susy Scott, Nastassja Kinski cover and pictorial, Meet the Mrs. featuring Marilyn Griffin and Marilyn Parver	(50; N/A) 3–6
	June	Joland Egger, Marianne Gravette cover and Playmate of the Year pictorial, Morganna, Debra Winger interview	(35; N/A) 5–10
	July	Ruth Guerri Playmate and cover, James Bond Girls Nude featuring Kim Bassinger and others, Erogenous Parts	(75) 4–8
	August	Carina Persson, Sybil Danning cover and pictorial, Permanent Vacation	(75; N/A) 4–8

Year	Issue	Description	Value ($)
1983	September	Barbra Edwards, Kym Herrin cover, The Girls of the Atlantic Conference	(40; N/A) 3–6
	October	Tracy Vacaro, Charlotte Kemp cover, Redheads pictorial, Loretta Martin: Brunette Ambition	(75; N/A) 3–6
	November	Veronica Gamba, Donna Ann cover, Women in White: Nurse pictorial, Jamie Lee Curtis, Sybil Danning	(100) 5–10
	December	Tery Nihen, Joan Collins cover and pictorial, Flash-dancers	(40; N/A) 3–6
1984	January	Sherry Arnett, Melanie Griffith and Don Johnson pictorial	(35; N/A) 4–8
	February	Julie McCollough, Michael Douglas	(75; N/A) 5–10
	March	Kim Morris, Sally Field	(50; N/A) 3–6
	April	Terri Weigel, Victoria Sellers pictorial	(75; N/A) 4–8
	May	Christine Ricjters, Kathleen Turner cover, interview and poster	(75) 3–6
	June	Rebecca Ferratti, Linda Evans pictorial, Kathy Shower	(75; N/A) 3–6
	July	Lynne Austin, Carrie Leigh pictorial, Tom Cruise	(50; N/A) 3–6
	August	Carina Persson, Terry More cover and nude pictorial	(55) 3–6
	September	Rebekka Armstron, Maral Collins, The Chicago Club	(100; N/A) 4–8
	October	Katherine Hushaw, The Girls of the Ivy League, Wendy O. Williams	(50; N/A) 4–8

Year	Issue	Description	Value ($)
1984	November	Donna Edmondson, Dolph Lungren pictorial	(100) 3–6
	December	Karen Valez, Suzanne Somers cover and special eight-page nude pictorial	(75; N/A) 5–10
1985	January	Joan Bennett, Goldie Hawn cover and feature	(35; N/A) 3–5
	February	Cheri Witter, Sybil Danning, Girls of Texas	(125) 3–5
	March	Donna Smith, Women in Lingerie pictorial	(55) 3–5
	April	Cindy Brooks, Playmate Sisters pictorial	(35; N/A) 3–5
	May	Kathy Shower, Vanity pictorial	(35; N/A) 3–5
	June	Devon De Vasquez, Roxanne Pulitzer pictorial	(40; N/A) 3–5
	July	Hope Marie Carlton, Grace Jones, Jamie Lee Curtis	(35; N/A) 3–6
	August	Cher Butler, Judy Norton	(35; N/A) 3–5
	September	Venice Kong, Madonna cover and fourteen-page pictorial, Brigette Nielsen	(35; N/A) 12–25
	October	Cynthia Brimhall, Jerry Hall pictorial	(N/A) 3–5
	November	Pamella Sanders, Women of Mensa	(50; N/A) 3–5
	December	Carol Fiscatier, Barbi Benton twelve-page pictorial, Vanity, Bruce Springsteen, Don Johnson	(35; N/A) 5–10
1986	January	Sherry Arnett, Melanie Griffith and Don Johnson pictorial	(35; N/A) 3–5
	February	Julie McCullough, Michael Douglas	(75; N/A) 4–8

Year	Issue	Description	Value ($)
1986	March	Kim Moris, Sally Field	(125) 3–6
	April	Terri Weigel, Victoria Sellers pictorial	(75; N/A) 4–8
	May	Christine Richters, Kathleen Turner cover, story and poster	(50) 3–5
	June	Rebecca Ferratti, Kathy Showers and Linda Evans pictorials	(75; N/A) 3–7
	July	Lynne Austin, Carrie Leigh pictorial, Tom Cruise	(50; N/A) 3–6
	August	Ava Fabian, Brigette Nielsen pictorial, Sigourney Weaver	(125) 3–5
	September	Rebekka Armstrong	(100) 3–6
	October	Sachiko, Women of the Ivy League, Wendy O. Williams	(40) 3–6
	November	Donna Edmondson, Dolph Lungren pictorial	(100; N/A) 3–6
	December	Laurie Carr, Brooke Shields· cover and feature, Women of the 7/11	(N/A) 4–8
1987	January	Luann Lee, Marilyn Monroe ten-page pictorial	(25) 5–10
	February	Julie Peterson, Stephanie Bachman ten-page pictorial	(25) 3–5
	March	Marina Baker, Janet Jones cover and pictorial, The Adventures of a Small-Town Sleuth	(40) 3–7
	April	Anna Clark, Ava Fabian cover, Here Comes Casanova pictorial featuring Faye Dunaway, Jean Dreams	(30) 3–7
	May	Kymberly Paige, Vanna White pictorial, Barbara Hershey	(30) 4–8

Year	Issue	Description	Value ($)
1987	June	Sandy Greenberg, Donna Edmondson cover and Playmate of the Year pictorial	(50; N/A) 4–8
	July	Carmen Berg, Beach Party Special featuring twenty pages of sun, surf and sex	(15) 3–6
	August	Sharry Knopski, Paulina Porizkova cover and pictorial, Women of Florida	(50; N/A) 4–8
	September	Gwen Hajek, Girls of James Bond: A Historical Pictorial of All the 007 Movies and Women . . . a sixteen-page special	(25) 4–8
	October	Bandi Brandt, Donna Mills cover and pictorial	(50; N/A) 4–8
	November	Pam Stein, Jessica Hahn cover and eight-page pictorial, Cher, Kelly McGillis	(10) 4–8
	December	India Allen, Brigette Nielsen pictorial, Jessica Hahn	(15) 4–8
1988	January	Kimberly Conrad, Kim Bassinger eight-page nude pictorial	(25) 3–5
	February	Kari Kennell, The Nude Girls of Britain	(10) 3–5
	March	Susie Owens, ten-page lingerie pictorial	(10) 3–5
	April	Eloise Broady, Vanity cover and nude pictorial	(10) 3–6
	May	Diane Lee, Denice Crosby nude pictorial, Cathy Shower pictorial	(10) 3–6
	June	Emily Arth, Theresa Russell pictorial	(10) 3–5

Year	Issue	Description	Value ($)
1988	July	Terri Lynn Doss, Cindy Crawford cover and nude pictorial	(20; N/A) 4–8
	August	Helle Michaelse, Kimberly Conrad nude pictorial	(10) 3–5
	September	Laura Richmond, Jessica Hahn cover and special nude pictorial	(40) 4–7
	October	Shannon Long, Nude College Girl pictorial	(10) 4–7
	November	Pia Reyes, Nude Women of Washington	(10) 3–5
	December	Kata Karkkainen, Samantha Fox, Cher, Vanessa Williams, Vanity, Jessica Hahn	(10) 3–6
1989	January	Fawna MacLaren, 35th Anniversary Special	(20) 3–6
	February	Simone Eden, Brazilian Sex Stars	(10) 3–5
	March	Laurie Wood, La Toya Jackson cover and nude pictorial	(10) 4–8
	April	Jennifer Jackson, Erika Eleniak cover, Girls of the Big East nude pictorial, Beach Blast pictorial, Wet Mischief pictorial	(10) 5–10
	May	Monique Noel, Natalya Negada cover and nude pictorial: "From Russia with Love," Christine Keeler pictorial	(10) 3–5
	June	Tawni Cable, Kimberly Conrad cover and Playmate of the Year, Dana Plato ("Different Strokes") nude pictorial	(10) 5–10
	July	Erika Eleniak, Broadcast Nudes . . . Shelly Jamison	(10) 3–5

Year	Issue	Description	Value ($)
1989	August	Gianne Amore, Brandi Brandt cover, Women of Wall Street nude pictorial, Off with Their Clothes pictorial	(10) 3–5
	September	Korin and Mirjam Von Breeschooten . . . playmates and cover, Reno Confidential, KC Winkler pictorial	(10) 3–5
	October	Karen Foster, first Pamela Anderson cover, Girls of the Southeastern Conference, Julie McCullough pictorial, Keith Richards interview	(35) 7–15
	November	Renee Tenison, Donna Mills cover and pictorial, Sex in the Cinema	(10) 3–6
	December	Petra Verkaik, Candice Bergen cover, Lethal Women: Nude Pictorial of America's Leading Ladies of Wrestling, Karen Mayo-Chandler nude pictorial	(40) 3–5
1990	January	Peggy McIntaggart, Joan Severance cover and nude pictorial, Andy Warhol's Playboy Art	(30) 3–5
	February	Pamela Anderson, Polish-born model Bogna cover and nude pictorial of the Women of Russia, The Year in Sex	(N/A) 5–10
	March	Deborah Driggs, Donald Trump and *Playboy* model Brandi Brandt cover, *Playboy*'s World Tour pictorial, Fax and Figures pictorial	(35) 3–5

Year	Issue	Description	Value ($)
1990	April	Lisa Matthews, Deborah Driggs cover, Girls of the A.C.C. pictorial, Tony Curtis's daughter Allegra Curtis nude pictorial	(75) 3–7
	May	Tina Bockrath, Margaux Hemmingway cover and pictorial, "Living Dangerously" pictorial	(20) 2–4
	June	Bonnie Marino, Playmate of the Year model Renee Tenison cover and pictorial, Wild Orchid	(75) 3–7
	July	Jacqueline Sheen, Sharon Stone cover and pictorial, Body Double pictorial Marilyn Monroe Look-alike Rhonda Ridley	(N/A) 3–5
	August	Melissa Everidge, *Baywatch* star Erika Eleniak cover and nude pictorial, The Girls of Canada	(N/A) 4–8
	September	Kerri Kendall, Rosanna Arquette cover and nude pictorial, World Cup Women pictorial	(N/A) 3–5
	October	Brittany York, Melissa Everidge cover, Girls of the Big West pictorial, gladiator Marisa Pare pictorial	(20) 3–6
	November	Lorraine Olivia, Teri Copley cover and pictorial, Sex in the Cinema	(10) 3–5
	December	Morgan Fox, Sherilyn Fenn cover and *Twin Peaks* pictorial, Sex Stars of 1990	(30) 3–5
1991	January	Stacy Leigh Arthur cover, *Playboy*'s Playmate Review,	

June 1953

December 1953

May 1952

Circa 1950

#10, 1959

March 1963

June 1959

January 1969

May 1968

Year	Issue	Description	Value ($)
1991	January	Here's Looking at You pictorial: Helmut Newton	(10) 2–4
	February	Cristy Thom, Pamela Anderson cover, Sheer Madness pictorial, The Year in Sex featuring Madonna, Cicciolina and Marla Maples, Flex Appeal pictorial: a pumped-up portfolio of beautiful bodybuilders	(35) 4–7
	March	Julie Anne Clarke, Stephanie Seymour cover and nude pictorial, Cuba Libre pictorial	(75) 3–7
	April	Christine Leardini, Julie Clarke cover, Women of the Women's Colleges, Spring Break pictorial	(10) 3–8
	May	Carrie Jean Yazel, Shannon and Tracy Tweed cover and pictorial, Free Agent: Liz Pasko pictorial	(10) 3–5
	June	Sasha Linssen, Playmate of the Year Lisa Matthews cover and pictorial, The Women of Comedy pictorial featuring Rhonda Shear and Rosanne Katon	(10) 4–7
	July	Wendy Kaye, Samantha Dorman cover, The Height Report: pictorial of tall women, Balkan Beauty pictorial	(10) 3–5
	August	Corina Harney, Caprice cover and California Dreamin' pictorial, Yesterday's Wild Child: Brit Amanda de Cadenet pictorial	(10) 3–5

Year	Issue	Description	Value ($)
1991	September	Samantha Leah Dorman, The Barbi Twins cover and pictorial, Not Your Average Working Girl pictorial, Tula pictorial	(10) 3–6
	October	Cheryl Bachman, Tai Collins cover and nude pictorial, The Girls of the Big Ten pictorial	(10) 3–5
	November	Tonja Christensen, La Toya Jackson cover and nude pictorial, Sex in the Cinema 1991	(10) 3–5
	December	Wendy Hamilton, Dian Parkinson cover and nude pictorial, Sex Stars 1991	(50) 3–5
1992	January	Suzi Simpson, The Swedish Bikini Team cover and nude pictorial, *Playboy*'s Playmate review	(50) 4–8
	February	Tonya Beyer, Supermodel Rachel Williams cover and nude pictorial, *Playboy*'s World Tour '92 pictorial	(10) 3–5
	March	Tylyn John, Vicki Smith cover, Bruce Weber pictorial, Society Darlings nude pictorial	(10) 2–4
	April	Cady Cantrell, Wendy Kaye cover, Girls of the Big Eight, Shelley Michelle "Double Vision" nude pictorial	(10) 3–6
	May	Vicki Smith, Elizabeth Ward Gracen cover and "Miss America" nude pictorial, A Pride of Brides pictorial	(N/A) 2–4
	June	Angela Meline, Corinna Harney cover and Playmate of the Year pictorial, Video Vamp pictorial	(35) 3–7

Year	Issue	Description	Value ($)
1992	July	Amanda Hope, Pamela Anderson cover and nude pictorial, Med Alert pictorial, Nicole Kidman	(75) 7–15
	August	Ashley Allen, Magie Murphy cover, Hail Columbia pictorial, Domestic Bliss	(10) 7–15
	September	Morena Corwin, Sandra Bernhard cover and nude pictorial, Fly Girls pictorial	(10) 2–4
	October	Tiffany Sloan, Cristy Thom cover, "Funny Girl" pictorial, Girls of the Big East pictorial	(10) 3–7
	November	Stephanie Adams, Joan Severance cover and nude pictorial, Sex in the Cinema	(10) 3–6
	December	Barbara Moore, Sharon Stone cover, Jessica Hahn nude pictorial, Bettie Page special, Sex Stars 1992 featuring photos of Demi Moore, Madonna, Geena Davis, Rachel Williams, Claudia Schiffer, Cindy Crawford, Pamela Anderson, Erika Eleniak and many others	(N/A) 6–10
1993	January	Echo Leta Johnson, Barbi Twins cover and nude pictorial, The Year in Sex	(15) 3–7
	February	Jennifer LeRoy, Stephanie Seymour cover and nude pictorial, Being in Nothingness	(10) 2–4
	March	Kinberly Donley, Mimi Rogers cover and nude pictorial, A Club of One's Own pictorial	(10) 2–4

Year	Issue	Description	Value ($)
1993	April	Nicole Wood, Tonja Christensen cover, Tattoo You pictorial, Student Bodies pictorial, Frank Zappa interview	(10) 3–6
	May	Elke Jeinsen, Dian Parkinson cover and pictorial, Susie Owens: From Playmate to Superhero	(10) 3–5
	June	Alesha M. Oreskovich, Nicole Smith cover and Playmate of the Year pictorial, All About Eden	(15) 3–5
	July	Leisa Sheridan, Charlotte Lewis cover and pictorial: Brit Force Lucky Stiff pictorial	(10) 2–4
	August	Jennifer J. Lavoie, Pamela Andersen and Dan Aykroyd cover, Lady Lifeguards pictorial, Like Mother/Like Daughters pictorial	(10) 3–5
	September	Carrie Westcott, Jennifer Driver cover, Show Stopper pictorial featuring the Girls of the South Beach	(10) 2–4
	October	Jenny McCarthy, Jerry Seinfeld cover and interview, The Girls of the PAC 10, Ronda Shear nude pictorial	(N/A) 5–10
	November	Julianna Young, Brazil's Amazing Triplets cover and nude pictorial, Sex in the Cinema	(10) 3–5
	December	Arlene Baxter, Erika Eleniak cover and pictorial: Beverly Hills Hot, Sex Stars 1993 featuring Madonna, Janet Jackson, Anna Nicole Smith,	

Year	Issue	Description	Value ($)
1993	December	Daryl Hannah, Cindy Crawford, Drew Barrymore, Elle MacPherson, Shannon Doherty, Jessica Hahn and others	(10) 3–5
1994	January	Anna-Maria Goddard, 40th Anniversary Issue Special, *Playboy*'s Playmate Review, Jenny McCarthy, pictorials of Cindy Crawford, Sharon Stone, Vanna White, Madonna, Kim Bassinger, Ursula Andress, Marilyn Monroe and Jayne Mansfield, 40 Memorable Years pictorial	(N/A) 10–20
	February	Julie Lynn Cialini, Anna Nicole Smith cover and special Valentine pictorial, The Year in Sex, Lord Byron (Byron Newman) pictorial	(10) 2–4
	March	Neriah Davis, Shannon Doherty cover and pictorial, *Playboy*'s Hottest International Playmates	(15) 5–10
	April	Becky Delas Santos, Heidi Mark cover, The Girls of Hooters pictorial, Playmate Revisited: Marianne Gravatte, Elizabeth Nottoli pictorial	(10) 3–5
	May	Shae Marks, Elle MacPherson cover and nude pictorial, Bunny's Honey's pictorial . . . featuring Bettie Page	(15) 3–7
	June	Elan Carter, Jenny McCarthy cover and Playmate of the Year pictorial, Female Firefighters pictorial	(N/A) 5–10

Year	Issue	Description	Value ($)
1994	July	Traci Adell, Patti Davis cover and pictorial, Playmate Revisited: Shannon Long	(10) 2–4
	August	Maria Checa NYPD's Carol Shaya cover and nude pictorial, Jean Harlow exclusive pictorial, Bunny Fashions 2000, Viva Milan pictorial	(10) 3–5
	September	Kelly Gallagher, Robin Givens cover and nude pictorial, A Walk on the Bi Side pictorial	(10) 2–4
	October	Victoria Niko Zdrok, Jennifer Lavoie cover, Paula Barbieri pictorial, Girls of the SEC	(10) 3–5
	November	Donna Perry, Pamela Anderson cover and pictorial, Elle MacPherson, Rock Girls, Christian Slater interview	(10) 5–10
	December	Elisa Bridges, Bo Derek cover and pictorial, John Bobbitt's Ex-Fiancée pictorial, Sex Stars of 1994, featuring Claudia Schiffer and others	(10) 3–5
1995	January	Melissa Holiday, Drew Barrymore cover and nude pictorial, Playmate Review, The Year in Sex	(10) 5–10
	February	Lisa Marie Scott, Victoria Jacobs cover, Life Begins at Forty nude pictorial	(10) 3–5
	March	Stacy Sanchez, Amber Smith cover and pictorial, Stunt Women pictorial	(10) 3–5

Year	Issue	Description	Value ($)
1995	April	Danella Folta, Shana Hiatt, Girls of Hawaiian Tropic, The Doctor Is In	(10) 3–5
	May	Cynthia Gwyn Brown, Nancy Sinatra cover and nude pictorial, Dreaming of Jeanie: Jeanie Buss	(10) 3–6
	June	Rhonda Adams, Julie Cialini cover and Playmate of the Year, The Immortal Mr. Meyer pictorial, Shannon Tweed: *Playboy* Gallery	(10) 3–5
	July	Heidi Mark, Sandra Taylor cover and pictorial, Little Women pictorial, Carol Shaya, Karen Foster: *Playboy* Gallery	(20) 3–5
	August	Rachel Jean Marteen, Shelly Jones cover, Girls of Radio, Traci Adell pictorial	(10) 3–5
	September	Donna D'Errico, Kimberley Conrad cover and pictorial, Jaid Barrymore nude, Cindy Crawford, Sandra Bullock	(75) 3–5
	October	Alicia Rickter, Lisa Boyle cover, Women of the Ivy League, Showgirls pictorial, Pamela Anderson: *Playboy* Gallery	(15) 3–5
	November	Holly Witt, Tahnee Welch cover and nude pictorial, Sex in the Cinema 1995, Barbara Edwards: *Playboy* Gallery, "X-Files" David Duchovny	(10) 3–5

Year	Issue	Description	Value ($)
1995	December	Samantha Torres, Farrah Fawcett cover and nude pictorial, Sex Stars of 1995, Tula: *Playboy* Gallery, Bettie Page pictorial, which includes rare full-page color	(75) 10–20
1996	January	Victoria Fuller, Pamela Anderson cover and The Ultimate Pam Anderson pictorial, Jenny McCarthy: *Playboy* Gallery, The Year in Sex, *Playboy*'s Playmate Review	(10) 4–7
	February	Kona Carmack, Leslie Nielsen with Sandra Taylor and Traci Andell cover, Naked Nielsen pictorial, Zap pictorial: TV's Roughest, Buffest Lady Warrior, Cameron Diaz: *Playboy* Gallery, Bruce Willis interview	(10) 3–5
	March	Priscilla Lee Taylor, Tracy Hampton nude pictorial, Playmate Revisited: DeDe Lind	(10) 3–5
	April	Gilian Bonner, Samantha Torres cover, Playmate Revisited: Lillian Muller, Tammi Alexander nude pictorial: Tammi and The Bachelor	(10) 3–5
	May	Shauna Sand, Cindy Crawford cover and Music and Supermodels pictorial featuring Cindy Crawford, Claudia Schiffer, Elle, Stephanie, Kate and others,	

Year	Issue	Description	Value ($)
1996	May	Electra pictorial, Debra Jo Fondren: *Playboy* Gallery, Ray Bradbury interview	(10) 5–10
	June	Karin Taylor, Stacy Sanches cover and Playmate of the Year pictorial, Twin Peaks pictorial featuring Pandora Peaks, Joyce Nizzari: Playmate Revisited, Julia Louis-Dreyfus	(15) 3–5
	July	Angel Lynn Boris, Jenny McCarthy cover and nude pictorial, The Girls of Venus Swimwear	(10) 7–15
	August	Jessica Lee, Leeann Tweed cover, The Women of Atlanta, Hard Bodies pictorial, Kathy Shower: Playmate Revisited, Janet Jones: *Playboy* Gallery	(10) 3–5
	September	Jennifer Allen, Uma Thurman cover and pictorial, Small Town Girls, Patti McGuire: Playmate Revisited	(10) 2–4
	October	Nadine Chanz, Jennifer Allen cover, British Rock Sensation Samantha Fox nude pictorial, The Girls of the Big Twelve, Playmate Revisited: Donna Michelle	(10) 5–10
	November	Ulrika Ericsson, Donna D'Errico cover and Hot New "Baywatch" Babe pictorial, Sex in Cinema Stripped Bare, Janet Pilgram: Playmate	(10) 3–6
	December	Victoria Silvstedt, Jenny McCarthy cover and	

Year	Issue	Description	Value ($)
1996	December	pictorial, Raquel Welch: *Playboy* Gallery, Crista Speck: Playmate Revisited, Saturday Night Specials . . . the females of Women: Stories of Passion	(10) 7–12
1997	January	Jami Farrell, Marilyn Monroe cover and nude special including her famous centerfold, The Year in Sex, Salvador Dali nudes, Lisa Winters: Playmate Revisited, *Playboy*'s Playmate Review, The Return of James Bond	(10) 4–10
	February	Kimber West, Echo Johnson/ Anna-Marie Goddard/Rachel Jean Marteen/Jami Ferrell cover, Love and Lingerie Special, Carol Vitale: Playmate Revisited, Brigitte Nielsen: *Playboy* Gallery, History of the Sexual Revolution	(10) 3–5
	March	Jennifer Miriam, Faye Resnick cover and pictorial, Sharry Konopski: Playmate Revisited, Brigitte Bardot: *Playboy* Gallery, Clint Eastwood	(10) 2–5
	April	Kelly Marie Monaco, Joey Heatherton cover and nude pictorial, Women of Dentistry pictorial, 20 questions with Vanessa Williams, James Bond, Playmate Revisited: Dolly Reed, *Playboy* Gallery: Dorothy Stratten	(10) 4–8

Year	Issue	Description	Value ($)
1997	May	Lynn Thomas, Claudia Schiffer cover and super-model pictorial, The Morrell Sisters pictorial, Cyndi Wood: Playmate Revisited, The New James Bond II	(10) 4–8
	June	Carrie Stevens, Victoria Silvstedt cover and Playmate of the Year nude pictorial, Carmen Electra pictorial, Playmate Revisited: Lisa Baker	(10) 5–10
	July	Daphnee Duplaix, Farrah Fawcett cover and nude pictorial, Daphnee Lynn Duplaix pictorial, History of the Sexual Revolution Part IV, Brandi Brandt: Playmate Revisited	(10) 5–10
	August	Kalin Olson, Nikki Ziering cover, Biker Babes, *Playboy* Gallery: Sophia Loren, Don't Touch That Dial pictorial	(10) 3–5
	September	Nikki Schieler, Pamela Anderson cover and nude pictorial, Sports Babes, Playmate Revisited: Karen Valez	(10) 5–10
	October	Layla Roberts, Stacy Fuson cover, Girls of the Big Ten, Cristina Barone, Spice Girls, Joan Severence: *Playboy* Gallery	(10) 3–5
	November	Inga Drozdova, Suzen Johnson cover and Tabloid Temptress pictorial, Sex in the Cinema 1997, Playmate Revisited: Bebe Buell	(10) 3–5

Year	Issue	Description	Value ($)
1997	December	Karen McDougal, Miss Canada cover and pictorial, The History of the Bra pictorial, Sex Stars of 1997, Candy Loving: Playmate Revisited	(10) 3–5
1998	January	Heather Kozar, Shannon Tweed cover and pictorial, "My Story" by Bettie Page, pictorial of Pietra Thornton, The Year in Sex, Playmate Review, Kim Bassinger: *Playboy* Gallery	(10) 3–5
	February	Julia Schultz, Daphne Deckers cover and pictorial, Couch Tomatoes, History of the Sexual Revolution Part VI, Victoria Valentino: Playmate Revisited	(10) 3–5
	March	Marliece Andrada playmate and cover, The Great Swimsuit Takeoff pictorial, Jamie Presley, Erika Eleniak: Playmate Revisited	(10) 3–5
1998	April	Holly Joan Hart, Linda Bravo cover and pictorial, Jody Watley nude pictorial, Monique St. Pier: Playmate Revisited	(10) 3–5
	May	Deanna Brooks, Ginger Spice cover and nude pictorial, Elizabeth Ward Gracen pictorial, Veronica Gamba: Playmate Revisited	(10) 5–10
	June	Marliece Andrada, The Babes of *Baywatch* cover and pictorial, Fly Girl, The	

Year	Issue	Description	Value ($)
1998	June	History of the Sexual Revolution Part VII	(10) 3–5
	July	Lisa Gergan, Karen McDougal cover and Playmate of the Year nude pictorial, The Helmut Newton Girls pictorial	(10) 3–5
	August	Angela Little	(10) 3–5
	September	Vanessa Gleason, "Melrose" Mom Lisa Rinna cover and Proud, Pregnant, and Beautiful cover and nude pictorial, Heidi Davies nude pictorial, Nina Hartley	(10) 5–10

All other issues to present		3–5

BEST FROM *PLAYBOY* (AND *PLAYBOY ANNUAL*)

(1954–1957 are hardcover, 1964 up are softcover)

Year	Issue	Value
1954		50–100
1955		40–80
1956		35–70
1957		50–100
1964	#1	15–30
1964	#1 Deluxe Edition	20–40
1968	#2	12–25
1969	#3	12–25
1970	#4	12–25
1971	#5	10–20
1972	#6	10–20

1973	#7	10–20
1975	#8	10–15
1978	#8	4–7
1982 up		4–7

PLAYBOY PRESENTS 50 BEAUTIFUL WOMEN

(A Special Collection)   **Value ($)**

1989	Maude Adams, Ursula Andress, Carroll Baker, Penny Baker, Bridgette Bardot, Sonia Braga, Barbara Carrera, Kimberley Conrad, Farrah Fawcett, Linda Evans, Jessica Hahn, Elke Jane Kennedy, Jayne Mansfield, Donna Mills, Victoria Principal, Marilyn Monroe, June Pointer, Dorothy Stratten, Vanna White and others	7–15
	Sugar and Spice—Brooke Shields (extremely rare)	50–125+

PLAYBOY SPECIALS

Playboy Special Editions are currently very popular with collectors. These issues in general are valued at $5 to $10 each and acquire a collector's value a few short months after being published. Issues that feature one or more photos of such noted females as Madonna, Vanity, Jessica Hahn, Vanna White, Patti McGuire, Dorothy Stratten, Jayne Mansfield, Marilyn Monroe, Janet or La Toya Jackson, Kimberley Conrad, Barbara Carrera, Tanya Roberts, Jenny McCarthy and any other star who is currently popular are valued at $7 to $15. It should be noted that *Playboy* magazine's back issue department offers many of these editions at a cost from $10 to $50 each.

Listed below are a few of the many titles that are *Playboy* specials:

Playboy's Holiday Girls
The Year in Sex
Nudes
Nude Celebrities
Playboy Photography
Playboy's Great Playmate Hunt
Playboy's Nudes
Women of Color
Women on the Move
Winter Girls
Girls of Winter
Girls of Summer
Girls of the World
Bathing Beauties
Hot Denim Daze
Playmates in Paradise
Playmates in the Spotlight
Playmates in Bed
Kimberley Conrad
Dian Parkinson
Playmate Review
Sex and Other Late
 Night Laughs
Sexy Ladies
Sexy Girls Next Door

Nude Playmates
Vanna White
Video Playmates
Playboy's Book of Lingerie
Sexy, Sassy & Sophisticated
College Girls
Classic Centerfolds
Real Sex
Girlfriends
Blondes, Brunettes
 and Redheads
Wet & Wild Women
Working Women
Entertaining Women
Pompeo Posar
Fantasies
Facts & Figures
International Playmates
21 Playmates
Men's Club
Cover Girls
Supermodels
Voluptuous Vixens
X-Girls

Swimsuit Magazines and Special Values

Swimsuit magazines, such as *Swimwear Illustrated, Swimwear U.S.A.* and *Swimsuit International,* as well as swimsuit special editions of *Sports Illustrated, Sports* and *Inside Sports* are extremely popular and whose value is based on the models shown in a particular issue. Swimsuit magazines from the '70s, '80s, and '90s generally have a value of $1–$3. Issues containing photographs of current popular female actresses, female athletes and models such as Kathy Ireland, Christie Brinkley, Paulina Porzikova, Elle MacPherson, Stephanie

Seymour, Cheryl Tiegs and others have a value of $5–$10, depending on how many photos and if there is a cover photo. *Sports Illustrated*'s swimsuit issues are currently the only title that holds a higher value to the collector. That is mostly due to the high quality of photography and the quality of photographs modeled by extremely popular models.

SWIMSUIT ISSUES/*SPORTS ILLUSTRATED*

1964	January 20	Babette cover	$15–30
1965	January 18	Sue Peterson cover	10–20
1966	January 17	Sunny Bippus cover	10–20
1967	January 18	Marilyn Tindal cover	10–20
1968	January 15	Turia Mau cover	7–15
1969	January 13	Jamie Becker cover	7–15
1970	January 12	First Cheryl Tiegs cover	12–25
1971	February 1	Tannia Rubiano cover	5–10
1972	January 17	Sheila Roscoe cover	5–10
1973	January 29	Dayle Haddon cover	5–10
1974	January 28	Ann Simonton cover	5–10
1975	January 27	Cheryl Tiegs cover	10–20
1976	January 19	Yvette and Yvonne Sylvander cover	6–12
1977	January 24	Lena Kansbod cover	6–12
1978	January 16	Maria Joao cover	5–10
1979	February 5	First Christie Brinkley cover	15–30
1980	February 4	Christie Brinkley cover	10–25
1981	February 9	Christie Brinkley cover	10–20
1982	February 8	Carol Alt	7–15
1983	February 14	Cheryl Tiegs cover	7–15
1984	February 13	First Paulina Porizkova cover	7–15
1985	February 11	Paulina Porizkova cover	5–12
1986	February 10	First Elle MacPherson cover	7–15
1987	February 9	Elle MacPherson cover	6–12
1988	February 15	Elle MacPherson cover	5–10
1989	February	25th Anniversary swimsuit issue, Kathy Ireland cover, issue shows every swimsuit	

January 27, 1975

January 19, 1976

February 4, 1980

February 9, 1981

February 8, 1982

February 13, 1984

February 10, 1986

February 11, 1991

Winter 1997

1989		cover and feature on the cover models today	6–12
1990	February 12	Rachel Hunter, Kathy Ireland and others	5–10
1991	February 11	Ashley Montana, Stephanie Seymour and others	5–10

All other swimsuit editions   3–5

Monster Magazines: Illustrated Horror, Monster/Science Fiction TV/Movie, and Related Magazines

In the late 1950s a new phenomenon appeared on newsstands across the United States. For the first time, fans of horror and monster movies had their own special movie magazine. This magazine did not feature Doris Day, Debbie Reynolds, Elizabeth Taylor, or other commonly seen cover stars; they featured the likes of *Frankenstein,* Bela Lugosi, Vincent Price, Boris Karloff, and other long-neglected horror film stars, monsters, and creatures of all kinds, who had their chance to meet the reading public. With the first issue of James Warren's *Famous Monsters of Filmland* in 1958, the die was cast for a whole new genre in magazine collecting. With the very first issue of *Famous Monsters,* editor Forest J. Ackerman sparked what has become a glowing flame in the hearts of collectors, both young and old. Most collectors of monster magazines are not content merely to collect the magazines, but can quite often branch out into collecting monster figures, gum cards, monster models, buttons, posters, horror videos, photos, autographs, and countless other related memorabilia. This hobby has shown tremendous growth in the past three decades evidenced in part by the increasing number of monster conventions being held throughout the United States and other countries. Values have risen and the number of new collectors entering the field is tremendous.

No other type of magazine has ever evoked such dedication or determination from the collector (quite often spanning decades of a collector's life) to acquire a complete run of one or more of the many different titles that have been created since that fateful day in 1958.

The term "monster magazine" covers a wide spectrum of magazine types, such as those specializing in a monster, horror, or science fiction theme. However, the "true" monster magazine in its purest form is a publication dedicated solely to monster and horror films. Examples of these "true" monster magazines are *Famous Monsters of Filmland, Monster World, Castle of Frankenstein, Monsters and Things, World Famous Creatures, The Journal of Frankenstein, 3D Monsters, Quasimoto's Monster Magazine, Monster Parade, Horror Monsters, Mad Monsters,* and *The Monster Times.* These monster magazines generally have excellent stories, interviews, and specials packed with photos on all the classic horror films and their stars from the past, right up to the latest sequel of *Scream* or the most recent episode of *Buffy the Vampire Slayer.* Quite often they include biographies and personal facts about the stars, directors, special effects, makeup, and production people.

Next come the science fiction/horror magazines with titles such as *Star Log, Starburst, Fantastic Films, Future Fantasy, Spacemen, Science/Fantasy Film Classics.* These magazines specialize mainly in science fiction movies and TV shows, with an occasional story on monsters or classic horror. For the most part, these magazines are very well done and service the collector's need to keep up on the current and upcoming science fiction movies, TV episodes, or cable specials.

Monster magazine collectors are often interested in science fiction and monster-related magazines. A related science fiction monster magazine is any nonhorror/science fiction magazine that contains a feature story or a cover with a horror, science fiction, or monster theme. It is not uncommon for the collector's value on these issues to increase quite quickly, especially if the magazine happens to be distributed regionally. An example of this is a recent issue of *Steppin' Out* magazine (published weekly as an entertainment magazine, and distributed free only in Northern New Jersey) that featured *Buffy the Vampire Slayer.* Most copies of this issue were read by noncollectors and then tossed into the trash the following week. Today copies of the *Buffy* issue are selling at horror conventions for an average of $20, and on Internet auction sites for as high as $65. This is just one example of a magazine that has all the components to make it highly desirable: low regional distribution, a readership not related to collecting, and a horror subject at its peak of popularity. Most science fiction monster magazines fall into the $3 to $5 price range, with many quite often selling for as high as $10 to $15.

A fanzine, as the name implies, is a fan magazine published and written by a fan and/or a fan club. These amateur magazines can range from just a few pages to well over a hundred pages, with a few topping two hundred pages. A great deal of enthusiasm goes into the design and creation of a fanzine. Many are extremely well done and are usually dedicated to one specific area of collecting, a certain movie or TV show, or a personality. The dozens of fanzines published in recent years devoted solely to *Lost in Space, Star Wars, Star Trek, Beauty and the Beast, The Outer Limits,* and *Godzilla* are wonderful examples. Today the collector can still find fanzines on such subjects as *Dark Shadows, The Munsters, Space 1999, Battlestar Galactica, Friday the 13th, Xena: Warrior Princess, Rocky Horror Picture Show,* and countless other shows and movies. A fanzine's value is based on its content, whether or not it contains an exclusive interview with a star (one that has not been published elsewhere), if it includes rare unpublished photos, the quality of stories and of the paper used in the magazine, and whether the cover is in color or black and white. Fanzines of the sixties are becoming more and more difficult to find and are now selling for an average of $10 to $50. Issues from the seventies at $10 to $30, and issues from the eighties and nineties sell for $2 to $5, with the more desirable valued at $7 to $10.

Prozines are basically fanzines that are published on a more professional level. A prozine can be the result of a fan's attempt to make a living from doing what he or she enjoys most, or of a small publishing company trying to expand its market. Prozines generally have a larger production budget, are often printed by a professional print shop, can be ordered through ads in other magazines, or can be purchased on a newsstand or at a collectors' shop. Examples of prozines would be such titles as: *Gore Creatures, Scary Monsters* (early issues), *The Japanese Fantasy Film Journal, The Old Dark House, The Late Show, Cinemagic* (pre-*Starlog*), *SPFX, Bizarre, Little Shop of Horrors, Midnight Marque, Children of the Night, Black Oracle, Spectre, Garden Ghouls Gazette,* and *Photon.* In our value section we will be listing some of the more notable titles. New titles are appearing on the collecting scene regularly and most only last for a few issues. The average prozine is valued at $3 to $10.

The last category of monster magazines is the monster/horror illustrated magazine. These magazines, most with extremely violent and horrific covers, have long been ignored by monster magazine dealers, and even excluded from monster magazine reference books and guides. After years of being overlooked, back issues of these magazines are eagerly sought by today's collectors and dealers alike. Collectors are appreciating the fine artwork and highly imaginative stories of such magazines as *Creepy, Eerie,* and *Vampirella.* Even more appreciated are the macabre artwork and terribly frightening stories of *Tales from the Tomb, Witches' Tales, Tales of Voodoo, Weird, Shock, Weird Mysteries, Vampire Tales,*

Weird Worlds, Tales from the Crypt, Terror Tales, and others. In just a few years, values on these issues have risen dramatically, in some cases, ten-fold. The collectors of monster magazines now actively include these frighteningly creative horror magazines in their collections. Certain illus-trated horror magazines have not been listed in this guide (for example, *Monsters Unleashed, Dracula Lives,* and a few others). These titles are more highly regarded by comic collectors than monster magazine collec-tors at present. If you wish to research illustrated horror magazines not listed in this guide, one excellent source is *The Overstreet Comic Book Price Guide* by Robert M. Overstreet, or you may call the Official Mon-ster Magazine Hotline, provided exclusively to readers of this guide, at 201-641-7212 or send an e-mail to henkellang@aol.com (during regular business hours, Eastern Standard Time).

Buying Monster Magazines

While most collectible magazines can be found by rummaging through old boxes at a garage sale or browsing the tables of a local flea market, monster and science fiction magazines are very rarely offered at these places. One reason for this is that monster magazine collectors take great pride in their collections and stay in close contact with the collect-ing world. When collectors decide to sell they will go to the same places where they bought their issues and expect to sell them for a fair price; these places are conventions, mail order catalogs, the Internet, or comic book and back issue magazine stores.

1. Monster and Science Fiction Conventions

A convention focusing on a horror, monster, or science fiction theme is a prime source for obtaining back issue monster magazines. Issues from the most common to the most rare are offered by many different dealers and in many different grades of condition. It is not uncommon for col-lectors to get together before, during, and after the show to trade issues. Prices can vary dramatically from dealer to dealer. It is not uncommon to find one dealer selling, for example, a number one issue of *Famous Monsters of Filmland* in fine condition for $300, and another dealer just a few tables away selling the same issue, in the same condition, for $800. When searching the conventions it is best to get there very early.

Some conventions offer an early bird admission to attendees at a higher price, which can pay off well if you're looking for the best buys. Sometimes there are hundreds of dealers offering thousands of magazines and related memorabilia. Conventions may also offer vintage horror and fantasy flicks rarely shown on network TV or cable stations, autograph and photo sessions with the stars, previews of new horror products and toys, and lectures by celebrities in the horror or science fiction field. In addition, they're a great place to make new friends. To learn of upcoming conventions, check with the trade publications offered at local newsstands, comic book, and back issue magazine stores, or from the larger book stores such as Barnes and Noble.

2. Comic Book and Back Issue Magazine Stores

Comic book and back issue magazine stores are including vintage monster and science fiction magazines to their inventory more than ever. Nearly all offer the most recent newsstand issues. However, it is becoming increasingly difficult to walk into a shop and find monster magazines published before 1975, and nearly impossible to see an issue from before 1963. The reason for this is many shop dealers are not yet accustomed to paying an acceptable price to collectors, so the collector will then sell his collection elsewhere—usually at a convention or through the mail. Also, some of the "old-timer" back issue shops don't always monitor their inventory carefully, so always remember to speak to the store's owner about the magazine you want. Too often collectors, not seeing monster magazines on display, will turn around and quietly walk out. But if you ask, you may be pleasantly rewarded, as I have discovered that many of these shop owners will price issues lower than their true value. This is generally because of the owner's lack of knowledge in the field of monster magazine collecting. At one time, this source was the most common way that a collector could find issues. Regrettably, in today's marketplace the comic book and back issue store is slowly fading away as the primary source for these magazines.

3. Mail Order and the Internet

The most reliable and common way collectors purchase monster magazines is through mail order dealers and auctions on the Internet. When selecting a mail order dealer it is helpful to be referred by another collector who has had a positive buying history with a specific dealer. Be sure to choose a dealer that offers return privileges (generally seven to fourteen days), as the seller's idea of acceptable condition may vary from your own. You should be truly satisfied with your purchase only when you have the magazine in your hands and can determine its condition for yourself. Some dealers will charge the top value for an old back issue with a cover in extremely fine condition without bothering to look inside to determine whether the contents have been clipped. However, most mail order dealers who have been in business awhile have learned to carefully inspect each page of the issues they are offering. Mail order dealers remain the collector's best source, since most keep complete runs of all titles in stock, in various degrees of conditions, and offer them on a continuous basis. If a mail order dealer does not have your issues in stock or an issue in the condition you are seeking, he will likely be able to locate that copy at a later date.

Collectors should also consider taking out their own classified ads in the many trade papers, want ad press, or penny-saver publications in their area.

The Internet auction is becoming a prime source for back issue monster and science fiction magazines. Prices have not yet gone through the roof, as has happened with many types of magazines. Most issues on the Internet can often be found at prices much lower than those offered by shop owners, mail order dealers, or sellers at conventions. The reason for this is that presently there is a good supply of titles being offered and the competition to buy has not yet been established. I expect this to change in the coming year or two, and prices will likely become out of reach for the beginning collector as the serious collector discovers this growing and dynamic marketplace. At present, the Internet auction can be fun and rewarding to the collector as long as the collector sets an affordable limit to the price he or she is willing to pay.

Selling Monster Magazines

When selling your monster magazines, first consider selling them through an inexpensive classified ad in a trade paper. This is where you will reach the beginning and seasoned collector and more often than not realize the highest price per issue for your collection. Ads in these publications usually cost from 20 to 30 cents per word and most times deliver good results. If you have an extensive collection, which is of high quality and quantity, you may consider advertising in one of the larger national newsstand trade magazines such as *Starlog, Filmfax,* or *Fangoria.* Ads here will run from $33 to $66 to list, in general, what you are offering. It is not unusual for collectors, while in the process of selling their collections, to find themselves enjoying becoming a part-time dealer. Many of today's most successful and respected monster magazine dealers started out in this manner.

Selling to a dealer is advisable if the seller wishes to sell the collection quickly and with the least amount of involvement. Do not expect very high values; most dealers are working with a great deal of overhead costs (cataloging, advertising, storage, printing, staff salaries, etc.) and must make a profit from the magazine's resale in order to stay in business. Dealers will usually offer anywhere from 10 to 50 present of an issue's resale value for common issues. Rarer issues will sell to a dealer for 25 to 75 percent. For example, if you are fortunate enough to offer a dealer vintage copies, in fine or better condition, of *Famous Monsters of Filmland* (numbers 1 through 38 and #114), *Monster Parade, Shock Tales, World Famous Creatures,* and *Thriller,* do not settle for less than 75 percent of the current resale value. These issues are at a premium, sell extremely well, and are quickly disappearing from the marketplace. Be patient, be flexible, and you will get a decent price from one dealer or another.

Again, conventions are the most exciting way to sell your collection or duplicate issues. Dealers' tables are available (depending on the show) on a first-come, first-served basis. Many of the better conventions have their tables reserved as early as one year in advance. Prices per table can cost from just a few dollars at a small local convention, to hundreds of dollars at a larger well advertised and established convention. When selling at many of the larger shows it is required by state and sometimes local law to have a sales tax number and card. Where required this is a must. Information regarding sales tax laws and sales rules can be obtained from the convention holders or by calling the state sales tax department. Conventions are not only great places to sell your magazines, you also share and enjoy the day with fellow fans. It is not unusual for sellers to end up spending all the money made by selling magazines on issues that they have been searching for for years. When selling at a convention, it is important to price your magazines competitively and be willing to offer a modest discount on larger purchases. If you do these things, you should have the experience of a lifetime.

Grading Monster Magazines

Unlike other areas of magazine collecting, the world of monster magazine collecting has pretty much established its own customized grading system. The grading of monster magazines is extremely important to the collector and should be equally as important to the dealer/seller. Properly grading monster magazines is an absolute must. Collectors want to know about every imperfection that may exist on the outside and on the inside of the magazine before they make their purchases. Collectors of other type magazines (rock and teen magazines, movie or adult magazines, for example) are much more tolerant of an issue's condition. For precise grading standards, refer to the grading section at the beginning of this book.

MONSTER/SCIENCE FICTION MAGAZINE VALUES

Year	Issue/Number	Description	Value ($)
Adventures into Horror **(Stanley Publications)**			
1970	#1		7–15
	#2		6–12
Alien **(Alien: The Movie One Shot, Published by Warren)**			
1979		Includes scenes cut from the film, special effects photos	5–10
All About Star Trek Fan Club **(Ego Enterprises)**			
1977	#1–5		5–10
Amazing Cinema **(Cinema Enterprises)**			
Publishing begins in 1981	All issues		5–10
Amazing Forries **(One Issue Published by Metropolis Publications)**			
1976		Dedicated to Forrest J. Ackerman . . . this is your life	20–40
American Cinematographer **(ASC Holding Co.)**			
1980	February	Star Trek: The Motion	

Year	Issue/Number	Description	Value ($)
1980	February	Picture cover and feature . . . "A Look Behind the Scenes"	3–6
1989	October	Lon Chaney cover and feature: Phantom of the Opera . . . The Legend Continues	3–5

***Ancient Astronaut Special Edition/Star Wars versus Alien* (Countrywide Publications)**

1979	Fall	"The Nightmare Worlds of Alien," "Behind the Scenes at Alien," "Star Wars: Droids Take Over," "Meet H. R. Giger: Horror"	3–6

Bananas

1979	#33	Star Trek cover and movie preview	5–10

Battlestar Galactica Official Poster Magazine

	#1–4		10–15

***Black Zoo* (Charlton Publications)**

1963		One shot of the movie, a picture-by-picture chiller mag	10–20

***Castle of Frankenstein* (Gothic Castle Publishing Company)**

1962–1975	#1		15–30
	#2	The many faces of Christopher Lee, superheroes, etc.	15–30
	#3	The Karloff story, the Frankenstein story, son of Chaney, etc.	15–30
	#4	Special vampire issue, Lon Chaney Jr., etc.	12–25
	#5	Edgar Rice Burroughs's Frankenstein, The Evil	

Year	Issue/Number	Description	Value ($)
1962–1975	#5	of Frankenstein, the Peter Lorre story, etc.	7–15
	#6	Christopher Lee returns in the Gorgon, radio horrors, Alfred Hitchcock interview, Dracula and the Wolfman, Lon Chaney Jr.'s monsters, another lost Frankenstein, etc.	7–15
	#7	Die, Monster, Die: a visit to the set . . . Boris Karloff's first monster role since 1929, the night Richard Burton turned into a monster, Bela Lugosi versus Christopher Lee, Dracula Prince of Darkness	7–15
	#8	Christopher Lee as Dracula cover, Fu Manchu: Behind the Scenes, David McCallum: The Man from M.O.N.S.T.E.R., Bela Lugosi's last days, Batman and Robin: from the serial to TV	10–20
	#9	Batman's TV Joker cover, TV villains: Catwoman, Fantomas, Boris Karloff, Victor Buono, and others, a Batman special	15–30+
	#10	TV's Green Hornet cover and feature, King Kong, Bela Lugosi's Tragic addiction, Christopher Lee and Lon Chaney exclusive interviews	10–20+
	#11	Leonard Nimony/Star Trek cover and feature, A Talk	

Year	Issue/Number	Description	Value ($)
1962–1975	#11	with Christopher Lee, The Man behind Marvel Comics, The Horror Chamber of Dr. Faustus, UFO: Flying Saucers and Worldwide Blackouts	15–30+
	#12	Raquel Welch/One Million Years B.C. cover and feature, Spock/Leonard Nimoy speaks, interview with Marvel Comics, etc.	7–15
	#13	Planet of the Apes cover and feature, 2001: A Space Odyssey, Ray Bradbury interview, Dark Shadows, etc.	10–20
	#14	Star Trek cover and feature: Star Trek is back, etc.	10–20
	#15	Witches and demons special, Planet of the Apes, etc.	7–15
	#16	Satanism and vampires issues, Dark Shadows cover and feature, the history of horror films, etc.	7–15
	#17	Magic and occult issue, history of fantasy and horror films, Ray Harryhausen's films, etc.	6–12
	#18	Frankenstein, The Night of the Living Dead, etc.	6–12
	#19	Ray Harryhausen special, etc.	6–12
	#20	Frankenstein, The Mummy, Wolfman, First Men on the Moon	6–12
	#21	Frankenstein, Sinbad	6–12

Year	Issue/Number	Description	Value ($)
1962–1975	#22	The Exorcist, Linda Blair cover and feature, exclusive interview with The Exorcist's director Bill Friedkin, The Exorcist: Behind the Scenes	10–20
	#23	Return to Planet of the Apes cover and special feature, Roger Corman interview, George Pal's Doc Savage, etc.	6–12
	#24	Memorial to Boris Karloff special, The Evil of Frankenstein, freaks and mutations, the $25,000 monster, The Exorcist Part II	6–12
	#25	The Time Machine cover and feature, The Night Stalker, Andy Warhol's Frankenstein, Mel Brooks's Frankenstein, Phantom of the Paradise, etc.	6–12
1967 Annual			10–20+

Chilling Monster Tales (MM Publishing, Ltd.)

1966	#1	Them: Giant Ants, Dracula's Lost Chapter, House of Frankenstein, Island of Dr. Moreau	10–20

Chilling Tales of Horror (Stanley Publications, Inc., Illustrated Horror)

1969	#1 (June vol. 1, #1)	After Death, Epitaph, The Shadows in the Mirror, The Bloodstone	10–20
	#2 (August vol. 1, #2)	The Book of Doom, Contract in Blood, Corpse in the Coffin, Vampire	10–20

Year	Issue/Number	Description	Value ($)
1969	#3 (October vol. 1, #3)	Ghostly Revenge, Rotting Flesh of the Dead, Twin of Terror, Curse of the Vampires	10–20
1970	#4 (June vol. 1, #4)	The Tomb of the Unseen, A Live Corpse for the Zombie, The Specter's Revenge, Payment in full	5–10
	#5 (August vol. 1, #5)		15–30+
	#6 (October vol. 1, #6)	The Demon Master, King of the Vampires, Howl of the Hunter, The Devil on Your Dial	5–10
	#7 (December vol. 1, #7)	Slave of the Living Hell, The Vampire's Fate, Within the Tomb of Terror, Wings of Darkness	5–10
1971	#8 (February vol. 2, #2)	The Day the World Died, Spirit of Frankenstein, The Vampire's Prey, The Man Who Tried to Live Forever	5–10
	#9 (April vol. 2, #2)	Face of the Fiend, Five Found Dead, The Flying Head, The Hands of Darkness	5–10
	#10 (June vol. 2, #3)	Priestess of the Sphinx, The Creekmore Curse, Deity of Death, Vampire's Bane, Phantom Fountain	5–10
	#11 (August vol. 2, #4)	Bride of the Beast, Assault from the Unknown, Vampire Cat, The Soul Collectors	5–10
	#12 (October vol. 2, #5)	The Winged Creatures of Satan, The Ghost Tiger, Subway Spectre, The Witch's Curse	5–10

Year	Issue/Number	Description	Value ($)

Cinefantastique (Frederick S. Clarke Publishing)

	Issue/Number	Description	Value ($)
	#1	*Note:* This title started out as a prozine with the first issue being mimeographed. This mimeographed first edition is extremely rare and if offered would easily be valued at over $100. When offered, it would be advisable to ask for bids. This would help the seller to determine its present market value better.	
	#1	Professionally published issue	15–30
	#2	Dark Shadows cover and feature	20–30
	#3	Review of horror, fantasy, and science fiction films	10–20
	#4	George Pal's The Time Machine cover and special	10–25+
	#5	Paul Wendkos interview, Film Animation	5–10
	#6	Planet of the Apes special	10–20+
	#7	Interview with George Romero	5–10
	#8	Amicus Films issue special	5–10
	#9	Christopher Lee special	5–10
	#10	The Golden Voyage of Sinbad	5–10
	#11	Zardoz special	5–10
	#12	The Exorcist special	6–12+
	#13	Christopher Lee: The Man with the Golden Gun	5–10
	#14	Phantom of the Paradise	5–10
	#15	The Films of Terence Fisher	5–10
	#16	The Day the Earth Stood Still special	5–10+

Year	Issue/Number	Description	Value ($)
	#17	A Boy and His Dog	4–8
	#18	Logan's Run special	10–20
	#19	The Omen	6–12
	#20	War of the Worlds special	5–10
	#21	Carrie special	6–12
	#22	Ray Harryhausen special, The Eye of the Tiger	6–12
	#23	The Wicker Man	4–8
	#24	Double issue special	10–20
	#25	Hans Salter cover and feature	3–5
	#26	Close Encounters special, a double issue	5–10
	#27	The Primevals	5–10
	#28	Forbidden Planet special, a double issue	10–20
	#29	Donner on Superman	3–5
	#30	Alien special	10–20
	#31	Salem's Lot special	5–10
	#32	The Black Hole, a double issue	3–5
	#33	John Carpenter: The Director Who Came in from the Fog	3–5
	#34	Alfred Hitchcock's The Birds	3–5
	#35	Clash of the Titans	3–5
	#36	The Explosive Films of David Cronenberg	3–5
	#37	Dick Smith: Altering States	3–5
	#38	The Filming of Altered States	3–5
	#39	Conan the Barbarian	3–5
	#40	Stop Motion Magician: George Pal	3–5
	#41	Ghost Story	3–5
	#42	The Filming of Conan the Barbarian	3–5

Year	Issue/Number	Description	Value ($)
	#43	Cat People	4–8
	#44	Double issue special with two different covers: Blade Runner and Star Trek II	7–15
	#45	The Scariest Men in America	3–5
	#46	Double issue special with two different covers: Krull and the Thing	3–12
	#47	The Dark Crystal	3–5
	#48	Something Wicked This Way Comes	3–5
	#49	Double issue special . . . 3-D	4–8
	#50	The Dead Zone	3–5
	#51	20,000 Leagues Under the Sea, Firestarter, Star Trek III	3–5
	#52	Dune, Filming Lynch's Era	3–5
	#53	2010 Odyssey Two, The Company of Wolves, The Last Star Fighter	3–5
	#54	Lord of Light, Cat's Eye	3–5
	#55	Lifeforce	3–5
	#56	The Return of the Living Dead special	7–15
	#57	Legend, Enemy Mine	3–5
	#58	Psycho III, Twilight Zone, Brazil, Invader from Mars	3–5
	#59	Highlander, Ray Bradbury, John Carpenter	3–5
	#60	Invaders from Mars, Howard the Duck	3–5
	#61	Alfred Hitchcock's Psycho	3–5
	#62	Little Shop of Horrors, Star Trek IV, Captain Eo	3–5
	#63	Star Trek special	10–20

Year	Issue/Number	Description	Value ($)
	#64	Star Trek: The Movie Trilogy, Harry & the Hendersons	3–5
	#65	Little Shop of Horrors, Superman IV, Robocop	3–5
	#66	Robocop, Batteries Not Included, Star Trek: The Next Generation, Prince of Darkness, Cyberpunk	3–5
	#67	Movie Poster Artists of The Fifties	3–5
	#68	Giger, Willow, Who Framed Roger Rabbit?	3–5
	#69	Freddy Mania and Nightmare on Elm Street, Remaking The Blob	3–5
	#70	Vincent Price: Horror's Crown Prince, Cocoon II, Who Drew Roger Rabbit?	3–5
	#71	Star Trek: Behind the Scenes of The Next Generation	3–5
	#72	The Adventures of Baron Munchausen	3–5
	#73	James Bond: Licence to Kill	3–5
	#74	Batman, Beetlejuice	3–5
	#75	Tales from the Crypt, Stephen King, Beauty & the Beast	3–5
	#76	The Handmaid's Tale, Captain America	3–5
	#77	Hollywood's Forgotten Monster Maker, Back to the Future, Star Trek	3–5
	#78	Robocop 2, Gremlins 2	3–5
	#79	Dick Tracy, Robocop 2	3–5

Year	Issue/Number	Description	Value ($)
	#80	Star Trek: The Next Generation, Night of the Living Dead	3–5
	#81	Dark Shadows, Two Evil Eyes, Stephen King, Night of the Living Dead	3–5
	#82	Stephen King, Misery, James Bond, Edward Scissorhands	3–5
	#83	Arnold Schwarzenegger: Terminator 2	3–5
	#84	Teenage Mutant Ninja Turtles, Robin Hood, Terminator 2	3–5
	#85	Star Trek: The Next Generation	3–5
	#86	Star Trek: The 25th Anniversary Note: This issue has two different covers	3–5
	#87	Silence of the Lambs, Stephen King	3–5
	#88	Star Trek VI, Stephen King	3–5
	#89	Alien 3, Hellrazer	3–5
	#90	Evil Dead, Batman Returns, Honey, I Blew Up the Kid	3–5
	#91	Star Trek: The Next Generation, Batman Returns, Silence of the Lambs	3–5
	#92	Dracula, Queen of Outer Space	3–5
	#93	Babylon 5, Ren & Stimpy	3–5
	#94	Star Trek: Deep Space Nine, Meteor Man	3–5

Year	Issue/Number	Description	Value ($)
	#95	Ren & Stimpy Note: There are two different covers for this issue	3–5
	#96	Jurassic Park, Robocop 3 Note: There are two different covers for this issue	3–5

Note: Double issue specials are generally valued at $3 to $6 or $4 to $8. A recent back issue can climb in value quite rapidly if the subject featured in that issue becomes popular with collectors, such as issues with specials on *Star Trek*, cult films, and so on.

Cinefax (Don Shay Publishing)
First Issue Published in March 1980

		Value ($)
#1	Star Trek	10–20
#2–7		5–10
#8–present		4–8

Cinemacabre (Prozine Published by George Strover)

#1		10–20
All other issues		5–10

Cinemagic (Prozine Published by Cinema Enterprises)

#1–3		10–20
#4–11		3–6

Cinemagic (Published by O'Quinn)

#1	Remaking Rocketship X-M	5–10
#2–37		2–4

Cinema Odyssey (One Issue Only)

1981	For Your Eyes Only, Raiders of the Lost Ark, and Superman II exclusive behind-the-scenes photos, meet the director of Revenge of the Jedi, sexy	

Year	Issue/Number	Description	Value ($)
1981		ladies of the silver screen, the new Rocky Horror flick, interviews with John Carpenter, Susannah York, and Ray Harryhausen	3–6

Cinefan

Year	Issue/Number	Description	Value ($)
1974	#1	King Kong, Max Steiner, 2001: A Space Odyssey, Lesley Ann Warren, the Toho legend	5–10

Close Encounters of the Third Kind
(Official Authorized Edition) Warren

Year	Issue/Number	Description	Value ($)
1977		All about the astonishing film with dazzling photos	1–3

Close Encounters of the Third Kind
(Official Collectors Edition) Warren

Year	Issue/Number	Description	Value ($)
1978		The fully authorized story packed with dozens of color photographs	1–3

Communicator, The

Year	Issue/Number	Description	Value ($)
1975	Fall	Star Trek	2–4

Cracked's Collectors' Edition/Those Cracked Monsters
(Major Magazines, Inc.)
(one issue only)

Year	Issue/Number	Description	Value ($)
1978			3–6

Cracked's For Monsters Only (Major Magazines, Inc.)
(Issued from 1965 through 1972 with One Issue Being Published in 1987)

Year	Issue/Number	Description	Value ($)
	#1	The Masters of Terror	6–12
	#2	Bela Lugosi, Boris Karloff, Lon Chaney, The Munsters,	10–20
	#3	The Horror Worlds of Boris Karloff	2–10
	#4	Two Kings of Terror: Vincent Price and Christopher Lee	5–10

Year	Issue/Number	Description	Value ($)
	#5	Jack Pierce: The Man Behind the Monsters, Peter Lorre	5–10
	#6	John Carradine, Frankenstein '68	4–8
	#7	Karloff and Lugosi, Vampire Hunt '69	4–8
	#8	Fantastic Films of the 'Forties Featuring Lon Chaney, Jr.	5–10
	#9	Trog, Blood Relations	5–10
	#10	Scream and Scream Again, Dark Shadows	6–12
1967	Annual		5–10
1972	Annual		5–10
1987	Single issue		3–5

Creepy (Warren; Illustrated Horror)

	#1		10–20
	#2–15		5–10
	#16, #17		3–6
	#18–23		4–8
	#48	1973 Annual	4–8
	#55	1974 Annual	4–8
	#65	1975 Annual	3–6
	All other issues		3–5

Creepy Annual

1971			5–10+
1972			5–10+

Creepy Yearbook

1968			6–12+
1969			6–12+
1970			7–15+

Cue

1975	December	Star Trek cover and feature: Can 1999 Match Trek	3–5

Year	Issue/Number	Description	Value ($)

Curse of Frankenstein/Horror of Dracula
(one shot published by Warren)

1964		Special magazine on the two great horror flicks	5–10

Dawn of the Dead Official Poster Book
(one shot published by MM Communications)

1979		Exclusive photos from George Romero's movie, behind-the-scenes look, magazine opens to become a giant color wall poster A. with movie title on poster	10–20
1979		B. with movie title on poster/signed by Tom Savini	25–50
1979		C. with movie title on poster	30–60+

Demonique (The Journal of Obscure Horror Cinema)

		All issues	5–10

Doctor Who Weekly (British Magazine Published by Marvel Comics)

Publishing begins in 1979		All issues	2–4

Dracula (Ideal Publishing)

1977		Frank Langella as Dracula cover and feature	3–5

Dracula Classic (One Issue Only Published by Eerie Publications, Inc.)

1976		Bela Lugosi: The man who made Dracula famous, a new generation of vampires, a history of vampires, Dracula's Guest by Bram Stoker	3–6

Year	Issue/Number	Description	Value ($)

Dracula Official Movie Magazine **(Merit Publications, Inc.)**

| 1979 | | (one shot featuring Frank Langella) | 4–8 |

Dracula '79 **(One Shot Publishing by Warren)**

| 1979 | | Christopher Lee cover, the film stars who created the Dracula legend: Bela Lugosi, Frank Langella, and others, vampires of the movies: a complete photo history | 3–6 |

Dragonslayer **(Marvel Super Special #2)**

| Official Movie Edition | | | 2–4 |

Dynamite

| | #65 | Star Trek: The Motion Picture | 2–4 |

Eerie **(Warren, Illustrated Horror)**

	#1	First printing	100–200+
	#1	Second printing	100–200+
	#2		10–20
	#3		10–20
	#4–50		4–8
	All other issues		2–4

Eerie Yearbook

1970			5–10
1971			5–10
1972			5–10

Electric Company **(Published by Children's Television Network)**

1980	January	Star Trek cover and feature: The Outer Space Creatures of Star Trek	2–4
1981	January	Flash Gordon	2–3
1982	June	Star Trek Rides Again	2–3

Elvira's Mistress of the Dark **(Illustrated Movie Adaptation)**

| | #1 | | 3–6 |

#13, 1975

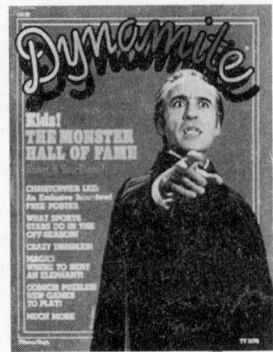

#15, 1975

#18, 1975

#25, 1976

#18

#20

#21

#22

#29

Year	Issue/Number	Description	Value ($)
Enterprise **(Star Trek)**			
	#1–13 All issues		2–4
Enterprise Incident **(Star Trek)**			
	#1, #2		10–20
	#3, #4, #12		6–12
	#5–11		5–10
	#13 and up		2–4
Enterprise Incident's Collectors' Edition			
	All issues		2–4
Enterprise Incident's Spotlight on Interviews with Star Trek Personalities			2–4
Enterprise Incident's **Spotlight on Leonard Nimoy**			2–4
Enterprise Incident's **Spotlight on the Technical Side**			2–4
Enterprise Incident's **Spotlight on William Shatner**			2–4
Enterprise Spotlight 2 **(Star Trek) One Issue Only**			
	#1		2–4
Famous Films			
1978	December	Leonard Nimoy cover and feature: Spock Speaks	4–8
Famous Monsters of Filmland **(Warren Publishing)**			
	#1	1958 . . . The behind-the-scenes story of Hollywood's House of Horrors, The 10 Most Frightening Faces Ever Filmed, Alice in Monsterland: A history of horror films, The Frankenstein Story, Out of This World Monsters, How Hollywood Creates Monsters, TV means	

#1

#2

#10

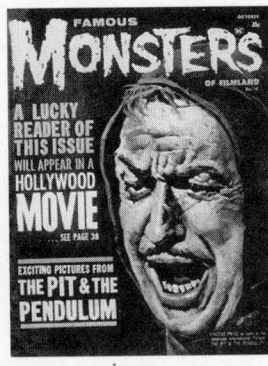

#14

#15

#16

#17

#28

#29

Year	Issue/Number	Description	Value ($)
		Terrifying Vampires, monster quiz	300–600+
	#1	British edition	250–500+
	#2	Monsters Are Badder Than Ever, The Monster Who Made a Man: Boris Karloff, Mad Magazine Creates a Monster, Girls Will Be Ghouls: All about Girls Who Have Made Good Being Bad Little Monsters, Public Vampire #1: Bela Lugosi, Terror-vision, Monsters of the World Unite, Message from the Monster	150–250+
	#2	British edition	150–200+
	#3	Photos never before seen: Boy into Monster, Frankenstein from Space	200–350+
	#4	Zacherly: How He Became King of the Ghouls in New York, The Mummy: Printed on Tanna Leaves, Christopher Lee: The Handsome Horror	200–400+
	#4	Ghoul's eye sticker cover issue	200–400+
	#5	The untold illustrated Black Lagoon story, Why They Had to Bring Back The Fly, Movies You Shouldn't See, photo contest: 10 best	200–350+
	#6	King Kong returns, sneak preview of 1960 horror films, Zacherly's shocking revival, exclusive: Secrets of The Time Machine	175–300+

Year	Issue/Number	Description	Value ($)
	#6	M. T. Graves sticker cover issue	225–375+
	#7	Zacherly: Zach comes out of his cave, cyclops and lollipops, Dr. Cyclops, mad laboratories: exclusive photos from Hollywood, Letter from a Vampire	100–170+
	#7	First pictures—tomorrow's monsters printed on cover	150–225+
	#8	Lon Chaney: Man of a Thousand Faces, What's the New Look in Monsters, 13 Ghosts photo preview, Monster Marketplace	100–200
	#9	Vincent Price from the Fall of the House of Usher cover and feature, A Strange Story about Lugosi, Rare Photos: Phantom of the Opera, how you can get monster masks by mail, giant Halloween special issue	100–150
	#10	Claude Rains is back in Phantom Returns, special movie preview special, First Time Ever: A Picture Story of Flash Gordon, a terrific article by the man who wrote Psycho	75–175
	#11	Gorgo: MGM's new release, a picture history: Dr. Jekyll and Mr. Hyde, Best Movies from Edgar Allen Poe	125–225
	#12	Curse of the Werewolf	125–225
	#13	Collector's 13th issue, Frankenstein cover,	

Year	Issue/Number	Description	Value ($)
	#13	preview: St. George and the Seven Curses, The Beasts of Tarzan, The Thing from Another World: The Monster Unmasked, The Incredible Shrinking Man, Claude Rains revealed, Rocket to the Rue Morgue, monsters in review	100–200+
	#14	Vincent Price cover and Pit and the Pendulum feature	75–150
	#15	Zacherly cover and feature: He's Back to Judge Our Makeup Contest, more mad robots issue, the return of things to come, Return of the Burn: Bob Burn, Invasion of the Body Snatchers	100–170+
	#16	Lon Chaney cover: the man who lost his face: Dick Smith, The Clown at Midnight: Robert "Psycho" Bloch Part I, The Mask, Cristiano's caricatures, Lon Chaney shall not die, free flight to Karloffornia	75–125
	#17	Elsa Lanchester as the Bride of Frankenstein cover, The Clown at Midnight: Conclusion, Lon Chaney shall not die, Glen Strange interview	50–100
	#18	Sardonicus Unmasked, War of the Colossal Beast with photos	65–100+

Year	Issue/Number	Description	Value ($)
	#19	Tales of Terror: Peter Lorre, Basil Rathbone, and Vincent Price	60–100+
	#20	Lon Chaney, The Man Who Saw King Kong Ninety Times	60–100+
	#21	The Bride of Frankenstein cover and photo filmbook, Route 66 Horror Show	100–175+
	#22	The Life and Times of Dracula: Photographs from Bela Lugosi's Own Scrapbook, eye-popping news on all future horror films, 5th anniversary special	100–175+
	#23	The most unusual Frankenstein photo ever, Son of Kong: Final Chapter, Karloff Speaks exclusive interview	50–100
	#24	Werewolf of London, a forbidden look inside the house of Ackerman, a return visit to the Phantom	50–100
	#25	King Kong: special photo filmbook . . . a photographic record never before published	60–100
	#26	Outer Limits exclusive: Things to See on TV's New Show, a new Dracula; from the other side of the world, the small and the tall of Hollywood's tiny terrors	75–125+
	#27	New fears: a preview of things and creatures to

Year	Issue/Number	Description	Value ($)
	#27	come, the voice of fiendom, conclusion of the King Kong story, Hall of Fame	50–75
	#28	Lon Chaney's Phantom Face Unmasked, The Most Exciting Collection of Horror Photos in Seven Years, two-faced monsters	50–75
	#29	The Flesh Eaters: exclusive sneak preview, Jerry Lewis attacked by monsters, Christopher Lee talks about monsters, The Mole People, The Seven Faces of Dr. Lao, The Mexicreatures	55–90
	#30	The Powers of Dracula: 25 facts about the most feared vampire of all time, Return of Frankenstein, how they made Godzilla: a report on all those great Japanese monsters, Menace of the Red Death: a hair-raising visit to the set of a new horror film	50–100
	#31	The Mummy, secrets you never knew about Lon Chaney Sr., Monster Eye: A Look at Things to Come, Return of the Creatures from South of the Border, Headlines from Horrorville	40–70
	#32	King Kong cover, the incredible Aurora—Famous Monsters Universal Pictures master monster-makers contest issue,	

Year	Issue/Number	Description	Value ($)
	#32	Horror of Dracula in comic strip, The Monsters Roll Out Their Blood-Red Carpet, The Horrible Sun Demon	50–100+
	#33	The Hunchback of Notre Dame complete photo story, Castle of Terror	15–25
	#34	Mr. Hyde, Horrors of Spider Island, Cheers for Chaney, The Stone Men Strike, Werewolf in a Girl's Dormitory, The Change of the Leech Woman, William Castle, Dr. Jekyll and Mr. Hyde filmbook	15–25
	#35	Bela Lugosi cover, When Dracula invaded England, Night of the Blood Feast, Godzilla: King of the Creatures, Headlines: All about Boris Karloff, Fay Wray, Bert Gordon, John Carradine and Velma the Vampire, Fantastic Frankensteins from France, The Gordons Will Get You: Hollywood's Monster-Making Brothers	10–20
	#36	The Mummy's Ghost, The House of Wax Face of Fire revealed, second annual amateur makeup contest issue, The Alligator People, St. George and the Seven Curses: Bert Gordon, The Return of The Fly	10–15

Year	Issue/Number	Description	Value ($)
	#37	Harryhausen's Horror from Venus, inside Lugosi's haunted house, see The Fiend Without a Face, the story of the terrifying giant monster Ymir, Village of the Giants, The Skull, the Hunch Facts of Notre Dame, 20 Million Miles to Earth filmbook, The Black Heart of Dorian Gray, Blood Creature	10–15
	#38	Curse of the Demon, Invasion of the Saucermen	75–150+
	#39	Frankenstein Conquers the World, Son of One Million Years B.C.: First Pix of Three New Harryhausen Dinosaurs, The Man who Killed The Fly: Farewell to Herbert Marshell, the men behind the monsters: a new department begins, what makes Luna tick: Carroll Borland, the 13 faces of Frankenstein: Willis O'Brien exclusive	10–15
	#40	40th Anniversary issue, Horror Hotel: Meet Its Ghastly Guest . . . Christopher Lee, dinosaurs, the Great Lugosi Mystery Solved, Mummy's Hand, Dracula after Midnight, The She Creature	8–15
	#41	The Werewolf of London, of the Mummy's tomb, the thin monster captured: exclusive interview with	

Year	Issue/Number	Description	Value ($)
	#41	John Carradine, The Black Zoo, Vampires 3: Bela Lugosi Bites Again, Farewell to Ford, Horror Hall of Fame: Favorite Fiends and Cool Scenes	6–10
	#42	Frankenstein Meets the Wolfman special, King Kong Returns, Carry on Screaming, Christopher Lee Talks about The Mummy and More	6–10
	#43	Christopher Lee as Dracula, Dracula Flies Again: It happened in Horrorwood, Fantastic Voyage, In the Days of the Dinosaurs: Lost Worlds of O'Brien and Harryhausen, Rathbone and Buster Crabbe, House of Dracula: Chaney, Atwill, Carradine and Strange, Verne Langdon Strikes Again	6–10
	#44	Willis O'Brien's King Kong, Karloff Without Makeup, Chamber of Horrors, Horror Castle: Christopher Lee, The Attack of Mr. Black, Tarantula, The Daleks Are Coming	6–10
	#45	The Projected Man, House of Wax, Vincent Price, Doctor Blood's Coffin, Return of the Vampire: Lugosi Lives Again, The Human Monster: Lugosi	6–10

Year	Issue/Number	Description	Value ($)
	#46	Vampire of the Opera, Boris Karloff in The Magic Castle, The Mummy's Shroud, The Vampire and the Ballerina, The Mole People	6–10
	#47	Phantom of the Opera: Claude Rains Comes Back, Photos of the Mad Fiend in the New James Bond Movie You Only Live Twice, Horror of Dracula, The Black Cat strikes again, Return of the Monster Ghidrah photo exclusive, Karloff: The Magic Castle	6–10
	#48	Santa Kharis, The Ghost of Frankenstein: Complete Story in Pictures, The Sorcerers, Monsterrific Movies of Tomorrow, The Monster from One Billion B.C.: A New Comic Strip	15–25
	#49	Henry Hull as the Werewolf of London, Bram Stoker's Dracula with Bela Lugosi, Hidden Horrors: The Son of Dr. Jekyl and Mr. Hyde, the Ghost of the Ghost of Frankenstein, Footsteps of Frankenstein: A Comic Strip	9–18
	#50	Gorgo: Filmbook for Prehistoric Buffs, Tarantula, Devil Bat: Bela Lugosi, Meet Mr. Nye: The Man Behind the Masks, Horror	

Year	Issue/Number	Description	Value ($)
	#50	of Dracula: A Comic Strip, 50th anniversary issue	7–15
	#51	The Wolfman: Lon Chaney in his greatest role, Curse of Frankenstein: A Comic Strip, Jane Fonda: Barbarella . . . New Pictures of the Female Flash Gordon, Boris Karloff Interviewed, Return of Kong, The Black Heart of Dorian Gray	10–15
	#52	Barnabas: The Vampire of Dark Shadows . . . exclusive photos and story, Planet of the Apes: Incredible Pictures, Death Visits Dr. Cyclops . . . Albert Dekker enters Monster Hall of Fame, Son of Frankenstein filmbook	15–25+
	#53	Flesh Crawling Monster issue	4–6
	#54	The Invasion of the Saucermen cover, Dear Mr. Lee: The British King of Monsters Talks about His Favorite Monster Movies, Lon Chaney Talks to You, Behind the Ape-Ball: Tarzan to the Rescue, King Kong returns: a special feature, Dracula 2000, Invasion of the Vampires	5–10
	#55	Land of the Giants exclusive, animals, creatures and things special	10–20+
	#56	Frankenstein: rare pictures,	

Year	Issue/Number	Description	Value ($)
	#56	all about Boris Karloff: his life in pictures, comments on Karloff's death by Christopher Lee and Peter Lorre and others, Vincent Price	35–65
	#57	The Green Slime, the original Frankenstein picture book, Invasion of the Vampires	5–10
	#58	Karloff as the Mummy, Rowan and Martin as the Werewolf in The Maltese Bippy, Lon Chaney in Return of the Vampire, Monster in the House: Karloff, the Maddest Doctor: Lionel Atwill, Frankenstein 1970	4–8
	#59	All about Barnabas Collins, Frankenstein Must Be Destroyed movie preview, Christopher Lee in Dracula Has Risen from the Grave, John Carradine exclusive interview, Lugosi's haunted house	10–20
	#60	Dorian Gray, White Zombie: Lugosi, Raland Bryce, Frankenstein Part 3, man-eating plants photo story	4–8
	#61	Mark of the Vampire: a tale of undead featuring the great Bela Lugosi	5–10
	#62	Dr. Jekyll and Mr. Hyde, The Thing, Mark of the Vampire	4–8

Year	Issue/Number	Description	Value ($)
	#63	The Fiendish Hands of Orlac featuring Peter Lorre, Boris Karloff in rare Frankenstein makeup photos	4–8
	#64	Bela Lugosi: Murders in the Rue Morgue, Boris Karloff's Grandchildren, Destroy All Monsters, Terrors of the Third Dimension: Those Great Eye-Popping 3-D Movies	4–8
	#65	The Mask of Fu Manchu: Karloff, The Phantom Stricks Again, The Seven Faces of Dr. Lao, The Man Who Made The Mummy Is No More: A Tribute to the Late Karl Freund, Beasts, Creatures and Things, When Karloff Played Chaney, girls and gouls gallery	4–8
	#66	The Old Dark House: A Filmbook on the Karloff Classic	4–8
	#67	Witches and Warlocks special issue featuring The Black Cat with Boris Karloff and Bela Lugosi	4–8
	#68	Mysterious Island issue	4–8
	#69	London After Midnight filmbook featuring Lon Chaney	4–8
	#70–79	No issues were published with the title Famous Monsters, instead numbers 70 to 79 were published under the title Monster	

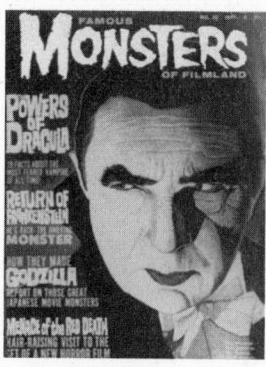

#30

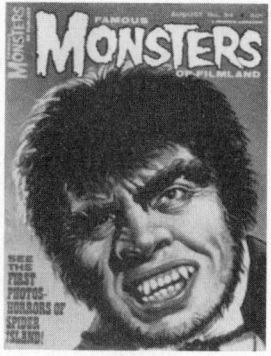

#34

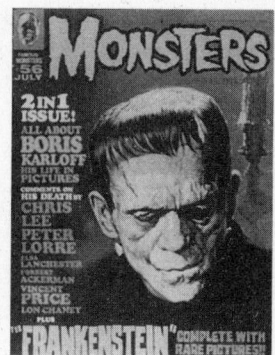

#56

#152

#163

#189

#11

1977

#1 (one shot)

Year	Issue/Number	Description	Value ($)
	#79	World and were numbered 1–10	
	#80	Beneath the Planet of the Apes, London After Midnight, Girls and Ghouls Gallery: portrait #7 . . . Florence Marly, Chasndu the Magician: Lugosi is Loose Again	15–25+
	#81	Jungle Captive cover, Island of Lost Souls filmbook, The Captive Wild Woman, Fires of Death, He Killed Dorian Gray, The House in the Twilight Zone: First of a Series	5–10
	#82	House of Dark Shadows special, Mummy's Tomb filmbook, Disneyland's House of Horrors	12–25+
	#83	The Mummy's Tomb, When Dinosaurs Ruled the Earth, The Hunchback of Notre Dame, The Raven	5–10
	#84	Christopher Lee, The Monster That Challenged the World, The Hunchback of Notre Dame, House of Dracula, The Raven: The Conclusion of the Great 1935 Universal Flick	6–12
	#85	Escape from the Planet of the Apes preview issue, Ghost of Frankenstein: Complete Story in Pictures, Faces that Launched a Thousand Shrieks	15–25

Year	Issue/Number	Description	Value ($)
	#86	The House that Dripped Blood with Christopher Lee, House of the Damned, Werewolf of London, The Masked Marvel of Monsterville: All about Don Post, Devil Bat: Bela Lugosi, Girls and Ghouls portrait #13, Fearjerkers	5–10
	#87	The She Creature, Curse of Frankenstein superspecial filmbook, photo-comics, Footsteps of Frankenstein comic strip, The Abominable Dr. Phibes	7–15
	#88	Night of Dark Shadows: First Photos of the New Movie, The Munsters, Michael Rennie: Farewell to the Master, In the Days of the Dinosaur, Blood of Kryon: Monster Comics	10–20+
	#89	Dracula versus Frankenstein, The Black Zoo, The Devil Commands, The Black Heart of Dorian Gray, Rip Van Dracula	5–10
	#90	Scream and Scream Again, Death of a Giant: Tor (Lobo) Johnson, The Black Sleep, Horror Castle, The Vampire Lovers, Attack of the Giant Tarantula, The Call of Dracula: Christopher Lee	5–10
	#91	Frogs, Godzilla versus the Smog Monster, Smile If	

Year	Issue/Number	Description	Value ($)
	#91	You Call Him Monster: The Late Basil Rathbone Interviewed, Count Yorga, Vampire, The Return of Count Yorga	10–20
	#92	Lugosi: The Life of Filmland's Dracula special issue, The Dracula Report, Public Vampire #1, The Great Lugosi Mystery, Unholy 13, Count Dracula's Vampire Ring	7–15
	#93	Tales from the Crypt cover, a special fearbook issue, The Mask: A Nightmare Movie in 3-D, Man-Eating Plants, Son of Kong, I Was a Tin Age Robot Part II, Lon Chaney Shall not die, King Kong Is Coming Back	7–15
	#94	Frankenstein, Dr. Jekyl and Sister Hyde, Shock-a-Bye Baby, How to Make a Mummy, In the Days of the Dinosaurs, Murders in the Rue Morgue, Dorian Gray Strikes Again, Fascinating Karloff Facts	5–10
	#95	Guess What Happened to Count Dracula, Attack of the Giant Insects, Conquest of the Planet of the Apes, Dr. Phibes Rises Again, Blacula	10–20
	#96	Special Wolfman issue, Letter to an Angel: Tribute to Chaney, Twins of Evil,	

Year	Issue/Number	Description	Value ($)
	#96	Hands of the Ripper, Frankenstein Meets the Wolfman, Dracula in Flames, Frankenstein and the Vampire, The Wolfman: Larry Talbot	4–8
	#97	Asylum: Attack by a Dead Hand, fight flicks in '73, Farewell to James Nicholson, Dracula after Death, Baron Blood	4–8
	#98	Invasion of the Saucermen cover, When Dracula Met the Vampires: Christopher Lee addresses the Count Dracula Society, The Black Sleep takes Tamiroff: Obituary for Akim, Blood from the Mummy's Tomb, The Thing with Two Heads, Spotlight on Lon Chaney Sr.: Happy Birthday Dear Phantom, Cheers for Chaney	2–6
	#99	Karloff, Lon Chaney Jr.: Carradine, Glenn Strange, J. Carroll Naish, House of Frankenstein sixteen-page bonus special, Blobs, Brains and Other Gooey Objects	4–8
	#100	100th great issue special, Alice in Monsterland, Farewell to Edward G. Robinson, Humorous History of Famous Monsters, The Return of Lugosi, The Bride of	

Year	Issue/Number	Description	Value ($)
	#100	Frankenstein: Mae Clarke Reminisces	20–40
	#101	Captain Marvel versus the Mysterious Scorpion, The Phantom's last fright: That Sad Day when Claude Rains Passed on to the Invisible World, Shazam, The Pit and the Pendulum, James Bond meets the Fiend, The Projected Man Revisited, Dracula 2000, Flash Gordon Attracts the World	5–9
	#102	Lon Chaney Sr.: An Incredible twenty pages on the legendary Chaney, the Diabolic Duo, Master of the Masks: Verne Langdon, Death Takes Horror Director Edgar G. Ulmer	5–10
	#103	The Creature from the Black Lagoon, Blacula Is Beautiful, the Loss of Captain Nemo: Robert Ryan, Beyond the Planet of the Apes, The Soul of a Gentle Man: This Was the Late George Macready, Farewell to Jack Hawkins, Lon is gone	10–15
	#104	The Fly, Robert Bloch, Frankennstin 1973, Son of Psycho: Bloch, The Vault of Horror	5–7
	#105	Christopher Lee Invades Los Angeles special issue,	

Year	Issue/Number	Description	Value ($)
	#105	Memorial to Glenn Strange, Abbott and Costello Meet Frankenstein, Tears for Chaney, Joe E. Brown: The Mouth That Roared	3–7
	#106	The Sun Demon cover, The Curse of the Katz-Man People: A Famous Producer Dies, The Living Ghost: John Agar, Dracula TV, The Golden Voyage of Sinbad, Vampire Circus, Witches and Demons Are Among Us	3–5
	#107	Westworld: The Frightening Amusement Park of the Future, The New Canadian Dracula, Kane Richard dies, Westmore Brothers Gone	3–5
	#108	King Kong special photo filmbook issue, The Battle for the Planet of the Apes	15–25
	#109	Vincent Price in Madhouse, Son of Kong, TV's Monsters Hall of Fame, Night of the Living Dead, Karloff Revisited	4–10
	#110	Karloff in The Ghoul, Vincent Price in The Pit and the Pendulum, The Trail of Dracula, Lon Chaney as Frankenstein, Japan's giants: Godzilla, Gigantis and Gorath, The Time Machine, Willis O'Brien farewell repeated from 1962	7–12

Year	Issue/Number	Description	Value ($)
	#111	The Exorcist, Zardoz: It's Wilder Than Oz, Young Frankenstein, Nosferatu: The Silent Vampire, Devils of Darkness	5–10
	#112	Bride of Frankenstein cover, A Unique Lugosi Feature: Such Men Are Dangerous, Warhol's Frankenstein, Fantastic Planet, End of Endora: The Death of Agnes Moorehead, Horror Express: Christopher Lee	7–12
	#113	The Mystery of the Wax Museum, Frankenstein and the Monster from Hell, Beauty Escapes the Beast: Fay Wray, Evelyn Ankers, and Barbara Steele, Otto Kruger: Time Stops, The Hunchback of Notre Dame Revealed, Return of the Ghoul, Sidney Blackermer Farewell	6–10
	#114	All of Japan monsters 100-page special issue, Godzilla: The King Kong of Kung Fu Goes Gung-ho, The Monster: Half Man and Half Monster, Frankenstein Conquers the World, Blue Kong, King Kong versus Godzilla, Mothra, The Return of Ghidrah, Boris Karloff, Lon Chaney Sr., Christopher Lee, Peter Cushing and Dwight Frye	50–100+

Year	Issue/Number	Description	Value ($)
	#115	A History of Jekyll and Hyde, Lugosi book Part I by his son, Famous Monster Convention report, Phantom of the Paradise	5–7
	#116	The Land That Time Forgot, Humphrey Bogart returns as Mr. X?, Japanese monsters, Lon Chaney's tribute to his feature	5–7
	#117	Tribute to Ray Harryhausen twenty-page special, Peter Cushing and Christopher Lee, Forrest Ackerman's Five Favorite Fright Films, Ray Harryhausen's birthday, 20 Million Miles: Part I	5–7
	#118	Ray Harryhausen's Cyclops cover, 20 Million Miles to Earth, the Peter Cushing story, 1974 Famous Monsters Convention	15–25
	#119	100-page superspectacular issue, Karloff, Lugosi, Christopher Lee, dinosaurs, Night of the Blood Beast, Horror Hotel	4–8
	#120	The Creature from the Black Lagoon cover, Never Seen Before Exorcist Pictures: The Return of Regan, Fantasy Filmcon 1975, The Devil's Rain, Fredric March tribute, Larry Vincent	5–10

Year	Issue/Number	Description	Value ($)
	#121	Boris Karloff as The Mummy cover, Those Weird Monsters from Mexico, Cher Is Frankenstein's New Bride, Rod Serling Farewell	4–8
	#122	Ingrid Pitt cover and feature, Famous Monsters Convention, The Man-made Monster filmbook, Beyond the Door, Monsters from Mexico	4–8
	#123	Special holiday issue, Plague of the Zombies cover, The Phantom lives: Lon Chaney honored, Bela Lugosi at the Deli, Go to the Devil photo feature, A Sound of Thunder, Monsters versus Stooges: The Three Stooges, Carreras and Hammer Films	5–7
	#124	Mexico vampire cover, Terror of Transylvania: Lugosi Still Lives, Frankenstein's director James Whale, The Daleks Are Coming, The Hindenburg, Monsters from Mexico	5–7
	#125	All about the New King Kong, Dark Shadows, Monsters from Mexico	5–7
	#126	Mr. Sardonicus grins again, King Kong's Colorful Crash, Lugosi's Transylvania Trip, Renfield Revisited at Last, Dr. Who	5–7

Year	Issue/Number	Description	Value ($)
	#127	New Bride of Frankenstein cover, Baby Frankenstein, The Golem's Gonna Getcha, Hammer's Horrific Monsters, The Unholy 2: Karloff and Lugosi, Exorcist Actor Dies: Lee J. Cobb, Marcel Delgado interview	5–7
	#128	Food of the Gods, Happy Birthday John Carradine, Revenge of the Zombies, The Art of Lugosi, Farewell to Freda Inescort	5–8
	#129	Futureworld cover and feature, Drac Invades England: Lugosi, At the Earth's Core, Witches and Demons, Daleks Invade England, Prehistoric Story, The Green Slime	5–7
	#130	Peter Cushing as Van Helsing cover, Specie 1999, The Mad Ghoul Part II, Squirm, The Time Travelers, Richard Arlen obituary	5–8
	#131	Christopher Lee in Horror of Dracula cover, Creatures of the Deep, Vultura: Last Chapter . . . Gene Roth Has Died, Lugosi's Hidden Films, Bride of the Monster, Bedlam: Boris Karloff	5–8
	#132	King Kong special, King Kong in New York, The Q Experiments, The Great	

Year	Issue/Number	Description	Value ($)
	#132	Lugosi, Old Kong Lives, Fritz Land: The Great Man Is Gone, Death Takes David Bruce, Here There Be Dragons	5–8
	#133	Forbidden Planet cover, Dracula after Midnight, 100 horror preview, Lugosi's last years, King Kong's Creator Dies: Marcel Delgado, The Outer Limits	5–10
	#134	Dr. Jekyl and Mr. Hyde cover, Outer Limits monsters, King Kong clashes, The Black Cat, Twin Titans of Terror, The Death of a Phantom: Jack Cassidy, Mysterious Lon Chaney	5–10
	#135	Godzilla versus Bionic Monsters, Terror Times Two, Lee Danforth, The Kentucky Fried Movie, The Black Cat Part II, Caligula and Dracula	5–10
	#136	Sinbad and the Eye of the Tiger, Close Encounters, Farewell Frankenstein, Dale Van Sickel, The Empire of the Ants, A Star is Re-Born: Robert Clarke, The Werewolf Dies: Henry Hull	4–7
	#137	Star Wars special issue, 1977 yearbook, Horror in the Lighthouse: Poe and Bloch, The Call of	

Year	Issue/Number	Description	Value ($)
	#137	Dracula: Christopher Lee, 6 Monsters for the Price of One, Black Heart of Dorian, The Mysterious Island, Devil Bat, The Unholy 13, Horror Hall of Fame, Brontosaurus Battle	7–10
	#138	Star Wars: What Science Fiction Experts Say about It, special giant summer issue, all about the amazing new Dr. Moreau, A Look at the Golden Years of Terrorvision, Stephen Boyd: His Last Voyage, Tales of Frankenstein, Reunited with Chaney, The Vampire Killers	5–10
	#139	Star Wars special: More about It, The Vampire Killers Part II, Ricardo Cortez: He Walked with Death, Werewolves, Invaders from Space, The Tribe, 50-Foot Woman Dies: Allison Hayes	7–12
	#140	The Most Hellish Frankenstein, The Incredible Films to Come, War of the Worlds Refought, When Worlds Collide Again, Star Wars rare pix, Tim Barr Is Gone	5–7
	#141	Close Encounters of the Third Kind, Godzilla, Sinbad, Alien	5–7
	#142	Star Wars cover and feature . . . Star Wars	

Year	Issue/Number	Description	Value ($)
	#142	Revisited, The Aliens Are Coming, Twilight Zone House, Starship Invasions, Star Trek, Horror Hall of Fame, Richard Carlson: Gone to the Other Side	5–7
	#143	The Mummy, Some Close Encounters, The Alien Factor, R Is for Revenge, Starcrash Flash, Twilight Zone House II	4–6
	#144	The Mummy Part II, A Lark with Quark, Special Effects, Dr. Paul Bearer	3–6
	#145	The Incredible Melting Man cover, Star Wars 2, Monster Maker's Queen, Fire, Felines Demons, Blood Banquet, Star Trek: 23rd Century, Corroll Luna Ill, Gertrude Astor Gone	3–6
	#146	Jaws versus Ape, Star Wars: Christopher Lee Talks about the Movie, Star Wars 2, Peter Cushing interview, Lost Continent	4–8
	#147	Star Wars special, Pinnacle of Terror, Carrie Fisher: Starry-Eyed Warrior, Benign King Boris, Vampire Death: Barry Atwater, Mr. Special Effects Arnold Gillespie	4–7
	#148	Darth Vader special	5–10
	#149	Battlestar Galactica special: All about Galactica, Mars Invades the Earth, Luna Lives:	

Year	Issue/Number	Description	Value ($)
	#149	Carroll Borland, Black Cat Strikes Again, Under Planet of Apes, House of Wax	5–7
	#150	Battlestar Galactica or Star Wars . . . Which One Is the Best?, Mighty Joe Young breaks loose, Dracula Quartet, Joe Bonomo Dies, Return of Frankenstein, Dear Dracula: Christopher Lee	4–8
	#151	Star Wars contest winners issue, Lord of the Rings, John Dykstra, Superman movie, Body Snatchers, Fantasy Film Festival, Warlords of Atlantis, Mighty Joe Young	4–8
	#152	Superman special issue Valerie Perrine Talks, Wide World of Monsters, Among the Vamps, Florence Marley Dies, John Carradine, Boris Karloff Lives	3–6
	#153	Nosferatu: The Terror of Transylvania, David Prowse interview, Creatures from the 7 seas	3–5
	#154	Love at First Bite, Moonraker, Alien, Amityville Horror, Meteor, All the New Vampire Films	3–5
	#155	Doctor Who, Starcrash, Alien movie preview	5–7
	#156	Alien: terrifying photos from the movie, Star Wars	

Year	Issue/Number	Description	Value ($)
	#156	2 feature with giant color foldout, Moonraker: James Bond Blasts Off	10–15+
	#157	The New Dracula: Frank Langella, Moonraker's Jaws	5–7
	#158	Alien issue, exclusive interview with H. R. Giger, The 3-D Horrors, Star Wars, Golem, House that Bled, Godzilla versus the Badair, John Chambers: Men Behind Monsters, Fascinating Facts about the First Film Frankenstein	10–15+
	#159	More on the Alien movie, All about Time after Time	10–15+
	#160	Meteor, Exclusive Buck Rogers interview, The Martian Chronicles: Science Fiction TV, The Brood, Nosferatu	4–7
	#161	Star Trek the Motion Picture, Disney's Super Space Thriller: The Black Hole, Buck Rogers, Christopher Lees New Film: Arabian Adventure	5–8
	#162	The Black Hole: A Closer Look at This Sensational Film, Star Trek: The Motion Picture special	3–6
	#163	Friday the 13th exclusive, The Fog, New Fright Films Photos	15–30
	#164	Saturn 3, The Humanoids, The Crimson Cult, Manikins of Menace	4–8

Year	Issue/Number	Description	Value ($)
	#165	The Empire Strikes Back special, Darth Vader interview	5–10
	#166	The Empire Strikes Back special	5–10
	#167	The Empire Strikes Back special, The Inside Story on Godzilla, All about The Shining	5–7
	#168	Close Encounters of the Third Kind special and 1981 yearbook	5–7
	#169	Ray Harryhausen, Alien on Earth, Fantasy Film Forecast	4–6
	#170	Battle beyond the Stars, Meet Ming the Merciless in Flash Gordon, The Awakening	3–6
	#171	Fabulous photos of the legendary Lon Chaney Sr., Flash Gordon, TV's Alien Invasion, Why Sammy Davis Jr. Loves Monster Movies	5–7
	#172	The Incredible Shrinking Women, The Omen III, Fiend, Scanners	4–6
	#173	The Devil and Max Devlin, The Funhouse, Meet Famous Film Monsters in the flesh	3–6
	#174	Star Wars special: The Empire Strikes Back	5–10
	#175	Superman II: First Photos and Story, Clash of the Titans, Raiders of the Lost Ark	5–8

Year	Issue/Number	Description	Value ($)
	#176	The Mutations cover, monster maker Terence Fisher Dead, Mindwarp, Dragonslayer, Rodan, Excalibur	5–7
	#177	Superman II, The Empire Strikes Back featuring an exclusive interview with Boba Fett, Outland Revisited, Raiders of the Lost Ark, James Bond's new flick: For Your Eyes Only	5–8
	#178	Raiders of the Lost Ark revisited, American Werewolf in London exclusive, Superman II: Terence Stamp talks, Dracula: the filmbook of the Bela Lugosi classic, Frankenstein I, II and III	5–8
	#179	Superman II, Raiders of the Lost Ark Revisited, a special interview with Zod the Villain Leader from Superman II	4–6
	#180	Frankenstein cover, The Grim Reaper, American Werewolf in London interviews, Linda Blair's Hell Night, The Mad Ghoul	5–10
	#181	Heartbeeps, The Origin of the Lost Ark, Inside the Mausoleum, Ghost Story	4–6
	#182	Mausoleum: Exclusive Photos, Ray Harryhausen's views on Clash of the	

Year	Issue/Number	Description	Value ($)
	#182	Titans, Caroline Munroe interview: story and photos, special feature: The Bloodiest Films of 1981	6–12
	#183	Swamp Thing, The Lost World	5–8
	#184	Dragonslayer, Conan, Hercules, Samson, Goliath and Atlas: Famous Barbarians of Filmland	5–8
	#185	The Mummy cover, Star Trek: The Wrath of Khan, Blade Runner, The Thing, Poltergeist, Conan, Mutant	5–7
	#186	Poltergeist, Tron, The Road Warrior, Beastmaster, Star Trek: The Wrath of Khan	6–10
	#187	Star Trek: The Wrath of Khan special	6–10
	#188	Fearbook special, Frankenstein, Mummy's Ghost, Dr. Jekyl and Mr. Hyde, The Phantom Strikes: Lon Chaney, Monster Marathon	4–8
	#189	Close Encounters of the Third Kind: Steven Spielberg the Dream-Maker, the Magic of 3-D Revealed, The Incubus, Halloween III, The Legendary John Carradine	4–7
	#190	The Empire Strikes Back, Superman III: An Exclusive Preview, Moldy Mummy Movies, Future	

Year	Issue/Number	Description	Value ($)
	#190	Fantasy Films, Wells's Time Machine, The Best Within	7–12
	#191	The Dark Crystal: An Enlightening Look, great moments reviews	5–8

Famous Monsters of Filmland Convention Magazine

1974			30–60
1975			60–120+

Famous Monsters of Filmland Do-It-Yourself Monsters Makeup Handbook (Dick Smith's)

1965	One issue only		15–25

Famous Monsters of Filmland Paperbacks

1964	#1	The Best from Famous Monsters of Filmland	60–120+
	#2	Son of Famous Monsters of Filmland	70–120+
1965	#3	Famous Monsters of Filmland Strikes Back	30–60+

Famous Monsters of Filmland Yearbook

1962			100–165+
1964			40–70
1965			30–55
1966			20–35
1967			15–25
1968			10–15
1969			10–15
1970			15–25
1971			15–25
1972			25–45+

Year	Issue/Number	Description	Value ($)

Famous Monsters Game Book (Warren)

1982		One issue only	5–10

Famous Monsters Star Wars Spectacular (Warren)

1977		How they did the special effects and other Star Wars features	10–15

Fangoria (Published by O'Quinn Studios)
1979–present

Note: Fangoria back-issue values are greatly influenced by Fangoria's back-issue department. Many back issues are available directly through Fangoria at very reasonable prices; however, when an issue is no longer offered by Fangoria the value on that particular issue can increase considerably. In some cases, if a collector shops around or attends conventions, copies can be purchased for less than the Fangoria back-issue price

Year	Issue/Number	Description	Value ($)
1979–present	#1	25 years with Godzilla, Alien photo preview, Christopher Lee interview, The Making of The Creature from the Black Lagoon, Battlestar Galactica's Lost Aliens, Dr. Who	20–30
	#2	Prophecy, Robert Bloch and Richard Matheson Interviewed, Carl Lundgren, The Making of Phantasm, War of the Worlds, Dracula, issue includes a Dr. Who poster	4–6
	#3	Christopher Lee: Arabian Adventure, Night Stalker episode guide, The Brood, the art of Mike Sullivan, Jack Arnold: Tales of the	

Year	Issue/Number	Description	Value ($)
1979–present	#3	Unexpected, issue includes a giant Alien poster	4–6
	#4	Star Trek: Spock and the New Aliens, Salem's Lot TV special, A Talk with Caroline Munroe, The Robots of Disney's The Black Hole, issue includes giant robot poster	15–25
	#5	Saturn 3, The Coming, The Fog, Monsters of Star Command, The Art of Dennis Anderson, issue includes a 16-page posterbook	7–12
	#6	Anthony Daniels in The Empire Strikes Back, Vincent Price Remembers, Count Fangor introduction, Friday the 13th: A Day for Terror, Stephen King, George Romero, Quatermass, issue includes a giant poster . . . A Tribute to Hammer Films	7–12
	#7	Jack Nicholson in The Shining, The Terror Factor, Alien Creatures from Galaxina, Savini Strikes Back: Maniac, The Hitchcock Legacy Films	4–6
	#8	Zombie, from the producers of Halloween and Fade to Black, George Pal, Escape from New York: A Talk with John Carpenter, Force Five, Horror of Dracula	5–10

Year	Issue/Number	Description	Value ($)
1979–present	#9	Motel Hell, The Howling, Terror Train, The Elephant Man, Conan	60–120
	#10	Scanners, Mother's Day, Outer Limits, Altered States, Mighty Joe Young, Hammer and Sangster	12–22
	#11	Funhouse, The Howling, My Bloody Valentine, Excalibur	12–22
	#12	Friday the 13th Part II, Hammer on TV, The Hand, Clash of the Titans, Romero's Knightriders, Tobe Hooper	12–22
	#13	Dragonslayer, The Beast Within, An American Werewolf in London, the George Romero interviews	12–22
	#14	An American Werewolf in London, The Power, Dead and Buried, Caveman, John Carpenter on Halloween II and The Thing, Shock FX special	15–25
	#15	Halloween II, On the set of Swamp Thing, Alfred Hitchcock's Television Legacy, Siskel and Ebert Talk Back, The Beast, Jamie Lee Curtis: An End to Terror, Incredible Creatures of Ray Harryhausen, Beyond Rocky Horror . . . Shock Treatment	15–25+
	#16	Ghost Story, Basket Case, Creations of Chris Tucker,	

Year	Issue/Number	Description	Value ($)
1979–present	#16	The Legendary Dick Smith, Rick Baker's EFX	4–6
	#17	The Grisley Independents . . . Pranks, The Deadly Spawn and Bloody Pulp, Ghost Story, Cat People's Screenwriter Alan Ormsby, White Doc, Dark Shadows: The Gothic Soap	4–8
	#18	Cat People: FX by Burman, Rest in Peace, John Carpenter's The Thing, The Beast Within, on the set of George Romero's Creepshow	4–8
	#19	Poltergeist, Road Warrior: Mad Max Returns, Parasite, The Thing	4–6
	#20	Creepshow's E. G. Marshall, Stephen King and George Romero, Joe Dante: After The Howling, The Scaly Star of Death Bite, The Undiscovered Joe Blasco, Fear on Film: Carpenter, Landis and Cronenberg	7–12
	#21	Rob Botton and the FX of The Thing, Friday the 13th Part III, The Sword and the Sorcerer, The Great Zacherly, Monsters versus Wrestlers	4–8
	#22	Halloween III/Season of the Witch, George Romero on Creepshow, Friday the 13th Part III: The FX, Pink Floyd's The Wall, Elvira, Ingrid Pitt	4–8

Year	Issue/Number	Description	Value ($)
1979–present	#23	Evil Dead, Poltergeist, Halloween III: The Effects, The Dreaded Incubus, Texas Chainsaw Massacre	7–12
	#24	XTRO, The Grisly FX of Steve Neilli, Larry Cohen's Q, The Sender, Poltergeist's FX, Klaus Kinski	4–8
	#25	Videodrome: TV with Guts, Tom Savin, Scalps, Gordon on Wood, The Editorial Famous Monsters Wouldn't Print	4–8
	#26	The Hunger's Dick Smith's FX, Ed French, Amityville II FX, issue includes Scream Greats poster #1	4–8
	#27	Grande Illusions: Gore and Me by Tom Savini, The Timewalker, Evil Dead, Psycho II, Forrest J. Ackerman on Lon Chaney	4–8
	#28	Spasms, On the Set of The Dead Zone and Psycho II, The Deadly Spawn, Veronica Carlson, Fullerton and Buechler, Scream Greats poster #3 . . . Friday the 13th Part III	3–6
	#29	Gates of Hell, Jaws 3-D, Brain of Blood, Rotted Flesh, Twilight Zone: Behind the Scenes, The Dead Zone, An American Werewolf in London, Dead of Night, Scram Greats poster #4 . . . An American Werewolf in London	3–6

Year	Issue/Number	Description	Value ($)
1979– present	#30	The Nightmare Effects of Twilight Zone, John Carpenter on Halloween, Cujo: Behind the Scenes, Joe Dante Speaks, Freda Francis, James Herbert, Vincent Price, Scream Greats poster #5 . . . The Beast Within	3–6
	#31	Amityville 3-D, Dead Zone, Exorcist FX, The Keep, Matheson, Scream Greats poster #6 . . . The Funhouse	3–6
	#32	Christine, Scorsese on Cronenberg, Cujo FX, C.H.U.D., Stan Wilson, Friday the 13th poster	4–6
	#33	The SFX of The Keep, Christine, Splatter, Futurekill, Strange Invaders FX, Ed French, Italian Zombies, The Shining poster	4–7
	#34	The Terror of Mutant, Stephen King's Firestarter: On the set, Chainsaw's Ed Neal, The Hills Have Eyes, Reardon and Dreamscope, Videodrome poster	3–6
	#35	Ozzy Osbourne's Bark at the Moon, Stephen King's Children of the Corn, Firestarter, Baker, Twilight Zone: The Movie poster	3–6
	#36	Friday the 13th: The Final Chapter, Stephen King's Firestarter, The Brood poster	3–6

Year	Issue/Number	Description	Value ($)
1979– present	#37	Gremlins: Interview with Joe Dante, Dick Miller, The Hills Have Eyes, Mark Shostrom FX, Creepshow poster	8–12
	#38	The Fantastic Gremlins FX, Friday the 13th, The Mutilator, Jonathan Haze, Salem's Lot poster	4–8
	#39	The Makeup FX of V, Ghostbusters FX, Jason versus Michael Meyers, Attack of the 50-Foot Women, Gremlins FX, Dreamscape, Amityville 3-D poster	3–6
	#40	Return of the Living Dead, Ghostbusters FX, Nightmare on Elm Street, Night of the Comet, Arnold Schwarzenegger on The Terminator, Michael McDowell, Hammer's Vamps, Ghostbusters poster	7–12
	#41	Ghoulish FX of The Jacksons Torture, Christopher Lee Speaks, The Terminator, C.H.U.D., Darkside, Larry Buchanam, Motel Hell poster	3–6
	#42	The Nightmare World of Company of Wolves, Stephen King and Peter Straub on The Talisman, Body Double, Blood Simple Christopher Lee, Silent Night, Deadly Night	3–6

Year	Issue/Number	Description	Value ($)
1979– present	#43	Day of the Dead: On the Set, Cat's Eye, House on Haunted Hill, Silver Bullet, John Ashley Rambaldi FX, Creepshow poster	3–6
	#44	Friday The 13th: A New Beginning, After the Fall of New York, Return of the Living Dead, Nightmare on Elm Street, Jonathan Frid, Company of Wolves, Friday the 13th poster	3–6
	#45	Friday the 13th: A New Beginning, Elm Street's Scream Queen: Heather Langenkamp, Elvira, Creepshow poster	3–6
	#46	Lifeforce: Interview with Tobe Hooper, The re-Animator, Day of the Dead, Night of the Living Dead, Zombies, Caroline Munroe Nightmare on Elm Street poster	3–6
	#47	Day of the Dead: Tom Savini's FX, Mad Max Beyond Thunderdome, Lifeforce FX, Fright Night, Terminator poster	3–6
	#48	Return of the Living Dead, Tales from the Darkside, Fright Night, Silver Bullet, Stephen King revisited, Day of the Dead poster	3–6
	#49	Nightmare on Elm Street: Freddy's Revenge, Fright Night: Makeup FX,	

Year	Issue/Number	Description	Value ($)
1979–present	#49	Creepers, Silver Bullet, The Howling II, Fright Night poster	3–6
	#50	Nightmare on Elm Street II, The Re-Animator, Hammer Monster Secrets, Tom Savini, The Twilight Zone, Angelo Rossitto	3–6
	#51–Present		3–6

Fangoria: Bloody Best of

	#1–4		10–20
	#5		5–10
	#6		10–15
	#7		5–10
	#8 up		5–10

Fangoria/Freddy:
The Official Magazine of Nightmare on Elm Street   5–10

Fangoria Postcards Magazine

	#1		5–8

Fangoria Poster Magazine
Each issue contains 10 color wall posters

	All issues		5–8
	Volume I up		5–7

Fantastic Films (Blake Publishing Corporation, Fantastic Films Magazine, Inc.)

Year	Issue/Number	Description	Value ($)
1978–1985	#1	Close Encounters of the Third Kind, Star Wars, The Day the Earth Stood Still	7–12
	#2	Superman, Close Encounters of the Third Kind	7–9
	#3	Special Effects issue	8–12
	#4	Metamorphoses, The Lord of the Rings, Greg Jein Interview	5–7

Year	Issue/Number	Description	Value ($)
1978–1985	#5	Battlestar Galactica, Star Trek, The Outer Limits	5–10
	#6	Battlestar Galactica, The Lord of the Rings	4–8
	#7	The Selling of Superman, Star Wars, The Lord of the Rings	5–10
	#8	Superman, Star Wars	5–10
	#9	First Alien issue	10–15
	#10	First All-Alien Cover	15–20
	#11	Second All-Alien cover	15–20
	#12	Alien Feature	5–10
	#13	Godzilla and His Creators, Meteor	5–8
	#14	Star Trek, The Black Hole	4–8
	#15	The Black Hole, Star Trek	4–8
	#16	Saturn 3, The Fog	4–8
	#17	The Empire Strikes Back	3–6
	#18	The Empire Strikes Back	3–6
	#19	The Empire Strikes Back	3–6
	#20	Special Collectors Edition . . . Clone Wars Explained	3–6
	#21	Special Collectors Edition . . . Asteroid Worm Captured/Forbidden Planet	3–6
	#22	The Very Best of Fantastic Films, Star Wars, Empire Strikes Back	4–8
	#23	Special . . . From Star Wars to The Empire Strikes Back	4–8
	#24	Star Wars, Excalibur	4–8
	#35	Return of the Jedi	5–10+
	#25–46		3–6

Fantastic Monsters of the Films (Black Shield Publications)

1962–1963	#1		30–60
	#2, #3		35–65
	#4–7		25–45

Year	Issue/Number	Description	Value ($)
Fantastic Worlds			
	All issues		7–12
***Fantasy Empire* (Dedicated to Dr. Who and Published by New Media Publishing, Inc.)**			
	All issues		5–10
***Fantasy Enterprises* (One Issue Only)**			
1985	*Star Trek*		3–6
***Fantasy Film Guide Book: 1969* (Zine Published by The Sci-Fi Club)**			
1968	#1		10–20
***Fantasy Film Journal* (Published by Quarterly Nostalgia Graphics)**			
1977	#1	Special Star Wars issue including an interview with John Dykstra	4–8
Fantasy Image			
1985	March #2	Star Trek	4–8
Fantasy Magazine Index			
1976			12–22
	All other issues		4–8
***Fear of Darkness* (Bizarre and Unusual Cinema)**			
	All issues		7–12
Femme Fatale			
1992	#1, #2, #3		7–12
***Film Fantasy Yearbook* (Warren Publishing)**			
1982	#1	Raiders of the Lost Ark, Dragonslayer, Superman II, An American Werewolf in London, The Howling, Outland, Clash of the Titans, Wolfen, Friday the 13th Part II	5–10
1983		E.T., Star Trek II, Tron, The Thing, Halloween III, The Road Warrior, Conan, Creepshow, Poltergeist	4–8

Summer #1, 1992

#14

#1

May (one shot) 1977

#1

September #10, 1979

#1

#1

Winter 1978

Year	Issue/Number	Description	Value ($)

***Filmfax* (Michael Stein Publishing)**

Year	Issue/Number	Description	Value ($)
1986	#1	Space Patrol: Behind the Scenes with the Original Cast and Crew, actor Dick Miller: His Early Years with Roger Corman, The Bowery Boys: The Director Tells It, Cult Films . . . Plan 9 from Outer Space and Tobor the Great	100–150+
	#2	Invaders from Mars: The 1953 Classic versus the 1986 Remake, Space Patrol Part II, Abbott and Costello, Gumby Animator	65–125+
	#3	All Horror issue special, Bela Lugosi: The Final Years, Gloria Stuart on The Old Dark House, Dark Shadows' Vampire Jonathan Frid, Classic Scare Comedies, Reginald Leborg, Shock and Schlock of William Castle	15–25+
	#4	The Men in The Grey Rubber Suit special edition, Space Patrol, Plan 9 from Outer Space, The Adventures of Captain Midnight, Forrest J. Ackerman, Dick Miller, Candid Horror Photo Album, Films of Ed D. Wood Jr., Tobor the Great	15–25+
	#5	Little Shop of Horrors, The Big Bug Films of the 1950s	30–60+

Year	Issue/Number	Description	Value ($)
1986	#6	Beverly Garland: Her Early Years, Forrest J. Ackerman on Elsa Lanchester, Gimmick Films, Friends of Ed D. Wood Jr.	30–60
	#7	Four decades of Horror Noir film classics	35–65
	#8	Special flying saucer anniversary edition, First UFO Film, The Flying Saucer, Earth versus the Flying Saucers, The Three Stooges in Orbit, Battle in Outer Space, Flying Disc Man from Mars	25–45+
	#9	The Best of Filmfax 100-page special, Space Patrol TV, Adventures of Captain Marvel, Plan 9 from Outer Space, Tobor the Great, Candid Horror Photo Album, Films of Ed D. Wood Jr.	15–25+
	#10	Special 100-page anniversary issue, Bob Hope interview on his early career, The Films of Allison Hayes and Ed D. Wood, Night of the Ghouls, Robert Stack on Colorization, Cat and the Canary, Space Patrol	15–25+
	#11	Detour Retrospective, Films of Edgar Ulmer: Part 1, Moe's Daughter Remembers the Three Stooges, Tom Neal Jr., Lost City of the Jungle,	

Year	Issue/Number	Description	Value ($)
1986	#11	The Death of TV Superman George Reeves	15–25+
	#12	The Man from Planet X, The Bat Whispers, Douglas Fairbanks Jr. interview, The Films of Edgar Ulmer: Part 2, Tod Browning's Freaks, Jungle Girl serial, Virginia Karns and Lois Laurel interviews on Laurel and Hardy	20–35+
	#13	Boris Karloff, A History of TV Horror Hosts, Superman overview and interviews with cast, The Ritz Brothers and the Gorilla, Ben Welden interview, One Step Beyond and the John Newland interview, Curt Siodmak interview	20–35+
	#14	Zacherly interview, John Carradine tribute, the Marx Brothers' lost sitcom, Stanley Kramer interview, Veronica Carlson interview, Jungle Jim, Mad Love, Curt Siodmak interview	20–35+
	#15	Mel Blanc interview, Robinson Crusoe on Mars, Monogram Pictures, Ken Tobey interview, The Making of The Attack of the B Movie Monster, Perils on Nyoka, Ingrid Pitt interview, Return to Robin Hood's Sherwood Forest	8–15+

Year	Issue/Number	Description	Value ($)
1986	#16	The Complete History of Batman . . . Serials and TV, Adam West, Yvonne Craig, Gorilla Stuntman Steve Calvert, Carnival of Souls, The Lost Worlds of Willis O'Brien, Sabu Colossus of New York	8–15+
	#17	Science Fiction Theatre, Richard Webb interview, Captain Midnight, The Day the Earth Stood Still, Michael Rennie, The Angry Red Planet, Glamour Girls from Outer Space, The Queen of Outer Space	10–15+
	#18	The Monster of Piedras Blancas, Bela Lugosi's Last Screen Rites, Brain Movies, The Brain That Wouldn't Die, Great Horror Detectives	10–15+
	#19	Rocky Jones, Space Ranger, Arthur Dagwood Lake, Barbara Steele, The Monster That Challenged the World, William Bakewell on Douglas Fairbanks Sr., Thief of Bagdad	10–15+
	#20	Lon Chaney Jr.'s last interview, TV's Rocky Jones, Space Ranger: Part 2, Serial King Henry Macrae, Hazel Count, Robert Campbell on Working with Roger Corman, Jock Mahoney	10–15+

Year	Issue/Number	Description	Value ($)
1986	#21	Men into Space TV Science Fiction Docudrama, SPFX Makeup Artist Harry Thomas, Lon Chaney Jr. Remembered: Part 2, The History of Dick Tracy, Virginia Christine interview, Forrest J. Ackerman on His Late Wife Wendayne	7–15+
	#22	I Was a Teenage Werewolf exclusive, Abbott and Costello Meet-Movies, director Gene Fowler and actor Whit Bissel interviewed, Laurette Luez star of Prehistoric Women interviewed, Dick Tracy Part 2, B Movies' Hidden Heroines	7–12+
	#23	Mamie Von Doren, Bwana Devil: A 3-D Classic, Huntz Hall, Sylvia Sydney interview, Tugid Teen Films, Ackerman's Hellvision, Prehistoric Women, Sam Abarbanel	7–12+
	#24 up		7–12+

Note: Prices for *Filmfax* are greatly influenced by the publisher, which offers many issues through its back-issue department. Most of these publisher-offered issues are priced at $10 to $15 each for mint copies only one month after they are off the newsstands or have been sent out via subscription. When a back issue is no longer offered by *Filmfax,* that particular issue can easily double or even triple in value.

Year	Issue/Number	Description	Value ($)

Films Fortnightly **(British Magazine Published by London Publications)**

1971	April 3	Godzilla cover and feature, Science Fiction Film special	15–20+

Frankenstein Classic **(Modern Day Periodicals)**

1977	One issue only		5–7

Future/Future Life **(O'Quinn Studios)**

1978–1981	#1	Close Encounters of the Third Kind Special Effects	4–6
	#2–31		3–4

Future Fantasy **(Cousins Publications, Inc.)**

1978	(published in February, April, and June) #1	Beautiful Space Heroines, Close Encounters of the Third Kind, Captain Cosmos, William Shatner: Spider Fighter, Futuristic Sounds of the Rock Group Kiss, Pink Floyd, Todd Rundgren, Robert Takeover, Science Fiction Art	7–12

Note: Issue #1's value is based more on its popularity with collectors of the rock group Kiss than collectors of monster magazines

	#2	Close Encounters of the Third Kind, Flying Saucer in Fact and Fantasy, Authentic UFO Photos, Peter Frampton Meets R2D2, Godzilla, Captain Cosmos, Dammation Alley	4–8
	#3	Close Encounters versus Star Wars, The Resurrection of Star Trek	4–8

Year	Issue/Number	Description	Value ($)

Galactic Journal (One Issue Only)

1987		Director Paul Verhoeven on Robocop, Star Trek: The Next Generation and Robin Curtis on the Old Generation	6–12

Ghoul Tales (Stanley Publications, Inc., Illustrated Horror)

1970	#1 (November vol. 1, #1)	The Bogeyman, The Voice of Doom, Terror on TV, Destiny's Double Deal	10–20
1971	#2 (January vol. 1, #2)	You Look Good Enough to Eat, The Curse of the Pirate's Gold, Bloody Spawn of the Cat, The Evil Eye	8–15
	#3 (March vol. 1, #3)	Corpse in the Coffin, Voodoo Dolls, The Witches' Curse, Eternal Death	6–12
	#4 (May vol. 1, #4)	Terror of the Deep, Bloodstone, Medusa's Head, Death Takes a Holiday	7–14
	#5 (July vol. 1, #5)	The Buried Curse Werewolfs of the Rockies, The Evil Secret of Black Hollow, Undying Brain	6–12

Gore Creatures (Prozine)

	#1, #2		20–35
	#2–9		15–30
	#10 up		6–12

Gorezone (O'Quinn Studios)

Note: Back issues of *Gorezone* can be purchased directly through the publisher.

	#1		4–8
	All other issues		3–6

Year	Issue/Number	Description	Value ($)

Gothism **(Prozine)**

| | All issues | | 5–12 |

Gremlins Souvenir Magazine **(Official Collector's Edition)**

| 1984 | | All about Gremlins with exclusive interviews | 3–6 |

Halls of Horror **(Formerly *House of Horror/House of Hammer*)**
Note: British monster magazine with American distribution

	#21	Christopher Lee, Boris Karloff, The Werewolf, Warlords of the Deep	6–12
	#22	Christopher Lee/The Mummy	5–10
	#23	Enemy from Spece, Frankenstein	5–10
	#24	Seven Shock-Filled Creature Classics special . . . Aliens, Vampires, Dragons, and Monsters	5–10
	#25	The Spawn of Psycho: The Robert Bloch Interview, Hammer's Psycho Screamers, The History of Slash Movies	5–10
	#26	Masters of the Macabre special . . . Karloff, Lugosi, Pleasence, Carradine, and Lorre, Barbara Steele interview, The House of the Long Shadows	5–10
	#27	Special Blood Hunters edition featuring Jaws 3-D and The Night Stalker, Brides of Dracula	5–10+
	#28	Vincent Price on film and Video, Close-up on Ingrid Pitt, Brides of Dracula, H. G. Lewis	5–10+

Year	Issue/Number	Description	Value ($)
	#29	Mad Max: The Day After, The Poetry of Evil: Vincent Price, Mutant	6–12
	#30	Horror Fantasy and Science Fiction: An A-to-Z Guide	5–10

Heidi Saha (an Illustrated History of, Published by Warren)

	One shot		20–40

Horror Monsters (Charleton Publications)

Year	Issue/Number	Description	Value ($)
1961–1965	#1	How to Build Your Own Monster	20–40
	#2	The Pit and the Pendulum	20–40+
	#3	The Mask, The Devil's Hand, Bloodlust, The Stein of Frankenstein	15–30
	#4	Shock Theatre, Mummy's Curse, Bob Burns: Man of Horror	15–25
	#5	The Head: Peter Lorre . . . The Little Giant of Monsterland, Burn Witch Burn	12–25
	#6	Frankenstein 1970, Dracula	10–20
	#7	Werewolf in a Girls' Dorm	10–15
	#8	The Brain That Wouldn't Die, Where Monsters Walk, The Fly	12–25
	#9	The House on Haunted Hill, The Black Sleep, George Zucco	10–15
	#10	The Curse of Frankenstein, The Black Sleep, Vincent Price special	10–15

Horror Movie Yearbook (Warren Publishing)

Year	Issue/Number	Description	Value ($)
1981		Friday the 13th, Fade to Black, The Fog, The Changeling, The Shining,	

Year	Issue/Number	Description	Value ($)
1981		Without Warning, The Alien, Silent Scream, etc.	5–10

***Horror of Party Beach* (Warren Publishing)**

1964			6–12

***Horror Tales* (Eerie Publications: Illustrated Horror)**

Year	Issue/Number	Description	Value ($)
1969	#1 (June vol. 1 #7)	Satan's Plaything, Screams in the Night	10–20
	#2 (August vol. 1 #8)	Wall of Blood, This Head Is Mine	10–15
	#3 (November vol. 1 #9)	The Slime Creatures, Werewolf, Bury Her Deep	8–16
1970	#4 (January vol. 2 #1)	House of Monsters, The Witch and the Werewolf	6–12
	#5 (March vol. 2 #2)	Witches' Nightmare, Ghoul Without Pockets, The Slimy Gargoyle	5–10
	#6 (May vol. 2 #3)	Tombstone for a Ghoul, Monster Nightmare	5–10
	#7 (July vol. 2 #4)	Vampires from Beyond, The Doom Witch	5–10
	#8 (September vol. 2 #5)	Into the Land of Ghoulish Monsters, Vampires and Things from Beyond	5–10
	#9 (November vol. 2 #6)	Spine-Chilling Horror from the Edge of Darkness	5–10
1971	#10 (January vol. 3 #1)	The Terror of the Mummy, The Shocking Death of the Witch, The Terrifying Satan the Demon	5–10
	#11 (March vol. 3 #2)	Body Snatcher, Sawdust Banshee	5–8
	#12 (May vol. 3 #3)	The Bloody Thing, Zombie Magic	5–8
	#13 (July vol. 3 #4)	The Witches' Coven, Curse of the Vampire	5–8
	#14 (September	The Vampire Lives, The	

July 1970

January 1971

March 1971

April 1974

April 1973

August 1973

August 1974

October 1974

December 1970

Year	Issue/Number	Description	Value ($)
1971	vol. 3 #5)	Curse of the Dead Witch, The Nightmare	4–8
	#15 (November vol. 3 #6)	The Blood Demon, The Weird and Beastly Monsters, The Wild One	4–8
1972	#16 (January vol. 4 #1)	The House of Blood, The Monster, Satan's Corpse	4–8
	#17 (March vol. 4 #2)	The Hairy Beast, Walls of Fear	4–8
	#18 (April vol. 4 #3)	Special Total Shock Issue, The Terrifying Bloody Corpse, The Mad Ones	4–8
	#19 (June vol. 4 #4)	The Ghastly Terror of the Skeleton, The Rhyme of Shock	4–8
	#20 (August vol. 4 #5)	The Demon, Grotesque	4–8
	#21 (October vol. 4 #6)	The Ghoul, Bloody Nightmare	4–8
	#22 (December vol. 4 #7)	The Devil's Witch, The Corpse That Lives	4–8
1973	#23 (February vol. 5 #1)	The Blood-Chilling Flesh-Eaters, Terror Below	4–8
	#24 (April vol. 5 #2)	The Bloody Wolfman, Ghoul's Mansion	4–8
	#25 (June vol. 5 #5)	Blood-Sucking Vampires Strange Monsters and Evil Beings	5–10
	#26 (August vol. 5 #4)	The Manbeast, The Evil One	4–8
	#27 (October vol. 5 #5)	The Monster in Cloth, The Mad Witch	5–10
	#28 (December vol. 5 #6)	Circle of Terror, Deadman's Tomb, The Devil You Say?	4–8
1974	#29 (February vol. 6 #1)	The Grotesque Checkmate, The Spooks, The Tomb of Hate	3–7

Year	Issue/Number	Description	Value ($)
1974	#30 (April vol. 6 #2)	The Awesome Demons and Skeletons, Satan's Toys, Fang of Revenge	4–8
	#31 (June vol. 6 #3)	The Blood-Chilling, Living Dead, Head-Chopper, The Fighting Vampire	4–8
	#32 (August vol. 6 #4)	The Vampires, The Spirit of Evil, The Broomstick Witch	4–8
	#33 (October vol. 6 #5)	Skin Crawlers, Evil Idol	4–8
	#34 (December vol. 6 #6)		4–8
1975	#35 (February vol. 7 #1)	The Screaming Hell, Signed in Blood, The Creatures' Crypt	
1976	#36 (May vol. 7 #2)	Jumbo-size giant issue Never Kill a Corpse, Vampire Bride, Cats of Doom, Satan's Revenge, Horror with Fangs	6–12
	#37 (August vol. 7 #3)	Jumbo-size giant issue	6–12
	#38 (November vol. 7 #4)	Jumbo-size giant issue House of Blood, The Vampire Files, The Thing, The Supernatural, Satan's Demon, The Dead Demons	5–10
1977	#39 (May vol. 8 #2)	Jumbo-size giant issue Curse of the Vampire, Nightmare in Blood, Spirit of the Witch, Pool of Evil	6–12
	#40 (August vol. 8 #4)	The Head-Chopper, The Skeletons, The Fanged Freak	5–10

Year	Issue/Number	Description	Value ($)
1977	#41 (November vol. 8 #5)		5–10
1978	#42 (February vol. 9 #1)	The Demon, Tear 'em Apart, Bloodsucker, The Skull	5–10
	#43 (May vol. 9 #2)	The House of the Vampire, Head Full of Snakes, Black Light Terror	5–10
	#44 (August vol. 9 #3)	Swamp Monster, The Vampire, Voodoo Terror, Satan's Pit of Evil, Nightmare in Blood	5–10
	#45 (November vol. 9 #4)		5–10

House of Hammer
(British horror magazine dedicated to Hammer Films, published by Top Sellers, Ltd./Quality Communications)

	#1	Dracula: An Illustrated Adaptation	6–15
	#2	The Curse of Frankenstein, The Texas Chainsaw Massacre	6–12
	#3	All Monster special	6–12
	#4	Legend of the Seven Golden Vampires	6–12
	#5	Death in Space, Peter Cushing	6–12
	#6	Dracula: Prince of Darkness	10–15
	#7	Burn Witch Burn, Twins of Evil	6–12
	#8	Shandor, The Quatermass Experiment, King Kong, Christoper Lee's New Dracula Film, Jekyl and Hyde, Hammer's Science Fiction	5–10

Year	Issue/Number	Description	Value ($)
	#9	Carrie, King Kong, Squirm, Seizure	5–10
	#10	Curse of the Werewolf, Sentinel, Satan's Slave	4–8
	#11	Peter Cushing is Tender Dracula, Ray Harryhausen on Horror, Zoltan, The Gorgon	6–12
	#12	Witchfinder General, The Exorcist II: The Heretic, The Gorgon	6–12
	#13	Plague of the Zombies, Star Wars, Mansion of the Doomed, Victor Frankenstein, Blood City	10–15+
	#14	Raquel Welch: One Million Years B.C., John Carradine interview	15–20+
	#15–#18		5–10

House of Horror (Formerly House of Hammer)

Year	Issue/Number	Description	Value ($)
	#19	Revenge of the Blood Beast, The Yeti, Frankenstein, Dracula, The Reptile: The Full Film in Comic Form	6–12
	#20	Kronos, The Incredible Melting Man, The Mummy, Savage Bees	4–8

House of Horror (American Edition)
(Top Sellers, Ltd/Quality Communications)

Year	Issue/Number	Description	Value ($)
	#1	Curse of the Werewolf, Boris Karloff, Vincent Price, George Romero	10–20

House of Horror (Warren Publishing)

Year	Issue/Number	Description	Value ($)
	#1	Frankenstein cover	325–425

Note: Only 400 copies of this issue were printed and prices of over $600

Year	Issue/Number	Description	Value ($)

have been paid in the past. It is advisable to offer this issue as a bid item: this way the seller will attain the fairest current market value.

Incredible Science Fiction (Science Fantasy Film Classics, Inc.)

1978	#1	The Creature from the Black Lagoon, Five Million Years to Earth, Aliens and Monsters special	5–10

Journal of Frankenstein (Published by New World Enterprises, Syndicated, Inc.)

1959	#1	The Boris Karloff Story: Master of Horror, The History of Horror Movies: All Manner of Fantasies, House on Haunted Hill, John Zacherly	60–110

Journal of Popular Film and Television

1984	Summer	Star Trek	3–6

King Kong (Sportscene Publications)

1977		The Monster That Made History, issue contains an amazing King Kong poster	6–12

King of the Monsters (Cousins Publications)

1977		The New Kong Movie, Konga and the Monster Menagerie, Kogar the Ape, Kong on Stage	5–10

Kong (Countrywide Communications, Inc)

1976		The Most Famous Monster of All Time special, includes a poster	6–12

Larry Ives' Monster and Heroes (M & H Publications)

1967–1968	#1	A History of Frankenstein, Johnny Shefield Filmland's

Year	Issue/Number	Description	Value ($)
1967–1968	#1	Son of Tarzan, TV's Costume Heroes, Heroes of Radio, Bat-Men of Darkest Africa	12–22
	#2	The Monster Men of ERB, The Origin of Altron Boy, The Four Faces of Captain America, The Creators and Actors of Superman	10–17
	#3	The Creation of King Kong, Heroes of TV, Captain Video, The Burroughs Library	7–15
	#4	Movie Serials, Captain Marvel, Werewolves in the Movies	5–10
	#5	The Creation of Frankenstein, Radio's Captain Midnight, Boris Karloff	6–12
	#6	Flash Gordon, The World of John Carter, Buster Crabbe	5–10
	#7	The Green Hornet, The Mummy	20–40

Legend Horror Classics (British Monster Magazine)

	All issues		5–10

Mad Monsters (Charlton Publications)

Year	Issue/Number	Description	Value ($)
1961–1965	#1	Konga: A Picture Preview, Saint George and the 7 Curses, Reptilicus: The Evil Creature from a Time Long Dead, Black Sunday, The Truth about Monsters	15–25
	#2	The Creature from the Black Lagoon cover, Bela Lugosi: Horror Master,	

Year	Issue/Number	Description	Value ($)
1961–1965	#2	House of Horrors, The Brides of Dracula, Werewolf Album	15–20
	#3	Boris Karloff: The Master Monster Talks, She-Beasts on the Prowl, The Immortal Monster Caltoki, Mystery of Black Magic, Attack of the Mad Monsters: Beings from Outer Space	15–20
	#4	The Beast of Yucca Flats, The House of Frankenstein, Invasion of the Body Snatchers	15–25
	#5	Frankenstein Meets the Wolfman: Lugosi and Chaney, Abbott and Costello Meet the Monsters, The Three Stooges in Orbit, Journey to the Seventh Planet	15–25
	#6	Boris Karloff: Man of a Million Horrors, Anthony Quinn in The Hunchback of Notre Dame, The Day of the Triffids full-length feature, The Black Zoo Party, Monster on the Campus	15–25
	#7	I Married a Monster from Outer Space, Corridors of Blood, King Kong versus Godzilla	15–25
	#8	Lon Chaney Jr.: Champion of Chills, The Strangler: Mad Monster on the Loose, The Giant	

Year	Issue/Number	Description	Value ($)
1961–1965	#8	Behemoth, Devil Bat: A Chilling Classic	15–23
	#9	Vincent Price: The Masque of the Red Death, Witness the Creation of the Devil Wolf of Shadow Mountain, Chill to Goliath and the Vampires, The Bat	15–22
	#10	Zombies: The Incredibly Strange Creatures, Cult of Horror special, Basil Rathbone: Demon of Distinction, The Mummy	30–60+
1981		Christopher Lee cover and feature, Altered States, The Howling's Success, Raiders of the Lost Ark	20–40+

Magus (RGM Publications)

1981	One issue only		25–60+

Media Spotlight (IRJAX Enterprises, Inc.)
Publishing begins in 1976

	#1	Star Trek Lives Again, Gene Roddenberry and the Star Trek movie	6–12
	All other issues		4–8

Midnight Marque (Prozine)

	#1		20–40
	#2–4		15–30
	#5, #6		15–25
	#7–15		10–15
	#16 up		10–15

Modern Monsters (Prestige Publications)

1966	#1	King Kong, A New Look at Frankenstein, That Other Werewolf	15–30

#1

#4

#5

#6

#8

#2, 1962

#5, 1963

#6, 1963

#9, 1964

Year	Issue/Number	Description	Value ($)
1966	#2	Count Dracula, Blood, Bullets and Bond, Nick Adams interview	15–25
	#3	The Mummy, The Cosmis Cliffhangers	15–25
	#4	The Invisible Man, King Kong: A Double Take, Spy Smasher, The Green Hornet Strikes	15–25

Mole People, The **(Warren Publishing)**

1964		A Terrifying Story Told in 500 Photos from the Film	5–10

Monsterama **(Forrest J. Ackerman's)**

1991	#1	Karloff, Lugosi, Chaney, the Wolfman	5–10+
	#2		4–8+

Monster Attack
(Illustrated horror and movie photos and stories.)

	All issues		3–6

Monster Fantasy **(Mayfair Publications)**

1975	#1	The Vampire Book: The Legends, The Movies and Terrifying Reality, My Father Peter Lorre: An Exclusive Interview, Sea Creatures and Space Ghouls, Frankenstein's Latest Monster, Horror Headguarters: London Report	5–10
	#2	The Book of the Mummy: A Full-Length Bonus, The Strange Death of Lon Chaney, Satan and Salem: The Witchcraft Movies, Horror's First Lady; Elsa	

Year	Issue/Number	Description	Value ($)
1975	#2	Lanchester, The Hindenburg, The Thing That Was Killing The Girls (fiction)	3–5
	#3	The Space Monster Book featuring Forbidden Planet, etc., The Phantom of the Opera, Monsters from TV's Star Trek and The Outer Limits, The Tragic Life of Laird Cregar, Alfred Hitchcock	4–8
	#4	Lon Chaney Jr.: book-length bonus feature, Zombie: Movies of the Living Dead, The Horror Films of Jack Nicholson, Abbott and Costello Meet the Monsters	3–6

Monster Howls (Humor Vision, Inc.)

1966	#1	Monster movie photos and illustrations presented in a humorous horror vein . . . one issue only	15–25

Monster Madness (Monster Movie Humor with Original Photos, Published by Marvel)

1972–1973	#1	Frankenstein cover	3–6
	#2	Frankenstein, Igor, and Basil Rathbone cover	3–6
	#3	The Bride of Frankenstein cover	3–5

Monster Mag (British Monster Poster Magazine Published by Top Sellers Ltd.)

1973	#1	Christopher Lee	10–15
	#2, #3		6–12

Year	Issue/Number	Description	Value ($)
1973	#16	Christopher Lee, Vampire Circus, Death Line, Blood and Bullets	5–10
	All other issues		4–8

Monster Mania (Renaissance Productions)

Year	Issue/Number	Description	Value ($)
1967	#1	Christoper Lee cover, Dracula: Power of Darkness, The Reptile, Rasputin: The Mad Monk, The Peter Cushing Story, interview with Jack Pierce	15–30
	#2	Tribute to Hammer Films special	15–25
	#3	Peter Cushing Returns in Frankenstein Created Woman, The Wolfman, Revenge of Frankenstein	20–40

Monster Monthly (Marvel)

Year	Issue/Number	Description	Value ($)
1982	#1	Saturn III cover, Robot Monsters	6–12
	All other issues		4–10

Monster Parade (Magnum Publications)

Year	Issue/Number	Description	Value ($)
1958	#1	Issue is marked volume 2, #1	175–325+
	#2	Issue is marked volume 1, #2	125–250+
	#3	Issue is marked volume 1, #3	100–200
1959	#4	Issue is marked volume 1, #4	75–125

Monster and Things (Magnum Publications)

Year	Issue/Number	Description	Value ($)
1959	#1	The Vampire Legend, Rodan, Frankenstein 1970	100–200
	#2	The Story of Frankenstein, movie monster pinups	125–225

Year	Issue/Number	Description	Value ($)

Monsters of the Movies (Marvel)

Year	Issue/Number	Description	Value ($)
1974–1975	#1	King Kong special, The Night Stalker, Christopher Lee, Boris Karloff, Bela Lugosi, Lon Chaney	10–12
	#2	The Frankenstein Monster, Count Yorga, King (Boris) Karloff	5–10
	#3	Special Vampire issue, Inside Hammer Films, Barnabas Collins, Blackula, Count Yorga, Bela Lugosi	5–10

Monster Times: The (Tabloid Published by Monster Times Publishing)

Year	Issue/Number	Description	Value ($)
1972–1976	#1	The Man Who Saved King Kong, Mushroom Monsters, The End of the World	10–15
	#2	Special Star Trek issue . . . The William Shatner interview, Star Trek Production Secrets, the Star Trek Photo Story	10–20
	#3	Bug issue special, King Kong, Man-Eating Plants	5–10
	#4	The Bride of Frankenstein, Tales from the Crypt, Green Lantern and Green Arrow, Dracula Goes to Court	5–10
	#5	Creature from the Black Lagoon, Star Trek special, The Return of Dr. X, Mushroom Monsters, DC's Tarzan of the Apes	5–10
	#6	Special all-zombie issue, Tales of the Living Dead	3–6
	#7	Godzilla: King of the Monsters issue, King Kong	

Year	Issue/Number	Description	Value ($)
1972–1976	#7	Meets the Giant Bug, Batman for President	10–20
	#8	Hammer Horror Films special, Horror of Dracula, Curse of the Werewolf, Christopher Lee exclusive interview, Aurora's Dr. Deadly Toys: Terror Toys Invade London	5–10
	#9	This Island Earth, Buck Rogers, Flash Gordon	3–5
	#10	EC comic special	3–5
	#11	The Planet of the Apes special, exclusive Dracula interview	10–20
	#12	Gorgo Speaks, Behind the Planet of the Apes, Steranko's History of the Comic	10–15
	#13	Meet Marvel's Marvelous Spiderman, Colossal Monsterous Movie Mistakes, Good Vibes from Dr. Phibes, Shazam	5–10
	#14	The Wolfman, exclusive interview with Peter Cushing	5–10
	#15	The Valley of Gwangi, How to make a Monster, Dracula in Comix, Godzilla	5–10
	#16	Attack of the Planet Monster, Godzilla, memoirs of Mighty Joe Young, the return of Dr. Phibes and Count Yorga	5–10
	#17	Super science fiction issue, Forbidden Planet filmbook,	

Year	Issue/Number	Description	Value ($)
1972–1976	#17	Rod Serling Speaks, Meet the Mysterious Mysterians, Asylum, King Kong's Komeback	6–12
	#18	Christopher Lee: Dracula A.D. 1972, King Kong Komix, The Monster of Piedras Blancas	4–8
	#19	Tarantula, The Return of EC, Movies That Don't Die, Monsterous Movie Ads	3–6
	#20	20 Million Miles to Earth, Fu Manchu, Star Trek: A Super Salute, A Warped Neal Adams	6–12
	#21	The Total Frankenstein, includes a Frankenstein filmbook, Frankenstein's castle and a Frankenstein film list	10–20
	#22	Inside the Vault of Horror, The Green Slime, Godzilla versus Ghidrah	4–8
	#23	Godzilla: The King of the Monsters, meet The Rat	10–20
	#24	Theatre of Blood, Rodan: The Flying Monsters, Last of The Planet of the Apes, Mad Basie Wolverton, Return of the History of Comics	6–12
	#25	Horror Heroines special, The Trouble with Star Trek, King Kong Fu, Werewolves on Wheels, Captain Marvel's Maker, Batman and Superman, The Fly	6–12

Year	Issue/Number	Description	Value ($)
1972–1976	#26	Destroy All Monsters special, The Return of Star Trek exclusive, Superman Slept Here	4–8
	#27	Bela Lugosi: The Decline and Fall, The Screeb's Strangest Vampires, Blackula Bites Back, Dreaming of Dracula, The World's Best Vampire Story	6–12
	#28	Hammer's House of Horror issue, Great Movie Death Scenes, The Legendary Lon Chaney, Plastic Man	4–8
	#29	The Truth about the Abominable Snowman, EC Lives, Sinbad Sales Again, Japanese Monsters, The House of Frankenstein	4–8
	#30	Special Werewolves and Monsters issue	4–6
	#31	Special All-Martian issue, War of the Worlds, Making Martian Monsters	6–12
	#32	The Beast from 20,000 Fathoms, Marvel's Mightiest Monsters, Werewolf of Washington, Mexican Monsters, Questor, Bruce Lee Lives, Godzilla	4–6
	#33	The Planet of the Apes, All-Ape special issue, The Complete Saga of The Planet of the Apes, History of Celluloid Simians	15–20+

Year	Issue/Number	Description	Value ($)
1972–1976	#34	Female Fiends, Star Trek's Captain Kirk Speaks, Zardoz, Underground Horrors, The Time Machine, Swamp Thing	5–10
	#35	The Return of Godzilla, Female Fiends Revisited, Makeup Masters, Supernatural Superheroes, Toho's Titans of Terror	5–10
	#36	Curse of the Werewolf, Star Trek's Mr. Spock Speaks, Robert Monsters, Martians Attack	4–6
	#37	Gammera, The Apes (Planet of the Apes) Invade TV	10–15
	#38	A Giant History of Giant Film Giants, Sinbad's Golden Voyage, Conan, Beware the Blob Maker	4–6
	#39	Who Is King . . . Godzilla or King Kong, Dracula, Frankenstein, Planet of the Apes, Ghidrah, Gammera, The Wolfman, The Creature from the Black Lagoon, Rodan, The Mummy, Destroy All Monsters	5–10
	#40	The Phantom of the Opera, Son of Kong, Fay Wray Remembers, Bela Lugosi Lives	4–8
	#41	The Six Frankensteins of Filmdom, The Terror from Beyond Space, Andy Warhol's Dracula, How to Make a Mummy	4–6

Year	Issue/Number	Description	Value ($)
1972–1976	#42	Godzilla versus The Thing, Star Trek Returns, The Unsinkable Shrinking Man, Horror Movie Comics, Werewolves	4–8
	#43	All-Demon issue, Star Trek's Captain Kirk, The Exorcist	6–12
	#44	One Million Years B.C., Raquel Welch cover, Dinosaur issue special, Cave Girls	10–15
	#45	Jane Fonda as Barbarella cover and feature, A Talk with Long John Carradine, Star Trek's Bill Shatner, The King Kong Disaster, The Worst Fright Film Ever Made, Shriek of the Mutilated, Bugs	5–10
	#46	All-Dracula issue, The Real Dracula, A Conversation with Christopher Lee, Star Trek: The Final Frontier	4–8
	#47	Star Trek versus Space 1999 special, Flash Gordon, Science Fiction Comics	5–10
	#48	Special Bionic issue, Six Million Dollar Man, The Bionic Woman, Meet Jamie the Bionic Woman	4–8

Monster Times Collector's Issue

	#3	Godzilla and King Kong: Who Is the King?, issue includes 10 wall posters	10–20

Year	Issue/Number	Description	Value ($)
Monster Times/Star Trek Lives			
	#1	Star Trek, UFO, Lost in Space, The Outer Limits, etc.	15–20
	#2	Inside profiles on all the people who made Star Trek, exclusive stories and photos	10–20
Monsterland, Forrest J. Ackerman's (New Media Publishing)			
1985–1987	#1	Forrest Ackerman talks to Steven Spielberg, The Complete Godzilla, Night of the Living Dead, The Hills Have Eyes II, The Company of Wolves	30–55+
	#2	Elvira, Sybil Danning and Jane Badler cover and feature, A Talk with Stephen King, Sting Meets the Bride, Vincent Price, The New Godzilla	20–35+
	#3	Godzilla, the creature of George Pal, Nightmare on Elm Street, Lifeforce	10–20
	#4	Fright Night: The Director's Story, Day of the Dead, The Tragic Life of Bela Lugosi, Makeup Master John Carl Buechler, Filmfests	15–25
	#5	Roddy McDowall, Sting and Jennifer Beals, Day of the Dead, Japan's Frankenstein versus Gammera, Boris Karloff: Titan of Terror, On the set of The Re-Animator,	

Year	Issue/Number	Description	Value ($)
1985–1987	#5	Christopher Lee exclusive interview	10–15
	#6	Werewolves, Vampires and Nightmares, The Return of Freddy Krueger, Caroline Munroe exclusive interview, The Dead Girls, Building Godzilla '85	6–12
	#7	Elvira cover and feature, Psycho III, The Last Day of Lon Chaney, Trolls, Twilight Zone: Behind the Scenes, The Time Machine	15–25
	#8	Psycho III, The Amazing Stories Story, Twilight Zone	5–10
	#9	Creature Invasion issue, Invaders from Mars, the Godzilla book, The Fly Flies Again, Peter Lorre, Creating the Killbots, Enemy Mine	4–8
	#10	Poltergeist II, Tobe Hooper: Director from Mars, Big Trouble in Little China, The House That Dripped Blood, Labyrinth, Curse of Frankenstein	4–8
	#11	Aliens, The Dark Shadows of Barnabas Collins, The Boy Who Could Fly, The Beast from 20,000 Fathoms, John Carpenter	6–12
	#12	Critters, The Outer Limits, Invaders from Mars, The Secrets of Freddy Krueger, Aliens' Sigourney Weaver	5–10

Year	Issue/Number	Description	Value ($)
1985–1987	#13	Poltergeist II, The Creature from the Black Lagoon, On the Set of Aliens, The Hunt for Cherry 2000, Vincent Price: Meet the Grand Master, The Original King Kong	5–10
	#14	King Kong: Censored Scenes, The Flight of the Navigator, Master of Fright: Peter Cushing, The Seventh Voyage of Sinbad, The Boy Who Could Fly, Greg Cannon	4–8
	#15	Elvira cover and feature with poster, Stephen King, Make Your Own Star Trek Costume	12–25
	All other issues		5–10

Monster Scene Journal
Publishing begins in 1992

	All issues		4–8

Monsters to Laugh With (Non-Pereil Publications)

1964–1965	#1–3		10–15

Monsters Unlimited (Formerly Monsters to Laugh With, Magazine Management, Inc.)

1965–1966	#1	Marked #4	5–10
	#2	Marked #5	5–10
	#3	Marked #6	5–10
	#4	Marked #7	5–10

Monster World (Mayfair Publishing)

1975	#1	Vampires of the Screen, Dracula Lives, Monsters Gone Ape, Darren McGavin: The Night Stalker	6–10

Year	Issue/Number	Description	Value ($)
1975	#2	The Many Faces of Lon Chaney, Vincent Price Unmasked, The Making of King Kong, Nightmare Theatre	3–8

Monster World (Warren)

Note: Numbers 1 through 10 are considered issues 70 through 79 of *Famous Monsters of Filmland*

Year	Issue/Number	Description	Value ($)
1964–1966	#1	The Wolfman cover, Battle of the Frankensteins, monster comics, etc.	10–15
	#2	TV's The Munsters cover and feature with exclusive photos, Monster Comics	10–20
	#3	The She Creature, Battle of the Giant Beetle, Curse of Frankenstein	25–50
	#4	Frankenstein 1970, Horror in the Lighthouse, The Munsters and Their Car, A Letter to Christopher Lee, The Faces of 7 Great Fiends	10–15
	#5	Boris Karloff's Newest Horror Film, The Monsters of Hammer Films, Bela Lugosi in the Bride of the Monster	6–12
	#6	Horrific Holiday issue, The Revenge of the Zombies, Return of the Vampires	6–12
	#7	Son of Frankenstein special . . . complete with rare photos	6–12
	#8	Dr. X, Jesse James Meets Frankenstein's Daughter,	

Year	Issue/Number	Description	Value ($)
1964–1966	#8	Billy the Kid versus Dracula	6–12
	#9	Meet the Addams Family: cover and special feature	10–15
	#10	Reptiles, Batman and the Superheroes, The Ghost in the Invisible Bikini	4–8

Movie Aliens Illustrated (Warren)

1979	#1	Darth Vader and others, including Alien, the movie	3–6

Movie Maker (Fountain Press)

1971	December	Christopher Lee in I Monster cover and feature, Horror Movies: Methods and Mystigue	6–12

Movie Monster Poster Book (Published by Watermill Press)

1979		Crammed with information and facts about all kinds of movie monsters: Frankenstein, The Mummy, Gorgo, The Lost Continent, King Kong, This Island Earth, The Creature from the Black Lagoon, Godzilla on Monster Island: magazine opens to become a full-color giant-size wall poster of the first King Kong	6–12

Movie Monsters (S. J. Publications)

1981	#1	Star Wars, Vampires: The Walking Dead, Dracula: The King of the Vampires, The Female Vampire, Darth Vader Turns Vampire	6–12

Year	Issue/Number	Description	Value ($)
1981	#2	Star Wars, Boris Karlof: The Man Who Made Frankenstein's Monster Famous, The Bride of Frankenstein, King Kong, Bela Lugosi	4–8
	#3	The Legend of Darth Vader: Fact and Fiction Superman: The Movie That Made 'Em Forget the Comic, Fantastic Animation: Making Monsters Come to Life Bugs on the Munch	4–8

Movie Monsters (Seaboard Periodicals)

	Issue/Number	Description	Value ($)
	#1	Planet of the Apes, Dracula, The Exorcist, Gorgo	6–15
	#2	Planet of the Apes, 2001: A Space Odyssey, Doc Savage, Frankenstein, Rodan, One Million Years B.C.	6–15
	#3	Phantom of the Opera, The Wolfman, Godzilla, Boris Karloff, Batman, Forbidden Planet, Jack the Giant Killer	6–10
	#4	The Thing, Flash Gordon, Lon Chaney Jr., Lost Worlds, The Loch Ness Monster, The Walt Disney Monsters, The Day the Earth Stood Still, The Star Trek Phenomenon, 20 Million Miles to Earth	6–12

Year	Issue/Number	Description	Value ($)
Munsters: The Official Magazine (Twin Hits, Inc.)			
1965		One Shot magazine dedicated to TV's The Munsters, issue includes a Munster calendar and an episode not seen on TV	50–100+
Original Monsters (Prozine)			
	All issues		12–22+
Newsweek (Newsweek, Inc.)			
1977	June 24	Star Wars cover and feature . . . Why America Loves the Star Wars Heroes	5–10
1978	September 11	TV's Battlestar Galactica cover and feature, Son of Star Wars	5–10
1986	December 22	Spock cover and Star Trek feature	4–8
Nightmare (Illustrated Horror, Published by Skywald Publishing Co.)			
1970–1975	#1		6–12
	#2–7		3–6
	#8	Tales from the Crypt reprint stories	6–12
	All other issues, including annual, yearbook, and special		3–6

Omni (Omni Publications International, Ltd.)
Note: A high-quality science fact and fiction magazine often collected by collectors of monster, science fiction, and horror magazines

#1 October 1978		12–25
#2–12		6–12
All other issues		2–4

Year	Issue/Number	Description	Value ($)
Original Monsters (Prozine)			
	All issues		12–25
Photon (Prozine)			
	All issues		6–12+
Prevue (Formerly *Mediascene, Supergraphics*)			
1980–present	#42	First Preview issue, The Empire Strikes Back	12–22
	#46	Morgan Fairchild cover and feature	6–12
	#52	Debbie Harry cover and feature (Note: popular issue with rock fans)	12–22
	#57	Harrison Ford cover and feature . . . The Temple of Doom	5–10
	All other issues		4–8
Psycho (Skywald Publishing)			
1971–1975	#1		6–12
	All other issues, including annual, yearbook, and special		3–6
Quasimodo's Monster Magazine (Mayfair Publications)			

Note: Issues 1 and 2 are titled *Monster World*

Year	Issue/Number	Description	Value ($)
1975–1976	#3	First Quasimodo issue, Christopher Lee exclusive interview, Lugosi: The Man and the Vampire, Earthquake, Nightmare Theater, A Look at Phase IV	5–10
	#4	Son of Chaney: The Story of Lon Chaney Jr., The Making of the Exorcist, The Land That Time Forgot: exclusive interview with Doug McClure, Space	

Year	Issue/Number	Description	Value ($)
1975–1976	#4	1999: Part 1, The Films of Roger Corman	5–10
	#5	Jekyl and Hyde: Through the Years, Heroes of Horror, Space 1999: Part 2, The Master of Radio Horror . . . Himan Brown and Mystery Theatre, The Lorre [Peter] Story	5–10
	#6	Introducing Esmeralda, William Shatner on Star Trek, Karloff: King of Monsters, John Carradine, Life and Death in Death Race 2000	5–10
	#7	The Wolfman, Leonard Nimoy: Star of Star Trek, Bug, Splat Films, Monsters Gone Ape	5–10
	#8	The Invisible Man, Star Trek biographies, All about the Mummy	4–8

Questar (W. G. Wilson/MW Communications)

Year	Issue/Number	Description	Value ($)
1978–1981	#1	Star Wars cover and feature	30–60
	#2	Capricorn I, Phoenix, What's Right with Space 1999, Science Fiction Cinema	10–20
	#3	Superman the Movie, Battlestar Galactica, Invasion of the Body Snatchers, Dawn of the Dead, Lord of the Rings	6–12
	#4	Forrest J. Ackerman's Just Imagine . . . Jeannie, George Romero interview, Buck Rogers	10–20

Year	Issue/Number	Description	Value ($)
1978–1981	#5	Alien: A Detailed Look at the Most Devastating Thriller, Moonraker: Bond in Space, Star Trek the Movie preview, Kiss up close	15–25
	#6	The Black Hole, Star Trek, Don Post exclusive interview, The Rocky Horror Picture Show	10–15
	#7	A. E. van Vogt interview, Conan movie preview, Caroline Munroe Portrait Album featuring a full-color wall poster	10–15
	#8	Star Wars: Mark Hamill on The Empire Strikes Back, Bigfoot Lives, Robert Bloch, What's Keeping the Space Shuttle	6–12
	#9	Ray Bradbury, Night of the Living Dead retrospective, Battle Beyond the Stars	4–8
	#10	Somewhere in Time, Scared to Death, Battle Beyond the Stars	3–6
	#11	The Art of Boris, Robby the Robot	3–6
	#12	Logan's Run creator interviewed, Star Blasters, Time Machine	3–6
	#13	Isaac Asimov interview, Eroticism in the Fantasy Cinema . . . Barbarella and others	6–12

Reel Fantasy (Reel Fantasy, Inc)

| 1978 | #1 | Star Wars cover and feature, The Spy Who | |

Year	Issue/Number	Description	Value ($)
1978	#1	Loved Me, Lynda Carter: Wonder Woman	10–15

***Revenge of Dracula* (Eerie Publications)**

1977	one shot		6–12

Ripley's Believe It or Not . . . True Weird

	All issues		7–20

Rocky Horror Official Poster Magazine

	#1	Tim Curry: Not Just a Pretty Transvestite	6–12
	#2	Another Serving of Curry Please, Brien Talks to O'Brien about Rocky Sequel	6–12

Rocky Horror Picture Show Official Magazine

1979	one shot	Exclusive interviews with Richard O'Brien and Richard Hartley, Brian Thompson on the set design, Sue Blaine on the costume design, news of the sequel, on the road with Rocky Horror	8–15

***Scarlet Street* (R. H. Enterprises)**

1990	#1	Dark Shadows: From The Winds of War to the Wings of Bats, The Flash: Barry Allen Is Alive and Well on CBS, Frankenstein: Unreleased?, Hounded by Holmes: Hounds Abound in Many Versions, Robin Takes Wings, Universal Horrors, Sherlock Holmes Meets Jack the Ripper, Superboy Plays Hooky	100–175

Year	Issue/Number	Description	Value ($)
1990	#2	Hound of the Baskervilles, Dark Shadows, DC Comics TV Gallery of Villains, Atlantis: The Lost Continent, Horror Italian Style, The Black Museum, The Silence of the Lambs, The Golden Years of Sherlock Holmes	25–50
1991	#3	Barbara Steele: Black Sunday, Tarzan Returns, Collinwood Revisited, SCTV Meets the Addams Family, The Mad Doctor, Night of the Hunter, The Women Who Played The Woman, All about Batman, The 90 Year History of the Hound of the Baskervilles, Rococo: Horror Redefined	20–40+
	Reprint Issue		5–10
	#4	Superboy Speaks Up, The Return of Dracula, By Lovecraft Possessed, The Crucifer of Blood, Zack and Ach Are Back, Interview with Ex-Vampire	20–40
1992	#5	Barbara Hale, Patrick Macnee, Jack Larson, The House That Screamed Blood, Universal vs. Hammer Films, Batman Returns, Jeremy Brett, Christopher Lee, The Solitary Cyclist, Star Trek, The Addams Family, Mr. & Mrs. North	6–12+

Year	Issue/Number	Description	Value ($)
1992	#6	Circus of Horror, Noel Neill, David Nelson, Black Sabbath, The Big Circus, Vampire Circus, The Crooked Man, Batman, Gorgo, Freaks, Berserk, Nightmare Alley, Strangers on a Train	4–8+
	#7	Vincent Price, John Moulder-Brown, Yvette Vickers, Tomb of Ligeia, The Sussex Vampire, Bluebeard, Batman Returns, House of Wax, The Raven, They Do It with Mirrors, The Invisible Man Returns, Laura, Innocent Blood, Joan Hickson	4–8+
	#8	Dracula, Dracula's Daughter, Son of Dracula, Sherlock Holmes Confesses: An Exclusive Interview with Peter Cushing, Vampires over Hollywood: Bram Stoker's Dracula, Vampires over Pittsburgh: John Landis on Innocent Blood, Sherlock Holmes as Dracula: Jeremy Brett, Rebecca Eaton, Fangs for the Memories: 20 Vampire Classics and Not-So-Classics, Dark Shadows on Videotape	4–8+
1993	#9	Danny DeVito: Fine Feathered Fiend, Thomas	

Year	Issue/Number	Description	Value ($)
1993	#9	Beck, The Black Scorpion: Richard Denning and Carlos Rivas, Mornings with Peter Cushing, Veronica Carlson, The Cushing Collection, Joan Bennett	4–8+
	#10	Animated Bat Talk, Kevin Conroy, Loren Lester, Karloff and Lugosi's Lost Film, Beverly Garland, Sherlock Holmes Meets The Twilight Zone, Richard Dempsey: I Was a Teenage Vampire, The Alligator People, The Hardy Boys	4–8

Scary Monsters

	All Issues		4–8

Science and Fiction Film Classics (Science and Fantasy Film Classics Inc.)

Year	Issue/Number	Description	Value ($)
1977–1978	#1	Star Wars cover and feature, including a 22-by-32-inch full-color Star Wars wall poster, 2001: A Space Odyssey, Forbidden Planet	6–12
	#2	Close Encounters of the Third Kind special issue, Silent Running, War of the Worlds	3–6
	#3	Star Trek special issue, Laserblast, This Island Earth	4–8
	#4	Battlestar Galactica special issue, Journey to the Far Side of the Sun, When Worlds Collide	4–8

Year	Issue/Number	Description	Value ($)

Science Fiction, Horror and Fantasy (DW Enterprises)

1977–1978	#1	The Making of Star Wars, a Star Wars special issue, Christopher Lee, Ray Harryhausen	6–12
	#2	Star Wars: Creators Reveal Production Secrets, Mark Hamill Reveals the Problems in Making Star Wars, Douglas Trumball: Film Genius, Leonard Nimoy: Invasion of the Body Snatchers, Christopher Lee, Superman, Meteor, Ray Bradbury, The Swarm, Witch Mountain	4–8

Science Fiction Illustrated (LC Print Publications)

1977	#1	King Kong: The Ninth Wonder of the World, Sinbad and the Eye of the Tiger: Ray Harryhausen's Newest Creation, The Making of Star Trek, The Future of Logan's Run	5–10

Scream (Illustrated Horror, Skywald Publishing Corp.)

1973–1975	#1		5–10
	#2–11		4–8

Screen Chills (Pep Publishing)
One issue only

1957		I Was a Teenage Werewolf, Dead That Walk	200–400+

Screen Monsters (S. J. Publications)

1981	#1	Frankenstein special issue	5–10

Year	Issue/Number	Description	Value ($)

Screen Thrills Illustrated (Warren Publishing)

	#1	The 13 Faces of Tarzan, The Saga of Superman, The Three Stooges Meet Hercules	15–25
	#2–4		15–25
	#5	Batman's Boy Wonder Robin, The Beverly Hillbillies, James Cagney	7–15
	#6	The Phantom, Charlie Chan, Robert Taylor	7–15
	#7	Captain America, Humphrey Bogart, Kings of Comedy	6–12
	#8	Sinister Spider, The Marx Borthers, Sabu	5–10
	#9	Zorro, Alan Ladd, Superheroes	6–12
	#10	James Bond, The Lone Ranger, The Beatles, The Three Stooges	15–30

Screen Superstar/Star Wars Special

	#8	The full story, a special expanded edition packed with full-color photographs from the film	7–15

SF Movieland

1985	All issues		3–5

SFTV (HJS Publications)

1984–1985	All issues		6–12

Shock (Stanley Publications, Inc., Illustrated Horror)

1969	#1 (May vol. 1 #1)	Voodoo Dolls, Eternal Death, Witch's Curse, Cremation	15–30
	#2 (July vol. 1 #2)	Curse of the Zomboori, Swamp Monster, The	

Year	Issue/Number	Description	Value ($)
1969	#2 (July vol. 1 #2)	Other World, More Deadly Than the Male	15–30
	#3 (September vol. 1 #3)	The Hidden Horror, Artist of Evil, Within the Tomb, Snake Goddess, Million Year Monster	10–20
	#4 (November vol. 1 #4)	The Flapping Head, Claws of the Hungry Demon, The Destroyer Fiend of Midnight	7–15
1970	#5 (January vol. 1 #5)	The Grave Robber, The Ghost's Revenge, Only the Evil Need Fear the Bogeyman, A Hex on My Brother	6–12
	#6 (March vol. 1 #6)	Evil Returns, Ghostly Destroyer, The Land of Living Myths, Fangs of the Fiend	6–12
	#7 (May vol. 2 #2)	Terror House, The Evil Secret of Black Hollow, The Undying Brain	6–12
	#8 (July vol. 1 #8)	Vampire's Castle, The Howling Head, The Noose of Pearls, Hypnotist of Death	6–12
	#9 (September vol. 2 #4)	The Mark of the Monster, The Spectral Sister, Vampire Master, Sleep of Death	6–12
	#10 (November vol. 2 #5)	Tomb of the Cursed Corpse, Vision of Death, Vampire Swoops, Killers from Hell	6–12
1971	#11 (January vol. 2 #6)	The Vampire's Bones, Were-Fiends of Filmland, The Girl Who Died Twice,	

Year	Issue/Number	Description	Value ($)
1971	#11 (January vol. 2 #6)	Haunt of the Hyena, The Bat and the Brain	6–12
	#12 (March vol. 3 #1)	Vigil of the Vampires, Three Hours to Doom, Fiend of the Undead, The Floating Coffin	4–8
	#13 (May vol. 3 #2)	Queen for the Voodoo Chief, The Ghost in the Show Window, Lady of Death, The Faceless Legion	4–8
	#14 (July Vol. 3 #3)	Grave of Doom, The Spectral Bride, Vampire Castle, Madman's Manor	6–12
	#15 (September vol. 3 #4)	A Living Corps for the Zombie, the Pulverizing Peril, Murder Stalks New York, An Unknown Universe, The Vanishing Submarine	6–12

Shock Tales (MF Enterprises)

1959	#1	Funeral for a Vampire, The Most Perfect Monster	175–300+

Shriek (Acme News)

1965–1967	#1	Vincent Price: Sovereign of the Sinister, The Flesheaters, Girl Vampire, Secret of Blood Island, Horror Hags: Joan Crawford and Bette Davis, History of the Horror Movie, Die Die My Darling	30–55
	#2	My Life of Terror: An Interview with Boris Karloff, Devils of Darkness, Vincent Price in	

Year	Issue/Number	Description	Value ($)
1965–1967	#2	Wargods of the Deep, Dr. Terror's House of Horror, Devil Doll	30–55
	#3	Dracula: Prince of Darkness, The Face of Fu Manchu, Rasputin the Mad Monk, The Reptile, The Zombies, The Psychopath	25–50
	#4	Frankenstein Conquers the World, The Brides of Fu Manchu, The Mask, Daleks Invade the Earth, Carrying on Screaming, Munsters Go Home	25–50

***Silver Screen Horror, Vincent Price Presents* (Globe Communications Corp.)**

1977	May #1 (One issue only)		7–15

Slaughter House Magazine

	All issues		4–8

Spaceballs: the Magazine | | | 3–5 |

***Spaceman* (Warren Publishing)**

	Issue	Description	Value
	#1	When Worlds Collide, Voyage of the Space Eagle, space ships, monsters	125–200
	#2	H. G. Wells's Things to Come, space movie previews	75–125
	#3	Girl in the Moon	100–175
	#4	Flash Gordon	50–75
	#5	Yesterday's Spacemen, The First Buck Rogers on Film, Radar Men from the Moon	20–40
	#6	Rocketman, Metropolis	20–40

Year	Issue/Number	Description	Value ($)
	#7	Hollywood's Astronauts, King of the Lost Planet, Rocketmen, Twins from Other Worlds	20–40
	#8	Boris Karloff: Out of This World, The Farenheit Chronicles, 20 Million Miles to Earth	15–30
1965 Yearbook			30–60

Space: 1999 Magazine (Charlton Publications)

	#1–8		7–15

Space Trek (Stories and Layouts Press)

1978–1979	#1	Battlestar Galactica special, Superman, Star Trek, Earth versus the Flying Saucers, Japanese Weirdos	3–6
	#2	The Incredible Hulk, Battlestar Galactica, Superman, Flash Gordon, Strange Demonic Children in the Monster Movies, Clones: A Look at Futuristic Flicks	3–6
	#3	Battlestar Galactica versus Star Wars special, Flying Saucer Attack, Superman, The First Men in the Moon, Star Trek	5–10

Space Wars (Stories and Layouts Press)

1977–1979	#1	Star Wars special: The Science Fiction Movie of the Decade, 2001: A Space Odyssey, Flash Gordon, The Return of Star Trek, Famous Movie Robots	6–12
	#2	Silent Running, The	

Year	Issue/Number	Description	Value ($)
1977–1979	#2	Greatest Collection of Spaced-Out Movie Posters Ever Spawned, Star Wars	4–8
	#3	Mars Attacks, Robots: The Metal Horde in Film, Sexy Space Ladies, Bizarre Monsters: The History of the Pulps	4–8
	#4	Close Encounters versus Star Wars, Mars Attacks Revisited	2–7
	#5	H. G. Wells's Things to Come	3–7
	#6–11		3–7
	#12	Star Wars special, Invasion of the Body Snatchers, Superman II, Build Your Own Daggit	6–12

Spectre (Horror Filmzine)

	All issues		5–10

SPFX (SPFX Publications)

1977	#1	The War of the Worlds special	10–20
	#2	The Day the Earth Stood Still special	6–12

Splatter Times, The (Taboid)

	All issues		15–35

Star Battles (Stories and Layouts)

1978–1979	#1	Superman extra, Battlestar Galactica versus Buck Rogers	5–7
	#2	Star Wars: How to Meet Luke Skywalker and R2D2, Battlestar Galactica, Superman II	3–6

Year	Issue/Number	Description	Value ($)
Star Blaster			
	All issues		5–7
Starblazer (Liberty Communications, Inc.)			
1984	All issues		4–7
Starburst (Starburst Magazine, Ltd.)			
1977–	#1	Star Wars special	15–25
present	#2	Space Cruiser, The Prisoner, Star Wars, Close Encounters	6–12
	#3	Close Encounters of the Third Kind, Logan's Run, Star Trek, Star Wars	5–10
	#4	The Hulk, War of the Worlds, Star Trek, Tolkien, Merlin	4–7
	#5	The Filming of Superman the Movie, Battlestar Galactica, Dark Star	3–5
	#6	Close Encounters of the Third Kind, Message from Space, Silent Running, Superman, Dalek index	3–5
	#7	Battlestar Galactica special, Superman the Movie, Invasion of the Body Snatchers	6–12
	#8	Space 1999 special Superman II, Alien, Leonard Nimoy, Star Wars II	6–12
	#9	The Making of the Lord of the Rings, Invasion of the Body Snatchers, Forbidden Planet, Tales of the Unexpected	3–5
	#10	Dr. Who, Star Trek: The Motion Picture, Aliens in	

Year	Issue/Number	Description	Value ($)
1977–present	#10	the Cinema, The Shapes of Thing to Come, Lost in Space	5–7
	#11	Star Wars, Inside Star Trek the Motion Picture, Lord of the Rings, James Bond special effects exclusive, The Humanoid: Behind the Scenes	4–6
	#12	Bond in Space: Special Effects, The China Syndrome, The Spaceman and King Arthur, 007's Jaws Interviewed, Screen Robots portfolio	4–7
	#13	Buck Rogers in the 25th Century, The Art of Space 1999, The Omega Man, Alien, Moonraker, The Avengers	4–7
	#14	Alien special, Dr. Who special effects, The Avengers, The Time Machine	12–20
	#15	Alien effects, Gandahar, Quatermass, Dr. Who, Sapphire and Steel, Serial Superheroes	3–5
	#16	The Black Hole, Alien Art, Planet of the Apes, Kronos	3–5
	#17	Star Trek the Movie special	5–10
	#18	Meteor, Blake 7, Movie Aliens, George Pal, Project UFO	3–4
	#19	Science Fiction Movie Bonanza, Star Trek, Saturn 3, The Black Hole, Meteor, Tom Baker	4–7

Year	Issue/Number	Description	Value ($)
1977–present	#20	Fantasy Females special, Blake 7, Star Trek versus The Black Hole, 20,000 Leagues Under the Sea, The Thing, The Outer Limits	15–25
	#21	Special Effects spectacular, Jules Verne, Battlestar Galactica	4–8
	#22	The Empire Strikes Back special	6–12
	#23	The Empire Strikes Back special	6–12
	#24–33		2–6
	#34	Special Werewolf issue, The Howling, Movie Wolewolves, Outland Special Effects, For Your Eyes Only	4–8
	#35–42		2–6
	#43	Star Wars special	5–10
	#56	Fantasy Females special issue	6–12
	#59	Return of the Jedi special	6–12
	#71	Indiana Jones and the Temple of Doom special	4–8
	#86	The Emerald Forest	4–7
	#87	Mad Max III, Tina Turner cover	4–6
	#100	Michael Jackson: Captain Eo cover and feature	4–7
	All other issues		2–6

Star Encounters (Stories and Layouts)

Year	Issue/Number	Description	Value ($)
1978–1979	#1	Star Wars	5–10
	#2	Star Wars, Close Encounters of the Third Kind, The Rocky Horror Picture Show, Meat Loaf Capricorn I	5–10

Year	Issue/Number	Description	Value ($)
1978–1979	#3	Beyond Star Trek, Star Wars, First Cloning of Apes, Ray Bradbury, Swarm: Killer Bees	2–4

Star Force (Reliance Publications)

Year	Issue/Number	Description	Value ($)
1978	#1	Lynda Carter: Wonder Woman cover and feature, The Incredible Melting Man, Close Encounters of the Third Kind, Star Trek	5–10
	#2	The Empire Strikes Back Special Edition	4–8
	All other issues		4–8

Star Invaders (Liberty Communications)
Publishing Begins in 1984

	Issue/Number	Description	Value ($)
	All issues		3–5

Starlog (O'Quinn Studios)

	Issue/Number	Description	Value ($)
	#1	Star Trek, Space 1999, The Bionic Woman, David Bowie	15–30
	#2	Space 1999, Star Trek, H. G. Wells	15–25
	#3	Star Trek, The Six Million Dollar Man, Space 1999	10–20
	#4	The Six Million Dollar Man, Nick Tate interview, The Bionic Woman	10–20
	#5	UFO episode guide, Star Trek, Space 1999	10–20
	#6	The Making of Destination Moon, Star Wars, Special Effects Part I, Fantastic Journey Interview, Star Trek the Movie, Space 1999	10–20
	#7	Star Wars, Robby the Robot, Rocketship XM, Star Trek	10–20

#7

#11

Vol. 17, 1992

#1, 1979

#2, 1979

#2

#4

#9

#10

Year	Issue/Number	Description	Value ($)
	#8	Model Animation special, Star Wars, Saturday Morning TV, The Fly	6–12
	#9	TV's Logan's Run, Patrick Duffy, Lynda Carter, Jared Martin, William Shatner, a special all-TV issue	20–30+
	#10	George Pal exclusive interview, Isaac Asimov, Close Encounters of the Third Kind, Space 1999 set designs	10–20
	#11	The Makeup Men special, The Prisoner, Close Encounters of the Third Kind, the Superman Movie, Science Fiction Comics, The Incredible Shrinking Man	6–12
	#12	The Making of Close Encounters of the Third Kind, Star Trek's Enterprise	6–12
	#13	Exploring the Planets special, David Darth Vader Prowse interview, Close Encounters of the Third Kind	6–12
	#14	Special Effects . . . Star Trek's Final Voyage	5–10
	#15	This Island Earth, Blood Beast, Rod Serling's Twilight Zone	5–10
	#16	Buck Rogers, Leonard Nimoy in Invasion of the Body Snatchers, The Invaders	5–10
	#17	Battlestar Galactica, The	

Year	Issue/Number	Description	Value ($)
	#17	Incredible Hulk, Dr. Strange	5–10
	#18	Hollywood Halloween issue special . . . Special Effects, Wizards, Tricks and Treats, The Star Wars Sequel, Star Trek, Vampire Movies	5–10
	#19	Star Wars TV special, Athena, Leonard Nimoy: Body Snatchers Return, TV's Buck Rogers, The Lord of the Rings, Superman, Roger Corman: Master of the B Movies	5–10
	#20	Superman the Movie Arrives, Mindy Talks about Mork, Buck Rogers's 50th Anniversary, Jason of Star Command	5–6
	#21	Buck Rogers the Movie, Mark Hamill, Venus Movies, Lost in Space episode guide, Stop-Motion Animation	4–5
	#22	Moonraker, Science Fiction Films in '79, Lorne Green, The Shape of Things to Come	5–10
	#23	Alien, Darth Vader, Dr. Who	10–25
	#24	Starlog Through the Years, Science Fiction Spectacular	6–12
	#25	Star Trek, Alien, The Thing, Ray Bradbury interview	6–12
	#26	The Making of Alien	15–25
	#27	Battlestar Galactica, Alien:	

Year	Issue/Number	Description	Value ($)
	#27	The Special Effects, Star Trek: The Special Effects, The Black Hole: A Day on the Set, Time after Time	6–11
	#28	Buck Rogers, TV's Wonder Woman, Battlestar Galactica, The Hulk	5–8
	#29	Meteor, Space 1999, TV's Buck Rogers, The Incredible Shrinking Man	3–6
	#30	Star Trek Movie Preview, The Incredible Science Fiction Stuntwomen	10–15
	#31	The Black Hole, The Empire Strikes Back, Star Trek, 20,000 Leagues Under the Sea	4–8
	#32	Star Trek exclusive, Meteor, Buck Rogers, Robots on Film	4–8
	#33	Saturn 3, Harlan Ellison on Star Trek, Voyage to the Bottom of the Sea	4–8
	#34	Battlestar Galactica 1980, The Alien Returns exclusive, interview with the directer of The Empire Strikes Back, Twikki: Buck Rogers's Robot, The Martian Chronicles, Dr. Who	4–6
	#35	Darth Vader Returns: The Empire Strikes Back, Star Blazers, The Black Hole, Battle Beyond the Stars	6–12
	#36	Science Fiction spectacular	4–8
	#37	Harrison Ford exclusive interview, Star Trek, Dr. Who	5–10

Year	Issue/Number	Description	Value ($)
	#38	Close Encounters of the Third Kind: Inside the Mothership, The Empire Strikes Back, Buck Rogers, Star Trek	4–8
	#39	Buck Rogers: Exciting Changes, Battlestar Galactica, Mork and Mindy, The Hulk, Battle Beyond the Stars, Star Trek, Tom Corbett	4–6
	#40	The Empire Strikes Back, Mark Hamill, Gene Roddenberry on Star Trek, Buck Rogers, Space 1999	5–10
	#41	The New Flash Gordon Movie, 3-D SFX, Escape from New York, The History of Science Fiction Comics Part I, The UFO Chronicles	4–8
	#42	Star Trek's Other Aliens: An Exclusive Interview with Mark Leonard, Dr. Who, The Wild Wild West Revisited	4–8
	#43	Scanners, Farewell to the Empire: Gary Kurtz, Altered States, Popeye	3–5
	#44	Altered States, Flash Gordon, The Incredible Shrinking Woman	3–6
	#45	Buck Rogers's New Alien Hero, Outland, Apes on TV	4–8
	#46	Clash of the Titans, Superman II, Altered States	4–8

Year	Issue/Number	Description	Value ($)
	#47	Superman II, Dr. Who, Outland, Sarah Douglas interview	3–6
	#48	5th Anniversary Special, exclusive George Lucas interview	3–6
	#49	For Your Eyes Only: James Bond Is Back, Escape from New York	4–8
	#50	The Empire Returns: Boba Fett Unmasked, Outland, Heavy Metal: Sound and Vision, The Six Dr. Whos	10–15
	#51	Lawrence Kasdan, William Shatner on the New Star Trek Project	4–8
	#52	Blade Runner, Heart Beeps, H. R. Giger Art	4–8
	#53	Heart Beeps, The Greatest American Hero Returns, Patrick Macnee: The Avengers, Ray Bradbury on His Science Fiction Films of the Past and Present	3–6
	#54	3-D issue special, The Greatest American Hero, Special Effects of Raiders of the Lost Ark, Star Trek	5–7
	#55	Time Bandits, Quest for Fire, Star Trek	2–5
	#56	The Empire Strikes Back Special Effects Secrets, The Time Machine, Forbidden Planet, Things to Come, 20,000 Leagues Under the Sea, The Thing, The Invisible Man, The	

Year	Issue/Number	Description	Value ($)
	#56	Black Hole, This Island Earth	6–12
	#57	The Empire Strikes Back, The Return of the Lost in Space Robot	6–12
	#58	Blade Runner, Should Spock Die?, John Carpenter's The Thing, Battlestar Galactica, Star Trek bloopers	6–12
	#59	Conan, Tron, Star Trek, Krull, Filming the Thing	6–12
	#60	Science Fiction Spectacular special issue, Star Trek, Tron, E.T., Star Trek, The Thing, Blade Runner, Poltergeist	4–7
	#61	Star Trek special: On the Set and Behind the Scenes, Revenge of the Jedi, The Thing, Road Warrior	10–15
	#62	Star Trek II: An Interview with Kirk, Tron, Conan, Star Wars	4–7
	#63	E.T., Beastmaster, Android, Kurt Russell interview	4–6
	#64	E.T., Star Trek, The Thing	4–6
	#65	Mark Hamill, E.T. SFX, 2010: Odyssey Two	6–12
	#66	The Dark Crystal, Dune, The Time Tunnel, Raiders of the Lost Ark	4–6
	#67	Superman III, Exclusive Interview with the Man Who Killed Spock, William Shatner, Star Trek II	4–6

Year	Issue/Number	Description	Value ($)
	#68	007 Is Back . . . a special double Bond issue: Sean Connery and Roger Moore, Star Trek III and Beyond	5–10
	#69	Return of the Jedi	10–15
	#70	Blue Thunder, Space Hunter, Something Wicked This Way Comes	4–6
	#71	Return of the Jedi special issue	10–15+
	#72	Sci-Fi Spectacular special	4–7
	#73	Superman III, Octopussy's Maud Adams	3–6
	#74	Return of the Jedi, Jaws 3-D, Never Say Never Again, War Games	6–12
	#75	Never Say Never Again, The Art of Return of the Jedi	5–10
	#76	Summer Films special	4–6
	#77	The Right Stuff, Brainstorm, Dr. Who Turns 20	3–6
	#78	Brainstorm, The Right Stuff, Arthur C. Clarke Meets Indiana Jones	4–6
	#79	Knight Rider interview, The Right Stuff, Fiona Lewis, Never Say Never Again	4–8
	#80	Return of the Jedi Special Effects special, Star Trek III, The Last Starfighter	5–10
	#81	Greystoke: The Ultimate Tarzan, Indiana Jones and the Temple of Doom	4–6
	#82	Star Trek III, Conan,	

Year	Issue/Number	Description	Value ($)
	#88	Return of the Jedi Special Effects	5–10
	#89	V: The Vistors, Starman, Return of the Jedi	6–12
	#99	Star Wars and the Droids, Amazing Stories, Mad Max	4–7
	#109	Sigourney Weaver/Aliens, Star Trek IV, Space Camp	6–12+
	#115	Alien's Viva Vasquez exclusive interview, Superman IV, Tom Baker	5–10
	#120	Star Wars, 100-page sci-fi special issue	5–10
	#124	TV's New Star Trek: The Next Generation, 100-page sci-fi spectacular	4–8
	All other issues		4–6

Starlog, The Best of
	All issues		3–10

Starlog Photo Guidebooks
	All issues		5–15

Starlog Specials
(including poster magazine, Addams Family special, etc)
	All issues		5–15

Starscene (Tabloid Published by Ptolemy Publications)
	All issues		3–6

Star Trek Official Poster Monthly
	#1		15–25
	#2		10–15
	#3–10		8–12
	All other issues		6–10

Star Trek: The Next Generation (O'Quinn Studios)
	All issues		4–8

Year	Issue/Number	Description	Value ($)
Star Warp **(Stories, Layout and Press, Inc.)**			
1978	#1		3–5
	#2	Star Wars, The Girls of Star Trek, etc.	4–8
	#3–4		3–5
Star Wars Official Poster Monthly			
	All issues		10–20
Star Wars Return of the Jedi Official Collectors Edition			
1983			10–12
Star Wars Spectacular **(Warren)**			
1977	One shot		10–15
Star Wars The Empire Strikes Back Official Collectors Edition Magazine			
1980			10–12
Stark Terror **(Stanley Publications: Illustrated Horror)**			
1970	December #1	The Executioner, In the Snake Pit, Hallucinations, The Gorilla	15–25
1971	February #2	Black Cat from Hell, The Devil Walks on Halloween	10–15
	April #3		7–15
	June #4		7–15
	August #5		7–15
Strange Galaxy **(Eerie Publications, Inc.: Illustrated Horror)**			
1971	#1 (February vol. 1 #8)	The Unknown, Space Monsters, The Moon Is Red	20–30+
	#2 (April vol. 1 #9)	Dimension X, Human Monster	20–30+
	#3 (June vol. 1 #10)	The Space Demons, The Planetoid Monsters, Metal Terror	15–30+

Year	Issue/Number	Description	Value ($)
1971	#4 (August vol. 1 #11)	The Black Void Beyond	15–30+

Strange Unknown (Tempest Publications)

1969	May #1		10–20+
	July #2		10–15+

Superheroes (Warren)

1966	#1		10–25

Supernatural (Dorset Publishing)

1969	#1, #2		15–30+

Suspense (Suspense Publications)

1959	#1–4		60–120+

Tales from the Crypt (Eerie Publications, Inc.: Illustrated Horror)

1968	#1 July		15–30

Tales from the Tomb (Eerie Publications, Inc.: Illustrated Horror)

Year	Issue/Number	Description	Value ($)
1969	#1 (July vol. 1, #6)	He Rose from the Grave and Became a Terror Among Us, The Hell Below, Werewolf	10–20
	#2 (September vol. 1, #7)	Three Times Dead, The Corpse Came Home	5–10
1970	#3 (January vol. 2, #1)	Gruesome Shock, The Bloody Thing, The Corpse Macabre	6–12
	#4 (April vol. 2, #2)	Ghouls' Graveyard, The Swamp Monsters	6–12
	#5 (June vol. 2, #3)	The Thing from the Grave, Fire Monster	4–8
	#6 (August vol. 2, #4)	Zombies from Another World	4–8
	#7 (October vol. 2, #5)	The Creatures, The Call of the Monsters, The Slimy Corpse	5–10
	#8 (December vol. 2, #6)	Killer Creatures, Food for Ghouls	6–12
1971	#9 (February vol. 3, #1)	Zombie, Werewolf, The Blood Totem	5–10

March 1970

November 1970

March 1971

June 1971

October 1970

February 1973

November 1973

March 1974

May 1974

Year	Issue/Number	Description	Value ($)
1971	#10 (April vol. 3, #2)	Vampire, The Deadly Demon	6–12
	#11 (June vol. 3, #3)	The Night of the Vampire, The Strange Secret of Torture Castle	4–8
	#12 (August vol. 3, #4)	The Living Horror of Worlds Unknown	6–12
	#13 (October vol. 3 #5)	Blood Goddess, The Weird House, The Ghosts	6–12
	#14 (December vol. 3, #6)	The Spine-Chilling Zombies, The Gruesome Cannibal, The Hair-Raising Deadman, Ghouls and Werewolfs	4–8
1972	#15 (February vol. 4, #1)	The Ghoul, Satan's Blood Bath	5–10
	#16 (March vol. 4, #2)	A Horrorama of Terrifying Vampires, Ghouls and Demons	5–10
	#17 (July vol. 4, #3)	The Corpse, The Cat Is Evil, The Blood-Sucking Vampires	5–10
	#18 (September vol. 4, #4)	The Weird Corpse, Naked Horror, The Strange Friend	5–10
	#19 (November vol. 4, #5)	The Demon Strikes, Cup of Death	10–15
1973	#20 (January vol. 5, #1)	The Monster of Darkness, A Coffin for Two	6–12
	#21 (March vol. 5, #2)	A Chillerama of Blood-Draining Horror: Blood-Sucker, The Open Grave	4–8
	#22 (May vol. 5, #3)	The Bloody Thing, Seat of Doom	4–8
	#23 (July vol. 5, #4)	The Fiendish Savagery of the Blood Cult, The Monster	4–8
	#24 (September vol. 5, #5)	The Fleshless Corpse, Fingers of Doom	4–8

Year	Issue/Number	Description	Value ($)
1973	#25 (November vol. 5, #6)	The Dead Can't Sleep, The Monster Is Hunger, A Thing of Flesh and Wire	5–10
1974	#26 (January vol. 6, #1)	The Spider, The Mummy's Evil Eyes, Chop Their Heads Off	5–10
	#27 (March vol. 6, #2)	Where the Flesh-Eaters Dwell, The Hanged, The Bloody Vampire	5–10
	#28 (May vol. 6, #3)	The Curious Coffin, A Tomb of Ice, Burn Witch Burn	5–10
	#29 (July vol. 6, #4)	Heads of Horror, The Demon, The Skin-Rippers	6–12
	#30 (September vol. 6, #5)	A Living Corpse, The Skull, Horror Doll	6–12
	#31 (November vol. 6, #6)	A Dead Thing Among Us, Monster, Terror in Black	6–12
1975	#32 (February vol. 7, #1)	Head-Chopper, The Skeletons, The Fanged Freak	10–15

Tales of Terror (Eerie Publications: Illustrated Horror)

1964	#1	Summer	20–40

Tales of Voodoo (Eerie Publications: Illustrated Horror)

1968	#1 (November vol. 1, #11)	Eerie Bones, Bloody Mary, Crack-Up	12–25
1969	#2 (February vol. 2, #1)	Death Strikes Four, Hairee, Dragon Egg	10–15
	#3 (May vol. 2, #2)	Chant of the Dead, Skeletons Have No Secrets, Drums of Doom	6–12
	#4 (July vol. 2, #3)	The Bloody Ax, Witches' Curse	6–12
	#5 (September vol. 2, #4)	Corpses of the Jury, The Dead Went Marching By, Murder on the Floor	6–12

Year	Issue/Number	Description	Value ($)
1970	#6 January vol. 3, #1)	Signed in Blood, Voodoo Terror, House of Shock	6–12
	#7 (March vol. 3, #2)	The Slimy Snake Man, The Old Crone's Voodoo	6–12
	#8 (May vol. 3, #3)	The Devil's Zombie, Demons and Vampires	5–10
	#9 (July vol. 3, #4)	Blood-Hungry Vampires, Terrifying Creatures, Flesh-Eating Ghouls	5–10
	#10 (September vol. 3, #5)	The Witch's Pit, Bloody Head, Horrible Thing	5–10
	#11 (November vol. 3, #6)	The Demon Is a Hangman, The Shocking Gutless Thing	5–10
1971	#12 (January vol. 4, #1)	The Spider, Voodoo Witch, Deadman's Duel	5–10
	#13 (March vol. 4, #2)	Blacklight Monsters, Terror of the Dead	5–10
	#14 (May vol. 4, #3)	The Shocking Horror of the Twisted Brain, There Is a Blood-Sucker Among Us	5–10
	#15 (July vol. 4, #4)	The Incredible Terror of the Mummies, Witch of Doom, A Thing of Horror	5–10
	#16 (September vol. 4, #5)	An Inferno of Shocking—Weird and Bizarre Tales of the Supernatural	5–10
	#17 (November vol. 4, #6)	Step into the Scarifying World of Bizarre Monsters, Vampires and Ghouls	5–10
1972	#18 (January vol. 5, #1)	Zombie Maker, The Bloody Creature	5–10
	#19 (March Vol. 5, #2)	Demons and Things from the Chilling Pit of Voodoo Horror	5–10
	#20 (April vol. 5, #3)		5–10

Year	Issue/Number	Description	Value ($)
1972	#21 (June vol. 5, #4)	The Cave of Vampires, The Transparent Ones	5–10
	#22 (August vol. 5, #5)	The Pit of the Monsters, Horror Bells	5–10
	#23 (October vol. 5 #6)	The Blood-Dripping Head, The Cat of Horror	5–10
	#24 (December vol. 5, #7)	Satan's Dead Demons, The Bloody Horror	5–10
1973	#25 (January vol. 6, #1)	The Blood-Dripping Scarecrow, Horror Face	5–10
	#26 (March vol. 6, #2)	The Monster Cloud, Force of Horror	5–10
	#27 (May vol. 6, #3)	A Horror Spectacular of Blood-Dripping Terror	5–10
	#28 (July vol. 6, #4)	From Out of the Coffin, Pit of Horror, The Ice Monsters	5–10
	#29 (September vol. 6, #5)	Tear Him Apart, Man-Rat	5–10
	#30 (November vol. 6, #6)	A Garden of Corpses Satan's Bloody Pearls	5–10
1974	#31 (January vol. 7, #1)	Pool of Evil, Midnight Hag, The Blood Slave	5–10
	#32 (March vol. 7, #2)	Vampire, Satan's Demon Horror with Four Legs	5–10
	#33 (May vol. 7, #3)		5–10
	#34 (July vol. 7, #4)		5–10
	#35 (September vol. 7, #5)	The Rats Are Coming, Horror in Jade	6–12
	#36 (November vol. 7, #6)	Its Fangs Cried for Blood, Lighthouse Terror, The Monsters	6–12

Talking Pictures Magazine

1965	#2	The Addams Family and The Munsters: A Special Issue	15–25

Year	Issue/Number	Description	Value ($)

Terrors of Dracula (Modern Day Periodicals: Illustrated Horror)

Year	Issue/Number	Description	Value ($)
1979	#1 (May vol. 1, #3)	The Blood-sucking Vampire, The Files	6–12
	#2 (August vol. 1, #4)	The Strange Vampire Rises Thirsty, Horror without a Head	4–8
	#3 (November vol. 1, #5)	Vampire, Evil Black Cats, The Spider, The Alien Monsters	4–8
	#4 (February vol. 2, #1)	Fangs of Horror, The Strange Vampire Plague, The Flesh-Eaters	4–8
1980	#5 (May vol. 2, #2)		4–7
	#6 (August vol. 2 #3)		4–7
	#7 (November vol. 2, #4)		4–7

Terror Tales (Eerie Publications: Illustrated Horror)

Year	Issue/Number	Description	Value ($)
1969	#1 (March vol. 1, #7)	Skulls of Doom, Sales of Death	15–30
	#2 (May vol. 1, #8)	Meet Me in the Tomb, The Shelf of Skulls, Death Claws	12–22
	#3 (July vol. 1, #9)	The Deadly Ghouls, Satan's Vault of Horror	10–20
	#4 (November vol. 1, #10)	Vampire, Dig Me a Grave	10–20
1970	#5 (January vol. 2, #1)	The Hanging Ghoul, The Vampire Files	6–12
	#6 (March vol. 2, #2)	The Vampire Monster Trap, The Dead Demons	6–12
	#7 (May vol. 2, #3)	The Zombie's Vault	6–12
	#8 (July vol. 2, #4)	The Evil Monsters, The Isle of Deamons	6–12
	#9 (September vol. 2, #5)	Unearthly Creature Features & Monsters From Worlds Beyond	6–12

Year	Issue/Number	Description	Value ($)
1970	#10 (November vol. 2, #6)	The Bloody Ax, The Shrunken Glass Corpes	6–12
1971	#11 (January vol. 3 #1)	The Zombie's Cave, The Jungle Ghost	6–12
	#12 (March vol. 3 #2)	Creature of Evil, The Corpse They Couldn't Bury	6–12
	#13 (May vol. 3, #3)	The Strange Horror of the Wooden Menace, The Evil Ones	6–12
	#14 (July vol. 3, #4)	The Tomb, The Unknown, House of Worm	6–12
	#15 (September vol. 3, #5)	Uncanny, Spine-Shattering Weird Tales from Beyond the Dark Shadows	6–12
	#16 (November vol. 3, #6)	The Blood-Chilling Werewolf	6–12
1972	#17 (January vol. 4, #1)	The Demon's Night, The Swamp Devils	6–12
	#18 (March vol. 4, #2)	Shrieking Vampires, Monsters and Strange Tales from the Unknown	6–12
	#19 (April vol. 4, #3)	Creatures, Strange Monsters	5–10
	#20 (June vol. 4, #4)	The Bloody Vampires, Things of Horror	5–10
	#21 (August vol. 4, #5)	The Graveyard, A Feast for Rats	5–10
	#22 (October vol. 4, #6)	The Gruesome Creatures, Chamber of Horrors	5–10
	#23 (December vol. 4, #7)	The Monster, A Thing of Horror	5–10
1973	#24 (February vol. 5, #1)	Stage of Horror, Torture, The Shape of Evil	5–10
	#25 (April vol. 5, #2)	Curse of the Mummy, The Monster	5–10

November 1969

May 1971

August 1973

October 1974

July 1977

March 1971

May 1971

July 1971

#65

Year	Issue/Number	Description	Value ($)
1973	#26 (June vol. 5, #3)	A Shocking Explosion of Horror Where Demons, Evil Fiends, and Dead Things Live	5–10
	#27 (August vol. 5, #4)	The Werewolves, Pool of Horror	5–10
	#28 (October vol. 5, #5)	Lighthouse of Horror	5–10
	#29 (December vol. 5, #6)	The Hunger Corpsemakers, The Horror Bugs	5–10
1974	#30 February vol. 6, #1	The Undead, The Demon Ghost	5–10
	#31 April vol. 6, #2	The Buried, The Skeletons	5–10
	#32 June vol. 6, #3	Zombies Coast to Coast	5–10
	#33 August vol. 6, #4	Satan's Revenge, Give Me Back My Brain	5–10
	#34 (October vol. 6, #5)	The Spider, The Seven Skulls	5–10
	#35 (December vol. 6, #6)	The Flesh-Ripper	5–10
1976	#36 (April vol. 7, #1)	Beyond the Grave, The Flesh-Eaters	6–12
	#37 (July vol. 7, #3)	Blood Bath, Voodoo Terror, Skin-Rippers	6–12
	#38 (October vol. 7, #4)		6–12
1977	#39 (April vol. 8, #1)	House of Blood	6–12
	#40 (July vol. 8, #2)	Ghoul's Mansion	6–12
	#41 (October vol. 8, #3)	The House That Dripped Blood	6–12
1978	#42 (January vol. 9, #1)		5–10

Year	Issue/Number	Description	Value ($)
1978	#43 (April vol. 9, #2)	Fangs of Horror, The Spider, The Seven Skulls	5–10
	#44 (July vol. 9, #3)		5–10
	#45 (October vol. 9, #4)		5–10

3-D Monsters (Fair Publications)

1964	#1		25–60

Thriller (Tempest Publishing)

1962	#1	The Vampire Was a Sucker, Her Blood Ran Hot	80–225+
	#2	The Monster That Ate Candy, The Mummy Who Wanted a Daddy	80–225+
	#3	Necking with a Vampire, Werewolves Are Funny, Monsters for Hire	80–225+

True Twilight Tales

1964	One issue only		6–12

True Weird

Note: Collected by some monster magazine collectors for its strange and fantastic true stories

1955–1956	All issues		12–25

TV Greats' Space Stars

1978		Superman versus Wonder Woman, Battlestar Galactica special 12-page section, The Incredible Hulk, The Scoop on the New Star Trek, Mork & Mindy, The Who's Who in Space, Star Wars	5–10

Year	Issue/Number	Description	Value ($)

TV Science Fiction Monthly **(British Poster Magzine Published by Sportscene Ltd.)**

	all issues		4–9

Twilight Zone Magazine **(TZ Publications)**
Publishing begins in 1980

	#1		5–10
	All other issues		3–6

Vampirella **(Warren)**

Year	Issue/Number	Description	Value ($)
1969–1988	#1		60–125+
	#2		30–60+
	#3		60–110+
	#4		40–60
	#5		25–45
	#6		25–45
	#7		25–45
	#8		25–45
	#9		25–25
	#10		20–35
	#11		20–35
	#12		15–30
	#13		15–30
	#14		15–30
	#15		15–30
	#16		15–30
	#17		10–20
	#18		10–20
	#19	1973 annual	10–20
	#20		10–20
	#21		10–20
	#22		10–20
	#23		10–18
	#24		10–18
	#25		7–15
	#26		7–12
	#27	1974 annual	7–12
	#28		6–12
	#29		6–12

Year	Issue/Number	Description	Value ($)
1969–1988	#30		10–18
	#31		10–18
	#32		6–12
	#33		5–10
	#34		5–10
	#35		5–10
	#36		5–10
	#37	1975 annual	6–12
	#38		5–10
	#39		5–10
	#40		5–10
	#41		4–8
	#42		4–8
	#43		4–8
	#44		4–8
	#45		4–8
	#46		6–12
	#47		4–8
	#48		4–8
	#49		4–8
	#50		4–8
	#51–113		4–8

Vampirella Annual
1972			75–125+

Vampirella Special
1977	#1		10–20

Vampire Tales, Stan Lee Presents (Illustrated Horror, Marvel)
1973–1975	#1		6–12
	#2–11		3–6
	#1 1975 Annual		3–6

Web of Horror (Major Magazine, Illustrated Horror)
1969–1970	#1		15–25
	#2, #3		10–20

Weird (Eerie Publications, Illustrated Horror)
1966	#1		15–25

Year	Issue/Number	Description	Value ($)
1966	#2	Vampires, Werewolves, and Monsters special	6–12
	#3	Black Death, Blood Blossom, Fanged Terror	6–12
	#4	Tiger-Tiger, Fatal Scalpel	6–12
1967	#5	Fiends from the Crypt	6–12
	#6	Ghoul for a Day, Horror in the Mine, Gruesome Garden	6–12
	#7	The Ghostly Guillotine	10–15
1968	#8	Secret Coffin	6–12
	#9	Careless Corpse	6–12
	#10	Werewolf Castle	10–15
	#11	Death Makes Three, Skull Scavenger, House of Chills	6–12
	#12	Torture Garden, Idol of Evil, Death on Ice	6–12
1969	#13	Nightmare Mansion	6–12
	#14	Monster Mill, The Empty Coffin	6–12
	#15	Ghoul's Castle, Horror Hour	6–12
	#16	Fanged Horror, Now I Lay Me Down to Die	6–12
	#17	Blackness of Evil, Blood Bath	6–12
1970	#18	The Sewer Werewolves, The Vampire Witch	6–12
	#19	Zombie for a Day	6–12
	#20	The Shrunken Monster	6–12
	#21	Vampire Ghouls, Werewolf	6–12
	#22	Feast for Vampires	6–12
	#23	The Angry Vampire	6–12
1971	#24	The Terror of the Swamp Monster, Feast for Rats	5–10
	#25	Devil Statues, The Wax	6–12

October 1970

February 1971

August 1971

July 1973

September 1974

February 1975

February 1971

August 1974

April 1971

Year	Issue/Number	Description	Value ($)
1971	#26	The Beast from Below	5–10
	#27	Vampire Files, The Best	5–10
	#28	Satan's Warlock	5–10
	#29	The Weird World of Zombies, Vampires and Monsters	6–12
1972	#30	Beyond Evil, Thing in the Box, Death Demon	5–10
	#31	Demons and Vampires special	5–10
	#32		5–10
	#33	The Stone Monsters, The Beast	5–9
	#34	The Bloody Corpse, The Mummies	5–9
	#35	Mask of Horror, Dead Man's Rope	5–9
	#36	The Skin-Crawlers	5–9
1973	#37	From the Grave Below	5–9
	#38	Poison of Evil, The Geek	4–8
	#39	The Rotting Ghouls, Jaws of Terror	4–8
	#40	A Head Full of Snakes	5–10
	#41	The Flesh-Rippers	5–9
	#42	The Swamp Creature	5–9
1974	#43	A Storm of Blood	5–9
	#44	Scream in Terror	4–8
	#45	The Shape of Evil	4–8
	#46	Tomb of Horror, Monster Maker	4–8
	#47	The Evil Black Cats	5–9
	#48		5–9
1975	#49	A Thing with Fangs, Coils of Terror, Blind Monsters	8–15
1976	#50	The Fleshless Corpse, The Living Dead	6–12

Year	Issue/Number	Description	Value ($)
1976	#51	Mask of Horror	6–12
	#52	The Vampire Lives	6–12
1977	#53	Vampire, The Coffin	6–12
	#54		6–12
	#55	Cave of Vampires,	6–12
1978	#56	Werewolf, Cat of Evil	4–8
	#57	The Monster from Saturn	4–8
	#58	Stay out My Grave	4–8
	#59	Vampire, Give Me Back My Brain	6–12
1979	#60		5–9
	#61		5–9
	#62		5–9
1980	#63	Bloody Thing	6–12
	#64	The Hairy Beast	6–12
	#65	Claws of Horror	6–12
	#66		6–12
1981	#67		6–12
	#68		6–12
	#69	The Bloody House	6–12

Weird Vampire Tales **(Modern Day Periodicals, Illustrated Horror)**

Year	Issue/Number	Description	Value ($)
1979	#1	It Cried for Blood	5–10
	#2		5–10
	#3		5–10
1980	#4	Bloodsucker, Fanged Freak, The Demon	5–10
	#5		5–10
	#6	The Fanged Flies	5–10
	#7		5–10
1981	#8	Fangs and Claws, The Flesh-Rippers, Werewolf	4–8
	#9	The Bloodsucking Vampire Strikes	4–8
	#10		6–12

Year	Issue/Number	Description	Value ($)
Weird Worlds (Eerie Publications, Inc Illustrated Horror)			
1970	#1	The Space Vampire	15–30
1971	#2	The Hungry Brain	15–25
	#3	The Demon Star	10–15
	#4	The Metal Replacements	10–15
	#5	Gut-Clutching Tale of Shocking Terror	10–20
Weird Worlds (Scholastic Inc.)			
Publishing begins in 1980			
	All issues		5–10
Werewolves and Vampires (Charton Publishing)			
1962	One shot		15–35
Witches' Tales (Eerie Publications, Inc.: Illustrated Horror)			
1969	#1	Ghost-Bait, Broom for a Witch, Green Horror	15–25
	#2	A Taste of Blood	8–17
	#3	Devil's Monster	8–17
1970	#4	The Mummies,	10–15
	#5	Claws of Horror, Monster in White	10–15
	#6	House of Vampires	6–12
	#7	Special Bewitching Issue	10–15
	#8	The Skeleton, Vampire	6–12
	#9	Winged Monsters, The Hungry Vampire	6–12
1971	#10	The Weird Terror of the Zombie Manikins	6–11
	#11	The Evil Black Cats	6–12
	#12	Mask of Horror	6–12
	#13	The Bloody Blob	6–12
	#14	One Step Beyond	6–12
	#15	The Conjurer, Jeb's Bloody Ghost	6–12
1972	#16	House of Vampires	10–15
	#17	Shocking Horror Tales of	

Year	Issue/Number	Description	Value ($)
1972	#17	Strange Monsters 'n' Evil Things	6–12
	#18	The Witch's Horror	5–10
	#19	Monsters of Evil	5–10
	#20	Evil Is the Witch	5–10
	#21	Stay Out of My Grave	8–15
1973	#22	The Monster That Burns	5–10
	#23	Web of Horror	5–10
	#24	The Cave Monsters	5–9
	#25	The Fiend from the Outside	5–9
	#26	A Horror in Wood, The Vampire	10–15
	#27	Eat the Flesh, Drink The Blood	8–15
1974	#28	The Vampire	5–10
	#29	The Screaming Things	8–16
	#30		6–12
	#31		5–10
	#32	Horror Without a Head	5–10
	#33	The Thing that Screamed	10–20
1975	#34	Gruesome Nightmare	8–17

World Famous Creatures (Magsyn Publications)

1958–1959	#1	The World's Most Frightening Horror	125–175+
	#2	The She Demon	100–175+
	#3	Bela Lugosi's Life Story	100–175+
	#4	How to Buy Hollywood Monster Equipment	100–150+

World of Horror (Dallruth Publishing)

1972	#1–6		15–25
	#7–9		10–15

Rock and Roll
and Teen Magazines

✠

Teen and rock magazines have always played an important role in America's youth culture. Since the early fifties, teenagers and young adults have been drawn to pop music magazines with their eye-catching full-color covers, pinups, posters, and inside facts and scoops on the most current pop personalities.

In the fifties, it was Buddy Holly, Johnny Mathis, Annette Funicello, Elvis Presley, and others who stirred the emotions of the young. In the sixties, it was the Beatles, the Rolling Stones, Sonny and Cher, the Monkees, and many others. At present it's the Spice Girls and Britney Spears that receive all the attention from the new millennium fan. Today these magazines appeal to teenagers and adults as well. Unlike many other publications, back issue teen/rock magazines have not faded into obscurity, but are highly prized by their owners. Today's teens find themselves listening and rocking to many of the same pop performers that their parents, and even grandparents, enjoyed in past decades and continue to enjoy today.

With the increased popularity of pop music during the past four decades, thousands of radio stations and record shops throughout the world service these fans daily. This is one indication of how important music and music stars are in the lives of fans. They want to know more about their favorites, and they have a need to obtain pinups and posters. Their prime source for the past forty years has been the rock/teen magazine.

By nature, the rock and teen magazine was not designed to last beyond the first few hours with the magazine purchaser. In the past, as well as today, fans who buy rock/teen magazines will take them home or remove them from their mailboxes and start clipping all the photos and pulling out the posters. These clipped photos and posters generally end up in scrapbooks, on a bedroom wall, or in a fan's school locker. Regrettably, this procedure renders the rock/teen magazine totally worthless. Few teen magazines from the fifties and sixties survived this practice, making complete copies from these two decades very much sought after and very expensive to purchase when found. It does not always take decades for a rock magazine's value to rise beyond its cover price. Current issues, issues perhaps just a few months old, can appreciate by as much as 50 to 200 percent. This is usually owing to the quality of photos, posters, and story on a particular star and the overall distribution of the magazine. In today's market, with the many Internet auction sites, a recent teen/rock magazine that may be common and easy for one collector to acquire can be nearly impossible for a fan on the other side of the world to purchase. This is just one example of why many issues, including the latest issues, can have a high value.

The primary element in determining the value of a rock/teen magazine is its content—who is on the cover; what or whom the feature articles are about; how long, interesting, or unusual the articles are and whether they include interviews; how many and how rare the photos are; and whether or not color pinups or posters are included.

If a pop star or group is currently enjoying some measure of success, the demand for rock/teen magazines on the personality or group increases. In short, the greater the star (stars), the greater the demand for magazines on the star, thus increasing the value of the magazine.

When an older group (The Bee Gees, for example) makes a comeback with a tour or a new album, values of magazines featuring them can double or even triple in a very short time. Tribute films and movies at the theater and on cable TV also play a major role in determining who is currently popular.

Condition also determines a rock/teen magazine's value, and in most cases the issue must be complete. After completeness, physical condition of the magazine is next in importance. Unlike monster magazines, comics, coins, and many other collectibles, however, rock and teen magazines are not held to such a strict form of grading. A very good and a very fine copy of an older issue will usually have the same value. Truly mint copies from the fifties and sixties are extremely rare and considerably more valuable.

Buying and Selling Rock/Teen Magazines

Current issues of rock/teen magazines can be found on just about any newsstand or purchased directly by subscription, and many back issues can be ordered through a magazine publisher's back-issue department. When back issues are no longer available from the publisher, however, it is necessary to find other sources.

Record dealers are increasingly including pop music magazines with their inventory, and quite often they offer the latest hard-to-find specialty and foreign rock magazines. When visiting a record shop, it is best to talk to the manager about your magazine needs. If he does not have your particular magazine in stock, he will, at least, be conscious of your needs the next time he purchases a magazine collection.

Garage sales and flea markets are also prime collecting sources, and, best of all, the unexpected goodies you find there can usually be purchased at a fraction of their real value. Trade papers that specialize in pop records, magazines, and memorabilia, however, will be your most reliable sources. Dealers and collectors from all over the United States and many foreign countries regularly offer a continuing supply of back-issue pop magazines. These publications are also excellent places for the collector to advertise his or her needs when attempting to add to a collection or sell a collection.

Internet auctions are quickly becoming The Place to buy back-issue teen and rock magazines. Prices on these auctions run generally from real buys to record-setting highs. For example, a 1993 issue of *Sixteen Magazine* featuring Leonardo DiCaprio, which would normally sell at a convention, back-issue magazine store, or through the mail for maybe $1 to $2, sold for $27. If you don't mind a little excitement, and have a set price that you're willing to pay for an issue, then this new marketplace can be a lot of fun.

Comic-book shops, back-issue magazine stores, and record shows and conventions are also great places to acquire music magazines. A collector of Kiss or Beatle magazines, for example, would be wise to attend a Kiss or Beatles convention. Hundreds of pop music conventions are held in the United States and abroad annually. These conventions are not only fine sources for adding much sought after issues to your collection, but are doubly rewarding as places to meet other enthusiasts, and sometimes the pop performers themselves. You should also seriously consider joining a fan club both as a means of acquiring back issues, and for the additional benefit of being kept informed of upcoming events relating to your favorite performer.

In the recent past, mail-order dealers specializing in rock and teen magazines have become the most reliable means of acquiring magazines at a set price. Many mail-order dealerships, such as The Back Issue (P.O.

Box 743, Ridgefield Park, NJ 07660) purchase magazine collections every day and maintain active inventories of thousands of issues. If a mail-order dealer does not currently have your back issue in stock, often the dealer will keep your want list on file and inform you at a later date of its availability.

Before purchasing any rock or teen magazine, however, it is extremely important that you inspect each page for missing pinups, stories, and clippings. Furthermore, when posters are included in an issue, examine the issue closely to see if they are all there, are reasonably intact, and are indeed the posters that belong to that particular issue. Many magazines with beautiful, glossy color covers will appear to be in fine condition. Be cautious, however, it is easy to assume that the entire magazine is this way, but you cannot always judge a teen/rock magazine by its cover. When buying through the mail, ask for return privileges in the event the issue purchased is not complete.

Selling rock and teen magazines involves basically using the same sources that you used in acquiring issues. Highest prices will be attained when marketing your collection to collectors of your particular group or personality. I strongly suggest that you experiment with selling your issues on an Internet auction site. The cost to place a back issue magazine up for bid on the Internet is nominal and the rewards can be great. Internet auctions, trade papers, fan-club newsletters, and conventions are where the most active buyers are found. In trade papers and newsletters, an inexpensive classified ad will tell thousands of collectors that your collection is up for sale. When placing your ad to sell magazines, clearly state the title, issue number, the cover subject, the feature stories, and if the issue contains pinups and or posters. Also state the magazine's condition, your mailing terms, and your asking price.

AVERAGE ROCK/TEEN MAGAZINE VALUES

(Not Featuring the Most Collectible Stars)

Issues	Value ($)
1957	15–30
1958	12–25
1959	10–20
1960–1962	10–20

1963–1966	7–10
1967–1969	7–20
1970–1971	5–10
1972–1975	4–8
1976–1980	4–8
1981–1989	2–5
1990–present	1–2

MOST COLLECTIBLE ROCK AND ROLL
STARS/GROUPS OF THE FIFTIES

	Value ($)			
Subject	Cover and Feature	Cover Only	Feature Only	Cameo
Chuck Berry	20–40	20–40	10–20	10–20
Dick Clark/ American Band Stand	25–65	25–50	20–40	10–20
Dion & The Belmonts	50–100	50–75	15–30	15–25
Bobby Darin	20–40	15–25	10–20	10–20
James Dean (teen idol)	25–50	20–40	15–30	10–20
Fats Domino	15–30	15–25	10–20	10–20
Connie Francis	25–45	20–35	20–30	10–20
Annette Funicello	25–50	20–40	20–40	10–20
Buddy Holly	25–100	25–100	25–50	20–30
Brenda Lee	25–40	20–30	20–30	10–20
Roy Orbison	30–60	25–50	15–30	10–20
Elvis Presley	30–80	20–40	20–35	10–20
Conway Twitty	20–40	20–40	20–35	10–20

MOST COLLECTIBLE ROCK AND ROLL STARS/GROUPS OF THE SIXTIES

Subject	Value ($)			
	Cover and Feature	Cover Only	Feature Only	Cameo
Beach Boys	20–40	20–35	15–30	10–20
Beatles	25–50	20–40	15–30	10–20
Bee Gees	25–50	20–40	10–20	10–20
Bobby Darin	20–40	15–30	12–25	10–20
Dion	25–50	25–50	20–40	10–20
Doors/Jim Morrison	25–100	15–50	20–40	10–20
Grateful Dead	25–50	20–40	20–40	12–20
Bob Dylan	20–40	20–40	20–40	12–20
Shelley Fabares	15–30	15–30	10–25	10–20
Fleetwood Mac	20–40	15–30	15–30	10–20
Connie Francis	15–30	15–30	15–30	10–20
Bobby Fuller	25–50	20–50	20–40	12–25
Annette Funicello	15–35	15–35	10–30	10–20
Jimi Hendrix	25–100	20–60	25–75	15–30
Jan and Dean	25–50	25–50	25–50	20–30
Jefferson Airplane	20–30	20–30	10–25	10–20
Janis Joplin	25–100	25–50	20–40	10–20
Led Zepplin	15–30	10–20	15–30	10–20
Brenda Lee	15–25	15–20	10–20	10–20
Little Anthony & The Imperials	50–100	50–75	15–30	15–25
Johnny Mathis	50–100	50–75	15–30	15–25
Hayley Mills (teen idol)	15–30	15–30	15–30	10–20
Monkees	20–40	20–30	10–20	10–20
Ricky Nelson	25–60	20–50	15–30	12–25
Roy Orbison	20–30	15–20	10–20	10–20
Elvis Presley	30–60	35–50	10–20	10–20
Rolling Stones	25–50	20–40	15–35	10–20

Subject	Value ($)			
	Cover and Feature	Cover Only	Feature Only	Cameo
Rolling Stones/ Brian Jones	25–100	25–75	25–50	10–20
Sonny and Cher	20–40	20–40	10–25	12–20
Supremes/ Diana Ross	20–40	15–30	10–25	10–20
Ritchie Valens	50–100	50–75	15–30	15–25
The Who	20–30	20–30	10–20	10–20

MOST COLLECTIBLE ROCK AND ROLL STARS/GROUPS OF THE SEVENTIES

Subject	Value ($)			
	Cover and Feature	Cover Only	Feature Only	Cameo
Beach Boys	8–20	8–20	8–15	5–10
Beatles	5–20	5–10	5–12	5–10
Bee Gees	10–25	10–25	5–10	4–8
Blondie/ Debbie Harry	10–30	10–30	5–25	5–25
David Bowie	5–20	5–20	5–20	4–8
Brady Bunch (teen idols)	15–30	15–30	10–20	10–20
David Cassidy/ Partridge Family	15–30	15–30	10–20	10–20
Cher	5–15	5–15	5–15	4–8
Alice Cooper	5–30	5–25	5–20	4–8
Doors/Jim Morrison	10–100	10–100	5–40	5–10
Grateful Dead	5–30	5–30	5–25	5–10
Bob Dylan	5–25	5–25	5–20	3–7
Fleetwood Mac	10–30	10–25	5–20	5–10
Fleetwood Mac/ Stevie Nicks	15–30	10–25	5–25	5–10
Heart	5–15	5–15	5–15	5–10
Jackson Five	5–25	5–25	5–25	5–10

Subject	Value ($)			
	Cover and Feature	Cover Only	Feature Only	Cameo
Jimi Hendrix	5–100	5–100	5–50	5–20
Jefferson Airplane	5–20	5–50	5–20	5–10
Joan Jett/Runaways	5–20	5–20	5–20	4–8
Olivia Newton-John	10–25	10–25	5–10	4–8
Janis Joplin	5–75	5–50	5–60	5–10
Kiss	5–30	5–20	5–25	5–10
Led Zeppelin	5–20	5–15	5–15	4–8
Osmonds/Donny and Marie	10–25	10–25	10–25	5–10
Suzi Quatro	10–20	10–20	10–20	5–10
Santana	10–20	10–20	5–10	4–8
Ramones	10–20	10–15	10–20	5–10
Rolling Stones	5–40	5–40	5–25	5–10
Diana Ross	5–20	5–20	5–20	4–8
Sex Pistols	10–20	10–20	10–20	5–10

MOST COLLECTIBLE ROCK AND ROLL STARS/GROUPS OF THE EIGHTIES

Subject	Value ($)			
	Cover and Feature	Cover Only	Feature Only	Cameo
Lee Aaron	5–15	5–15	5–12	4–8
Bee Gees	10–20	10–20	5–10	4–10
Pat Benatar	5–15	5–10	5–10	4–8
Blondie/Debbie Harry	12–25	12–25	10–20	5–10
David Bowie	4–8	3–7	3–7	3–5
Belinda Carlisle	5–8	4–8	4–8	2–4
Cher	5–10	5–10	5–10	3–5
Alice Cooper	3–7	3–6	3–6	3–5
Doors/Jim Morrison	5–20	5–10	5–15	3–5
Grateful Dead	4–8	4–7	4–8	2–4
Fleetwood Mac	8–20	8–20	5–10	2–4
Fleetwood Mac/ Stevie Nicks	10–20	10–20	5–10	4–10

Subject	Value ($)			
	Cover and Feature	Cover Only	Feature Only	Cameo
Andy Gibb	15–25	15–25	10–20	5–10
Nina Hagen	10–20	5–10	5–10	4–8
Heart	5–10	5–10	5–10	2–4
Jimi Hendrix	5–10	5–10	5–10	2–4
Olivia Newton-John	10–20	10–20	5–10	4–10
Joan Jett	5–10	5–15	5–20	2–4
Kiss	5–15	5–10	5–12	2–4
Madonna	10–20	10–20	5–10	2–4
Marie Osmond	10–20	5–10	5–10	2–4
Rolling Stones	5–10	5–10	4–10	2–4
Diana Ross	4–8	3–6	3–5	2–4

ROCK/TEEN MAGAZINE VALUES

Year	Issue/Number	Description	Value ($)
Circus Magazine (Formerly *Hullabaloo*)			
1969	March	Jimi Hendrix	50–100
	May	Janis Joplin	50–100
	June	Frank Zappa	25–50
	July	Rock and Revolution	15–40
	August	Johnny Cash/Bob Dylan/ The Byrds	20–40
	September	The MC5	25–50
	October	The Beatles	25–50
	November	Bob Dylan	20–40
	December	John Lennon and Yoko Ono	30–60
1970	January	The Doors	50–100
	March	The Grateful Dead	30–60
	April	John Lennon and Yoko Ono	35–75
	May	Ten Years After	20–40
	June	Grace Slick	20–40
	July	Steve Winwood	20–40
	August	Joe Cocker	20–40
	September	The Band	25–50

#145, 1976

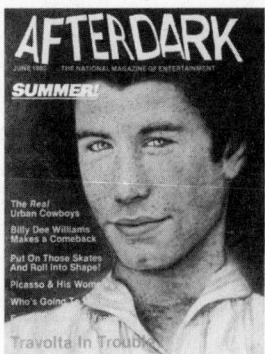

June 1980

#2, 1977

February 1978

July 1978

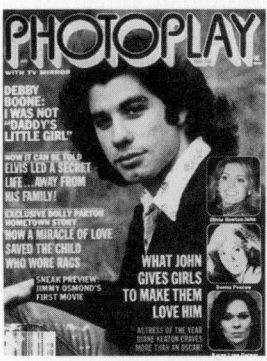

May 1978

July 1985

February 1993

#189, 1978

Year	Issue/Number	Description	Value ($)
1970	October	Janis Joplin	40–80
	December	Jimi Hendrix memorial	50–100
1971	January	Grand Funk Railroad	25–50
	Febuary	Leon Russell	25–50
	March	Jerry Garcia	35–70
	April	Crosby, Stills, Nash, and Young	20–40
	May	James Taylor	20–40
	June	Alice Cooper	25–50
	July	Cat Stevens	20–40
	August	Paul McCartney	20–40
	September	Jim Morrison death issue	50–110
	October	George Harrison	20–40
	November	Ringo Star	20–35
	December	John Lennon	30–65
1972	January	The Doors	35–75
	February	Ray Davies	25–50
	March	Emerson, Lake, and Palmer	20–35
	April	Ian Anderson	20–40
	May	Humble Pie	20–40
	June	Graham Nash	20–40
	July	Stephen Stills	20–40
	August	Alice Cooper	25–50
	September	Leon Russell	40–80
	October	Marc Bolin	20–40
	November	Cat Stevens	20–40
	December	Moody Blues	30–60
1973	January	Carole King	15–30
	February	Edgar Winter	20–40
	March	Carly Simon	15–30
	April	Elton John	20–40
	May	Steve Marriot	15–25
	June	Rod Stewart	15–30
	July	David Bowie	15–30
	August	Rick Wakeman	15–25
	September	Ian Anderson	15–30
	October	Robert Plant	15–25

Year	Issue/Number	Description	Value ($)
1973	November	Uriah Heep	15–25
	December	Elton John	20–40
1974	January	Alice Cooper	15–30
	February	The Band	10–20
	March	Johnny Winter	10–20
	April	Jeff Beck	10–25
	May	Mark Farner	10–20
	June	Ian Hunter	10–20
	July	Edger Winter	10–20
	August	David Byron	10–20
	September	Jim Dandy	10–20
	October	Gregg Allman	15–30
	November	Peter Wolf	10–20
	December	The State of Future Rock	10–20
1975	#102	Elton John	10–20
	#104	Jimmy Page	10–20
	#106	Peter Gabriel	7–15
	#108	David Bowie	7–15
	#110	Alice Cooper	10–25
	#112	Rick Derringer	7–10
	#114	Todd Rundgren	10–20
	#116	Mick Jagger	10–25
	#118	Ron Wood	10–20
	#120	Gregg Allman	10–20
	#122	Rod Stewart	8–16
	#124	Ian Anderson	8–16
	#125	Linda Ronstadt	10–20
1976	#126	Ray and Dave Davies	5–10
	#127	Bob Dylan	6–12
	#128	Bruce Springsteen	10–20
	#129	Lou Reed	5–10
	#130	Kiss	15–30
	#131	David Bowie	6–12
	#132	Robert Plant	5–10
	#133	Mick Jagger and Keith Richards	7–15
	#134	Steven Tyler	5–10
	#135	Emerson, Lake, and Palmer	6–12

Year	Issue/Number	Description	Value ($)
1976	#136	Jeff Beck	5–10
	#137	King Kong	5–10
	#138	Alice Cooper	7–15
	#139	Caroline Kennedy	5–10
	#140	Saturday Night Live cast	6–20
	#141	Lindsay Wagner	6–12
	#142	Clint Eastwood	6–12
	#143	The Captain and Tennille	7–15
	#144	Cherrie Currie	7–15
	#145	John Travolta	10–20
	#146	ZZ Top	5–10
1977	#147	Breakouts	10–20
	#148	Kris Krisofferson	5–10
	#149	Lindsay Wagner	5–10
	#150	David Bowie	6–12
	#151	Paul Rogers	5–10
	#152	Christine McVie	10–20+
	#153	Ian Anderson	6–12
	#154	Keith Emerson	5–10
	#155	Alice Cooper	6–12
	#156	Sex and Today's Teenager	6–12
	#157	Jimmy Page	6–12
	#158	Ted Nugent	5–10
	#159	Linda Blair	7–15
	#160	Sissy Spacek	5–10
	#161	Kiss	12–25
	#162	Peter Frampton	7–15
	#163	Rick Wakeman	6–12
	#164	The Fonz	6–12
	#165	Keith Richards	6–12
	#166	Hall and Oates	6–12
	#167	Linda Ronstadt	7–15
	#168	TV's Logan's Run	10–20
	#169	Nancy Wilson	6–12
	#170	Cindy Williams	5–10
	#171	Gene Simmons	12–25
1978	#172	Dolly Parton	5–10
	#173	Freddie Mercury	10–20

Year	Issue/Number	Description	Value ($)
1978	#174	The Bee Gees	15–30+
	#175	Linda Ronstadt	6–12
	#176	Jackson Browne	6–12
	#177	Ted Nugent	6–12
	#178	Barry Gibb	12–25+
	#179	Peter Criss	15–30
	#180	Grace Slick	7–15
	#181	Paul Stanley	20–30
	#182	Paul McCartney	7–15
	#183	Carly Simon	10–20
	#184	Robbie Robertson of The Band	5–10
	#185	John Travolta	10–20
	#186	Foghat	5–10
	#187	Bob Seger	5–10
	#188	Andy Gibb	15–30
	#189	Texas Jam	5–10
	#190	Peter Frampton	6–12
	#191	Barry Gibb	10–20+
	#192	The Beatles	5–10
	#193	Shaun Cassidy	5–10
	#194	Kiss	10–20
	#195	25 Years of Rock	6–12
	#196	Linda Ronstadt	6–12
	#197	Ian Anderson	4–8
	#198	Billy Joel	4–8
	#199	Elton John	5–10
	#200	Ted Nugent	4–8
	#201	Steve Tyler	4–8
	#202	Freddie Mercury	10–20
	#203	Alice Cooper	7–15
1979	#204	Steve Martin	4–8
	#205	David Lee Roth	4–8
	#206	Marijuana	4–8
	#207	Rod Stewart	4–8
	#208	Mork and Mindy	4–8
	#209	Robert Plant	4–8
	#210	Sex in America	3–6

V12, #8, 1986

V4, #1, 1987

V4, #3, 1987

October 1968

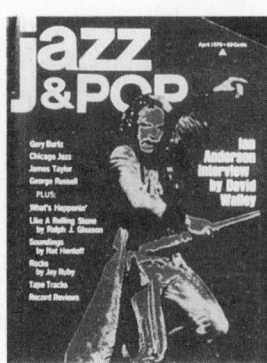

April 1970

June 1970

August 1973

August 1978

May 1984

May 1988

June 1990

#66, 1991

1990

August 1990

May 1989

July 1988

August 1988

November 1973

Year	Issue/Number	Description	Value ($)
1979	#211	Dan Aykroyd and John Belushi	5–10
	#212	Animal House	3–6
	#213	Eddie Money	3–6
	#214	The Bee Gees	10–20
	#215	Cheryl Ladd and Miss Piggy	5–10
	#216	Elvis Presley	3–6
	#217	Debbie Harry	10–20+
	#218	Bucky Dent	3–6
	#219	Jane Fonda	3–6
	#220	Stockard Channing	5–10
	#221	Hair's Donnie Dacus	3–6
	#222	Patti Hansen	3–6
	#223	Ron Wood and Keith Richards	5–10
	#224	Cher	5–10
	#225	Summer Movie Magic	3–6
	#226	Most Influential People	3–6
	#227	The Best of Circus	3–6
	#228	Woodstock	5–10
	#229	Gilda Radner	5–10
	#230	Robert Plant	3–6
	#231	Ric Ocasek	5–10
	#232	Stevie Nicks	15–30+
	#233	Steve Martin	2–5
	#234	Cheap Trick	4–6
	#235	Styx	4–6
	#236	Foreigner	4–8
1980	#237	Debbie Harry	10–20+
	#238	Debbie Harry and Robert Plant	10–20+
	#239	Steve Tyler	4–8
	#240	Rush	5–10+
	#241	Pink Floyd	5–10
	#242	David Lee Roth	4–8
	#243	Bob Seger	4–8
	#244	Summer Rock special	3–6

Year	Issue/Number	Description	Value ($)
1980	#245	Journey	4–8
	#246	Black Sabbath	4–8
	#247	Freddie Mercury	10–20+
	#248	Kiss	10–20
	#249	Ric Ocasek	4–8
	#250	Year-End special	5–10
1981	#251	Jim Morrison	6–12
	#252	Awards issue	4–8
	#253	Rush	5–10
	#254	Ritchie Blackmore	4–8
	#255	The New British Invasion	4–8
	#256	Ozzy Osbourne	5–10
	#257	AC/DC	5–10
	#258	Tom Petty	4–8
	#259	The Moody Blues	7–15+
	#260	12th Anniversary special	4–8
	#261	The Rolling Stones	5–10
	#262	Stevie Nicks	15–30+
1982	#263	Phil Collins	4–8
	#264	Pat Benatar	5–10
	#265	Angus Young	3–6
	#266	Ozzy Osbourne	5–10
	#267	Richie Blackmore	3–6
	#268	Rock and tour issue special	3–6
	#269	Debbie Harry	10–20
	#270	REO Speedwagon	4–8
	#271	David Lee Roth	3–7
	#272	Ozzy Osbourne	4–8
	#273	Rush	3–7
	#274	The Year in Review	3–6
1983	#275	Led Zeppelin	3–7
	#276	David Lee Roth	3–7
	#277	Ozzy Osbourne	3–7
	#278	Steve Perry	3–6
	#279	David Lee Roth	3–6
	#280	Rock on the Road	3–6
	#281	Def Leppard	4–8
	#282	Def Leppard	3–6

Year	Issue/Number	Description	Value ($)
1983	#283	Def Leppard	3–6
	#284	14th Anniversary special	3–6
	#285	Quiet Riot	3–6
	#286	The Year in Rock	3–6
1984	#287	Quiet Riot	3–6
	#288	Joe Elliot	3–6
	#289	Vince Neil	4–8
	#290	Heavy Metal special	3–6
	#291	David Lee Roth	3–7
	#292	Rock on the Road special	3–6
	#293	Klaus Meine	3–6
	#294	Motley Crue	3–7
	#295	Stephen Percy	3–6
	#296	Ratt	3–7
	#297	Dee Snider	3–7
	#298	Stephen Percy	3–6
1985	#299	Bruce Dickinson	3–7
	#300	Paul Stanley	5–10
	#301	Vince Neil	4–8
	#302	Gene Simmons	5–10
	#303	Paul Stanley	5–10
	#304	Kiss	5–10
	#305	Queensryche	3–6
	#306	Dokken	3–6
	#307	Motley Crue	3–7
	#308	Motley Crue	3–7
	#309	Jon Bon Jovi	4–8
	#310	Nikki Sixx	3–6
1986	#311	Paul Stanley	5–10
	#312	Vince Neil	3–6
	#313	Ratt	3–6
	#314	Motley Crue	3–6
	#315	Ozzy Osbourne	4–8
	#316	Eddie Van Halen	3–7
	#317	Judas Priest	3–6
	#318	Bon Jovi	3–7
	#319	David Lee Roth	3–6

Year	Issue/Number	Description	Value ($)
1986	#320	Motley Crue	3–6
	#321	Motley Crue	3–6
	#322	Cinderella	3–6
	#323	Motley Crue	3–6
	#324	Bon Jovi	3–6
	#325	Bon Jovi	3–6
1987	#326	Bon Jovi	3–6
	#327	Bon Jovi	3–6
	#328	Bon Jovi	3–6
	#329	Motley Crue	2–4
	#330	Bon Jovi	3–5
	#331	Bon Jovi	3–5
	#332	Bon Jovi	3–5
	#333	Def Leppard	2–4
	#334	The Year in Rock	2–4

1988–
present

Circus Magazine Pinups

Year	Issue/Number	Description	Value ($)
1975	#1	Mick Jagger	25–50
	#2	The Rolling Stones	20–30
	#3	Elvis Presley	15–30

Circus Raves

Year	Issue/Number	Description	Value ($)
1974	#1 February	Johnny Winter	20–40
	#2 March	Roger Daltry	15–30
	#3 April	Paul McCartney	15–30
	#4 June	Noddy Holder	15–30
	#6 August	Keith Emerson	15–30
	#7 September	Bill Wyman	15–30
	#8 October	Eric Clapton	12–25
	#9 November	Ian Anderson	12–25
	#10 December	Rod Stewart	12–25
1975	#101	Ritchie Blackmore	10–20
	#103	Mark Farner	12–25
	#105	Freddie Mercury	20–40
	#107	Robin Trower	10–20
	#109	Steve Marriot	10–20
	#111	David Bowie	12–15

Year	Issue/Number	Description	Value ($)
1975	#113	Paul Rogers	8–15
	#115	Elton John	10–20
	#117	David Byron	8–15
	#119	Ozzy Osbourne	10–20
	#120	Edgar Winter	10–20
	#123	Pete Townshend	10–20

Circus Rock Immortals Magazine

1980	#1	Jim Morrison	15–20

Creem

1967	Vol. 1, #1		75–200
	All other issues		30–60
1968	Vol. 2, #1–7		25–50
	#8	Adolf Hitler	15–30
	#9	Ted Nugent	30–60
	#10	Scot Richardson	20–40
	#11 (issue marked vol. 2 #10)	The Rationals	15–30
1969	All issues		20–40
1970	All issues		20–40
1971	January–July		20–40
	August, September, October		15–30
	November	Grand Funk Railroad	12–25
	December	Pete Townshend	15–30
1972	January	Alice Cooper	20–40
	February	Bob Dylan	25–40
	March	John Lennon	30–60
	April	Smokey Robinson	15–30
	May	T. Rex	15–30
	June	Black Sabbath	15–30
	July	The Beach Boys	20–40
	August	Rod Stewart	15–20
	September	The Rolling Stones	20–40
	October	Humble Pie	15–30
	November	Allman Brothers	20–40

Year	Issue/Number	Description	Value ($)
1972	December	Leon Russell	15–30
1973	January	The Rolling Stones	15–30
	February	Chuck Berry	10–20
	March	Edgar Winter	12–20
	April	Amazing Spiderman	10–20
	May	Jethro Tull	10–20
	June	Alice Cooper	12–25
	July	Johnny Winter	12–25
	August	David Bowie	12–25
	September	Led Zeppelin	12–25
	October	Guitar Special	10–20
	November	Jimi Hendrix	15–35
	December	The Rolling Stones	15–30
1974	January	Pete Townshend	10–20
	February	Elton John	10–25
	March	Emerson, Lake, and Palmer	10–20
	April	Iggy Pop	15–25
	May	Alice Cooper	10–20
	June	David Bowie	10–20
	July	The Rolling Stones	10–25
	August	Alice Cooper	10–20
	September	Rick Wakeman	10–20
	October	Rod Stewart	10–20
	November	The Allman Brothers	15–30
	December	Frank Zappa	15–30
1975	January	David Bowie	10–20
	February	Jimmy Page	10–20
	March	Lou Reed	10–20
	April	Gregg Allman	12–20
	May	Elton John	12–20
	June	Gallery of Rock Graves	15–30
	July	Alice Cooper	10–20
	August	Mick Jagger	10–20
	September	Pete Townshend	7–15
	October	The Rolling Stones	10–20
	November	Rod Stewart	6–12
	December	David Bowie	6–12

Year	Issue/Number	Description	Value ($)
1976	January	John Denver	15–20
	February	Bob Dylan	6–12
	March	Kiss	15–30
	April	The Beatles	7–10
	May	Led Zeppelin	7–15
	June	The Rolling Stones	6–12
	July	Kiss	10–20
	August	Paul McCartney	7–15
	September	Rod Stewart	5–10
	October	The Rolling Stones	6–12
	November	Sex and Rock and Roll	6–12
	December	Steve Tyler	5–10
1977	January	Kiss	10–20
	February	Peter Frampton	6–12
	March	Jefferson Airplane	6–12
	April	Jimmy Page	5–10
	May	Queen	10–20+
	June	Keith Richards	6–12
	July	Robert Plant	5–10
	August	Kiss	10–20
	September	Ted Nugent	5–10
	October	Peter Frampton	6–12
	November	Rod Stewart	4–8
	December	Grace Slick	5–10
1978	January	Mick Jagger	5–10
	February	Jimmy Page	5–10
	March	Johnny and Edgar Winter	6–12
	April	Johnny Rotten	4–8
	May	Ted Nugent	3–6
	June	Jethro Tull	4–8
	July	Mick Jagger	5–10
	August	Bob Seger	4–8
	September	David Bowie	5–10
	October	Bruce Springsteen	5–10
	November	The Who	5–10
	December	Mick Jagger and Keith Richards	5–10

Year	Issue/Number	Description	Value ($)
1979	January	Ted Nugent	4–8
	February	Led Zeppelin	5–10
	March	Debbie Harry	10–20
	April	The Blues Brothers	6–12
	May	Elvis Costello	5–10
	June	Debbie Harry	10–20
	July	Cheap Trick	5–10
	August	The Rolling Stones	5–10
	September	The Who	4–8
	October	Aerosmith	4–8
	November	Jimmy Page	4–8
	December	Cheap Trick	4–8
1980	January	Joe Jackson	4–8
	February	Debbie Harry	10–20
	March	Debbie Harry	10–20
	April	The Knack	5–10
	May	Debbie Harry	10–20
	June	The Clash	5–10
	July	David Lee Roth	4–8
	August	The Pretenders	5–10
	September	Bob Seger	4–8
	October	Judas Priest	4–8
	November	Pete Townshend	4–8
	December	Cheap Trick	4–8
1981	January	Bruce Springsteen	4–8
	February	Rockpile	4–8
	March	Bruce Springsteen	4–8
	April	The Police	5–10
	May	Eddie Van Halen	5–10
	June	Debbie Harry	10–20
	July	Angus Young	4–8
	August	Judas Priest	3–6
	September	Journey	4–8
	October	Van Halen	4–8
	November	Pat Benatar	4–8
	December	Ray Davies	4–8

Year	Issue/Number	Description	Value ($)
1982	January	Mick Jagger	5–10
	February	Keith Richards	5–10
	March	Pat Benatar	4–8
	April	The Police	4–8
	May	The Cars	4–8
	June	Joan Jett	7–12
	July	The B-52's	5–10
	August	Debbie Harry	7–15
	September	David Lee Roth	4–8
	October	Robert Plant	3–6
	November	John Cougar	3–6
	December	The Who	4–8
1983	January	Mick Jagger	4–7
	February	Keith Richards	3–6
	March	Pat Benatar	4–7
	April	Tom Petty	3–6
	May	Prince	3–7
	June	Michael Jackson	4–8
	July	Joan Jett	5–10
	August	Ray Davies	3–6
	September	David Lee Roth	2–6
	October	Robert Plant	2–6
	November	The Police	4–8
	December	Brian Setzer	3–7
1984	All issues		3–6
1985	All issues		3–6
1986	All issues		3–6
1987	All issues		3–6
1988	All issues		3–6

Hit Parader

1957	All issues		15–30
1958	All issues		15–30
1959	All issues		15–30

Year	Issue/Number	Description	Value ($)
1960	All issues		10–25
1961	All issues		10–20
1962	All issues		10–20
1963	All issues		10–20
1964	All issues		15–30
1965	All issues		15–30
1966	All issues		15–30
1967	All issues		20–40
1968	All issues		20–40
1969	All issues		20–40
1970	January	Jimi Hendrix	35–70
	February	Mick Jagger and Keith Richards	35–70
	March	Joe Cocker	10–20
	April	Grace Slick	12–25
	May	The Beatles	15–30
	June	Harry Nilsson	10–20
	July	Alvin Lee	12–25
	August	John Lennon and Yoko Ono	25–50
	September	Janis Joplin	20–40
	October	Paul McCartney	10–20
	November	The Who	12–25
	December	Blood Sweat and Tears	10–20
1971	January	Mick Jagger	12–25
	February	Neil Diamond	10–20
	March	Eric Burdon and War	8–20
	April	Melanie	10–20
	May	Jethro Tull	12–25
	June	The Kinks	10–20
	July	Grand Funk Railroad	10–20
	August	John Lennon and Yoko Ono	20–40

Year	Issue/Number	Description	Value ($)
1971	September	James Taylor	10–20
	October	Janis Joplin	20–40
	November	Paul McCartney	10–20
	December	Blood, Sweat and Clayton	10–20
1972	January	Mick Jagger	10–25
	February	John Lennon and Yoko Ono	15–30
	March	The Beach Boys	10–25
	April	Carole King	8–20
	May	Mick Jagger	10–20
	June	Melanie	8–20
	July	Rod Stewart and Faces	8–20
	August	Marc Bolan	10–20
	September	Bangladesh	10–20
	October	Elton John	10–20
	November	David Cassidy	10–20
	December	Elvis Presley	10–20
1973	January	Alice Cooper	10–20
	February	David Bowie	8–15
	March	Blood, Sweat and Tears	7–15
	April	David Cassidy	10–20
	May	Alice Cooper	10–20
	June		
	December		5–10
1974	All issues		5–10
1975	January	Jimmy Page	5–10
	February	Bad Co.	5–10
	March	John Lennon	5–10
	April	Keith Richards	5–10
	May	Paul and Linda McCartney	5–8
	July	Ian Anderson	5–10
	August	Mick Jagger	5–10
	September	Ian Anderson	5–10
	October	Edgar Winter	5–10
	November	Elton John	6–12
	December	Freddie Mercury	10–20

Year	Issue/Number	Description	Value ($)
1976	January	Eric Clapton	5–10
	February	Roger Daltry	5–10
	March	The Who	7–15
	April	Bryan Ferry	5–10
	May	Aerosmith	5–10
	August	Bad Co.	6–12
	September	Mick Jagger	6–12
	October	Led Zeppelin	5–10
	November	Elton John	6–12
	December	Peter Frampton	4–8
1977	January	Lynyrd Skynyrd	6–12
	February	Led Zeppelin	6–12
	March	Kiss	10–20
	April	Rod Stewart	5–10
	May	Fleetwood Mac	10–20+
	June	Queen	10–20+
	July	Led Zeppelin	5–10
	August	Boston	5–10
	September	Peter Frampton	5–10
	October	The Beatles	4–8
	November	Led Zeppelin	5–10
	December	The Rolling Stones	8–15
1978	January	Elvis Presley	4–8
	February	Yes	5–10
	March	Linda Ronstadt	5–10
	April	Steely Dan	3–6
	May	Gene Simmons	7–15
	June	Rod Stewart	5–10
	July	The Bee Gees	15–30+
	August	Fleetwood Mac	15–30+
	September	Hall and Oates	5–10
	October	The Rolling Stones	5–10
	November	Elvis Costello	4–8
	December	Andy Gibb	15–30+
1979	January	Led Zeppelin	4–8
	February	Gene Simmons	7–15
	March	Boston	4–8

Year	Issue/Number	Description	Value ($)
1979	April	Aerosmith	4–8
	May	Neil Young	4–8
	June	Paul Stanley	7–15
	July	Foreigner	5–10
	August	Cheap Trick	5–10
	September	Ted Nugent	4–8
	October	Peter Townshend	4–8
	November	Paul Stanley	7–15
	December	Aerosmith	4–8
1980	January	Robert Plant	5–10
	February	Freddie Mercury	10–20+
	March	Jimmy Page	4–8
	April	Cheap Trick	4–8
	May	Led Zeppelin	5–10
	June	Tom Petty	4–8
	July	Debbie Harry	10–20
	August	Aerosmith	4–8
	October	Mick Jagger and Keith Richards	4–8
	November	Heart	5–10
1981	January	The Cars	4–8
	February	Cheap Trick	4–8
	March	David Lee Roth	3–6
	April	Fleetwood Mac	10–20
	June	Debbie Harry	10–20
	September	Van Halen	3–6
	October	Queen	10–20
	December	Debbie Harry	10–20
1982	All issues		4–6
1983	January	Ozzy Osbourne	3–6
	February	Pat Benatar	3–6
	March	Robert Plant	3–6
	April	Tom Petty	3–6
	May–August		3–6
	September	Def Leppard and Iron Maiden	2–4

January 1992

Spring 1992

#18, 1979

December 1991

March 1968

September 1968

July 1984

December 1987

January 1992

#1, 1965

October 1960

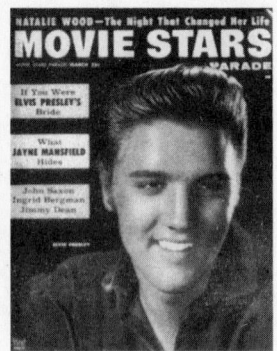

March 1957

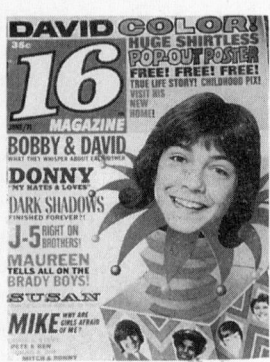

June 1971

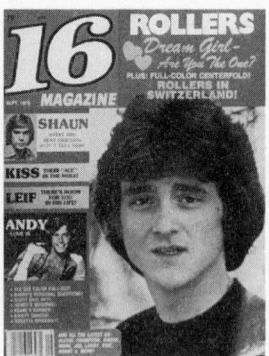

September 1978

February 1992

June 1970

May 1971

November 1963

Year	Issue/Number	Description	Value ($)
1983	October	Robert Plant	2–4
	November	AC/DC	2–4
	December	Judas Priest	3–6
1984–1989			2–4
1990–present			2–3

Rock Scene

Year	Issue/Number	Description	Value ($)
1973	March # 1	David Bowie	20–30
	May # 2	Ray Davies	12–20
	July # 4	Slade	10–20
1974	August #8	David Bowie	8–15
	October # 9	Mick Jagger	10–20
1975	January #10	Roxy Music	7–15
	March #11	Lou Reed	7–15
	May #12	Peter Gabriel	7–15
	July #13	Elton John	10–20
	September #14	Kiss	10–20
	November #15	Aerosmith	7–15
1976	January	Mick Jagger	10–20
	March	David Bowie	10–20
	May	Patti Smith	7–15
	July	Kiss	10–20
	September	Keith Richards	5–10
	November	The Rolling Stones	5–10
1977	January	Robert Plant	4–8
	March	The Ramones	6–12
	May	Ted Nugent	3–6
	June	Bryan Ferry	3–6
	July	Iggy Pop	4–8
	September	Television	3–8
	October	Joe Perry	3–6
	December	Johnny Rotten	4–8

Year	Issue/Number	Description	Value ($)
1978	January	Keith Richards	4–8
	March	The Ramones	4–8
	May	Queen	6–12
	June	Patti Smith	4–8
	July	David Johansen	3–6
	September	Kiss	10–20
	October	Bruce Springsteen	5–10
	December	Kiss	10–20
1979	February	Queen	6–12
	March	Meat Loaf	4–8
	May	Aerosmith	5–15
	July	Steve Tyler	5–15
	September	Debbie Harry	10–20
	November	The Clash	5–10
1980	January	Kiss	7–15
	March	Queen	5–10
	May	Led Zeppelin	4–8
	July	Dr. Hook	5–10
	September	Christie Hynde	4–8
1981	January	The Rolling Stones	5–10
	March	Talking Heads	4–8
	May	The Rolling Stones	5–10
1982	January	Debbie Harry	7–15

Rolling Stone

Year	Issue/Number	Description	Value ($)
1967	#1	John Lennon	250–500+
	#2	Tina Turner	150–250
	#3	The Beatles	125–250
	#4	Jimi Hendrix	200–400+
1968	#5	The Beatles	75–125
	#6	Janis Joplin	100–150
	#7	Jimi Hendrix	125–250
	#8	Lou Adler and John Phillips	50–100
	#9	The Beatles	50–100
	#10	Eric Clapton	40–80

Year	Issue/Number	Description	Value ($)
1968	#11	Baron Wolfman	40–80
	#12	Bob Dylan	40–80
	#13	Tiny Tim	35–70
	#14	Frank Zappa	40–80
	#15	Mick Jagger	50–100
	#16	The Band	50–100
	#17	Pete Townshend	40–80
	#18	Pete Townshend	40–80
	#19	Mick Jagger	50–100
	#20	The Beatles	40–80
	#21	The Beatles	40–80
	#22	John Lennon and Yoko Ono	75–100
	#23	The Beatles	35–70
	#24	The Beatles	35–70
1969	#25	MC 5	40–80
	#26	Jimi Hendrix	50–100
	#27	Groupies	25–50
	#28	Japanese Rock	25–50
	#29	Janis Joplin	50–100
	#30	American Revolution 1969	40–75
	#31	Sun Ra	40–75
	#32	Traffic	35–70
	#33	Joni Mitchell	25–50
	#34	Jimi Hendrix	75–100
	#35	Chuck Berry	25–40
	#36	John Lennon and Yoko Ono	40–80
	#37	Elvis Presley	25–50
	#38	Jim Morrison	100–200+
	#39	Brian Jones	100–200+
	#40	Jerry Garcia	50–100+
	#41	Joe Cocker	20–40
	#42	Woodstock	25–50
	#43	Bob Dylan	20–40
	#44	David Crosby	20–40
	#45	Tina Turner	25–50

April 1989

November 1991

July 1972

#8, 1984

#10, 1984

#6, 1984

February 3, 1990

October 17, 1988

December 22, 1980

Year	Issue/Number	Description	Value ($)
1969	#46	The Beatles	25–50
	#47	Bob Dylan	20–40
	#48	Miles Davis	20–40
	#49	Mick Jagger	25–50
	#50	The Rolling Stones	35–75
1970	#51	John Lennon	50–100
	#52	John Fogarty	25–40
	#53	The Grateful Dead	50–100+
	#54	Sly and the Family Stone	20–40
	#55	Abbie Hoffman	20–40
	#56	John Lennon	25–50
	#57	Paul McCartney	20–40
	#58	Captain Beefheart	20–40
	#59	Little Richard	25–50
	#60	George Harrison	20–40
	#61	Charles Manson	25–50
	#62	The Beatles	20–40
	#63	David Crosby	20–30
	#64	Janis Joplin	50–100
	#65	Mick Jagger	30–50
	#66	The Grateful Dead	30–60+
	#67	The Rascals	20–40
	#68	Jimi Hendrix	75–125
	#69	Janis Joplin	60–120
	#70	Grace Slick	25–50
	#71	The Beatles	25–50
	#72	Leon Russell	15–30
	#73	Rod Stewart	15–30
1971	#74	John Lennon	30–60
	#75	John Lennon	30–55
	#76	James Taylor	20–30
	#77	Bob Dylan	20–30
	#78	Mohammad Ali	15–30
	#79	Captain Beefheart	15–30
	#80	Joe Dellesandro	20–40
	#81	Michael Jackson	20–40
	#82	Peter Fonda	10–20
	#83	Country Joe McDonald	15–30

Year	Issue/Number	Description	Value ($)
1971	#84	Elton John	20–40
	#85	White House	10–20
	#86	John Lennon and Yoko Ono	25–50
	#87	Jethhro Tull	20–30
	#88	Jim Morrison	75–150
	#89	Keith Richards	30–60
	#90	George Harrison	25–50
	#91	The Incredible Hulk	10–25
	#92	Abbie Hoffman	10–20
	#93	Sly and the Family Stone	15–25
	#94	The Beach Boys	20–40
	#95	The Beach Boys	20–40
	#96	Duane Allman	20–40
	#97	Pete Townshend	20–30
	#98	Elvis Presley	15–30
1972	#99	Cat Stevens	15–25
	#100	Jerry Garcia	25–50+
	#101	The Grateful Dead	25–50+
	#102	Janis Joplin	30–60
	#103	Bob Dylan	10–25
	#104	Bob Dylan	10–25
	#105	Alice Cooper	10–25
	#106	Pete Seeger	10–18
	#107	Marvin Gaye	10–22
	#108	David Cassidy	25–50
	#109	Jane Fonda	8–20
	#110	Rod Stewart	10–20
	#111	Van Morrison	10–18
	#112	Mick Jagger	12–25
	#113	Paul Simon	10–20
	#114	Huey Newton	10–20
	#115	The Eagles	12–20
	#116	Randy Newman	10–20
	#117	Three Dog Night	10–20
	#118	The Grateful Dead	15–30
	#119	Sally Struthers	10–20
	#120	Jeff Beck	10–20

Year	Issue/Number	Description	Value ($)
1972	#121	David Bowie	10–20
	#122	Chuck Berry	10–20
	#123	Carlos Santana	10–20
	#124	Keith Moon	20–30
1973	#125	James Taylor and Carly Simon	12–25
	#126	Genesis	10–20
	#127	Diana Ross	20–30
	#128	Bette Midler	6–12
	#129	The Rolling Stones	10–20
	#130	Robert Mitchum	5–10
	#131	Dr. Hook	5–10
	#132	Truman Capote	5–10
	#133	Mark Spitz	5–10
	#134	Alice Cooper	10–20
	#135	Sonny and Cher	10–20
	#136	Yes	5–10
	#137	Rod Stewart	5–10
	#138	Paul Newman	5–10
	#139	Tatum O'Neal	5–10
	#140	Leon Russell	5–10
	#141	Elton John	6–12
	#142	Dan Hicks	4–10
	#143	Stevie Wonder	4–10
	#144	Stephen Stills	6–12
	#145	Art Garfunkel	6–12
	#146	Gene Autry	5–10
	#147	Liza Minnelli and Ronnie Spector	4–8
	#148	The Grateful Dead	10–20
	#149	The Allman Brothers	10–20
	#150	Hugh Hefner	4–8
	#151	The Who	6–12
1974	#152	Ringo Starr	5–10
	#153	Paul McCartney	5–10
	#154	Bob Dylan	5–10
	#155	David Bowie	5–10
	#156	Bob Dylan	5–10

April 1958

July 1965

November 1965

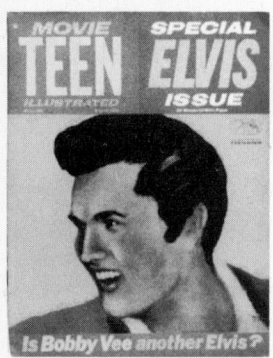

August 1961

November 1963

April 1973

October 1971

April 1971

June 1972

May 1979

September 1983

1980

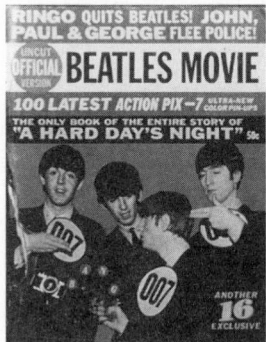

1964

#2, 1991

Summer 1980

September 1974

#382, 1991

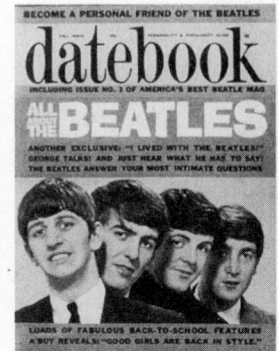

Fall 1964

Year	Issue/Number	Description	Value ($)
1974	#157	World's Sexiest Calendar issue	5–10
	#158	Marvin Gaye	5–10
	#159	Kris Kristofferson	5–10
	#160	Paul Getty	5–10
	#161	Jackson Browne	4–8
	#162	Gladys Knight and the Pips	12–20
	#163	James Dean	5–10
	#164	The Carpenters	10–20
	#165	Eric Clapton	5–10
	#166	Maria Mauldaur	5–10
	#167	Steely Dan	5–10
	#168	Crosby, Stills, Nash and Young	6–12
	#169	Jan and Dean	5–10
	#170	Tanya Tucker	6–12
	#171	Lily Tomlin and Richard Pryor	5–10
	#172	Lily Tomlin	5–10
	#173	Evel Knievel	5–10
	#174	Elton John	6–12
	#175	Dustin Hoffman	5–10
	#176	George Harrison	5–10
1975	#177	Suzi Quatro	10–20
	#178	Gregg Allman	10–20
	#179	Freddie Prinze	5–10
	#180	Les Paul	4–8
	#181	Loggins and Messina	4–7
	#182	Led Zeppelin	20–40
	#183	Linda Ronstadt	6–12
	#184	Roger Daltry	5–10
	#185	Peter Falk	4–8
	#186	John Denver	10–20
	#187	Carly Simon	10–20
	#188	Phoebe Snow	5–10
	#189	Stevie Wonder	4–8
	#190	LaBelle	4–8
	#191	The Rolling Stones	5–10

Year	Issue/Number	Description	Value ($)
1975	#192	Richard Dreyfuss	4–8
	#193	Neil Young	4–8
	#194	Doonesbury	4–8
	#195	Mick Jagger	5–10
	#196	The Eagles	6–12
	#197	Muhammed Ali	4–8
	#198	Bob Dylan	4–10
	#199	Rod Stewart and Britt Ekland	4–8
	#200	The Who	4–8
	#201	Jack Nicholson	4–8
	#202	Bonnie Raitt	4–8
	#203	Jefferson Starship	5–10
1976	#204	Bob Dylan	4–8
	#205	Pat Boone	4–8
	#206	David Bowie	4–8
	#207	Howlin' Wolf	4–8
	#208	The Osmonds	7–15
	#209	Mary Hartman	4–8
	#210	Robert Redford and Dustin Hoffman	4–8
	#211	Peter Frampton	5–10
	#212	Santana	7–15
	#213	Marlon Brando	3–5
	#214	Freddy Fender	3–5
	#215	Paul McCartney	4–8
	#216	Paul Simon	4–8
	#217	The Beatles	4–8
	#218	Loggins and Messina	4–8
	#219	Bob Marley	4–8
	#220	Aerosmith	4–8
	#221	Stephen Stills and Neil Young	4–8
	#222	Neil Diamond	5–10
	#223	Elton John	4–8
	#224	Electric Light Orchestra	3–5
	#225	Brian Wilson and the Beach Boys	4–8

Year	Issue/Number	Description	Value ($)
1976	#226	Janis Joplin	6–10
	#227	Linda Ronstadt	5–10
	#228	Jackson Browne	5–10
	#229	The Band	3–6
	#230	Rod Stewart	4–8
1977	#231	Jeff Bridges	2–4
	#232	Peter Frampton	3–5
	#233	Boz Scaggs	2–4
	#234	Princess Caroline	3–5
	#235	Fleetwood Mac	15–30+
	#236	Lily Tomlin	4–8
	#237	Hall and Oates	3–6
	#238	Keith Richards	3–5
	#239	Van Morrison	2–4
	#240	Crosby, Stills and Nash	3–6
	#241	Robert De Niro	3–6
	#242	Diane Keaton	2–4
	#243	The Bee Gees	10–20+
	#244	Heart	6–12
	#245	Diana Ross	5–10
	#246	Star Wars	10–20
	#247	O. J. Simpson	2–4
	#248	Elvis Presley	5–10
	#249	Paul McCartney and Wings	5–10
	#250	The Sex Pistols	4–8
	#251	The Rolling Stones	4–8
	#252	The Who	4–8
	#253	Steve Martin	3–5
	#254	10th Anniversary issue	3–6
	#255	James Taylor	3–6
	#256	Fleetwood Mac	12–25+
1978	#257	Bob Dylan	5–10
	#258	Jimmy Thudpucker	2–4
	#259	Rita Coolidge and Kris Kristofferson	3–6
	#260	Jane Fonda	2–4
	#261	Donna Summer	7–12

Year	Issue/Number	Description	Value ($)
1978	#262	Brooke Shields	7–14+
	#263	The Bee Gees	10–20+
	#264	Muhammad Ali	3–6
	#265	Jefferson Starship	5–10
	#266	Carly Simon	4–8
	#267	John Travolta	7–15
	#268	Mick Jagger	4–8
	#269	Willie Nelson	2–4
	#270	Patti Smith	3–6
	#271	John Belushi	3–6
	#272	Bruce Springsteen	3–6
	#273	The Rolling Stones	3–6
	#274	Buddy Holly	3–6
	#275	Steve Martin	2–4
	#276	Linda Ronstadt	3–6
	#277	Gilda Radner	3–6
	#278	Bob Dylan	3–6
	#279	The Who	3–6
	#280	Cheech and Chong	3–6
1979	#281/282	Richard Dreyfuss	1–2
	#283	The Cars	3–6
	#284	Neil Young	3–6
	#285	Dan Aykroyd	2–4
	#286	Ted Nugent	3–6
	#287	Johnny Carson	2–4
	#288	Michael Douglas	2–4
	#289	The Village People	3–6
	#290	Richard Pryor	2–4
	#291	The Bee Gees	10–20+
	#292	Jon Voight	2–6
	#293	Cheap Trick	3–6
	#294	Debbie Harry/Blondie	7–12
	#295	Paul McCartney	3–6
	#296	Joni Mitchell	3–6
	#297	Rickie Lee Jones	4–8
	#298	Robin Williams	3–6
	#299	James Taylor	3–6
	#300	The Doobie Brothers	3–6

April 1978

February 1989

May 1979

January 1988

July 1975

January 1991

December 1990

August 1979

July 1991

Year	Issue/Number	Description	Value ($)
1979	#301	Jimmy Buffet	2–4
	#302	Sissy Spacek	3–6
	#203	Martin Sheen	2–4
	#304	Bruce Springsteen	3–6
	#305	The Eagles	4–8
	#306	Bette Midler	3–6
1980	#307/308	The Year in Music special	3–6
	#309	Pink Floyd	6–15
	#310	Fleetwood Mac	10–20+
	#311	Tom Petty	3–6
	#312	Richare Gere	1–2
	#313	Bob Hope	2–5
	#314	Linda Ronstadt	3–6
	#315	The Clash	4–6
	#316	Bob Seger	3–6
	#317	Heart	5–10
	#318	The Pretenders	3–6
	#319	Hard Rock	3–5
	#320	Pete Townshend	3–6
	#321	John Travolta	6–12
	#322	The Empire Strikes Back	6–12
	#323	Jackson Browne	3–6
	#324	The Rolling Stones	3–6
	#325	Billy Joel	4–6
	#326	The Commodores	3–6
	#327	Robert Redford	1–3
	#328	Pat Benatar	4–8
	#329	The Cars	3–6
	#330	Mary Tyler Moore	3–6
	#331	Jill Clayburgh	2–4
	#332	Dolly Parton	3–5
	#333/334	The Beatles	3–6
	#335	John Lennon and Yoko Ono	5–10
	#336	Bruce Springsteen	4–8
	#337	The Police	3–7
	#338	Goldie Hawn	3–5

Year	Issue/Number	Description	Value ($)
1981	#339	Warren Zevon	3–5
	#340	Roman Polanski	2–4
	#341	Jack Nicholson	2–4
	#342	Gary U.S. Bonds	3–5
	#343	John Lennon	4–8
	#344	Susan Sarandon	2–4
	#345	James Taylor	3–5
	#346	Harrison Ford	3–6
	#347	Margot Kidder	2–4
	#348	Tom Petty	3–6
	#349	Rickie Lee Jones	3–6
	#350	Bill Murray	2–4
	#351	Stevie Nicks	25–45+
	#352	Jim Morrison	4–8
	#353	Yoko Ono	2–4
	#354	Meryl Streep	2–4
	#355	Elvis Presley	3–6
	#356	Keith Richards	3–6
	#357	Bill Hurt	2–4
	#358	Carly Simon	4–8
	#359/360	1981 Yearbook	2–4
1982	#361	John Belushi	4–8
	#362	Timothy Hutton	2–4
	#363	Steve Martin	3–6
	#364	Pete Wolfe	2–4
	#365	Simon and Garfunkel	5–10
	#366	Warren Beatty	1–2
	#367	Mariel Hemingway	3–6
	#368	John Belushi	4–8
	#369	Sissy Spacek	3–6
	#370	Natassja Kinski	3–6
	#371	David Letterman	1–2
	#372	Pete Townshend	3–6
	#373	Sylvester Stallone	3–6
	#374	E.T.	2–4
	#375	The Go-Go's	6–12
	#376	Tron	2–4
	#377	Elvis Costello	3–6

Year	Issue/Number	Description	Value ($)
1982	#378	Pink Floyd	3–6
	#379	Richard Gere	1–2
	#380	John Lennon and Yoko Ono	3–6
	#381	Billy Joel	3–6
	#382	The Who	3–6
	#383	Matt Dillon	2–4
	#384	Bette Midler	3–5
	#385/386	The Year in Music special	2–4
	#387	Paul Newman	1–2
	#388	Dustin Hoffman	1–2
	#389	Michael Jackson	5–10
	#390	Stray Cats	3–6
	#391	Jessica Lange	2–4
	#392	Dudley Moore	1–2
	#393	Joan Baez	3–6
	#394	Prince and Vanity	5–10
1983	#395	David Bowie	3–6
	#396	Sean Penn	1–2
	#397	Health Clubs	1–2
	#398	Men at Work	2–6
	#399	Eddie Murphy	1–2
	#400/401	Star Wars	10–20
	#402	John Travolta	6–12
	#403	The Police	4–8
	#404	Jackson Browne	2–6
	#405	Eurythmics	2–6
	#406	Chevy Chase	2–4
	#407	Sean Connery	3–6
	#408	Culture Club	3–6
	#409	Mick Jagger	3–6
	#410	Michael Jackson and Paul McCartney	4–8
	#411/412	Great Faces of '83	3–6
1984	#413	Eric Clapton	3–6
	#414	Duran Duran	3–6

Year	Issue/Number	Description	Value ($)
1984	#415	The Beatles	2–6
	#416	The Police	3–7
	#417	Michael Jackson	3–6
	#418	Jack Nicholson	2–4
	#419	Eddie Murphy	2–4
	#420	Daryl Hannah	2–6
	#421	Marvin Gaye	4–8
	#422	Cyndi Lauper	4–8
	#423	Culture Club	3–6
	#424	Bob Dylan	3–6
	#425	The Go-Go's	5–10
	#426/427	The Thompson Twins	3–6
	#428	Bill Murray	2–4
	#429	Prince	3–6
	#430	Huey Lewis	3–5
	#431	John Belushi	3–6
	#432	Tina Turner	3–6
	#433	David Bowie	3–6
	#434	Steve Martin	2–4
	#435	Madonna	5–10
	#436	Bruce Springsteen	3–6
1985	#437438	Great Faces of '84	3–5
	#439	Hall and Oates	3–6
	#440	Billy Idol	3–6
	#441	Mick Jagger	3–6
	#442	Bruce Springsteen	3–6
	#443	U2	3–6
	#444	Miami Vice	2–4
	#445	David Lee Roth	3–6
	#446	Richard Gere	1–2
	#447	Madonna and Rosanna Arquette	5–10
	#448	Phil Collins	3–6
	#449	Julian Lennon	2–4
	#450	David Letterman	1–2
	#451	Clint Eastwood	3–6
	#452/453	John Travolta and Jamie Lee Curtis	5–10

Year	Issue/Number	Description	Value ($)
1985	#454	Live Aid	3–5
	#455	Mel Gibson and Tina Turner	3–5
	#456	Prince	3–6
	#457	Sting	3–6
	#458	Bruce Springsteen	3–6
	#459	Steven Spielberg	1–3
	#460	Don Johnson	1–3
	#461	Dire Straits	3–6
	#462	Bob Geldorf	2–4
1986	#463/464	1985 Rock Yearbook	3–6
	#465	Michael Douglas	2–4
	#466	John Couger Mellencamp	3–6
	#467	Ricky Nelson	5–10+
	#468	Bruce Springsteen	5–6
	#469	Jim McMahon	1–2
	#470	Bruce Willis	1–2
	#471	Stevie Wonder	3–6
	#472	Wendy and Lisa of Prince	5–10
	#473	Whoopi Goldberg	2–4
	#474	Michael J. Fox	2–4
	#475	Madonna	5–10
	#476	Tom Cruise	2–4
	#477	Van Halen	3–6
	#478/479	Bob Dylan and Tom Petty	3–6
	#480	Jack Nicholson	1–2
	#481	Boy George	3–6
	#482	Paul McCartney	3–5
	#483	Don Johnson	1–2
	#484	Cybill Shepherd	2–4
	#485	Tina Turner	3–6
	#486	Billy Joel	3–6
	#487	Huey Lewis	2–4
	#488	Run DMC	2–4
	#489/490	1986 Yearbook special	2–4
1987	#491–500		3–6
	#501	Jimi Hendrix	4–8
	#502–514		3–6

Year	Issue/Number	Description	Value ($)
1987	#515/516	1987 Yearbook special	4–8
1988	#517–540		2–4
	#541/542	Bruce Springsteen	3–6
1989	#543–566		2–4
	#567/568		2–4
1990	All issues		2–4
1991	All issues		2–4
1992	All issues		2–4
1993–present			1–2
		X-Files and Madonna issues	5–10

16 Magazine

Year	Issue/Number	Description	Value ($)
1958	#1		50–100+
	#2		25–50+
1959	January–April		20–40
	May	Elvis Presley	40–60
	All issues		20–40
1960	All issues		20–30
1961	All issues		20–40
1962	January	Bobby Rydell	20–40
	All other issues		15–30
1963	All issues		15–30
1964	All issues		15–30
1965	All issues		15–35
1966	All issues		15–35
1967	All issues		20–40
1968	All issues		15–30
1969	All issues		10–30
1970	All issues		10–30

Year	Issue/Number	Description	Value ($)
1971	All issues		10–30
1972	All issues		10–25
1973	January–October		10–20
	November, December		5–10
1974	All issues		5–10
1975	All issues		5–10
1976	All issues		4–8
1977	All issues		4–8
1978	July, October		4–8
	All other issues		
1979	All issues		5–10
1980	All issues		5–10
1981	January–August		5–10
	September–December		4–8
1982	January–August		4–8
	September–December		4–8
1983	All issues		3–6
1984	All issues		3–6
1985	All issues		2–4
1986	All issues		2–4
1987	All issues		2–4
1988	All issues		2–4
1989	All issues		2–4
1990	All issues		2–4
1991	All issues		2–3
1992–present	All issues		1–3

Year	Issue/Number	Description	Value ($)
Song Hits			
1964	All issues		10–20
1965	All issues		10–20
1966	All issues		10–30
1967	All issues		15–30
1968	March	Jim Morrison	25–50
	All other issues		10–20
1969	May	The Doors	20–40
1970	All issues		10–20
1971	July		15–30
	All other issues		5–10
1972	All issues		5–10
1973	February	The Who	6–12
	July	Carly Simon	6–12
	December	The Carpenters	10–20
	All other issues		5–10
1974	May	Todd Rundgren	5–10
	August	Three Dog Night	5–10
	All other issues		4–8
1975	July	Olivia Newton-John	10–20+
	December	Jefferson Starship	6–12
	All other issues		4–6
1976	November	America	4–8
	All other issues		3–6
1977	September	Fleetwood Mac	15–30
	December	Kiss	10–20
	All other issues		3–6
1978	All issues		4–6
1979	March	Linda Ronstadt	4–8
	April	Jethro Tull	3–6

January 1990

June 1988

July 1988

December 1988

January 1989

February 1989

July 1989

February 1991

January 1992

October 1978

Spring 1979

Summer 1979

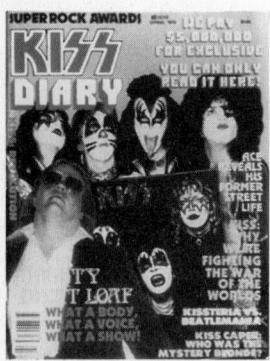

Spring 1979

August 1979

Spring 1978

#5, 1979

#3, 1979

#4, 1979

Year	Issue/Number	Description	Value ($)
1979	May	Queen	10–20
	July	The Bee Gees	10–20+
1980	January	Kiss	10–20+
	February	The Eagles	5–10
	April	Jefferson Starship	4–8
	August	Van Halen	4–8
	All other issues		3–5
1981	July, September		2–4
	All other issues		3–6
1982	April	Kiss	7–15
	All other issues		3–6
1985–1998			2–4
1989–present			1–3

Spin

Year	Issue/Number	Description	Value ($)
1985	May #1	Madonna	10–20
	June #2	Talking Heads	5–10
	July #3	Sting	5–10
	August #4	Annie Lennox	5–10
	September #5	Pat Benatar	6–12
	October #6	Keith Richards	5–10
	November #7	Bruce Springsteen	5–10
	December #8	Bob Dylan	5–10
1986	January	Debbie Harry	15–25
	Febuary	ZZ Top	3–6
	March	Mick Jones	3–6
	April	David Lee Roth	3–6
	May	Charlie Sexton	2–4
	June	Billy Idol	3–6
	July	Prince	3–6
	August	Mick Jagger	3–6
	September	Ozzy Osbourne	3–6
	October	R.E.M.	3–6
	November	Iggy Pop	3–6

Year	Issue/Number	Description	Value ($)
1986	December	Chrissie Hynde	4–8
1987	January	Janet Jackson	4–7
	February	Duran Duran	3–6
	March	The Beastie Boys	3–5
	April	Madonna	7–15
	May	Joan Jett	10–20
	June	Michael Jackson	4–8
	July	Susanna Hoffs	6–12
	August	Simple Minds	3–6
	September (no issues published for October or November)	John Cougar Mellencamp	3–5
	December	Sting	4–8
1988	January	Steven Tyler	3–6
	February	Inxs	3–5
	March	The Cure	3–5
	April	Sa-fire	2–4
	May	Run DMC	2–4
	June	Morrissey	2–4
	July	Belinda Carlisle	5–10
	August	Comics	2–4
	September	Tracy Chapman	1–2
	October	Jazzy Jeff and Fresh Prince	1–2
	November	Bon Jovi	3–6
	December	The Bangles	4–8
1989	January	U2	3–6
	February	Nick Cave	1–3
	March	Edie Brickell and the New Bohemians	2–4
	April	Madonna	5–10
	May	Elvis Costello	3–5
	June	John Cougar Mellencamp	2–4
	July	Elvis Presley	3–6
	August	Tom Petty	2–4
	September	10,000 Maniacs	2–4

April 1979

September 1984

November 1989

October 1988

August 1979

July 1991

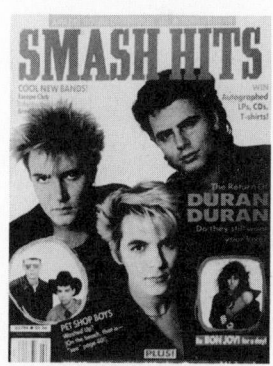

March 1994

1989

January 1989

Year	Issue/Number	Description	Value ($)
	October	Terence Trent D'Arby	2–4
1980–1982	All issues		1–3
1983–Present			1–3

Tiger Beat

Year	Issue/Number	Description	Value ($)
1965	September #1	Annette Funicello	30–60
	Octember #2	Annette Funicello	30–60
	November #3	Sonny and Cher	30–60
	December #4	Leslie Gore	20–40
1966	January–September		15–30
	October–December		10–25
1967	All issues		10–25
1968	All issues		12–25
1969	All issues		10–20
1970	All issues		10–20
1971	All issues		10–20
1972	All issues		8–15
1973	January–March		10–20
	April–December		7–15
1974	All issues		5–10
1975	All issues		3–8
1976–1981	All issues		3–6
1982–1986	All issues		2–4

Magazine Index

�

Most-Collectible Personalities Index